# CompTIA A+ Practice Tests Core 1 (220-1101) and Core 2 (220-1102)

Pass the CompTIA A+ exams on your first attempt with rigorous practice questions

**Ian Neil and Mark Birch**

BIRMINGHAM—MUMBAI

# CompTIA A+ Practice Tests Core 1 (220-1101) and Core 2 (220-1102)

**Authors**: Ian Neil and Mark Birch

**Reviewers**: Sahil Kumar, Sylvio Musto, and Amir Shetaia

**Senior Editor**: Ketan Giri

**Production Editor**: Shantanu Zagade

**Editorial Board**: Vijin Boricha, Megan Carlisle, Ketan Giri, Alex Mazonowicz, Aaron Nash, Abhishek Rane, and Ankita Thakur

**Production reference:** 1151123


Published by Packt Publishing Ltd.

Grosvenor House

11 St Paul's Square

Birmingham

B3 1RB

ISBN 978-1-83763-318-0

www.packtpub.com

# Contributors

## About the Authors

**Ian Neil** is one of the world's top trainers of Security+. He is able to break down information into manageable chunks so that people with no background knowledge can gain the skills required to become certified. He has recently worked for the US Army in Europe and designed a Security+ course that catered to people from all backgrounds (not just IT professionals), with an extremely successful pass rate. He is an MCT, MCSE, A+, Network+, Security+, CASP, and RESILIA practitioner that has worked with high-end training providers over the past 23 years and was one of the first technical trainers to train Microsoft internal staff when they opened their Bucharest Office in 2006.

**Mark Birch** is an experienced courseware developer and teacher in both information systems and cyber-security. Mark has been developing content and teaching CompTIA A+ classes for more than 20 years and understands the subject area in great depth. Mark began his career working within the aerospace industry (for a major defense contractor) and has over 30 years' experience consulting, engineering, and deploying secure information systems. He has spent over 20 years working with the United States Military and United Kingdom Armed Forces, helping many students attain their learning goals. Mark has ensured that soldiers, officers, and civilians have had the best opportunities to gain cyber-security accreditation.

# About the Reviewers

**Sahil Kumar** is a software engineer driven by an unwavering passion for innovation and a keen aptitude for problem-solving. With an impressive career spanning eight years, Sahil has honed his expertise in various domains, including IT systems, cybersecurity, endpoint management, and global customer support.

His experience in the tech industry is marked by a commitment to continuous learning and professional growth, as evidenced by his numerous certifications. Sahil holds coveted certifications such as CompTIA A+, CompTIA Security+, ITIL V4, OCI 2023 Foundations Associate, Microsoft SC-200, AZ-900, and a Certificate in Cyber Security (ISC2). This extensive certification portfolio reflects his dedication to staying at the forefront of technology and security trends.

Sahil's proficiency extends beyond the realm of cybersecurity; he is also well-versed in DevSecOps, demonstrating his versatility in tackling multifaceted challenges within the IT landscape. Currently, Sahil is pursuing a master's degree in cybersecurity at New York University, a testament to his commitment to academic excellence and staying at the top of his field. He holds a bachelor's degree in electrical and electronics engineering from Kurukshetra University.

**Sylvio Musto** is a technical trainer with over 13 years of experience in Information Technology, Information Security, Cyber Risks, and Auditing. He holds MBAs in Information Security Management as well as Leadership and Strategic People Management.

Sylvio currently works as the Supervisor of Internal Audit at MercadoLivre, one of the leading companies in the e-commerce and technology market in Latin America.

Throughout his career, Sylvio has made significant contributions to the field of Information Technology, working with renowned companies in software development, healthcare, insurance, and financial markets.

In addition to his professional accomplishments, Sylvio is also a dedicated educator. He currently serves as a professor at the Fundação Vanzolini and CompTIA, sharing his knowledge and experience with the next generation of IT professionals.

Sylvio Musto is recognized for his solid credentials, including ITIL v3, Cobit v5 Foundation, CompTIA Security+, CompTIA CySA+, and ISO 27001 Foundation certifications. His commitment to enhancing information security and strategically leading teams makes him a respected authority in the field of Information Technology.

Outside of work, Sylvio has a strong interest in automobiles and recently devoted his time to restoring a collector's vehicle he owns in Brazil.

**Amir Shetaia** is a dedicated professional with a profound passion for embedded systems, robotics, and self-driving vehicles. His career journey is marked by substantial achievements and contributions to the field.

Amir's practical experience includes serving as an Embedded Systems Intern at Valeo, a global automotive technology leader, and successful freelancer on Upwork. He is well-versed in programming languages such as C and Python and possesses expertise with various microcontrollers, including ARM Cortex, PIC, and AVR.

Amir's leadership qualities shine through his role as the Founder and Club Leader of the Mansoura Robotics Club, which has empowered over 1000 students, fostering a deep understanding of robotics fundamentals. He also excels as an Embedded Systems Mentor at CIS Team MU and an Embedded Systems Instructor at UCCD Mansoura Engineering, where he imparts his knowledge and expertise to aspiring engineers.

Amir's impact extends beyond his immediate community, as exemplified by his team's remarkable third prize victory in the Cloud practice exam at the Huawei ICT Competition Global Final. This achievement underscores his unwavering dedication and technical prowess on an international stage.

Amir is a professional who embodies a relentless pursuit of excellence and an unquenchable thirst for knowledge. His commitment to personal and professional growth is evident through his internships at prestigious organizations like Siemens Digital Industries Software, Information Technology Institute (ITI), and Bright Network. These experiences have honed his skills in areas such as Embedded Software Engineering, RTOS, Automotive Protocols, Artificial Intelligence, and more. Amir's journey is a testament to his exceptional grasp of embedded systems and Artificial Intelligence and his passion for sharing knowledge and fostering innovation.

# Table of Contents

# 3

# Hardware                                                    43

# 4

# Virtualization and Cloud Computing                          67

# 5

# Hardware and Network Troubleshooting                        79

6

# Mock Exam: Core 1 (220-1101)                                              99

7

# Operating Systems                                                         111

8

# Security                                                                  143

# 9

## Software Troubleshooting                                        167

# 10

## Operational Procedures                                          183

11

# Preface

Welcome to the practice test book on CompTIA A+, meticulously crafted for those seeking to pass the exam and gain a clear, concise understanding of the foundational concepts, technologies, and practices that underpin modern computer systems.

## Who This Book Is For

This A+ practice test book is written for individuals who are preparing to take the CompTIA A+ certification exam. This certification is often sought after by individuals aiming to start or advance their careers in the field of IT and technology support. The book caters to a wide range of individuals, including the following:

- **Aspiring IT professionals**: Those who are new to the IT industry and looking to gain the necessary knowledge and skills to enter the field

- **Entry-level technicians**: Individuals who are already working in IT support roles and wish to validate their skills and knowledge by obtaining the A+ certification

- **Career changers**: People coming from other industries who are interested in transitioning into a career in IT and require a foundational understanding of computer hardware, software, and troubleshooting

- **Students**: Students studying computer science, information technology, or related fields who want to enhance their learning and increase their employability

- **Self-learners**: Individuals who prefer self-paced learning and want to improve their technical skills on their own time, potentially with the aim of changing careers or advancing within their current role

- **IT enthusiasts**: Hobbyists and technology enthusiasts who wish to deepen their knowledge and skills in computer systems and hardware

- **Job seekers**: Those actively seeking employment in IT support or technician roles, as the A+ certification is often a prerequisite or advantage in job applications

- **Military personnel**: Military personnel transitioning to civilian roles in the IT sector, as the A+ certification can aid in their reintegration into the workforce

- **Professional development**: Individuals already in IT roles who are seeking to enhance their skills, stay updated with industry trends, and potentially pursue higher-level certifications in the future

Overall, the CompTIA A+ practice test book serves as a valuable resource for anyone looking to prepare for the CompTIA A+ certification exam and establish a solid foundation in IT hardware, software, troubleshooting, and customer service skills.

## What This Book Covers

*Chapter 1, Mobile Devices*, prepares you to test your knowledge of all aspects of mobile devices, laptops, tablets, and smartphones, from installation and connectivity to the management of devices.

*Chapter 2, Networking*, helps you test your knowledge of all aspects of networking, including protocols and ports through to different networking devices and the types of connectivity.

*Chapter 3, Hardware*, tests your knowledge of all aspects of hardware, cable types, devices, and the appropriate memory.

*Chapter 4, Virtualization and Cloud Computing*, tests your knowledge of all aspects of virtualization, including client-side virtualization, the use of resources, and security. In addition, it helps you to prepare to work with cloud models and services.

*Chapter 5, Hardware and Network Troubleshooting*, tests your knowledge of the best practices for troubleshooting, then examines how to troubleshoot different aspects of networking and hardware.

*Chapter 6, Mock Exam: Core 1 (220-1101),* offers a comprehensive assessment of your understanding of A+ Core 1 (220-1101) objectives. Challenge your problem-solving abilities and exam preparedness with an authentic set of CompTIA A+ exam questions.

*Chapter 7, Operating Systems*, tests your skills regarding installing and supporting the Windows operating system, including the command line and client support. We will also test the skills you will need for system configuration imaging and troubleshooting on macOS, Chrome OS, Android, and Linux OS.

*Chapter 8, Security*, evaluates your readiness for the exam by focusing on identifying and selecting controls used to mitigate security vulnerabilities for devices and their network connections. Wireless security, threats, and vulnerabilities including common methods of social engineering are also covered in this chapter.

*Chapter 9*, *Software Troubleshooting*, assesses your knowledge when troubleshooting PC and mobile device issues, which can include common operating systems, malware, and security issues.

*Chapter 10*, *Operational Procedures*, assesses your competence in adhering to best practices related to safety, environmental impact, communication, and professionalism. Important elements such as change management, backup and recovery, and privacy concepts are also covered in this chapter.

*Chapter 11, Mock Exam: Core 2 (220-1102),* provides you with a thorough evaluation of your grasp of the A+ Core 2 (220-1102) exam objectives. You can test your problem-solving skills and exam readiness against a realistic selection of CompTIA A+ exam questions.

## Conventions Used

New terms and important words are shown like this: "Cloud computing refers to the provisioning of resources without the need for capital expenditure, in which the **Cloud Service Provider** (**CSP**) provides all of the hardware and customer lease access."

## Get in Touch

Feedback from our readers is always welcome.

**General feedback**: If you have any questions about this book, please mention the book title in the subject of your message and email us at *customercare@packt.com*.

**Errata**: Although we have taken every care to ensure the accuracy of our content, mistakes do happen. If you have found a mistake in this book, we would be grateful if you could report this to us. Please visit www.packtpub.com/support/errata and complete the form.

**Piracy**: If you come across any illegal copies of our works in any form on the Internet, we would be grateful if you could provide us with the location address or website name. Please contact us at *copyright@packt.com* with a link to the material.

**If you are interested in becoming an author**: If there is a topic that you have expertise in and you are interested in either writing or contributing to a book, please visit authors.packtpub.com.

## Practice Resources – A Quick Tour

> **IMPORTANT:**
>
> **Before you start using the free online resources, you'll need to unlock them.** Unlocking **takes less than 10 minutes, can be done from any device**, and **needs to be done only once.** **Head over to the beginning of** *Chapter 10, Operational Procedures* **for unlock instructions.**

This book will equip you with all the knowledge necessary to clear the exam. As important as learning the key concepts is, your chances of passing the exam are much higher if you apply and practice what you learn in the book. This is where the online practice resources come in. With interactive questions, flashcards, and exam tips, you can practice everything you learned in the book on the go. Here's a quick walkthrough of what you get.

### A Clean, Simple Cert Practice Experience

You get a clean, simple user interface that works on all modern devices, including your phone and tablet. All the features work on all devices provided you have a working internet connection. From the Dashboard (*Figure 0.1*), you can access all the practice resources that come with this book with just a click. If you want to jump back to the book, you can do that from here as well.

Figure 0.1: Dashboard interface on a desktop device

## Practice Questions

The **Quiz Interface** (*Figure 0.2*) is designed to help you focus on the question without any clutter. You can navigate between multiple questions quickly and skip a question if you don't know the answer. The interface also includes a live timer that auto-submits your quiz if you run out of time. Click **End Quiz** if you want to jump straight to the results page to reveal all the solutions.

> **Pro Tip**
>
> One way to perfect your exam skills is to try the same quiz multiple times but focus on different aspects of the test-taking process each time. First, try answering all questions correctly without worrying about the time limit. Review the solutions for your incorrect answers and then reattempt the quiz. This time, try to answer all questions correctly in the shortest time possible. Review the solutions to your incorrect answers. Now, reattempt with correctness as your focus. Repeat this process multiple times till you feel ready.

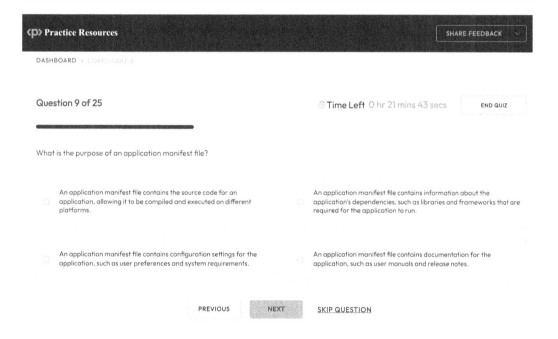

Figure 0.2: Practice Questions Interface on a desktop device

Be it a long train ride to work with just your phone or a lazy Sunday afternoon on the couch with your tablet, the quiz interface works just as well on all your devices as long as they're connected to the internet. *Figure 0.3* shows a screenshot of how the interface looks on mobile devices:

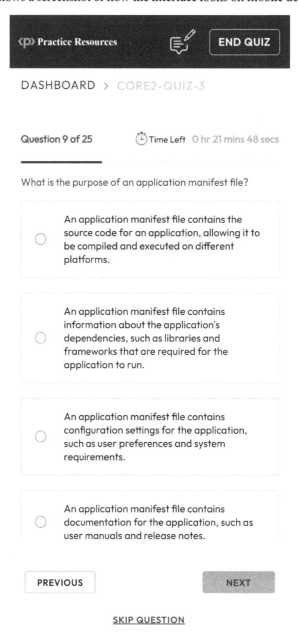

Figure 0.3: Quiz interface on a mobile device

## Flashcards

Flashcards are designed to help you memorize key concepts. Here's how to make the most of them:

1.  We've organized all the flashcards into stacks. Think of these like an actual stack of cards in your hand.

2.  You start with a full stack of cards.

3.  When you open a card, take a few minutes to recall the answer.

4.  Click anywhere on the card to reveal the answer (*Figure 0.4*).

5.  Flip the card back and forth multiple times and memorize the card completely.

6.  Once you feel you've memorized it, click the **Mark as memorized** button on the top-right corner of the card.

7.  Repeat this process as you move to other cards in the stack.

8.  You may not be able to memorize all the cards in one go. That's why, when you open the stack the next time, you'll only see the cards you're yet to memorize.

9.  Your goal is to get to an empty stack ensuring you've memorized each flashcard in the stack.

Figure 0.4: Flashcards interface

## Exam Tips

Exam Tips (*Figure 0.5*) are designed to help you get exam-ready. From the start of your preparation journey to your exam day, these tips are organized such that you can review all of them in one go. If an exam tip comes in handy in your preparation, make sure to mark it as helpful so that other readers.

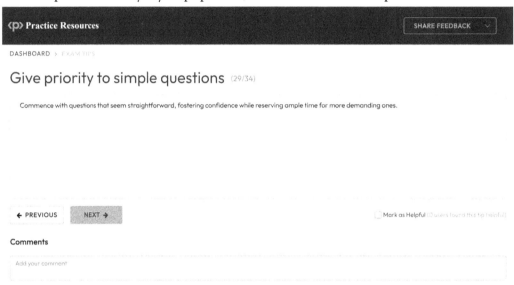

Figure 0.5: Exam Tips Interface

## Share Feedback

If you find any issues with the platform, the book, or any of the practice materials, you can click the **Share Feedback** button from any page and reach out to us. If you have any suggestions for improvement, you can share those as well.

## Back to the book

To make switching between the book and practice resources easy, we've added a link that takes you back to the book (see *Figure 0.6*). Click it to open your book in Packt's online reader. Your reading position is synced so you can jump right back to where you left off when you last opened the book.

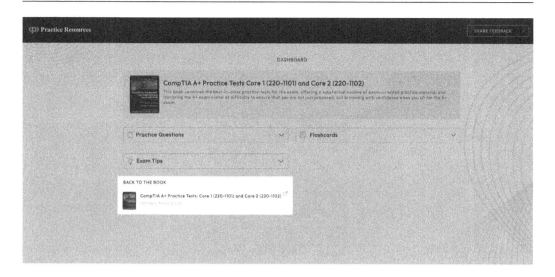

Figure 0.6: Jump back to the book from the dashboard.

**Note**

After the publishing of this book, certain elements of the website might change over time and thus may end up looking different from how they are represented in the screenshots.

## Share Your Thoughts

Once you've read *CompTIA A+ Practice Tests Core 1 (220-1101) and Core 2 (220-1102)*, we'd love to hear your thoughts! Scan the QR code below to go straight to the Amazon review page for this book and share your feedback.

https://packt.link/r/1837633185

Your review is important to us and the tech community and will help us make sure we're delivering excellent quality content.

# How to Use This Book

The purpose of having a practice test book is to facilitate your preparation for the CompTIA A+ exam. Prior to attempting a practice test, it's advisable to have either a digital document or a blank sheet of paper at your disposal. While taking the test, it's beneficial to jot down any subjects that are unfamiliar to you or questions you've answered incorrectly. This practice will help pinpoint areas where your understanding is lacking. Following the test, it is recommended that you revisit your study guide to address the identified gaps.

## Approach for Navigating Multiple-Choice Queries

Embrace this strategy to effectively tackle multiple-choice queries:

- **Thorough reading**: Immerse yourself in the questions and absorb their nuances
- **Elimination game**: Discard incorrect choices, systematically narrowing your options
- **Refinement process**: Evolve from a 50-50 stance to a 60-40 perspective through a meticulous review
- **Unveil the optimal**: Opt for the finest or most plausible choices when multiple correct answers exist
- **Precision in choice**: Align your selection with the specific query at hand

## Exercising Caution in Testing

Avoid these counterproductive actions during your testing endeavor:

- **Overthinking pitfall**: Steer clear of overanalyzing; maintain a balanced mindset
- **Rushing dilemma**: Eschew hasty scanning or racing through the test; maintain a composed pace
- **Doubt's detriment**: Refrain from second-guessing or doubling back; trust your initial instincts
- **Choice constancy**: Resist altering your answers; initial choices often prove sound
- **Comprehensive consistency**: Spare yourself from re-reading the entire test; stay focused on the task at hand

# Advice on Additional Resources – Practical Exercise

An additional preparatory resource that could prove valuable is the CompTIA Official Labs. These cloud-based labs offer a practical approach to exam readiness by directly addressing the topics covered in the exam. Particularly beneficial for individuals with minimal or no prior IT experience, these labs serve as excellent tools for gaining hands-on familiarity.

In the context of CompTIA A+, a solid grasp of hardware concepts is essential, and the labs effectively facilitate this understanding. A noteworthy aspect is the 12-month access granted, allowing ample time for exploration and learning. Notably, Packt Publishing has secured a substantial discount on the CompTIA official labs and the exam voucher, the details for which are at the back of the book.

## What You Will Learn in the CompTIA Official Labs

Once you have paid and signed up for the CompTIA CertMaster Labs for both A+ Core 1 (220-1101) and Core 2 (220-1102), you will have access to hands-on practice and skills development using real equipment and software accessed through a remote, browser-based lab environment. Aligned with Official CompTIA courseware and the CompTIA A+ exam objectives, CertMaster Labs make it easy for learners to practice and apply their skills in real workplace scenarios in preparation for the certification exam. All lab activities include gradable assessments, offer feedback and hints, and provide a score based on learner inputs, ultimately guiding you to the most correct and efficient path through job tasks.

There are two types of labs in the course:

- **Virtual Workbench Labs** provide learners with valuable hands-on practice installing, configuring, and troubleshooting computer hardware in an immersive 3D environment. Each scenario features a Tutorial Mode to guide the learner through step-by-step instructions, allowing learners to understand and practice 3D controls; an Explore Mode that enables learners to identify and manipulate hardware components in a sandbox environment; and an Assisted Mode that takes learners step by step through a procedure, offering help when needed. This hands-on environment gives learners the ability to learn the tangible aspects of IT and gain real-world experience. Learners can explore how the different components of a desktop, a laptop, and peripherals work together, and will get experience of working through different processes for installing and configuring computer components.

- **Virtual Machine Labs** utilize virtual machines built to simulate a server network so a learner can gain real-world, hands-on experience with tools, applications, and operating systems they would utilize in a job environment, such as Microsoft Windows or Kali Linux. Learners can compare network hardware using the GNS3 network simulator and configure a home router using OpenWRT.

Virtual Machine Labs are also available in different modes:

- **Assisted Labs** guide the learner step by step through tasks, offering assessment and feedback throughout a 10-15 minute experience, allowing the learner to correct any misunderstandings as they proceed through the activity.

- **Applied Labs** present a series of goal-oriented scenarios in a 20-30 minute experience covering multiple topics, scoring the learner's work at the end of the activity based on their ability to successfully complete each scenario. As a result, learners are forced to think critically about how to approach problems without a prescribed set of steps. Currently, Applied Labs are only available for Virtual Machine Lab activities.

The following labs are available for A+ Core 1 (220-1101):

- Assisted Lab: Exploring the Lab Environment
- Assisted Lab: Installing a Motherboard
- Assisted Lab: Installing Power Supplies
- Assisted Lab: Installing and Configuring System Memory
- Assisted Lab: Installing RAM
- Assisted Lab: Installing CPU and Cooler
- Assisted Lab: Upgrading and Installing GPU and Daisy-Chain Monitors
- Assisted Lab: Exploring the Virtual Machine Lab Environment
- Assisted Lab: Compare Networking Hardware
- Assisted Lab: Compare Wireless Network Technologies
- Assisted Lab: Configure a SOHO Router
- Assisted Lab: Compare Protocols and Ports
- Assisted Lab: Troubleshoot a Network #1
- Assisted Lab: Troubleshoot a Network #2
- APPLIED Lab: Troubleshoot a Network #1
- APPLIED Lab: Troubleshoot a Network #2
- Assisted Lab: Adding Expansion SSD in a Laptop
- Assisted Lab: Upgrading Laptop RAM

- Assisted Lab: Replacing Laptop Non-User Removable Battery
- Assisted Lab: Configuring Laptop Dock and External Peripherals
- Assisted Lab: Deploy a Printer

The following labs are available for A+ Core 2 (220-1102):

- Assisted Lab: Manage User Settings in Windows
- Assisted Lab: Support Windows 11
- Assisted Lab: Configure Windows System Settings
- Assisted Lab: Use Management Consoles
- Assisted Lab: Use Task Manager
- Assisted Lab: Monitor Performance and Event Logs
- Assisted Lab: Use Command-line Tools
- APPLIED Lab: Support Windows 10
- Assisted Lab: Perform Windows 10 OS Installation
- Assisted Lab: Perform Ubuntu Linux OS Installation
- Assisted Lab: Install and Configure an Application
- Assisted Lab: Troubleshoot a Windows OS Issue
- Assisted Lab: Configure Windows Networking
- Assisted Lab: Configure Folder Sharing in a Workgroup
- Assisted Lab: Manage Linux using Command-line Tools
- Assisted Lab: Manage Files using Linux Command-line Tools
- APPLIED Lab: Support and Troubleshoot Network Hosts
- Assisted Lab: Configure SOHO Router Security
- Assisted Lab: Configure Workstation Security
- Assisted Lab: Configure Browser Security
- Assisted Lab: Troubleshoot Security Issues Scenario #1
- APPLIED Lab: Troubleshoot Security Issues Scenario #2
- Assisted Lab: Use Remote Access Technologies

- Assisted Lab: Implement Backup and Recovery

- Assisted Lab: Implement a PowerShell Script

- Assisted Lab: Implement Bash Script

- Assisted Lab: Manage a Support Ticket

## Accessing the Course Materials

You will receive an access key and registration instructions via email once you have paid and signed up for the CompTIA CertMaster Labs for A+ Core 1 (220-1101) and Core 2 (220-1102).

# 1

# Mobile Devices

## Introduction

Mobile devices are in abundance in the workplace, ranging from laptops to tablets and smartphones. It's therefore important that IT technicians have working knowledge of each type of device, including both the storage used and the method of its migration from legacy to modern storage.

Additionally, in your own career, you may have to enable security for smartphones that require you to set up multifactor or biometric authentication, set up cellular communications and mobile hotspots, or connect a corporate user's Bluetooth headset. And, for laptop queries, whether it requires the order of a new device for the engineering department, installation of a new wireless card, or troubleshooting of the display screen, your understanding of laptop hardware, components, and types and size of cards is crucial to ensuring the support you offer is reliable and effective.

In the CompTIA A+ Core 1 (220-1101) exam, Domain 1.0 Mobile Devices is further broken down into the following core objectives:

- 1.1 Given a scenario, install and configure laptop hardware and components
- 1.2 Compare and contrast the display components of mobile devices
- 1.3 Given a scenario, set up and configure accessories and ports of mobile devices
- 1.4 Given a scenario, configure basic mobile-device network connectivity and application support

The rest of this chapter is committed to practice. For each of the concepts defined above, you will be given a series of questions designed to test your knowledge of each core 1 objective as defined by the official certification exam guidance for this domain. Once you have completed these questions and ensured you understand the concepts behind them, you should be fully prepared to do the same in your CompTIA A+ Core 1 (220-1101) exam.

# Practice Exam Questions

## 1.1 Given a scenario, install and configure laptop hardware and components

1.  Which of the following is the most secure method to set up a laptop or desktop to use biometric readers?

    A.  Set up the laptop/desktop for the person who uses the device

    B.  Set up the laptop/desktop so everyone in the accounts department can log in

    C.  Allow other departments access to the laptop/desktop

    D.  Set up the laptop for user access and allow guest access

2.  A hardware engineer is going to upgrade the RAM in a laptop. Before installing the new RAM, which of the following tasks should the hardware engineer complete first?

    A.  Purchase a 256 GB DDR3 RAM

    B.  Take anti-static precautions by wearing an electrostatic discharge strap

    C.  Check the power voltage to the motherboard

    D.  Download any operating system updates for the laptop's operating system

3.  A user's laptop is working perfectly fine, but for some reason, when they attempt to use it in a coffee shop, it will not power up. The user confirms that the battery is plugged in but notices a small bump on the battery. Which of the following is the most likely cause of this problem?

    A.  The power adapter is faulty

    B.  The operating system is corrupt

    C.  The system fan is not working

    D.  The battery has failed, as it is defective and needs replacing

4.  What type of RAM would you purchase for a laptop computer?

    A.  DIMM

    B.  DDR3

    C.  SDRAM

    D.  SODIMM

5.  Which of the following safety precautions do you need to take prior to installing an SSD into a user's laptop? (Choose four)

    A.  Clear your desk

    B.  Shut down the system

    C.  Disconnect the power cable

    D.  Remove the battery

    E.  Ground yourself by wearing an ESD strap

6.  What types of biometric authentication do the iPhone 10 and iPhone 11 use? (Choose two)

    A.  Fingerprint

    B.  Touch ID

    C.  Face ID

    D.  Vein

7.  A user has put their phone on charging, but the battery is draining quickly and is recharging very slowly. The phone is also hot to the touch. What is wrong with the phone?

    A.  The charging cable is faulty

    B.  The digitizer is broken

    C.  The battery needs to be replaced

    D.  The battery is set to low power mode

8.  A laptop user tries to surf the internet but finds they have no connectivity. Running the ipconfig /all command produces the following output:

    ```
    IPv4 Address. . . . . . . . . . . : 169.254.10.1
    Subnet Mask . . . . . . . . . . . : 255.255.0.0
    Default Gateway . . . . . . . . . :
    DHCP Enabled                        Yes
    ```

    Which of the following is the source of this problem?

    A.  DNS

    B.  DHCP

    C.  NETBIOS

    D.  Static IP address

9. Which of the following stages do you need to take when migrating a Hard Drive (HDD) to a Solid-State Drive (SSD) in a laptop? (Select all that apply)

   A. Clean the files on your old hard drive and remove redundant data

   B. Connect and initialize the SSD

   C. Make a full backup of your system

   D. Resize the old HDD partition where your data resides to be smaller than the SSD

   E. Clone the old HDD partition

   F. Restore the data onto the SSD

10. A new door access system uses a 13.56-MHz short-band frequency. Which of the following can be used for authentication with this system on a mobile device?

    A. Biometrics

    B. Certificates

    C. OAuth token

    D. NFC

11. A computer technician is going to install a Solid-State Drive (SSD) in a laptop. What is the standard form factor of the drive that the computer technician needs to purchase?

    A. 3.5 inches

    B. 2.5 inches

    C. 5.25 inches

    D. 8 inches

12. John Smith plugged his iPhone into his bedside power socket prior to going to bed, but in the morning, the battery displays a 5% charge. He then goes to breakfast, boils the kettle for a cup of tea, and plugs the phone's charger into the kettle's socket. After 30 minutes, the phone still does not seem to be charging. The phone charger is not approved by Apple. Which of the following steps should he take first to investigate the issue?

    A. Delete unwanted apps

    B. Reset the phone to factory settings

    C. Check the power rating of the charger

    D. Set the battery to low power mode

13. A client wants to connect an external keyboard to an Android tablet. Which of the following connection types are appropriate for this task? (Choose two)

    A. Bluetooth

    B. Ethernet

    C. Lightning cable

    D. USB-C

14. What is the most common use of NFC?

    A. Making contactless payments

    B. Creating a hotspot

    C. Enabling touchscreen

    D. Creating a VPN

## 1.2 Compare and contrast the display components of mobile devices

1. Which of the following describes the function of a digitizer?

    A. It converts DC power to AC power

    B. It can support a contrast ratio of 2000:1

    C. It controls the brightness setting on an LCD monitor

    D. It is a piece of glass that is installed on a mobile device to enable the touchscreen to function

2. Which of the following is used by a smartphone to change the orientation of the screen?

    A. Bezel

    B. Digitizer

    C. Accelerometer

    D. Gyroscope

3. The external webcam attached to a laptop is switched on, but it is not producing any images. Which of the following can resolve this issue?

    A. Reboot the computer and try again

    B. Purchase a new webcam

    C. Uninstall and then reinstall the webcam software and ensure you have the most up-to-date drivers from the manufacturer's website

    D. Plug the webcam into another USB port

4.  What is the purpose of an inverter?

    A.  To convert AC to DC power

    B.  To enable touchscreen functionality

    C.  To convert DC to AC power

    D.  To increase readability in low-light conditions

5.  When using a high frame rate, the crystals twist or untwist giving the screen a quick response time that helps reduce ghosting and motion trail. Which of the following options is being described?

    A.  TN

    B.  IPS

    C.  VA

    D.  CRT

6.  You are having trouble with your voice recognition technology on your Windows 10 laptop. Which of the following tasks should you perform first to resolve this issue with minimal effort?

    A.  Reboot the laptop

    B.  Get an up-to-date driver for the voice recognition software

    C.  Enable apps to access your microphone

    D.  Purchase an external microphone

7.  A user is having trouble reading the screen on their legacy LCD monitor. The screen looks very dim. What do you think is most likely causing the problem?

    A.  The brightness has been turned down

    B.  The digitizer is broken

    C.  The backlight is failing

    D.  The VGA cable is damaged

8.  A user has a large dark area on their iPhone screen and has taken it to a mobile phone repair shop. The technician looks at the screen and sees that there is no physical damage. What does the technician determine to be the problem?

    A.  Water damage

    B.  Problem with the inverter

    C.  Brightness too low

    D.  Broken digitizer

9.  Which of the following displays is best for both gaming and graphic design?

    A.  LED

    B.  LCD

    C.  CRT

    D.  IPS

10. Which of the following displays is prone to ghosting and can support a contrast ratio of 2000:1?

    A.  OLED

    B.  VA

    C.  IPS

    D.  LED

11. What type of screen is used by monitors, tablets, smartphones, and TV screens and does not use a backlight?

    A.  CRT

    B.  LCD

    C.  OLED

    D.  LED

12. A user has plugged in two monitors (via a VGA cable and an HDMI cable) and wants to set up dual monitors. However, there does not seem to be an image on the second monitor. What should the user do first to enable dual monitors?

    A.  Go to Settings, Home, Display, Multiple Displays, and then select Duplicate these displays

    B.  Go to Settings, Home, Projecting to this PC, and then select Extend these displays

    C.  Go to Settings, Home, Projecting to this PC, and then select Duplicate these displays

    D.  Go to Settings, Home, Display, Multiple Displays, and then select Extend these displays

13. The sales team wants to play a promotional video from an iPhone 10 for the chief executive officer using Bluetooth speakers, but there does not seem to be any sound coming out of the Bluetooth speakers. The sales team has raised a ticket with the IT help desk. What actions should the support technician take to resolve the issue? (Choose two)

    A.  Under Settings, enable Bluetooth

    B.  Under General, enable Bluetooth

    C.  Ensure the phone is within 20 meters of the speakers

    D.  Ensure the phone is within 10 meters of the speakers

14. A computer technician is troubleshooting wireless connectivity on a laptop. Where do you think is the most likely location for the wireless antenna?

    A.  On the front of the laptop

    B.  On the rear of the laptop

    C.  On the top of the laptop

    D.  Near the fan on the base of the laptop

15. A lawyer left court carrying a large number of case files. They tripped and accidentally dropped some of their files along with their mobile phone that was resting on top. When the lawyer picked up the phone, the screen did not appear broken, but 10 minutes later, when they attempted to send an email from the phone, the mail icon was unresponsive. The same was true for every other app they attempted to access. What do you think happened?

    A.  The digitizer broke

    B.  There was no power

    C.  There were CPU issues

    D.  All of the above

16. The touchpad on your laptop is unresponsive. What should you do? (Choose two)

    A.  Reboot the laptop

    B.  Remove an external mouse that is plugged in

    C.  Update the driver

    D.  Turn off the gyroscope

## 1.3 Given a scenario, set up and configure accessories and ports of mobile devices

1.  What type of connection does an iPhone 10 charger use?

    A.  USB-B

    B.  USB-A

    C.  USB-C

    D.  Lightning

2.  A user is trying to plug a USB 3.0 memory stick into their old Windows 7 laptop but is having difficulty doing so. Which of the following could be causing the issue? (Choose two)

    A.  The USB 3.0 drive has a different form factor

    B.  The USB 3.0 drive is upside down

    C.  The laptop does not have a USB 3.0 port

    D.  The end of the USB 3.0 drive is damaged

3.  What type of connection does a Samsung Galaxy phone use?

    A.  USB

    B.  USB-C

    C.  Micro USB

    D.  Mini USB

4.  A user is finding it difficult to plug their phone charger into their cell phone, and so orders a new charger from Amazon. However, when the new charger is inserted, the same thing happens. It does not seem to fit. Which of the following is the cause and solution of the issue?

    A.  The port that the user is plugging the cable into has a build-up of lint, and they need to use compressed air to clear it

    B.  The port that the user is plugging the cable into has a build-up of lint, and they need to blow into the port to clear it

    C.  The port that the user is plugging the cable into has a build-up of lint, and they need to spray WD-40 into the port to clear it

    D.  The port that the user is plugging the cable into has a build-up of lint, and they need to use a long darning needle to clear it

5.  A user goes into a shop and purchases Bluetooth-capable earbuds so that they can listen to music when working out in the gym. However, when they turn on their smartphone and their earbuds, they find they cannot hear the music. What does the user need to do first to resolve this issue? (Choose two)

    A.  Install a driver on the phone

    B.  Enable Bluetooth

    C.  Pair the device

    D.  Turn on the music

6. Which of the following types of functionality would a docking station with DisplayPort provide for a laptop user? (Choose three)

   A. Keyboard and mouse

   B. Wi-Fi

   C. Ethernet connectivity

   D. Speakers

   E. Dual-monitor functionality

7. A user is working remotely from home and is due to participate in a Zoom conference call in 15 minutes. Unfortunately, when they boot up their laptop, they find their home wireless network is down. What can the user implement quickly so that they can participate in the conference call? Choose the solution that requires the minimum amount of effort.

   A. Travel 10 miles to the local Starbucks to use their wireless network

   B. Connect the laptop directly to the wireless router using an Ethernet cable

   C. Create a hotspot using a smartphone

   D. Reboot the wireless router

8. A laptop user has been complaining to the help desk that their laptop does not have that many ports. They would like a range of additional ports for a keyboard, a mouse, and a VGA projector. How can the support desk fulfill this request with the least amount of administrative work?

   A. Install a KVM switch

   B. Install a port replicator

   C. Install dual monitors

   D. Install a hub

9. When using a tablet with a touch pen, you get erroneous behavior such as an erratically moving cursor. Which of the following are the first three steps you should take to identify the problem?

   A. Check whether the screen is damaged

   B. Replace the touch pen battery

   C. Recalibrate the touch pen

   D. Clean the touchscreen

10. What type of connection was micro USB replaced by?

    A.  Serial

    B.  Lightning

    C.  USB-C

    D.  Parallel

11. What type of connection does an iPhone 14 charger use?

    A.  USB-A

    B.  USB-B

    C.  USB-C

    D.  Lightning

12. What type of interface uses a nine-pin RS-232 hardware port?

    A.  Parallel

    B.  RJ45

    C.  RJ11

    D.  Serial

13. A user is trying to connect to a Zoom session, but when they select the video option, it fails to open. They then go to the camera app on their desktop to test the webcam, but the webcam also fails to open. The webcam was working the previous day. Which of the following should be done to address this issue? (Choose two)

    A.  Ensure that in the camera privacy settings, Allow apps to access this camera is enabled

    B.  Unplug the webcam USB cable and try another USB port

    C.  Close any other video software applications and turn on the webcam to see whether it will launch

    D.  Purchase another webcam as the webcam is broken

14. The touchscreen feature on a Windows 10 computer has stopped working. Which of the following should a technician check?

    A.  That there are no air bubbles on the screen

    B.  Computer settings

    C.  Display settings

    D.  Power settings

15. Following an update to the operating system of their desktop computer, the user's webcam is no longer functioning. The user is due to join a Zoom session in 45 minutes time. Which of the following should be their first step to resolve the issue?

    A.  Quickly go to the shops and buy another webcam

    B.  Reboot their computer

    C.  Reinstall the webcam software including any driver updates

    D.  Update the operating system

16. A Cornish pasty vendor in Waterloo railway station is having difficulty taking contactless card payments. When the card is tapped, the contactless scanner does not read the card and process the transaction. The customers need to insert their card into the device and enter their pin to make payments. Which of the following technologies is at fault here?

    A.  Bluetooth

    B.  Wireless

    C.  NFC

    D.  Infrared

17. A member of the sales team contacts the support desk to say that their cell phone is overheating. Which of the following is causing this to happen? (Choose three)

    A.  A cracked screen

    B.  Using the phone as a Wi-Fi hotspot

    C.  A faulty battery

    D.  Using a cheap charging cable

    E.  Several outdated applications being left open

18. Which of the following cable types did the Lightning cable replace?

    A.  Apple 30-pin connector

    B.  Apple 20-pin connector

    C.  Apple 25-pin connector

    D.  USB-C

## 1.4 Given a scenario, configure basic mobile-device network connectivity and application support

1. A company issues their sales team smartphones under a CYOD policy. A salesperson decides to watch a film on Netflix when staying at a hotel because it is cheaper than subscribing to the hotel's video packages. After breakfast, they use their smartphone to find directions to the next customer's site, but the internet is not working. What is the most likely reason that the internet is not available?

   A. Network coverage is not available in the area

   B. The phone has a data cap

   C. The Mobile Device Management (MDM) solution pushed out an update that disabled the internet

   D. The company has defaulted on its monthly account payment

2. Which of the following types of authentication is two-factor?

   A. Retina and fingerprint

   B. Password and fingerprint

   C. Password and PIN

   D. Gait and swiping a card

3. A user received a new smartphone through the post and has managed to connect the phone to their wireless network to access the internet. However, when they leave home later that day, all internet access has been lost and they cannot make calls. What has the user forgotten to do when setting up the new phone?

   A. Install the SIM card

   B. Turn on mobile data

   C. Remove the film protecting the screen

   D. Activate Bluetooth

4. A regular gym user has just bought an Apple Watch so that they can monitor their exercise by completing the rings each day. To see their progress in the iPhone app, they will need to pair both devices. What is the easiest method of doing so?

   A. Pair manually using the four-digit Apple Watch passcode

   B. Use the camera on the Apple Watch app on the iPhone

   C. Pair manually using a six-digit passcode

   D. Enter the Apple Watch passcode

5.  A mobile salesperson has complained to the service desk that the latest changes to their calendar have appeared on their laptop but have failed to appear on their corporate mobile phone. What should the service desk do to resolve this issue?

    A.  Check that the corporate phone battery is above 50%

    B.  Reboot the corporate mobile phone

    C.  Check that the corporate password has been updated on the calendar application

    D.  Remotely wipe the corporate mobile phone

6.  What is the benefit of using a Global System for Mobile Communication-based phone?

    A.  It can only be used high up a mountain

    B.  The Subscriber Identity Card (SIM) is removable and can be inserted into an unlocked handset with the user's chosen provider

    C.  It can only be used with a satellite

    D.  It can only be used with a WPA3 wireless network

7.  In the past year, the sales team from a company has lost eight smartphones containing sensitive company information. Which of the following options would allow the company to remotely wipe any lost smartphone so that commercially sensitive data cannot be compromised?

    A.  WPA2 PSK

    B.  Disabling Bluetooth

    C.  Mobile Device Management (MDM) solution

    D.  Using a VPN on all company phones

8.  What is the purpose of a Mobile Application Management (MAM) solution? (Choose two)

    A.  Patch management

    B.  Prevent data transfer to personal apps

    C.  Set policies for apps that process corporate data

    D.  Remotely wipe devices

9.  Where does your Samsung Galaxy back up your data?

    A.  Gmail

    B.  Google Drive

    C.  Knox container

    D.  Office 365

10. A user tries to download an app from the Apple App Store onto their iPhone, but the installation fails. What do they need to do next?

    A.  Enter their Hotmail account details

    B.  Enter their Gmail account details

    C.  Enter their iPhone passcode

    D.  Enter their Apple ID and password

11. On the 70th anniversary of Edmond Hillary's climb to the summit of Mount Everest, a team from New Zealand plans to follow in his footsteps. Some of the locations that they will visit en route will have very poor connectivity for cell phones. Which of the following would you recommend that they use for communications?

    A.  Carrier pigeon

    B.  DSL

    C.  Hotspot

    D.  Satellite

12. A pop star on a worldwide tour has complained to you, their cell phone provider, that their iPhone battery is draining too quickly. They also find when running applications that the weather app is using the most power. What would you recommend they do to prevent battery drain but still allow them to get weather notifications?

    A.  Turn off location services

    B.  Connect to local wireless networks

    C.  Manually enter the locations in the weather app

    D.  Change the battery

13. A traveling salesperson was trying to use the GPS on their phone, but it stopped working. They took it to a cell phone store and the support technician took less than one minute to identify the source of the problem and advised the salesperson to change the battery. How did the technician resolve the issue?

    A.  Turned on Bluetooth

    B.  Turned off power conservation mode

    C.  Cleaned the touchscreen

    D.  Turned on Wi-Fi

14. A foreign government intends to track an intelligence agent's phone at all times while they travel abroad. Which of the following can prevent them from doing so?

   A.  Set location services to pause

   B.  Keep the device in a laptop bag

   C.  Turn off location services

   D.  Delete location services

15. Where does your iPhone back your files up to?

   A.  Boot Camp

   B.  Office 365

   C.  Google Drive

   D.  iCloud

16. How can you verify that Bluetooth is enabled on a Windows 10 phone?

   A.  The Bluetooth tile is blue

   B.  The Bluetooth tile is white

   C.  The Bluetooth tile is green

   D.  The Bluetooth tile is gray

17. What can you use to prevent PII and sensitive data from being shared outside the company over corporate email?

   A.  Legal hold

   B.  MailTips

   C.  Firewall

   D.  DLP

18. Comparing Global System for Mobile Communication (GSM)-based phones and Code Division Multiple Access (CDMA)-based handsets, which of the following statements is true?

   A.  Both GSM and CDMA phones have removable SIM cards

   B.  Neither GSM nor CDMA phones have removable SIM cards

   C.  GSM phones have removable SIM cards, while CDMA phones have no SIM cards

   D.  CDMA phones have removable SIM cards, while GSM phones have no SIM cards

19. A mobile salesperson has been asked to cover a different territory for a three-month period. On their first day working in the new territory, their smartphone cannot access the internet nor make any calls. Which of the following needs to be carried out so that the salesperson can use their smartphone?

    A.  Firmware update

    B.  PRL update

    C.  Turn on location services

    D.  Restart the smartphone

20. A user's smartphone is unable to make a 4G connection. What should they do to resolve this issue?

    A.  Go to Settings, then Mobile Data, and enable Wi-Fi calling

    B.  Go to Wi-Fi, then Mobile Data, and enable mobile data

    C.  Go to Settings, then Mobile Data, and enable mobile data

    D.  Go to Wi-Fi, then enable Wi-Fi calling

21. Which of the following are true about Google Workspace? (Select all that apply)

    A.  It is a subscription service with a 14-day free trial

    B.  You can create virtual machines

    C.  You can conduct video meetings

    D.  You can access Google Drive

    E.  There is at least 30 GB of storage per user

    F.  You need a live.com email to access it

22. The FBI informs a business that one of their employees might be carrying out some criminal activities. They want to ensure that any messages sent via corporate email are retained and not deleted as these emails might be needed as evidence for the case against the employee. Which of the following solutions will the system administrator implement?

    A.  Back up the employee's mailbox

    B.  Apply a legal hold

    C.  Set up a forensic toolkit

    D.  Maintain the chain of custody

23. Which of the following are valid ways to test a Bluetooth connection? (Choose three)

    A.  If you have earbuds, verify that the Bluetooth connect tile is blue

    B.  If you are wearing a headset, go into Zoom (or some other video calling service), then locate Audio Settings, Speaker, and select Test speaker

    C.  If you have earbuds, try playing music on your phone

    D.  If you are wearing a headset, go into Zoom (or some other video calling service), then locate Audio Settings, Microphone, and select Test mic

    E.  If you are wearing a headset, go into Zoom (or some other video calling service), then locate Video Settings, Speaker, and select Test speaker

    F.  If you are wearing a headset, go into Zoom (or some other video calling service), then locate Video Settings, Microphone, and select Test mic

# 2

# Networking

## Introduction

Modern technology is increasingly characterized by the interconnectivity of our devices. This means that to keep pace with this progress and provide consistent and effective support, it is imperative that IT professionals have a working knowledge of networking concepts ranging from IP addresses to the different types of wireless networks.

You will need to know what ports different applications use in order to open those ports on the firewall and allow them to communicate. IT administrators also need to know how to troubleshoot issues when users cannot connect to the network, whether the source of the problem is a DNS or IP error. Wireless networks are a common part of everyday life, and it is vital that you have the knowledge and experience to determine which type of wireless network is best for a given scenario. The practice test in this chapter will test the application of the information that you have gained from previous study.

In the CompTIA A+ Core 1 (220-1101) certification examination, Domain 2.0 Networking makes up 20% of the assessment and is therefore a vital component of a student's successful preparation. This domain is further broken down into the following core objectives:

- 2.1 Compare and contrast Transmission Control Protocol (TCP) and User Datagram Protocol (UDP) ports, protocols, and their purposes

- 2.2 Compare and contrast common networking hardware

- 2.3 Compare and contrast protocols for wireless networking

- 2.4 Summarize services provided by networked hosts

- 2.5 Given a scenario, install and configure basic wired/wireless small office/home office (SOHO) networks

- 2.6 Compare and contrast common network configuration concepts

- 2.7 Compare and contrast internet connection types, network types, and their features

- 2.8 Given a scenario, use networking tools

The rest of this chapter is committed to practice. For each of the concepts defined above, you will be given a series of questions designed to test your knowledge of each core 1 objective as defined by the official certification exam guidance for this domain. Once you have completed these questions and ensured you understand the concepts behind them, you should be fully prepared to do the same on your CompTIA A+ Core 1 (220-1101) exam.

## Practice Exam Questions

### 2.1 Compare and contrast TCP and UDP ports, protocols, and their purposes

1.  A systems administrator needs to use a protocol for secure remote access to network devices. Which of the following should they use?

    A.   Telnet TCP port 23

    B.   SSH TCP port 22

    C.   RDP TCP port 3389

    D.   SNMP UDP port 161

2.  When an online store alerts you that you are being redirected to a secure server, what protocol should be seen in the URL?

    A.   TFTP

    B.   HTTPS

    C.   HTTP

    D.   SSH

3.  Which of the following mail clients downloads the email, stores it on the local computer, and does not retain a copy on the mail server?

    A.   POP

    B.   IMAP

    C.   SMTP

    D.   SSH

4. Which application protocol is used in Windows operating systems for file and print sharing?

   A.  137-139

   B.  67/68

   C.  445

   D.  389

5. Which of the following standard ports is used by secure Post Office Protocol (POP)?

   A.  110

   B.  995

   C.  993

   D.  143

6. Which of the following protocols is connectionless and used for streaming video or audio?

   A.  TCP

   B.  RDP

   C.  UDP

   D.  TFTP

7. Which of the following ports is used by the secure version of the protocol that can provide statuses and reports of all network devices?

   A.  161

   B.  389

   C.  110

   D.  162

8. Which of the following protocols uses TCP ports 20/21 and transfers data in cleartext?

   A.  TFTP

   B.  FTP

   C.  SSH

   D.  FTPS

9.  Which of the following are default ports for HTTP and HTTPS traffic? (Choose two)

    A.  23

    B.  80

    C.  110

    D.  443

    E.  445

10. TCP is connection-orientated and uses a three-way handshake. What is the correct sequence of the handshake?

    A.  SYN, ACK, and SYN-ACK

    B.  SIGNAL, CONNECT, ACKNOWLEDGE

    C.  SYN-ACK, ACK, and SYN

    D.  SYN, SYN-ACK, and ACK

11. A system administrator is setting up a new firewall and needs to allow SMTP traffic to flow through. Which of the following TCP ports must be enabled for inbound traffic?

    A.  21

    B.  22

    C.  23

    D.  25

12. Which of the following standard ports is used by secure IMAP?

    A.  993

    B.  110

    C.  995

    D.  143

13. Which of the following is an unsecure remote access protocol that can have its password stolen by a protocol analyzer?

    A.  SSL

    B.  SSH

    C.  Telnet

    D.  RDP

## 2.2 Compare and contrast common networking hardware

QTYPE: MCQ-MULTI_ANSWER

1.  A junior network administrator has been asked to identify the front and back of a patch panel. Which of the following is true? (Choose two)

    A.  The front of the patch panel is where cabling running through the company terminates at the insulation displacement connector (IDC)

    B.  The back of the patch panel is where cabling running through the company terminates at the insulation displacement connector (IDC)

    C.  The front of the patch panel has prewired RJ45 ports

    D.  The back of the patch panel has prewired RJ45 ports

2.  Cloud Service Providers (CSP) need to be able to rapidly provision servers and networks using scripting. What type of networking provides this?

    A.  Wide area network (WAN)

    B.  Local area network (LAN)

    C.  Software-defined networking (SDN)

    D.  Storage area network (SAN)

3.  What type of firewall can perform URL filtering, content filtering, and malware inspection?

    A.  Stateless firewall

    B.  Host-based firewall

    C.  Stateful firewall

    D.  Unified Threat Management (UTM)

4.  What is the purpose of an Optical Network Terminal (ONT) installed at a customer's home?

    A.  It provides fiber to the curb (FTTC)

    B.  The ONT converts optical signals to electrical signals

    C.  The ONT converts electrical signals and converts them to optical signals

    D.  The ONT is located in a street cabinet

5.  Which of the following allows a host to pull power for a device through an ethernet cable plugged into a switch?

    A.  POE

    B.  Thunderbolt

    C.  Managed switch

    D.  Shielded twisted pair

6.  Which of the following network devices is used to reduce the size of broadcast domains in a LAN?

    A.  Load balancer

    B.  Managed switch

    C.  Router

    D.  Hub

7.  Which of the following technologies allows virtual servers to connect to high-speed storage?

    A.  SAN

    B.  PAN

    C.  Cluster

    D.  RAID 0

8.  A company wants to use POE as powering switches is more efficient than using an AC adapter and will help reduce the electricity bill. However, two of the switches do not support POE. Bearing in mind that cost is a concern, what can the network engineer do to solve this issue?

    A.  Purchase an uninterruptible power supply (UPS)

    B.  Purchase a generator

    C.  Install power injectors

    D.  Purchase two POE capable switches

9.  What type of switch is unpacked from the box, turned on, has either 4 or 8 ports, and is used in very small networks?

    A.  Managed switch

    B.  Aggregate switch

    C.  Power diode switch

    D.  Unmanaged switch

10. Which of the following legacy network hardware devices sends any incoming packets it receives to all ports connected to the device?

    A.  Load balancer

    B.  Switch

    C.  Router

    D.  Hub

11. If a network-based firewall is set up to allow HTTP and HTTPS traffic, what happens when a user tries to download a document using FTP?

    A.  Document will be downloaded

    B.  Document will be blocked by its host-based firewall

    C.  Implicit deny

    D.  Explicit deny

12. Which of the following statements about cable modems are true? (Select all that apply)

    A.  A cable modem is similar to a DSL router but uses coax

    B.  A cable modem is connected to the local router via an RJ45 port

    C.  A cable modem accesses the provider's network via a short segment of coax

    D.  The coax used by a cable modem is terminated using threaded F-type connectors

13. What are the THREE layers of an SDN?

    A.  Application layer

    B.  Transport layer

    C.  Control layer

    D.  Infrastructure layer

    E.  Data link layer

    F.  Physical layer

14. Which of the following is true concerning a network interface card used with a Cat 5 cable?

    A.  The NIC card will use a BNC connector

    B.  The NIC card will use an RJ45 connector

    C.  The NIC card will use an RJ11 connector

    D.  The NIC card will run at a speed of 10Mbps

15. What version of Power over Ethernet (POE) can draw power up to 25W?

    A.  802.11

    B.  802.3at

    C.  802.3bt

    D.  802.3af

16. Which of the following are true about different types of DSL? Select TWO.

    A.  ADSL provides the same upload and download speeds

    B.  ADSL provides a fast download but a slow upload speed

    C.  The symmetric version of DSL provides a fast upload and a slow download speed

    D.  The symmetric version of DSL provides the same upload and download speed

## 2.3 Compare and contrast protocols for wireless networking

1.  Which of the following bands work with radios that are single-band 2.4GHz? (Select all that apply)

    A.  Wi-Fi 6

    B.  Wi-Fi 5

    C.  802.11g

    D.  802.11b

    E.  Wi-Fi 4

2.  Which of the following wireless frequencies supports both 5GHz and 2.4GHz?

    A.  802.11b

    B.  802.11g

    C.  802.11a

    D.  802.11ax

3.  A user is trying and failing to get their Bluetooth earbuds to connect to their smartphone to listen to music. Which of the following actions should the user carry out? Select TWO.

    A.  Pair the device

    B.  Go to Settings | Wi-Fi, then enable Bluetooth

    C.  Go to Settings | Mobile Data, then enable Bluetooth

    D.  Go to Settings, then enable Bluetooth

4. Which of the following can be used as a bridge to connect two wireless networks over a distance of 25 miles?

    A. GPS

    B. Long-range fixed wireless

    C. Unlicensed wireless

    D. Licensed wireless

5. Which of the following wireless protocols can be used for contactless payments?

    A. Bluetooth

    B. RFID

    C. NFC

    D. Tethering

6. Which of the following standards supports only the 5GHz frequency band?

    A. 802.11a

    B. 802.11b

    C. 802.11g

    D. 802.11n

7. Which of the following statements about 2.4GHz wireless frequency is true? (Choose two)

    A. 2.4GHz is slower than 5GHz

    B. 2.4GHz is faster than 5GHz

    C. 2.4GHz covers a greater distance than 5GHz

    D. 2.4GHz covers a smaller distance than 5GHz

8. Which of the following wireless technologies has the fastest throughput?

    A. 802.11ac

    B. 802.11ax

    C. 802.11a

    D. 802.11b

9.  Which of the following wireless standards are backward-compatible with 802.11g?

    A.  802.11b

    B.  802.11a

    C.  802.11n

    D.  801.11ac

10. Which of the following statements about the 5GHz wireless frequency are true? (Choose two)

    A.  5GHz is more effective at propagating through solid surfaces than 2.4GHz

    B.  5GHz is less effective at propagating through solid surfaces than 2.4GHz

    C.  5GHz supports more individual channels and suffers less congestion than 2.4GHz

    D.  5GHz supports more individual channels and suffers more congestion than 2.4GHz

11. Which of the following standards supports MIMO technology?

    A.  802.11a

    B.  802.11b

    C.  802.11g

    D.  802.11n

## 2.4 Summarize services provided by networked hosts

1.  The helpdesk has been overwhelmed by network users saying that they cannot access any network resources. What server should the helpdesk ensure is up and running?

    A.  Domain controller

    B.  DNS server

    C.  DHCP server

    D.  Mail server

2.  If a home user has an internet connection but cannot connect to any websites and reports this to their ISP, what should the system administrator of the ISP check first?

    A.  The user's login credentials

    B.  The IP address of the user's device

    C.  The destination web servers

    D.  The DNS server settings

3.  What type of server can provide webpage caching?

    A.  File server

    B.  Proxy server

    C.  UTM firewall

    D.  Web server

4.  What type of network is used in oil or gas refineries?

    A.  Production network

    B.  Local area network

    C.  SCADA network

    D.  MAN

5.  Which of the following could be considered Internet of Things? (Choose two)

    A.  Alexa

    B.  Alarm clock

    C.  Smart meter

    D.  Headset

6.  Which of the following is true about spam gateways? (Select all that apply)

    A.  They use SPF, DKIM, and DMARC to verify the authenticity of the mail servers sending emails

    B.  They are used to send out spam to other organizations

    C.  They use a DLP system to stop PII and other sensitive information from leaving your network

    D.  They filter out incoming messages to prevent them from being delivered to users' mailboxes

7.  An organization has installed 20 web servers into an existing web array of 30 web servers. How can this array of web servers be optimized for faster response times?

    A.  Set up a cluster

    B.  Install a load balancer

    C.  Install a proxy server

    D.  Install a DNS server

8.  What type of server uses port 25?

    A.  DNS server

    B.  DHCP server

    C.  Proxy server

    D.  Mail server

9.  What type of content is hosted on a web server?

    A.  Stored files

    B.  Websites that contain home folders

    C.  Mailboxes

    D.  Authentication, authorization, and accounting information

10. A user has a mapped drive that shows a UNC path of \\server1\data. Which of the following network services are they accessing?

    A.  Print server

    B.  File share

    C.  Syslog

    D.  Proxy server

11. Which of the following can authenticate a supplicant without holding a copy of the relevant directory services?

    A.  Syslog server

    B.  DNS server

    C.  Proxy server

    D.  RADIUS server

12. A system administrator has installed a new laser printer for the customer service team. After installation, they attempt to print a test page, but it fails to print. What should they do first?

    A.  Calibrate the printer

    B.  Reboot the printer

    C.  Download the driver from the manufacturer's website

    D.  Change the toner cartridge

13. Which of the following servers centralizes log files from multiple servers?

    A.  Syslog

    B.  DHCP

    C.  File server

    D.  Domain controller

14. What is the first thing a home user should do when they purchase an IoT device such as a baby monitor?

    A.  Update the device

    B.  Disconnect the internet

    C.  Read the user manual

    D.  Reset the default password

## 2.5 Given a scenario, install and configure basic wired/wireless small office/home office (SOHO) networks

1.  What type of IP address should a server be given?

    A.  Dynamic

    B.  Static

    C.  Automatic Private Internet Protocol Addressing (APIPA)

    D.  Public

2.  What is the limitation of using a private IPv4 address?

    A.  It can only be used internally

    B.  It can only be used for networks of up to 1,000 hosts

    C.  It does not have a network ID

    D.  It does not have a host ID

3.  A systems administrator is configuring an IP address on the external port of the firewall that connects to the WAN. Which of the following IP addresses will they use?

    A.  131.107.1.1

    B.  192.168.1.1

    C.  169.254.1.223

    D.  172.16.5.13

    E.  10.10.15.6

4.  Which of the following is the default subnet mask for a Class B IPv4 address?

    A.  255.0.0.0

    B.  255.255.0.0

    C.  255.255.255.0

    D.  169.254.1.1

5.  If you work from home and need to connect to the internet, which of the following devices are you most likely to use?

    A.  Hub

    B.  Router

    C.  Switch

    D.  WAP

6.  Which of the following is a valid IPv4 address?

    A.  10.1.1.0

    B.  255.255.255.128

    C.  212.15.1.2

    D.  12.1.1.255

7.  A Windows server has been configured with both IPv4 and IPv6 addresses. What is this known as?

    A.  Double stack

    B.  Double IP addressing

    C.  Dual IP addressing

    D.  Dual stack

8.  Which of the following is the reason why a desktop might be allocated an IP address of 169.254.11.2? (Select all that apply)

    A.  The desktop might have a bad cable or cannot send its broadcast to the DHCP server

    B.  The desktop might not be able to contact a DNS server

    C.  The desktop might not be able to connect to a domain controller

    D.  The desktop might have been allocated a duplicate IP address

9. A user is unable to access the internet, and when the system administrator runs the ipconfig/
all command, they get the following output:

```
IPv4 Address. . . . . . . . . . . : 132.24.0.1
Subnet Mask . . . . . . . . . . . : 255.255.0.0
Default Gateway . . . . . . . . . :
```

Which of the following is the source of this problem?

A. DNS

B. Gateway

C. Private IPv4 address

D. Dynamic IP address

10. How many bits does an IPv4 address use?

A. 32

B. 8

C. 16

D. 64

11. Which of the following is an IPv6 address?

A. 10.1.1.1

B. B4-2E-99-C0-75-45

C. 169.254.1.5

D. 2001:0dC8:0000:0000:0abc:0000:def0:2311

12. An installation engineer has installed a new router in a SOHO network that consists of five
users. During testing, they noticed that all devices have APIPAs. Printers and file shares are still
working, but the hosts cannot access the internet. Which of the following has the installation
engineer MOST LIKELY forgotten to configure on the router?

A. NETBIOS

B. SMTP

C. DNS

D. SMB

13. How can you shorten the following IPv6 address:
2001:0dC8:0000:0000:0abc:0000:def0:2311?

   A.  2001:0dC8::0abc::def0:2311

   B.  2001:0dC8::0000:0abc:0000:def0:2311

   C.  2001:dC8::abc::def:2311

   D.  2001:dC8::abc:0:def0:2311

14. Which of the following is a public IPv4 address?

   A.  10.10.10.1

   B.  172.16.1.3

   C.  126.1.1.1

   D.  192.168.5.6

15. How many bits does an IPv6 address use?

   A.  16

   B.  32

   C.  64

   D.  128

## 2.6 Compare and contrast common network configuration concepts

1.  The financial director of an enterprise raised a ticket as they were unable to connect to any network resources. What should the system administrator check first?

   A.  DHCP server

   B.  SNMP

   C.  RADIUS server

   D.  DNS server

2.  What DNS record needs to be allocated to a host with an IP address of 2001:0436:2CA1:0057:0023:0567:5673:0005?

   A.  A

   B.  AAA

   C.  MX

   D.  TXT

3.  What is the default lease duration of a Microsoft DHCP server?

    A.  12 days

    B.  14 days

    C.  8 days

    D.  2 days

4.  Users in a small company cannot access the mail server on Monday morning. The system administrator had migrated the old mail server to a new version but did not update the DNS record for the mail server. What DNS records do they need to update?

    A.  MX

    B.  A

    C.  AAA

    D.  SRV

5.  What type of network would be a single site with all users in close proximity, secure, and connected by one or more switches?

    A.  WAN

    B.  MAN

    C.  LAN

    D.  CAN

6.  Which of the following uses cryptography to confirm that the source server that an email came from was legitimate?

    A.  SPF

    B.  DMARC

    C.  Syslog

    D.  DKIM

7.  One of the users in a company keeps raising support tickets for very minor issues. The IT team wants to be able to track him by his IP address. The company is using a DHCP server to dynamically allocate IP addresses. How can the IT team set this user up so that he gets the same IP address from the DHCP server?

    A.  Create a new scope for him

    B.  Create a customized lease duration for him

    C.  Create a static IP address for him

    D.  Create a reservation for him

8.  Which of the following technologies allows multiple networks to be created within a switch?

    A.  VLAN

    B.  Proxy Server

    C.  Firewall

    D.  Router

9.  The spam gateway was fooled by spam coming from many different fake domains. Which of the following can be implemented to prevent these emails from accessing the company network?

    A.  Firewall

    B.  Content filter

    C.  DMARC

    D.  Proxy server

10. A network administrator is planning to divide the company's network into three subnets. What do they need to configure in the DHCP server so that each subnet gets a certain range of IP addresses that are unique to that subnet?

    A.  Scope

    B.  Reservation

    C.  Lease

    D.  Superscope

11. What is the DNS record used by a host with an IP address of 131.122.14.12?

    A.  A

    B.  AAA

    C.  MX

    D.  SPF

12. What is the sequence of the DHCP handshake?

    A.  ACK, OFFER, REQUEST, DISCOVER

    B.  DISCOVER, OFFER, REQUEST, ACK

    C.  DISCOVER, REQUEST, OFFER, ACK

    D.  REQUEST, OFFER, DISCOVER, ACK

13. Which of the following is a method that can be used to securely connect a remote user's laptop to a corporate server from overseas?

    A.  WAN

    B.  SSL

    C.  DHCP

    D.  VPN

14. Which of the following tools can be used to prevent spear phishing or spam attacks? (Select all that apply)

    A.  Stateless firewall

    B.  SPF

    C.  DKIM

    D.  DMARC

## 2.7 Compare and contrast internet connection types, network types, and their features

1.  What type of network is the internet an example of?

    A.  MAN

    B.  PAN

    C.  WAN

    D.  LAN

2.  A mountaineering team is going to climb Mount Everest for charity. However, once they are 1,000 meters above the base camp, they find that they cannot use their cellular phones to communicate with the admin team back in the base camp. How can they climb the mountain and still communicate with the base camp?

    A.  Cable modem

    B.  Satellite

    C.  GPS

    D.  Wireless

3.  An organization using unshielded twisted pair cabling has been suffering from Electromagnetic Interference (EMI). What can the organization implement to protect from EMI and also provide high-speed communication at the same time?

    A.  Fiber

    B.  Coax

    C.  STP

    D.  10-BASE T

4.  What is the main type of connection used by an iPhone 11?

    A.  DSL

    B.  Wireless

    C.  Cellular

    D.  Satellite

5.  Which of the following statements are true about a Wireless Internet Service Provider (WISP)? (Choose two)

    A.  They manufacture the most modem wireless access points

    B.  They install long-range fixed-access wireless technology

    C.  They provide a bridge between the customer and their service provider networks

    D.  They monitor the wireless bandwidth for corporate customers

6.  Which of the following best describes a WAN?

    A.  An unsecure network over a very large geographical area

    B.  A secure fast network with all users in close proximity

    C.  A boundary network that protects the LAN

    D.  All of the above

7.  Which of the following technologies would allow a network host to be allocated an IP address based on its MAC address?

    A.  SMTP

    B.  DHCP

    C.  SSL

    D.  DNS

8.  A small solicitor's firm has just moved into a listed building. They are not allowed to drill into the walls and have paid a contractor to install a wireless router that connects all of the devices to the wireless network, meaning they do not need physical cables. What type of network has the contractor implemented?

    A.  LAN

    B.  PAN

    C.  WLAN

    D.  WAN

9.  A company's telephone line has failed due to adverse weather, and their internet connection has been subsequently lost. What type of internet access must they be using for this to occur?

    A.  DSL

    B.  Satellite

    C.  Fiber

    D.  Cable modem

## 2.8 Given a scenario, use networking tools

1.  Which of the following tools can be used to test a network card or switch port?

    A.  Crimping tool

    B.  Cable stripper

    C.  Punch-down tool

    D.  Loopback plug

2.  Which of the following tools will be used by a network administrator to score the cable jacket and remove it from the cable so that it can be attached to an RJ45 plug?

    A.  Crimper

    B.  Pliers

    C.  Cable stripper

    D.  Loopback plug

3.  What type of tool would be used to terminate wires into an IDC block?

    A.  Punch-down tool

    B.  Crimping tool

    C.  Cable stripper

    D.  Cable tester

4.  The CEO of a company is unable to obtain a network connection. The ports on the patch panel are not labeled. Which network tool will the system administrator use to identify the port that the CEO is using?

    A.  Crimping tool

    B.  Punch-down tool

    C.  Optical Time Domain Reflectometer (OTDR)

    D.  Toner probe

5.  Which of the following is the cheapest solution to monitor outbound traffic in an Ethernet network?

    A.  Network tap

    B.  Loopback plug

    C.  Spectrum analyzer

    D.  Toner probe

6.  A network engineer found that the RJ45 connection on an Ethernet cable had come loose and wanted to replace the RJ45 plug. Which of the following tools would they use to carry out this task?

    A.  Punch-down tool

    B.  Cable stripper

    C.  Crimping tool

    D.  Pliers

7.  A system administrator has a problem with their wireless access point. To troubleshoot the problem and measure the signal strength, what tool should they use?

    A.  Wi-Fi analyzer

    B.  Protocol analyzer

    C.  Bandwidth monitor

    D.  Radio frequency interference

8.  What tool should a network administrator use to measure whether a cable in a wall socket has a permanent connection to a patch panel?

    A.  Loopback plug

    B.  Cable tester

    C.  A bandwidth monitor

    D.  OTDR

# 3

# Hardware

## Introduction

In the vast realm of information technology, hardware serves as the solid foundation upon which the digital world thrives. From the tiniest microchip to the largest server, hardware is the tangible infrastructure that powers our digital existence. Understanding its intricacies is not only crucial for aspiring IT professionals but also essential for anyone seeking to navigate the digital landscape effectively.

In the CompTIA A+ Core 1 (220-1101) certification examination, Domain 3.0 Hardware makes up 25% of the assessment and is therefore a pivotal section. It is evident that mastering the principles of hardware is of paramount importance for success in this certification. This domain is further broken down into the following core objectives:

- 3.1 Explain basic cable types and their connectors, features, and purposes

- 3.2 Install the appropriate RAM given a scenario

- 3.3 Select and install storage devices given a scenario

- 3.4 Install and configure motherboards, CPUs, and add-on cards given a scenario

- 3.5 Install or replace the appropriate power supply given a scenario

- 3.6 Deploy and configure multifunction devices/printers and settings given a scenario

- 3.7 Install and replace printer consumables given a scenario

The rest of this chapter is committed to practice. For each of the concepts defined above, you will be given a series of questions designed to test your knowledge of each core 1 objective as defined by the official certification exam guidance for this domain. Once you have completed these questions and ensured you understand the concepts behind them, you should be fully prepared to do the same on your CompTIA A+ Core 1 (220-1101) exam.

# Practice Exam Questions

## 3.1 Explain basic cable types and their connectors, features, and purposes

1.  What is the main limitation of using copper cables for high-speed data transmission?

    A.  Signal attenuation

    B.  Interference from electromagnetic fields

    C.  Limited bandwidth

    D.  Insufficient insulation

2.  Which tool is commonly used to troubleshoot a fiber optic cable?

    A.  Optical Time Domain Reflectometer (OTDR)

    B.  Wire cutter

    C.  Ethernet cable tester

    D.  Multimeter

3.  When would you use an ST connector in networking and what is a key benefit?

    A.  Single-mode fiber

    B.  Multi-mode fiber

    C.  High-density networks

    D.  Coaxial cables

4.  What is the maximum distance limitation of Cat 5 cables for Ethernet networking?

    A.  100 meters

    B.  150 meters

    C.  200 meters

    D.  250 meters

5.  Which of the following tools is commonly used to add lines to the demarcation point (demarc)?

    A.  Punch-down tool

    B.  Wire stripper

    C.  Cable tester

    D.  Crimping tool

6.  In which of the following scenarios would you use an RJ11 connector?

    A.  Connecting a telephone handset to a wall jack

    B.  Connecting a computer to a router

    C.  Connecting a printer

    D.  Connecting a TV to a cable box

7.  When using a Gigabit network card, what is the maximum data transmission speed limitation of Cat 5 cables?

    A.  100 Mbps

    B.  1 Gbps

    C.  10 Gbps

    D.  40 Gbps

8.  Which operating system commonly utilizes Thunderbolt cables for high-speed data transfer and device connectivity?

    A.  macOS

    B.  Windows

    C.  Linux

    D.  Android

9.  What tool is commonly used to create an RJ45 cable?

    A.  Crimping tool

    B.  Wire stripper

    C.  Punch-down tool

    D.  Multimeter

10. In which scenario would you commonly use a Lightning to USB cable?

    A.  Charging an iPhone

    B.  Connecting a printer to a computer

    C.  Transferring data between two computers

    D.  Connecting a monitor to a laptop

11. What type of cable has a T568B connection on one end and a T568A connection on the other end?

    A.  Crossover cable

    B.  Straight-through cable

    C.  Coaxial cable

    D.  Fiber optic cable

12. What is the actual speed difference between USB and USB 2?

    A.  USB offers a speed of 12 Mbps, while USB 2 offers a speed of 480 Mbps

    B.  USB and USB 2 have the same speed of 480 Mbps

    C.  USB 2 offers a speed of 12 Mbps, while USB offers a speed of 480 Mbps

    D.  USB and USB 2 have variable speeds depending on the version

13. When should plenum-grade cables be used in networking installations?

    A.  Air-handling spaces

    B.  Outdoor environments

    C.  High-speed data transfer

    D.  Long-distance connectivity

14. When would you use Shielded Twisted Pair (STP) cables in networking installations?

    A.  High electromagnetic interference (EMI) environments

    B.  Outdoor installations

    C.  Long-distance connections

    D.  Low electromagnetic interference (EMI) environments

15. When are F-type connectors commonly used in networking?

    A.  Ethernet network connections

    B.  Fiber optic network connections

    C.  Cable television (CATV) connections

    D.  Wi-Fi network connections

16. A junior IT technician has inadvertently cut the end of an Ethernet cable with a sharp knife. What three tools do you need to repair it?

    A. Wire cutters, a crimping tool, and an RJ45 connector

    B. Screwdriver, electrical tape, and an RJ45 connector

    C. Soldering iron, heat shrink tubing, and an RJ45 connector

    D. Pliers, a multimeter, and an RJ45 connector

17. You are setting up a fiber optic network and need to choose between SC and LC connectors. Which connector type provides a higher density and is commonly used in data centers?

    A. SC connector

    B. LC connector

    C. ST connector

    D. FC connector

18. Which of the following interfaces is commonly used to connect external storage devices to a computer at high speeds?

    A. USB 2.0

    B. HDMI

    C. eSATA

    D. VGA

19. Which of the following is a primary advantage of using DisplayPort as a video interface?

    A. Simultaneous video and audio transmission

    B. Compatibility with older display devices

    C. Support for 4K and higher resolutions

    D. Lower cost compared to other interfaces

## 3.2 Install the appropriate RAM given a scenario

1. What is the primary purpose of virtual RAM (or virtual memory) in a computer system?

    A. To provide additional storage space for files and documents

    B. To improve system performance by extending available memory

    C. To create a backup of the system's physical RAM

    D. To facilitate faster data transfer between the CPU and GPU

2.  What is the primary reason for using DDR (Double Data Rate) RAM in computer systems?

    A.  Improved data transfer rates

    B.  Increased storage capacity

    C.  Enhanced power efficiency

    D.  Reduced latency

3.  Which type of memory module is commonly used in laptops and small form factor computers?

    A.  DIMM RAM

    B.  RIMM RAM

    C.  MicroDIMM RAM

    D.  SODIMM RAM

4.  What is the primary purpose of ECC (Error-Correcting Code) RAM in a computer system?

    A.  To provide faster data transfer between the CPU and RAM

    B.  To enhance graphics processing capabilities

    C.  To detect and correct memory errors

    D.  To increase the storage capacity of the RAM

5.  What is the primary benefit of using a dual-channel RAM configuration, which utilizes two differently colored memory slots, in a computer system?

    A.  Increased storage capacity

    B.  Faster data transfer rates

    C.  Improved graphics performance

    D.  Lower power consumption

6.  What is the primary advantage of using a quad-channel RAM configuration in a computer system?

    A.  Increased storage capacity

    B.  Enhanced multitasking capabilities

    C.  Improved data transfer rates

    D.  Lower latency in memory access

7. DDR RAM is a type of computer memory that offers improved data transfer rates compared to earlier memory technologies. Which of the following options correctly matches the lowest speed for each version of DDR RAM?

   A. DDR2 – 400 MHz, DDR3 – 800 MHz, DDR4 – 2,133 MHz

   B. DDR2 – 800 MHz, DDR3 – 1,600 MHz, DDR4 – 3,200 MHz

   C. DDR2 – 1,333 MHz, DDR3 – 1,866 MHz, DDR4 – 2,400 MHz

   D. DDR2 – 2,000 MHz, DDR3 – 2,400 MHz, DDR4 – 3,200 MHz

8. Which of the following options would be the best choice for a gaming PC in terms of disk, CPU, and RAM?

   A. HDD, AMD Ryzen 3, 8 GB DDR3

   B. SSD, Intel Core i5, 8 GB DDR4

   C. HDD, Intel Core i9, 32 GB DDR3

   D. SSD, Intel Core i7, 16 GB DDR4

## 3.3 Given a scenario, select and install storage devices

1. What is the primary advantage of installing an M.2 hard drive directly on the motherboard without using cables?

   A. Faster data transfer rates through the SATA interface

   B. Increased storage capacity through the NVMe interface

   C. Simpler and more secure connection without cable clutter

   D. Compatibility with legacy systems through the IDE interface

2. A user wants to replace the existing hard drive with the fastest possible 1 TB HDD. Which of the following drive types should the technician recommend as the BEST choice?

   A. eSATA

   B. 1TB NVMe SSD

   C. 1TB USB 3.0

   D. 1TB SATA SSD

3. Which of the following RPM options is commonly associated with slower rotational speeds for mechanical hard disk drives (HDDs)?

   A. 5,400 rpm
   B. 7,200 rpm
   C. 10,000 rpm
   D. 15,000 rpm

4. Which type of storage device is commonly used for portable data storage and transfer?

   A. Flash drive
   B. Memory card
   C. Optical drive
   D. Hard disk drive

5. When selecting a motherboard for a specific CPU, what is a critical consideration?

   A. Socket compatibility
   B. Memory type support
   C. Expansion slot availability
   D. Form factor compatibility

6. Which storage device uses laser technology to read and write data on optical disks?

   A. Flash drive
   B. Memory card
   C. Optical drive
   D. Solid-state drive (SSD)

7. How can you identify a SATA cable used in computer hardware?

   A. It has a small, L-shaped connector at one end and a flat connector at the other end
   B. It has a wide, rectangular connector at both ends
   C. It has a round, barrel-shaped connector at one end and a flat connector at the other end
   D. It has a triangular-shaped connector at one end and a small, rectangular connector at the other end

8. Which of the following rpm options is commonly associated with faster rotational speeds for mechanical hard disk drives (HDDs)?

   A. 5,400 rpm

   B. 7,200 rpm

   C. 10,000 rpm

   D. 15,000 rpm

9. You have three hard drives, sized 500 GB, 1 TB, and 2 TB. Which RAID configuration would provide both data redundancy and increased storage capacity?

   A. RAID 0

   B. RAID 1

   C. RAID 5

   D. RAID 10

10. When would you typically use the Peripheral Component Interconnect Express (PCIe) interface in computer hardware?

    A. Connecting high-speed graphics cards

    B. Expanding storage capacity with additional hard drives

    C. Connecting external peripherals such as printers or scanners

    D. Enhancing network connectivity with Wi-Fi or Ethernet adapters

11. You have four hard drives, sized 2 TB, 2 TB, 4 TB, and 4 TB. Which RAID configuration uses a minimum of four drives and would provide both data redundancy and increased storage capacity? (Choose two)

    A. RAID 6

    B. RAID 0

    C. RAID 5

    D. RAID 10

12. You have two hard drives of different sizes, a 1 TB drive and a 500 GB drive. Which RAID configuration would be most suitable for mirroring the data between the drives?

    A. RAID 0

    B. RAID 1

    C. RAID 5

    D. RAID 10

13. Which storage device is commonly used in digital cameras and smartphones for expanding storage capacity?

    A.  Flash drive

    B.  Memory card

    C.  Optical drive

    D.  Solid-state drive (SSD)

14. An IT support technician is upgrading their laptop to provide remote administration and run several programs at one time. The read-write speed needs to be the fastest possible. Which of the following options would fulfill their criteria?

    A.  2.5" SAS HDD

    B.  M.2 NVMe SSD

    C.  40 GB IDE HDD

    D.  mSATA SSD

15. What is a key difference between installing a 2.5" SSD and a 3.5" SSD on a desktop computer?

    A.  Form factor and size

    B.  Power requirements

    C.  Data transfer speed

    D.  Compatibility with drive bays

## 3.4 Given a scenario, install and configure motherboards, central processing units (CPUs), and add-on cards

1.  Which of the following statements best describes NVMe compatibility with a motherboard?

    A.  NVMe SSDs are compatible with any motherboard that has an M.2 slot

    B.  NVMe SSDs are only compatible with older motherboard models

    C.  NVMe SSDs require a specific NVMe-compatible motherboard with an M.2 slot

    D.  NVMe SSDs can be connected to any SATA port on a motherboard

2.  What is the maximum amount of RAM that x86 architecture can support?

    A.  2 GB

    B.  4 GB

    C.  8 GB

    D.  16 GB

3. A user is experiencing an issue where a dual-boot computer does not boot to the desired operating system. Which of the following troubleshooting steps can help resolve this problem?

   A. Check and adjust the boot order in the BIOS settings

   B. Perform a system restore to a previous working state

   C. Install the latest device drivers for the hardware components

   D. Upgrade the computer's RAM for improved performance

4. In a desktop computer, why are heat sinks and fans commonly used?

   A. To minimize the power consumption of the CPU

   B. To reduce the electromagnetic interference (EMI) in the system

   C. To increase the speed of data transfer between components

   D. To dissipate heat and prevent the CPU from overheating

5. In which scenario would you choose to use an ITX form factor for a computer?

   A. Building a compact and portable gaming PC

   B. Setting up a large-scale server farm

   C. Designing a high-performance workstation

   D. Creating a multimedia editing studio

6. What is the primary advantage of liquid cooling over air cooling in a computer system?

   A. Improved thermal efficiency

   B. Quieter operation

   C. Lower cost

   D. Simpler installation

7. After upgrading the motherboard, RAM, and video card, the hard drive is not booting, and the stored data cannot be accessed. The TPM (Trusted Platform Module) is active and hosting the encrypted key. What should the technician do to enable the system to boot again and gain access to the stored data?

   A. Enter the BIOS settings and disable the TPM functionality

   B. Restore the previous motherboard, RAM, and video card configuration

   C. Perform a TPM reset to clear the encryption key and reestablish a secure connection

   D. Contact the TPM manufacturer for guidance on recovering the encrypted data

8.  What is a potential cause of a clicking noise when booting up a computer?

    A.  Failing hard drive

    B.  Overheating CPU

    C.  Loose power cable

    D.  Malfunctioning graphics card

9.  Which of the following power connectors is commonly used to provide power to the CPU on a desktop motherboard?

    A.  8-pin EPS connector

    B.  4-pin Molex connector

    C.  6-pin PCIe connector

    D.  24-pin ATX connector

10. What is a potential consequence of operating a disk infrastructure in a degraded state?

    A.  Increased risk of data loss

    B.  Decreased power consumption

    C.  Improved system performance

    D.  Enhanced data security

11. What can happen if the CPU fan fails to function properly?

    A.  The CPU may overheat and lead to system instability or shutdown

    B.  The CPU's performance may decrease, causing slower operations

    C.  The system may emit a loud noise due to increased fan speed

    D.  The CPU may become physically damaged

12. When booting up a computer, which component can cause a continuous beeping noise if it is not properly seated?

    A.  RAM module

    B.  CPU

    C.  Power supply unit

    D.  Optical drive

13. What is the main difference between AT and ATX motherboards, and which one is considered legacy?

    A. Size and form factor

    B. Power connector design

    C. Expansion slots

    D. RAM type

14. If a heat sink is not effectively dissipating heat from the CPU, what can be done to address the issue?

    A. Check for dust accumulation and clean the heat sink

    B. Replace the thermal paste between the CPU and heat sink

    C. Ensure proper contact between the CPU and heat sink

    D. All of the above

15. A technician inserts an encrypted USB drive protected with BitLocker. When attempting to access the files on the USB drive through File Explorer, the technician encounters an error message stating that the drive is locked. Which of the following tools should the technician use to unlock and gain access to the encrypted drive?

    A. BitLocker Drive Encryption

    B. Disk Clean-up

    C. Windows Defender Firewall

    D. Task Scheduler

16. A student was able to successfully boot from a live Linux CD on a computer in the university library. This resulted in a data breach. Which of the following measures will be the most effective in thwarting this type of attack from occurring in the future?

    A. Implement secure boot and enable BIOS/UEFI password protection

    B. Restrict physical access to the computer and use lockable cabinets

    C. Install and configure a firewall with strict outbound traffic rules

    D. Enforce user access controls and limit administrator privileges

17. When you plug a device into your PC, the power to the PC goes down, and when you detach the device, the power is restored. What is the recommended solution for this situation?

    A.   Use a power supply with a higher wattage

    B.   Use a power supply with a lower wattage

    C.   Use a power supply with better voltage regulation

    D.   Use a power supply with a higher amperage

18. Which of the following are potential consequences of a CPU running at high temperatures due to worn thermal paste? (Choose two)

    A.   System instability and frequent crashes

    B.   Reduced CPU performance and slower system response

    C.   Increased power consumption and higher energy costs

    D.   Shortened lifespan of the CPU

19. Which of the following methods can improve system performance when multiple applications are being used simultaneously?

    A.   Upgrade the RAM to a higher capacity

    B.   Close unnecessary background processes and applications

    C.   Install a faster solid-state drive (SSD)

    D.   Increase the CPU clock speed

20. Which of the following options correctly describes a Molex connector?

    A.   The Molex connector is used to provide power to SATA drives

    B.   The Molex connector is primarily used for connecting fans and cooling devices

    C.   The Molex connector is a standard power connector for motherboards

    D.   The Molex connector is used to connect USB devices to the computer

21. What type of disk infrastructure is typically used in a degraded state?

    A.   RAID (Redundant Array of Independent Disks)

    B.   SATA (Serial ATA) disks

    C.   SSD (Solid-State Drive) disks

    D.   External USB disks

22. What is a potential cause when some keys on the keyboard do not work and there is no sign of physical damage?

   A. Software compatibility issues

   B. Incorrect keyboard layout settings

   C. Outdated keyboard drivers

   D. BIOS settings misconfiguration

23. What is the primary purpose of setting a boot password in a computer's BIOS settings?

   A. To prevent unauthorized access to the computer's BIOS settings

   B. To encrypt the data on the computer's hard drive

   C. To enhance the overall system performance

   D. To optimize the boot process for faster startup

24. What is the primary purpose of a Hardware Security Module (HSM)?

   A. Securely store and manage cryptographic keys

   B. Improve network performance

   C. Provide virtual machine encryption

   D. Enhance multi-threading capabilities

25. What is the purpose of multithreading in computer systems?

   A. Increase parallel processing and improve performance

   B. Provide secure storage for sensitive data

   C. Virtualize hardware resources for multiple applications

   D. Enhance network connectivity and speed

26. What should you do if virtual machines are not working on your computer, and you need to troubleshoot the issue?

   A. Update the BIOS firmware to the latest version

   B. Enable the "Virtualization Technology," "Intel VT-x," or "AMD-V" options in the BIOS settings

   C. Ensure that your computer meets the hardware requirements for running virtual machines

   D. Verify that the necessary drivers for virtualization are installed and up to date

27. What is the primary advantage of advanced risk computing?

    A.   Improved performance and efficiency

    B.   Enhanced security and data protection

    C.   Increased scalability and flexibility

    D.   Reduced power consumption and environmental impact

28. Which of the following best describes the purpose of Intel architecture in advanced computing?

    A.   Enabling high-performance computing applications

    B.   Providing advanced encryption and data security

    C.   Facilitating cloud computing and virtualization

    D.   Enhancing artificial intelligence and machine learning capabilities

29. What is a key benefit of multicore processors in advanced computing?

    A.   Increased parallel processing capabilities

    B.   Enhanced single-threaded performance

    C.   Improved power efficiency and heat management

    D.   Expanded memory capacity and bandwidth

30. For which type of devices are Intel Core M processors specifically designed?

    A.   High-performance desktop computers

    B.   Ultra-thin notebooks, tablets

    C.   Gaming consoles and graphics-intensive systems

    D.   Enterprise servers and data centers

## 3.5 Given a scenario, install or replace the appropriate power supply

1. When should you consider using a modular power supply in a desktop computer?

    A.   When you want to improve cable management and reduce clutter

    B.   When you need a power supply with a higher wattage capacity

    C.   When you want to enhance system cooling and airflow

    D.   When you require a power supply with multiple voltage outputs

2.  In the event of a power failure, what is the purpose of replacing a redundant power supply in a computer system?

    A.  Ensures an uninterrupted power supply

    B.  Increases storage capacity

    C.  Enhances CPU performance

    D.  Improves network connectivity

3.  When considering voltage levels for input and output connections, which of the following options correctly represents the typical voltage ranges for 3.3V, 5V, and 12V, along with their associated wire color?

    A.  3.3V: Orange or yellow; 5V: Red; 12V: Yellow or blue

    B.  3.3V: Red; 5V: Yellow; 12V: Orange or blue

    C.  3.3V: Blue; 5V: Red; 12V: Yellow or orange

    D.  3.3V: Yellow or orange; 5V: Red; 12V: Blue

4.  Which type of standard motherboard typically uses a 20-pin or 24-pin power connector?

    A.  ATX (Advanced Technology eXtended)

    B.  Mini-ITX (Information Technology eXtended)

    C.  Micro-ATX (Advanced Technology eXtended)

    D.  ITX (Information Technology eXtended)

5.  What is the primary advantage of a modular power supply?

    A.  Customizable cable management

    B.  Higher efficiency

    C.  Enhanced cooling performance

    D.  Increased power output

6.  When selecting the appropriate voltage input for electrical devices, which of the following options represents the correct voltage ranges for 110-120 VAC and 220-240 VAC?

    A.  110-120 VAC: Standard voltage in North America; 220-240 VAC: Standard voltage in Europe

    B.  110-120 VAC: Standard voltage in Europe; 220-240 VAC: Standard voltage in North America

    C.  10-120 VAC: Standard voltage for high-power devices; 220-240 VAC: Standard voltage for low-power devices

    D.  110-120 VAC: Standard voltage for low-power devices; 220-240 VAC: Standard voltage for high-power devices

7.  In an office environment where power failures can disrupt operations, what is the recommended solution to ensure a continuous power supply?

    A.  Implement a redundant power supply system

    B.  Increase the number of power outlets

    C.  Upgrade the office furniture

    D.  Install backup generators

8.  What wattage is the recommended power supply for a typical desktop computer?

    A.  300 W

    B.  500 W

    C.  750 W

    D.  1,000 W

## 3.6 Given a scenario, deploy and configure multifunction devices/printers and settings

1.  A company is experiencing an issue with its dot matrix printer that uses carbon paper. They report that the print on the first page is too light, while the subsequent pages are still legible. What is the most likely cause of this problem?

    A.  The print head pins are worn out, resulting in inconsistent printing

    B.  The carbon paper is not aligned properly in the printer, causing the first page to print lighter

    C.  The printer driver needs to be updated to ensure optimal printing quality

    D.  The printer's power supply is not providing sufficient voltage to the print head

2.  What happens during the charging stage of a laser printer?

    A.  Toner particles are attracted to the charged areas on the drum

    B.  The laser beam scans the photosensitive drum, creating an electrostatic image

    C.  Any residual toner or debris is removed from the drum and other components

    D.  The primary corona wire charges the photosensitive drum uniformly

3.  Which type of printer typically uses a laser beam or LED light source for image formation?

    A.  Laser printer

    B.  Dot matrix printer

    C.  Thermal printer

    D.  Impact printer

4.  When using the scan-to-email feature on a multifunction device (MFD), what configuration is required to send the scanned document as an email attachment?

    A.  Configuring the MFD with the IP address of an SMTP server

    B.  Enabling Wi-Fi connectivity on the MFD

    C.  Installing email client software on the MFD

    D.  Connecting the MFD to a network printer

5.  What is the purpose of a print server?

    A.  To manage the printing process and control print jobs

    B.  To provide network connectivity for printers

    C.  To share printers and enable print jobs from multiple computers

    D.  To store and manage printer drivers

6.  You notice that unauthorized individuals are using the printer without permission. This has resulted in the printer paper budget doubling in size. What should be implemented to address this security concern and reduce the paper budget?

    A.  User authentication and access control

    B.  Regular printer maintenance

    C.  Printer driver update

    D.  Network connection troubleshooting

7.  Which type of printer uses a series of pins striking an inked ribbon to create images?

    A.  Laser printer

    B.  Dot matrix printer

    C.  Thermal printer

    D.  Impact printer

8.  Which of the following is the correct sequence of a laser printer?

    A.  Charging, exposing, developing, transferring, fusing, and cleaning

    B.  Cleaning, exposing, developing, transferring, fusing, and charging

    C.  Charging, exposing, developing, fusing, transferring, and cleaning

    D.  Cleaning, exposing, developing, transferring, and fusing

9.  Which type of printer generates images by applying heat to special heat-sensitive paper that needs to be kept out of direct sunlight?

    A.  Laser printer

    B.  Dot matrix printer

    C.  Thermal printer

    D.  Impact printer

10. What could be the issue if printed documents have poor print quality? (Choose two)

    A.  The printer is low on ink or toner

    B.  The paper quality is low

    C.  The printer driver needs to be updated

    D.  The printer settings are incorrect

11. What happens during the fusing stage of a laser printer?

    A.  The toner on the paper is fused and melted into the fibers

    B.  Toner particles are attracted to the charged areas on the drum

    C.  Any residual toner or debris is removed from the drum and other components

    D.  The laser beam scans the photosensitive drum, creating an electrostatic image

12. You have a printer with two paper trays – the top tray contains paper, and the bottom tray contains labels. You notice that when printing, the documents are printed on labels instead of paper. What could be the issue? (Choose two)

    A.  The top paper tray has run out of paper

    B.  The paper tray selection is wrong

    C.  The printer driver needs to be updated

    D.  The ink or toner is low

13. How can a printer in a SOHO obtain the same IP from a wireless router running DHCP?

    A.  Enable DHCP reservation

    B.  Configure a static IP address for the printer

    C.  Restart the router regularly

    D.  Use a USB cable for network connectivity

14. When using the scan-to-folder feature on a multifunction device (MFD), what configuration is required to save the scanned document as a file on a shared network folder?

    A.   Configuring the MFD with the path to a suitably configured file server and shared folder

    B.   Enabling Bluetooth connectivity on the MFD

    C.   Installing file compression software on the MFD

    D.   Connecting the MFD to a USB storage device

15. When using the scan-to-cloud feature on a multifunction device (MFD), what does it mean to scan to the cloud?

    A.   Uploading the scan as a file to a document storage and sharing account in the cloud

    B.   Sending the scan as an email attachment to a cloud service provider

    C.   Printing the scan directly from the MFD to a cloud-based printer

    D.   Saving the scan on a local network server accessible from the cloud

16. You are experiencing issues where many print jobs are not getting picked up from the printer's paper trays. What can be implemented to prevent this issue?

    A.   Enable printing only when authorized users insert a PIN

    B.   Printer driver update

    C.   Clearing the print queue and restarting the printer

    D.   Replacing the printer's ink or toner cartridges

## 3.7 Given a scenario, install and replace the printer consumables

1.   Which component is responsible for the charging stage in a laser printer?

    A.   Toner cartridge

    B.   Drum unit

    C.   Corona wire

    D.   Fuser assembly

2.   Which type of USB connector is commonly used for connecting printers to a computer?

    A.   Type A

    B.   Type B

    C.   Type C

    D.   Micro-USB

3.  What could be the issue if a printed document is coming out landscape instead of portrait? How can we resolve this issue?

    A.  The printer driver is outdated

    B.  The wrong printer settings are selected

    C.  The printer's ink or toner is low

    D.  The paper size is incorrect

4.  When connecting a USB printer to a computer running Windows 10, what is the most important step to ensure proper functionality?

    A.  Selecting the appropriate printer model

    B.  Installing the latest printer driver compatible with Windows 10

    C.  Ensuring the USB cable is securely connected to both the printer and the computer

    D.  Configuring the printer settings to match the desired paper size

5.  How does wireless printing work in a network with multiple printers?

    A.  Each printer has its own dedicated Wi-Fi network for wireless printing

    B.  The printers are connected to a central print server that handles wireless print jobs

    C.  Each printer is assigned a unique IP address and communicates directly with devices on the network

    D.  Devices must physically connect to each printer using a USB cable for wireless printing

6.  Which type of 3D printing technology is commonly used with liquid resin materials?

    A.  Fused Deposition Modeling (FDM)

    B.  Stereolithography (SLA)

    C.  Selective Laser Sintering (SLS)

    D.  Digital Light Processing (DLP)

7.  Which of the following steps is required to set up print sharing and enable multiple computers to use a shared printer? (Select all that apply)

    A.  Connect the printer to a computer acting as the print server

    B.  Install the necessary printer drivers on each computer

    C.  Enable printer sharing in the printer's properties on the print server computer

    D.  Access the network settings on client computers and select the shared printer

    E.  Test the print-sharing functionality by sending a print job from a client computer

8.  When would you typically use Printer Control Language (PCL) in printing?

    A.  Printing documents with complex graphics and images

    B.  Printing text-based documents without complex formatting

    C.  Printing high-resolution photographs and images

    D.  Printing documents with advanced font rendering and color management

9.  When unboxing a new print device, which of the following actions should you perform? (Choose three)

    A.  Remove all protective tapes and packaging materials

    B.  A print device should normally be left to acclimate after removing the packaging materials

    C.  Install the necessary software and drivers

    D.  Load paper and adjust paper settings

    E.  Use a two-person lift technique for the printer

    F.  Perform a test print to ensure functionality

10. To replace the filament in a 3D printer, which of the following actions should the technician take? (Choose two)

    A.  Heat the extruder to a specific temperature to soften the filament and remove it manually

    B.  Navigate to the printer's settings menu and select "Filament Replacement"

    C.  Pull as much of the old filament out as possible, then push the new filament through

    D.  Use a specialized tool to unscrew the filament spool and replace it

11. Which type of 3D printing technology uses filament materials such as ABS or PLA?

    A.  Fused Deposition Modeling (FDM)

    B.  Stereolithography (SLA)

    C.  Selective Laser Sintering (SLS)

    D.  Digital Light Processing (DLP)

12. How does Wi-Fi direct printing work?

    A.  The printer connects directly to a Wi-Fi network for wireless printing

    B.  The printer creates its own Wi-Fi network for devices to connect and print wirelessly

    C.  The printer requires a physical connection to a device for wireless printing

    D.  The printer uses Bluetooth technology for wireless printing

13. What components are typically included in a printer maintenance kit?

    A. New fuser assembly, transfer/secondary charge roller, and paper transport rollers

    B. New toner cartridges and cleaning sheets

    C. Replacement ink cartridges and printheads

    D. Additional paper trays and feeder units

14. When would you typically use PostScript in printing?

    A. Printing documents with complex graphics and images

    B. Printing text-based documents without complex formatting

    C. Printing high-resolution photographs and images

    D. Printing documents with advanced font rendering and color management

# 4

# Virtualization and Cloud Computing

## Introduction

A new trend in the IT industry has seen an increasing number of companies moving their data online, taking advantage of the more cost-effective cloud and its features. Cloud computing refers to the provisioning of resources without the need for capital expenditure, in which the **Cloud Service Provider** (**CSP**) provides all of the hardware and customer lease access. The CSP is also responsible for disaster recovery, so that the customer only pays for the resources that they use.

Virtualization has also become increasingly popular within companies due to the ability to recover a desktop or server in minutes. Prior to virtualization, if a server crashed, it could take the system administrator half a day to recover it. Virtualization is used to provide desktops for cloud computers.

In the CompTIA A+ Core 1 (220-1101) certification examination, Domain 4.0 Virtualization and Cloud Computing makes up 11% of the assessment and is broken down into the following exam objectives:

- 4.1 Summarize cloud computing concepts
- 4.2 Summarize aspects of client-side virtualization

The rest of this chapter is committed to practice. For each of the previously defined concepts, you will be given a series of questions designed to test your knowledge of each core 1 objective as defined by the official certification exam guidance for this domain. Once you have completed these questions and ensured you understand the concepts behind them, you should be fully prepared to do the same on your CompTIA A+ Core 1 (220-1101) exam.

# Practice Exam Questions

## 4.1 Summarize cloud computing concepts

1.  What type of cloud service would you use if you wanted to move 100 desktops to the cloud?

    A.  SaaS

    B.  IaaS

    C.  SECaaS

    D.  MaaS

2.  In which type of cloud model does a company have most of its workforce on-premises and its mobile salesforce in the cloud?

    A.  Hybrid

    B.  Private

    C.  Community

    D.  Public

3.  An organization is expanding, and it needs to increase its storage space and compute resources to meet the demand of its customers. Most of the workforce operates as remote workers. Which of the following best describes the cloud service required?

    A.  PaaS

    B.  SaaS

    C.  IaaS

    D.  DRaas

4.  A company wants to migrate its email and business applications to the cloud. Which of the following cloud services will be used to meet the objective?

    A.  PaaS

    B.  SaaS

    C.  IaaS

    D.  MaaS

5.  The Chief Executive Officer wants to ensure that when the company moves to the cloud, it retains total control over the storage and management of proprietary data. Which cloud model is the best for this?

    A.  Hybrid cloud

    B.  Community cloud

    C.  Public cloud

    D.  Private cloud

6.  A salesperson from a Cloud Service Provider (CSP) is trying to sell a company metered utilization as part of a cloud package. Which of the following describes what they are selling?

    A.  Unlimited resources for free

    B.  A reserve pool of resources

    C.  Pay only for the resources consumed

    D.  Restriction on the allocation of critical resources

7.  Which of the following cloud models would allow three universities to share resources in a cloud environment?

    A.  Private cloud

    B.  Public cloud

    C.  Community cloud

    D.  Hybrid cloud

8.  A company is going to employ two consultants to help with data migration. The consultants will be able to connect to the desktops that the company allocates through a thin client to prevent anyone from downloading the company data. The configuration of each desktop must remain consistent. Which of the following will the IT team roll out to meet their needs and ensure the company has total control over the data?

    A.  Surface laptops

    B.  VDI

    C.  Terminal servers

    D.  IaaS

9. A company would like to enable its developers to create bespoke applications. These applications will require two separate servers, one for PHP and the other for MySQL. What cloud service should they purchase?

   A. SaaS

   B. IaaS

   C. PaaS

   D. Private cloud

10. What type of cloud model is known as multi-tenant?

    A. Private

    B. Community

    C. Hybrid

    D. Public

11. A law firm is going to migrate its currently on-premises infrastructure to the cloud. The firm stores a large number of wills and probates, property, and trust deeds. This data must be retained for a minimum of six years. What type of cloud model best fits this law firm's needs?

    A. Public cloud

    B. Private cloud

    C. Hybrid cloud

    D. Community cloud

12. Which of the following describes why a cloud provider would store hardware in its data center that is not dedicated to any single customer?

    A. Dynamic resource allocation

    B. Backup pool

    C. Shared resources

    D. System sprawl

13. Which of the following means that the server experiences very little downtime (also known as the "five nines")?

    A.  VDI

    B.  High Availability (HA)

    C.  Clustering

    D.  Shared resources

14. A famous toy company sees an increase in sales over the winter holidays and, consequently, needs to purchase more VDI and CPU resources to match customer demand leading up to Christmas. However, they need to be able to revert to normal resource consumption in January. What aspect of cloud computing would the toy company find useful?

    A.  Shared resources

    B.  Clustering

    C.  Rapid elasticity

    D.  Metered utilization

15. What type of cloud allows access to data even if the internet fails?

    A.  Private

    B.  Community

    C.  SaaS

    D.  Public

16. What type of cloud service is VDI?

    A.  SaaS

    B.  DaaS

    C.  PaaS

    D.  IaaS

17. What type of cloud model is known as single-tenant?

    A.  Hybrid

    B.  Private

    C.  Community

    D.  Public

18. Which of the following are only SaaS products? (Choose two)

    A. Office 365

    B. Developer tools

    C. Home Depot

    D. Spotify

19. Due to COVID, a financial company is moving all its workers to a work-from-home model. The company must ensure that stringent financial regulations are enforced at all times and that they can control users' desktops and prevent the exfiltration of data. Which of the following solutions will the company implement?

    A. VDI

    B. SaaS

    C. VPN

    D. RDP

20. Which of the following is an automated advantage of cloud storage?

    A. Resource exhaustion

    B. Dynamic resource allocation

    C. File sharing

    D. File synchronization

21. What is one of the disadvantages of using VDI on-premises?

    A. Recovering a virtual desktop using a snapshot is very slow

    B. Network failure means that no local processing of data can take place

    C. The connection can be achieved by using Citrix

    D. Disaster recovery is provided by the cloud provider

22. An IT company is going to move 10 servers and 50 desktops to the cloud. Which of the following cloud services will they migrate to?

    A. PaaS

    B. SaaS

    C. MaaS

    D. IaaS

23. New Zealand has just won the rugby World Cup final, and the official All Blacks online store cannot cope with the number of New Zealanders wanting to purchase their World Cup memorabilia. The store manager contacts their cloud provider for additional resources, which the cloud provider adds within 30 minutes. Which of the following concepts BEST describes what the cloud provider has just done?

   A. Rapid deployment

   B. Rapid elasticity

   C. Load balancing

   D. Metered service

## 4.2 Summarize aspects of client-side virtualization

1. What type of hypervisor runs on a bare-metal virtual platform?

   A. Type 1

   B. Type 2

   C. Type 3

   D. Type 4

2. A company is using VMware's ESX Server to provide its virtual network. It will be running five database servers, each of which will require an increase in CPU and RAM. How can this be achieved?

   A. Resource pooling

   B. System sprawl

   C. Network segmentation

   D. Metered utilization

3. An attacker gained access to a vulnerable guest computer and managed to attack the hypervisor, which resulted in a total failure of the virtual network. What type of attack was carried out?

   A. Pivoting

   B. VM sprawl

   C. Snapshot

   D. VM escape

4.  What type of hypervisors will Oracle VirtualBox for Windows 10 run on?

    A.  Type 3
    B.  Type 2
    C.  Type 5
    D.  Type 1

5.  What are the THREE main reasons that an IT team would create a sandbox?

    A.  To help prevent fires from spreading
    B.  To test new versions of software
    C.  To test new hardware
    D.  To examine applications that potentially contain malware
    E.  To ensure that new software patches do not have an adverse effect on business applications

6.  A manufacturer of pressure-relieving mattresses has a legacy application that tests cell movement. It needs to run on a Windows 98 operating system, which is a legacy system that is no longer supported. The company is updating all of the servers to Server 2022, with Windows 11 desktops, and plans to outsource the rewriting of the legacy application so that it is Windows 11 compliant. What should the manufacturer do in the meantime? (Choose two)

    A.  Build a Linux workstation and use it to run the legacy application
    B.  Create a sandbox for the legacy application
    C.  Build a virtual machine with the Windows 98 operating system
    D.  Install Hyper-V on one of the Windows 11 desktops in the manufacturing department
    E.  Install the application on a SQL server

7.  What is the purpose of using Second Level Address Translation (SLAT)?

    A.  It improves the performance of virtual memory when multiple guest machines are installed
    B.  It improves the performance of virtual networking when multiple guest machines are installed
    C.  It prevents the use of virtual memory when multiple guest machines are installed
    D.  It throttles the processor on multiple guest machines

8. Which of the following describes cross-platform virtualization?

    A. Installing virtual machines on Hyper-V, ESX, and Xen

    B. Installing and networking multiple sandboxes

    C. Testing multiple software applications, one after another, in a single sandbox

    D. Testing software applications under multiple operating systems and workloads

9. A company has a virtual network running 10 host machines, each with 50 guest machines. Yesterday, an attacker successfully connected to the host's physical network card and exchanged packets directly with a guest operating system, bypassing the host operating system. Which of the following BEST describes how the attacker gained access?

    A. The attacker used a NAT

    B. The attacker joined the local area network of the host

    C. The attacker used a virtual private network

    D. The attacker used a bridged network

10. A university professor teaches a computer class 10 times a week. The professor wants to ensure that they have a rapid solution to set the desktops up for their next group at the end of each session. To do this, they plan to build a master image of the operating system that can be rolled out so that all desktops will reset once the students have logged off. Which of the following technologies should the professor implement? (Choose two)

    A. They should create a ghost image so that they can reimage each machine

    B. They need to build a virtual machine environment and take a snapshot

    C. They need to take a system image and roll it out between classes

    D. They need to create a data backup

    E. They need to implement a VDI environment that utilizes VDE

11. Which of the following BEST describes virtual machine sprawl?

    A. A virtual machine overutilizing resources

    B. An isolation virtual machine for application testing

    C. An unmanaged virtual machine on the network

    D. The host machine is running out of resources due to overconsumption

12. A system administrator plans to implement VDI and wants to ensure that the storage for the virtual machine is both fault tolerant and has fast disk access. Which of the following should the administrator implement to fulfill these requirements?

    A. RAID 0 using SSD

    B. LAN

    C. Fiber Channel SAN

    D. RAID 5 using HDDs

13. If you wanted to separate a guest machine from the host or another virtual machine, which of the following would you implement?

    A. DMZ

    B. Isolation

    C. Docker

    D. Snapshot

14. A company's virtual network has been flooded with rogue virtual machines, which were not been patched when the other virtual machines were updated. This is a security risk as these unmanaged devices could be used to gain access to the company's network. The company has now employed a security consultant to remedy the situation. Which of the following is the consultant most likely to recommend? (Choose two)

    A. Deploy virtual machines using an image template

    B. Install anti-virus software on unmanaged virtual machines

    C. Deploy SolarWinds Virtualization Manager

    D. Remove the unmanaged virtual machines

15. A network administrator plans to deploy another virtual host server with 15 TB of memory and quad processors onto their virtual network. However, after building the host server, they find that the hypervisor fails to run. Which of the following is the BEST choice to resolve this issue?

    A. VT-x

    B. Multi-cores

    C. VT-d

    D. Intel GVT

16. Why would a network administrator ensure they use an Uninterruptible Power Supply (UPS) when deploying a new virtual host server? (Choose two)

    A.  It provides power for the virtual host in the event of total power loss

    B.  It provides power for the virtual host for 5 minutes so that the host can be shut down gracefully

    C.  It provides temporary power for the virtual host should there be a power loss for a few seconds

    D.  It provides power for booting the virtual host

17. What is the benefit of using container virtualization?

    A.  It allows you to create a virtual machine backup

    B.  It allows you to test malware

    C.  It allows you to separate your applications from the infrastructure and deploy and test code rapidly

    D.  It prevents virtual machine escape

18. What is application virtualization?

    A.  Putting an application into a sandbox for testing

    B.  Installing an application locally on a virtual machine

    C.  Putting the application inside a container

    D.  Running an application from a remote server that has additional resources

# 5

# Hardware and Network Troubleshooting

## Introduction

Understanding the importance of hardware and network troubleshooting is vital for any IT professional. Efficient troubleshooting minimizes downtime, optimizes system performance, and extends the lifespan of hardware. It enhances the user experience, safeguards data and security, and builds a reputation for reliability and expertise. Moreover, mastering troubleshooting opens doors to career advancement and equips you to handle emergencies with confidence. Throughout this chapter, you'll gain practical knowledge to tackle various hardware and network challenges, empowering you as a skilled problem solver in the dynamic world of IT.

In the CompTIA A+ Core 1 (220-1101) certification examination, Domain 5.0 Hardware and Network Troubleshooting makes up 27% of the assessment and is further broken down into the following exam objectives:

- 5.1 Given a scenario, apply the best practice methodology to resolve problems

- 5.2 Given a scenario, troubleshoot problems related to motherboards, RAM, CPU, and power

- 5.3 Given a scenario, troubleshoot and diagnose problems with storage drives and RAID arrays

- 5.4 Given a scenario, troubleshoot video, projector, and display issues

- 5.5 Given a scenario, troubleshoot common issues with mobile devices

- 5.6 Given a scenario, troubleshoot and resolve printer issues

- 5.7 Given a scenario, troubleshoot problems with wired and wireless networks

The rest of this chapter is committed to practice. For each of the concepts defined above, you will be given a series of questions designed to test your knowledge of each core 1 objective as defined by the official certification exam guidance for this domain. Once you have completed these questions and ensured you understand the concepts behind them, you should be fully prepared to do the same on your CompTIA A+ Core 1 (220-1101) exam.

## Practice Exam Questions

### 5.1 Given a scenario, apply the best-practice methodology to resolve the problem

1.  A systems administrator is given a ticket by the help desk to deal with the chief executive officer's printer. Their secretary said that it will not print, a light is flashing, and they think the printer paper is the issue. What should the systems administrator do first?

    A.  Verify the printer's full system functionality

    B.  Test a theory to determine the cause of the printer issue

    C.  Identify the problem with the printer

    D.  Establish a plan of action to resolve the email server issue

2.  A junior administrator was given a verbal warning by the IT manager following an incident where they patched the exchange server during working hours. This resulted in rebooting the server and 600 users not having access to their email for 15 minutes. Which of the following BEST describes the junior administrator's actions?

    A.  Patch management

    B.  Poor communication with users

    C.  Standard operating procedure violation

    D.  Establishing a plan of action

3.  A user has a problem with their laptop and a second-line support technician has arrived. The support technician knows that they must try and identify the problem. Which of the following should the support technician do first? (Choose two)

    A.  Back up all of the data

    B.  Ask the user whether they made any recent changes

    C.  Ask the user what they were doing before the incident occurred

    D.  Search the vendor's website for guidance

4. A systems administrator took 4 hours to identify and then implement a solution. The systems administrator then implemented the repair and tested full functionality. What should the administrator do next?

    A. Establish a theory of probable cause

    B. Implement preventative measures

    C. Document the findings, actions, and outcomes in the call center database

    D. Test the theory to determine the cause

5. A system administrator has determined that a user's laptop has the wrong screen resolution. They believe that a recent Windows update has caused the problem. What stage in the troubleshooting process have they just carried out?

    A. Establishing a theory of probable cause

    B. Identifying the problem

    C. Establishing a plan of action

    D. Testing the theory to determine the cause

## 5.2 Given a scenario, troubleshoot problems related to motherboards, RAM, CPU, and power

1. What safety precautions should I take when replacing Random Access Memory (RAM) on Windows Server 2022? (Choose two)

    A. Hot-swap the RAM

    B. Turn off the power

    C. Put the machine in standby mode

    D. Wear an electromagnetic static wrist strap

2. A user raises a ticket with the help desk as their desktop computer will not start. On arrival, the computer technician reboots the computer, and it beeps continuously. Which of the following is the problem with the desktop computer?

    A. A motherboard problem

    B. A RAM problem

    C. A power supply problem

    D. A video adapter problem

3.  A computer technician needs to upgrade the Central Processing Unit (CPU) in an AutoCAD computer. What is the first thing they should do?

    A.  Turn off the power

    B.  Search the manufacturer's website for the socket type

    C.  Wear an electromagnetic static wrist strap

    D.  Back up the data

4.  A computer technician has just installed additional RAM in a desktop computer and it has not been recognized. What should the computer technician do next? (Choose two)

    A.  Check the computer's BIOS

    B.  Wear an electromagnetic static wrist strap

    C.  Reboot the computer

    D.  Reseat the memory modules

5.  A computer technician has received a desktop computer from the customer services department. The customer services technician stated that the desktop computer recently had maintenance carried out by the second-line technician. They plug the computer into the main power but when they switch the desktop computer on, there is a black screen. They can hear the internal fans spinning, so they know there is power to the desktop computer. Which of the following could have caused this error? (Choose two)

    A.  An incorrectly orientated storage adapter cable

    B.  A motherboard error

    C.  The computer monitor is not switched on

    D.  A faulty Power Supply Unit (PSU)

6.  A user has complained to the help desk that the time on her computer is inaccurate. She has changed the time twice in the last week, but the computer clock keeps falling behind. The system administrator arrives and confirms that the clock time is inaccurate. What should the system administrator do to rectify the problem?

    A.  Change the power cable to the computer

    B.  Change the PSU

    C.  Change the complementary metal-oxide semiconductor (CMOS) battery

    D.  Search on the manufacturer's website to see whether there is an update to the BIOS

7.  A computer technician is carrying out annual maintenance on a desktop computer. When inspecting the motherboard, they notice that one of the capacitors is swollen. They take the computer back to their repair room to replace the capacitor. What is the purpose of capacitors located on the motherboard?

    A.  The capacitor circulates the airflow

    B.  The capacitor prevents power spikes

    C.  The capacitor stores data

    D.  The capacitor is used to power the real-time clock

8.  A user was issued with a new laptop computer running Windows 10. They raised a ticket with the help desk as their fingerprint reader is now not working following a recent Windows update. Which of the following is the next step?

    A.  Update the BIOS

    B.  Clear the Trusted Platform Module (TPM)

    C.  Restore a system image

    D.  Reboot the laptop

9.  A computer technician is diagnosing a problem with a desktop computer. When they reboot the computer, they hear 1 long beep, followed by 2 short beeps. What does the computer technician diagnose the problem as?

    A.  A motherboard problem

    B.  A normal post

    C.  A power supply problem

    D.  A video adapter problem

10. A computer technician has just been called out to the customer services department as one of the desktop computers has no power. The computer technician pushes the power button and there is no power and they cannot hear any noise from the internal fans. Which of the following should the computer technician carry out when diagnosing the problem? (Choose three)

    A.  Check the plug socket is turned on

    B.  Change the memory modules

    C.  Replace the power cable

    D.  Plug a lamp into the power socket

11. What has caused the following problem? (Choose two)

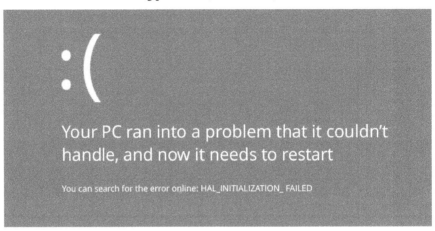

A. A system memory fault

B. A motherboard problem

C. An operating system corruption

D. A RAM problem

12. A user has reported to the help desk that they can smell burning coming from their computer. The help desk technician tells the user to immediately turn off the computer and unplug the power from the wall socket. Which of the following could have caused the burning smell? (Select all that apply)

A. The CPU fan is not working

B. The heatsink is not fitted properly

C. The PSU is overheating

D. The fan vents are clogged with dust

13. Which of the following could cause a computer to perform "sluggishly"?

A. The keyboard is not plugged in

B. A recent configuration has been made incorrectly

C. The mouse is not connected

D. The computer has no CPU

14. Which of the following would produce a grinding noise? (Choose two)

    A.  A problem with the RAM

    B.  A problem with a toner cartridge on an inkjet printer

    C.  A problem with the hard drive

    D.  A problem with the motherboard

15. A user reports to the help desk that they are having problems with their keyboard. The keyboard appears to be undamaged but when the computer technician tried the keyboard, some letters were not working. What should the computer technician do first?

    A.  Vacuum the keyboard

    B.  Wipe the keyboard with a wet cloth

    C.  Clean the keyboard with compressed air

    D.  Disable sticky keys

## 5.3 Given a scenario, troubleshoot and diagnose problems with storage drives and RAID arrays

1.  A customer has called an IT support company to provide a storage solution to a customer. The customer has purchased three 20-TB hard drives and the solution must provide fast read access and redundancy. Which of the following solutions would be the best to implement?

    A.  RAID 0

    B.  RAID 1

    C.  RAID 5

    D.  RAID 6

2.  A system administrator receives an alert from their mail server that one of the disks has failed. They log in to the server and can only see four out of their five disk sets. They have a hardware RAID 5 solution and therefore they can hot-swap out the failed disk. What risk if, any, will the system administrator encounter when replacing the failed disk?

    A.  RAID 5 is redundant and there is no risk at all

    B.  Pull the disks out one at a time and look for the SCSI ID of the failed disk

    C.  Look on the RAID array and look for the disk with the red light

    D.  If you remove a healthy disk, you will lose all your data

3.   A user boots up their computer and receives the following SMART error:

> SMART Hard Disk Error
> The SMART hard disk check has detected an imminent failure
> Please backup the content immediately and run Hard Disk Test

What should the user do next?

A.   Launch "Advanced > SMART settings > SMART self-test"

B.   Go to Disk Management and format the disk to get rid of errors

C.   Swap out the disk for a new disk

D.   Disable SMART monitoring

4.   A computer technician is trying to find out why a computer cannot boot. They take out the hard disk and connect it to a computer with recovery software. They are able to see the data. What should the computer technician do next?

A.   Put the disk back into the computer and boot from it

B.   Format the disk using Disk Management

C.   Back up the data

D.   Put the disk back into the computer and then install the recovery software

5.   A manager is working from their laptop computer and installs an encrypted USB drive containing a number of Excel spreadsheets that are confidential. They raise a ticket with the help disk. A support technician arrives to resolve the problem. What will the technician do to resolve the issue?

A.   They will use Disk Management

B.   They will convert the USB into New Technology File System (NTFS)

C.   They will turn on BitLocker on the C drive

D.   They will turn on BitLocker on the USB drive

6.   A computer technician is receiving disk errors from SMART monitoring. The computer boots normally and when they look at disk management, it states that all disks are in a healthy state. What is the cause of this error?

A.   Disk management is not functioning properly

B.   The filesystem is NTFS

C.   SMART monitoring is malfunctioning

D.   A disk is missing from the RAID 5 system

7.  A user's computer fails to boot up and they notice the hard drive LED is a solid orange. Which of the following could be causing this issue?

    A.  The computer has a memory problem

    B.  There is a hardware problem with the hard disk drive

    C.  The computer has a processor problem

    D.  SMART monitoring has been disabled, causing the computer to freeze

8.  A computer technician runs a performance test against a computer's hard drive. The test reveals that the disk is suffering from extended read/write times. What should the technician do next?

    A.  Launch "Advanced > SMART settings > SMART self-test"

    B.  Run the system diagnostic program that was supplied with the computer

    C.  Swap out the disk with a new disk

    D.  Disable SMART monitoring

9.  A computer that is configured with RAID 5 receives an alert that one of the disks is in a degraded state. Which of the following is causing this error and how does it affect the data on the disk? (Choose two)

    A.  One of the disks in the RAID 5 set needs to be formatted to NTFS

    B.  One of the disks in the RAID 5 set has failed

    C.  The data is no longer available

    D.  The data is still available

10. A computer technician boots up a computer and gets the error message "missing operating system." Which of the following is causing this error?

    A.  There is a disk missing from a RAID set

    B.  The computer is having a Windows update

    C.  The disk with the operating system has failed

    D.  The CMOS battery is failing

11. How can you tell if a storage device's performance is degrading?

    A.  There will be a solid orange light

    B.  Check the IOPS

    C.  Check Disk Management

    D.  There will be a flashing green light

## 5.4 Given a scenario, troubleshoot video, projector, and display issues

1.  A technician has been called to a classroom as the projector is very dim. Which of the following is causing the problem?

    A.  The inverter is broken

    B.  They need to adjust the display settings

    C.  The digitizer is failing

    D.  A burned-out bulb

2.  A technician is setting up a projector in a conference room and gets an error saying "no signal." What could be the cause of this issue?

    A.  The cable to the projector is faulty and needs to be replaced

    B.  The projectors' bulb needs to be replaced

    C.  The computer's monitor is broken

    D.  The computer needs to have its display set to "extend this display"

3.  A professor at a university connects their laptop to the projector in a theatre. The image being projected is fuzzy. Which of the following is causing this issue?

    A.  The cable is defective

    B.  The laptop display setting needs to be adjusted

    C.  The projector lens needs to be adjusted

    D.  The projector bulb needs to be replaced

4.  A presenter is trying to play a video that is on a DVD in their laptop. They can hear the sound but get an error on the projector stating "COPY PROTECTION: THE DVI/HDMI OUTPUT IS BLOCKED." Which of the following is causing this issue?

    A.  The HDMI cable is faulty

    B.  The protector is not HDCP-compatible

    C.  The display settings need to be adjusted

    D.  There is a problem with the DVD player

5.  A computer technician has connected a laptop to a projector in a lecture hall but an image is not being projected on the screen. They go back to their workshop and bring cables that they know are working. After swapping the cables, they get a "no source found" error. What should the computer technician do next? (Choose two)

    A.  Replace the projector's bulb

    B.  Check the connection on the HDMI cable

    C.  Run displayswitch.exe and select either duplicate or extend

    D.  Go to display settings on the laptop, choose multiple displays, and duplicate these displays

6.  A computer technician has been called out to a conference room where a presentation is due to take place. The presenter informs the computer technician that the images were flashing but it now looks like they are flickering. The computer technician notices some bright spots at the edge of the screen. What is causing this issue? (Choose two)

    A.  Check the cable connectors at both ends

    B.  Check the display settings

    C.  The backlight on the laptop is starting to fail

    D.  Reboot the laptop

7.  A new TV and video soundbar system has just been set up in a boardroom. The TV is being used to play videos from a presentation laptop. Sound is coming from the laptop and from the TV but the video soundbar is not producing any audio. Which of the following is causing the problem?

    A.  The soundbar is not turned on

    B.  The soundbar volume is too low

    C.  The High-Definition Multimedia Interface-Audio Return Channel (HDMI-ARC) port on the TV is not connected to the soundbar

    D.  The video resolution is too low

8.  A user has called the help desk as their monitor is showing a purple tinge. Which of the following is most likely causing the problem?

    A.  Display burn-in

    B.  A faulty graphics card

    C.  A bad cable

    D.  A burned-out bulb

9.  A user complains that the cursor on her screen keeps drifting, and she cannot control it. What should be done to resolve this issue?

    A.  Check the video cable

    B.  Calibrate the screen

    C.  Roll back the graphics driver

    D.  Change the screen resolution

10. A computer technician has been called out to a conference room where the projector is intermittently rebooting. What will the computer technician do next? (Choose two)

    A.  Change the power cable

    B.  Check the vents are dust-free and that there are no obstructions

    C.  Check that the projector fan is working properly

    D.  Check that the projector can handle the display resolution

11. The plasma screen in a conference room is displaying an image for about 60 seconds after it is shown on the screen. The presenter is using a presentation that is stored on their laptop via an HDMI cable. Which of the following is causing this issue?

    A.  Display burn-in

    B.  Dead pixels

    C.  A faulty cable

    D.  The laptop freezing

12. What is the primary purpose of testing the output resolution in a system?

    A.  To ensure accurate color representation

    B.  To optimize image quality

    C.  To verify compatibility with different display devices

    D.  To enhance system performance

13. A museum is experiencing issues with the touch-screen functionality on their Windows devices. Which of the following should be checked?

    A.  The battery status

    B.  The network connection

    C.  The display settings

    D.  The keyboard settings

## 5.5 Given a scenario, troubleshoot common issues with mobile devices

1.  A computer is experiencing issues during the POST process. What component should be checked?

    A.  RAM modules

    B.  The CMOS battery

    C.  The hard drive

    D.  The graphics card

2.  A network device is not receiving power through the Ethernet connection. What should be done to resolve the issue?

    A.  Check the network cable connections

    B.  Restart the network device

    C.  Install a Power over Ethernet (PoE) injector

    D.  Reset the network settings

3.  What could be the cause of a phone becoming excessively hot?

    A.  The phone is running resource-intensive apps

    B.  The phone is exposed to direct sunlight for a long time

    C.  The phone's battery is defective

    D.  The phone's operating system needs an update

4.  What is the most appropriate action to take if a phone has been exposed to liquid?

    A.  Immediately turn on the phone to check whether it is still functioning

    B.  Place the phone in a bag of rice for several hours to absorb the moisture

    C.  Use a hairdryer on low heat to dry the phone quickly

    D.  Take the phone to a professional repair service for assessment and cleaning

## 5.6 Given a scenario, troubleshoot and resolve printer issues

1.  How can a duplex printer help reduce excessive paper usage?

    A.  It automatically prints on both sides of the paper

    B.  It prints at a slower speed, conserving paper

    C.  It uses recycled paper for printing

    D.  It has a larger paper tray, reducing the need for frequent refills

2. What could be the potential cause of printed text not sticking to the paper?

   A. The printer is using low-quality ink cartridges

   B. The paper being used is not compatible with the printer

   C. The printer's fuser unit is not functioning properly

   D. The printer's temperature settings are too low

3. What could be the potential cause of a new printer with a duplex unit only being able to print on one side at a time?

   A. The printer's firmware requires an update

   B. The printer's duplex unit is not properly set up

   C. The printer's paper tray is not properly aligned

   D. The printer's ink cartridges are low on ink

4. What could be the potential cause of print quality issues, including marks on the printing paper? (Choose two)

   A. The printer's firmware requires an update

   B. The printer's drum unit is damaged

   C. The printer has dirty feed rollers

   D. The printer's ink cartridges are low on ink

5. When paper fails to feed properly in a printer, what is the most likely cause?

   A. The paper tray is empty

   B. The paper is too thick for the printer

   C. The printer driver needs to be updated

   D. The ink cartridges are low on ink

6. What is the most likely cause of a paper jam in a printer?

   A. The paper tray is empty

   B. The paper is wrinkled or folded

   C. There are obstructions in the paper path

   D. The ink cartridges are low on ink

7. To minimize paper waste and enhance print job control, what measures can be implemented?

   A. Load a large stack of paper into the tray

   B. Print double-sided documents whenever possible

   C. Require a login for print jobs

   D. Avoid using paper trays and feed paper manually

8. How does the failure of air conditioning in the printing environment affect a thermal printer, particularly regarding blank spots or missing text, and how can this issue be resolved?

   A. Causes overheating and damage to the print head; implement adequate ventilation and cooling solutions

   B. Results in increased ink consumption for thermal printing; adjust printer settings for optimized ink usage

   C. Causes blank spots or missing text on thermal paper; clean the print head

   D. Leads to decreased print speed and slower output; upgrade the thermal printer to a higher-performance model

9. Why does a projector power down unexpectedly during operation?

   A. Overheating caused by a dirty air filter

   B. Insufficient power supply to the projector

   C. A malfunctioning lamp in the projector

   D. A loose connection between the projector and power source

10. Why is a printer printing blank receipts?

   A. Empty ink or toner cartridges

   B. Paper feed issues or incorrect paper loading

   C. Overheating of the print head

   D. Outdated printer driver software

11. What type of printer typically uses a ribbon?

   A. An inkjet printer

   B. A laser printer

   C. A thermal printer

   D. A dot matrix printer

12. Why does a dot matrix printer produce documents with missing words?

    A.  Worn ribbon in the printer

    B.  Paper feed issues or misalignment

    C.  Overheating of the print head

    D.  Outdated printer driver software

13. Which of the following is the most important factor to prevent the print head from becoming too hot during printing?

    A.  Excessive heat can damage the print head and lead to poor print quality

    B.  The print head needs to be cold to ensure proper ink flow

    C.  Increased temperature enhances the printing speed

    D.  Excessive heat can increase the risk of printer malfunctions

14. A user is experiencing gaps in the printed labels from their label printer. What is the MOST likely cause of this issue?

    A.  Low ink or toner levels in the printer

    B.  Incorrect label alignment or positioning

    C.  A paper jam inside the printer

    D.  Outdated printer drivers or firmware

15. What could be the cause of a laser printer producing a ghost image on the printed page?

    A.  An insufficient fuser temperature

    B.  A low toner level

    C.  A dirty or damaged imaging drum

    D.  A loose connection between the printer and the computer

16. What should you do if you encounter a situation where paper is stuck to the fuser in a newly installed printer?

    A.  Use a pair of tweezers or pliers to carefully remove the stuck paper

    B.  Turn off the printer, allow it to cool down, and then gently pull the paper out in the direction of the paper path

    C.  Ignore the problem and continue printing, as it will likely resolve itself

    D.  Contact the printer manufacturer or a technician for assistance

17. A technician is troubleshooting an issue where lines appear down copied pages, but the printed pages sent directly to the copier render as intended. What is the MOST likely cause of this issue?

    A.   A clogged printer head

    B.   An overheated fuser

    C.   Damaged scanning glass

    D.   An incompatible toner

18. A laser printer is consistently printing garbled text instead of clear, readable text. What is the MOST likely cause of this issue?

    A.   Low ink or toner levels in the printer

    B.   Outdated printer drivers or firmware

    C.   Damaged printer cables or connections

    D.   Incorrect printer settings or font compatibility

19. In a digitization project, which of the following devices would be MOST suitable for capturing electronic images of a large collection of historical handwritten documents?

    A.   An NFC device

    B.   Flatbed scanner

    C.   Digital camera

    D.   QR scanner

20. A laser printer consistently prints a line from the top of the page down to the bottom on every sheet. What is the MOST likely cause of this issue?

    A.   Low ink or toner levels in the printer

    B.   A malfunctioning paper feed mechanism

    C.   Outdated printer drivers or firmware

    D.   Dust or debris on the imaging drum

21. A printer is producing a grinding noise during printing. What is the MOST likely cause of this issue?

    A.   Low ink or toner levels in the printer

    B.   A paper jam or obstruction in the printer

    C.   Outdated printer drivers or firmware

    D.   Network connectivity issues

## 5.7 Given a scenario, troubleshoot problems with wired and wireless networks

1.  You are experiencing issues with your wireless network, and you are unable to select a specific channel for your router. What is the MOST likely cause of this issue?

    A.  Interference from nearby devices or networks

    B.  Outdated firmware on the wireless router

    C.  Incorrect network configuration settings

    D.  Insufficient signal strength from the router

2.  You have implemented MAC filtering on your wireless network, but some devices are still able to connect without being on the approved list. What is the MOST likely cause of this issue?

    A.  Incorrect MAC addresses entered in the filter list

    B.  Outdated firmware on the wireless router

    C.  Interference from neighboring wireless networks

    D.  An incompatible wireless encryption protocol

3.  What action should be taken to resolve limited or no connectivity for a wireless client in a network due to an IP address issue?

    A.  Release and renew the IP address

    B.  Update the network adapter drivers

    C.  Adjust the wireless channel

    D.  Flush the DNS cache on the computer

4.  Which of the following best describes the use of the licensed band in wireless communication?

    A.  A reserved frequency spectrum for authorized users

    B.  A publicly accessible frequency spectrum

    C.  Temporary allocation for experimental purposes

    D.  An unlicensed frequency spectrum for general use

5.  In a wireless network setup with two routers, what can be done to avoid high latency issues?

    A.  Channel bonding

    B.  Separate wireless channels, each with its own IP address range

    C.  The use of wired connections

    D.  Implementation of Quality of Service (QoS)

6.  When remotely accessing the company network, which option provides a secure connection to the company LAN?

    A.  A Virtual Private Network (VPN)

    B.  Enhanced internet speed

    C.  Public IP address assignment

    D.  Firewall protection

7.  What is a possible solution to address a wireless connection that keeps dropping in an office environment?

    A.  Relocate the wireless router

    B.  Increase the internet bandwidth

    C.  Disable other wireless devices

    D.  Change the wireless encryption method

8.  What is the purpose of using a Wi-Fi analyzer to troubleshoot wireless connectivity issues?

    A.  Identifying signal interference sources

    B.  Increasing Wi-Fi speed

    C.  Changing the Wi-Fi password

    D.  Expanding wireless network coverage

9.  What could be a potential cause of poor Voice over Internet Protocol (VoIP) quality?

    A.  Outdated hardware

    B.  Low battery on the device

    C.  Insufficient bandwidth

    D.  Inadequate microphone sensitivity

# Mock Exam: Core 1 (220-1101)

The official CompTIA A+ Core 1 (220-1101) certification exam gives you 90 minutes to complete the test. Hence, it is advisable to set a timer before starting this mock exam to have a good assessment of your preparation level.

1. Which of the following is true about the M.2 form factor?

    A. M.2 supports only the SATA interface

    B. M.2 is exclusively used for graphics cards

    C. M.2 allows faster data transfer rates compared to traditional hard drives

    D. M.2 cannot be used as a boot device

2. What is a characteristic of RAID 5?

    A. Requires a minimum of three drives

    B. Provides the highest level of fault tolerance

    C. Offers increased read performance compared to RAID 0

    D. Requires dedicated parity drives

3. Which of the following flash memory card formats is commonly used in digital cameras?

    A. CompactFlash (CF)

    B. Secure Digital (SD)

    C. Memory Stick (MS)

    D. eXtreme Digital (xD)

4.  Which of the following statements about ATX motherboards is true?

    A.  ATX motherboards are exclusively designed for Intel processors

    B.  ATX motherboards typically have fewer expansion slots compared to microATX

    C.  ATX motherboards use the 20-pin ATX power connector

    D.  ATX motherboards support dual-channel memory architecture

5.  Which of the following is a security feature provided by the UEFI (Unified Extensible Firmware Interface)?

    A.  Secure Boot

    B.  BIOS password

    C.  CMOS clear jumper

    D.  Trusted Platform Module (TPM)

6.  Which of the following is a primary benefit of using an expansion sound card in a computer?

    A.  Increased CPU performance

    B.  Enhanced audio quality and capabilities

    C.  Improved cooling efficiency

    D.  Expanded storage capacity

7.  What is the purpose of cooling fans in a computer system?

    A.  To increase the display resolution

    B.  To provide wireless connectivity

    C.  To regulate the temperature of components

    D.  To improve sound quality

8.  What is the function of a heat sink in a computer?

    A.  To amplify audio signals

    B.  To provide additional storage space

    C.  To dissipate heat from a component

    D.  To improve network performance

9. What are motherboard connector headers used for?

   A. To store system configuration settings

   B. To provide additional power to the CPU

   C. To connect peripheral devices

   D. To control the display output

10. What is a key feature of multisocket motherboards?

   A. They support multiple graphics cards simultaneously

   B. They provide advanced overclocking capabilities

   C. They can accommodate multiple CPUs

   D. They offer extensive expandability options

11. What is the main advantage of using PostScript printing?

   A. Faster printing speed

   B. Higher print resolution

   C. Greater color accuracy

   D. Enhanced printer security

12. What is the primary benefit of duplexing in printing?

   A. Reduced paper waste

   B. Faster printing speed

   C. Improved print quality

   D. Increased printer durability

13. What is an important consideration when properly unboxing a device?

   A. Keeping the original packaging materials for future use

   B. Removing all protective films and covers before powering on

   C. Disregarding the instruction manual as it is not necessary

   D. Plugging in the device immediately without inspecting for damage

14. What does adjusting the printer tray settings refer to?

    A.  Changing the color settings for printed documents

    B.  Configuring the network connectivity of the printer

    C.  Adjusting the paper size and type for printing

    D.  Aligning the print heads for better print quality

15. What is an important consideration when selecting printer paper for optimal print quality?

    A.  Paper weight and thickness

    B.  Paper color and texture

    C.  Paper brand and manufacturer

    D.  Paper price and affordability

16. What does inkjet calibration involve?

    A.  Adjusting the ink cartridge settings for optimal performance

    B.  Aligning the print heads to ensure precise ink placement

    C.  Changing the inkjet printer's connection settings

    D.  Cleaning the inkjet carriage to remove debris and dust

17. What is the function of an inkjet carriage belt in a printer?

    A.  Transferring ink from the cartridge to the printhead

    B.  Controlling the movement of the printhead assembly

    C.  Ensuring proper paper feed and alignment

    D.  Maintaining optimal ink flow and print quality

18. Which of the following is a primary function of a firewall?

    A.  Data encryption

    B.  Virus scanning

    C.  Network traffic filtering

    D.  User authentication

19. What is the main purpose of overclocking a computer component?

    A. To extend the component's lifespan

    B. To reduce power consumption

    C. To increase the component's performance

    D. To improve compatibility with software

20. Which wireless network standard offers the highest data transfer rates?

    A. 802.11a

    B. 802.11b

    C. 802.11g

    D. 802.11ac

21. What is the primary purpose of Network Address Translation (NAT) in networking?

    A. To encrypt network traffic for secure communication

    B. To translate domain names into IP addresses

    C. To assign unique IP addresses to each device on a network

    D. To map private IP addresses to public IP addresses

22. Which port is commonly used for transferring files between a client and a server?

    A. 143

    B. 80

    C. 21

    D. 25

23. Which network protocol is used for secure remote access and secure file transfers?

    A. Secure Shell (SSH)

    B. Simple Network Management Protocol (SNMP)

    C. Post Office Protocol (POP)

    D. Network Time Protocol (NTP)

24. Which network protocol is commonly used for insecure remote command-line access to a server?

    A.  Domain Name System (DNS)

    B.  HyperText Transfer Protocol (HTTP)

    C.  Simple Network Management Protocol (SNMP)

    D.  Telnet

25. Which network protocol is primarily used for sending and receiving email messages?

    A.  File Transfer Protocol (FTP)

    B.  Simple Mail Transfer Protocol (SMTP)

    C.  HyperText Transfer Protocol (HTTP)

    D.  Post Office Protocol (POP)

26. Which network protocol is responsible for translating domain names into IP addresses?

    A.  Domain Name System (DNS)

    B.  Dynamic Host Configuration Protocol (DHCP)

    C.  HyperText Transfer Protocol (HTTP)

    D.  Simple Network Management Protocol (SNMP)

27. Which network protocol is responsible for automatically assigning IP addresses to devices on a network?

    A.  Simple Network Management Protocol (SNMP)

    B.  Domain Name System (DNS)

    C.  HyperText Transfer Protocol (HTTP)

    D.  Dynamic Host Configuration Protocol (DHCP)

28. Which feature allows mobile devices to determine their geographic location?

    A.  Global Positioning System (GPS)

    B.  Wi-Fi connectivity

    C.  Bluetooth technology

    D.  Near-Field Communication (NFC)

29. Which technology allows cellular networks to estimate the location of a mobile device?

   A. Wi-Fi positioning

   B. Cellular tower triangulation

   C. Bluetooth proximity detection

   D. GPS satellite tracking

30. What is the primary purpose of Mobile Device Management (MDM) and Mobile Application Management (MAM) solutions?

   A. To encrypt mobile device communications

   B. To secure mobile devices against physical theft

   C. To manage and control mobile device configurations and applications

   D. To provide remote wipe functionality for lost devices

31. Which protocol is commonly used for corporate email configuration on mobile devices?

   A. POP3 (Post Office Protocol version 3)

   B. IMAP (Internet Message Access Protocol)

   C. SMTP (Simple Mail Transfer Protocol)

   D. LDAP (Lightweight Directory Access Protocol)

32. What is the primary purpose of two-factor authentication (2FA)?

   A. To encrypt data during transmission

   B. To provide secure physical access to devices

   C. To verify the identity of users with an additional authentication factor

   D. To prevent unauthorized access to corporate applications

33. What is the purpose of the remote wipe feature on a stolen mobile phone?

   A. To physically retrieve the stolen device

   B. To track the location of the stolen device

   C. To delete all data on the stolen device remotely

   D. To disable the stolen device's network connectivity

34. What is the purpose of enabling Bluetooth on a device?

    A.  To establish a wireless internet connection

    B.  To pair and connect with other Bluetooth devices

    C.  To enable GPS navigation

    D.  To increase battery life

35. What action needs to be taken to enable pairing on a Bluetooth device?

    A.  Pressing a specific button on the device

    B.  Installing Bluetooth drivers

    C.  Connecting the device to a power source

    D.  Updating the device's operating system

36. What does the process of finding a device for pairing in Bluetooth involve?

    A.  Scanning for nearby Bluetooth devices

    B.  Connecting to a Wi-Fi network

    C.  Syncing data between devices

    D.  Enabling location services

37. What action should be taken to enable or disable the wireless/cellular data network on a mobile device?

    A.  Access the device's settings and toggle the data network option

    B.  Contact the mobile service provider for activation or deactivation

    C.  Restart the device to automatically enable or disable the data network

    D.  Update the device's operating system to enable or disable data connectivity

38. Which two wireless/cellular technology standards are commonly used for voice and data communication?

    A.  3G and 4G

    B.  GSM and CDMA

    C.  Bluetooth and Wi-Fi

    D.  LTE and WiMAX

39. What does the hotspot feature on a mobile device allow you to do?

    A. Create a secure wireless network for nearby devices to connect

    B. Enable high-speed data connectivity in remote areas

    C. Share the device's internet connection with other devices

    D. Connect to public Wi-Fi networks automatically

40. What is the purpose of Preferred Roaming List (PRL) updates on a mobile device?

    A. To enable international roaming capabilities

    B. To update the device's network security protocols

    C. To improve the device's call and data connection quality

    D. To optimize the device's battery usage during roaming

41. Which type of IP address is assigned to devices that are connected to the internet?

    A. Private addresses

    B. Loopback addresses

    C. Reserved addresses

    D. Public addresses

42. What is the maximum data transfer rate supported by USB 2.0?

    A. 480 Mbps

    B. 1 Gbps

    C. 5 Gbps

    D. 10 Gbps

43. What is the maximum data transfer rate supported by USB 3.0?

    A. 480 Mbps

    B. 1 Gbps

    C. 5 Gbps

    D. 10 Gbps

44. Which type of network is typically confined to a small geographic area, such as an office building or campus?

    A.  Local Area Network (LAN)

    B.  Wide Area Network (WAN)

    C.  Personal Area Network (PAN)

    D.  Metropolitan Area Network (MAN)

45. Which type of network spans a large geographical area and connects multiple LANs?

    A.  Local Area Network (LAN)

    B.  Wide Area Network (WAN)

    C.  Personal Area Network (PAN)

    D.  Metropolitan Area Network (MAN)

46. What is the maximum data transfer rate typically supported by Fast Ethernet (100BASE-TX) technology?

    A.  10 Mbps

    B.  100 Mbps

    C.  1 Gbps

    D.  10 Gbps

47. Which Ethernet standard supports a maximum data transfer rate of 10 gigabits per second (Gbps)?

    A.  10BASE-T

    B.  100BASE-TX

    C.  Gigabit Ethernet (1000BASE-T)

    D.  10 Gigabit Ethernet (10GBASE-T)

48. What is the maximum data transfer rate supported by the Cat 5 cable?

    A.  10 Mbps

    B.  100 Mbps

    C.  1 Gbps

    D.  10 Gbps

49. Which range of IP addresses is reserved for use as private IP addresses within internal networks?

    A.   10.0.0.0 – 10.255.255.255

    B.   179.16.0.0 – 179.30.255.255

    C.   212.16.0.0 – 212.16.255.255

    D.   169.254.0.0 – 169.254.255.255

50. What is the purpose of Automatic Private IP Addressing (APIPA) in a network?

    A.   To assign globally routable IP addresses to devices in a private network

    B.   To automatically assign public IP addresses to devices in a network

    C.   To provide temporary IP addresses when a DHCP server is unavailable

    D.   To enable communication between devices in different private networks

# 7

# Operating Systems

## Introduction

It is important that the exam candidate understands typical usage scenarios for different mainstream operating systems and specialist mobile operating systems. In an enterprise environment, it is important that support technicians can support and troubleshoot many different devices. Modern enterprise networks need to tailor their approach for many different end-user scenarios, from on-premises support to remote and mobile users. Devices may connect to applications and services using various network media, including Bluetooth, cellular and wired connections, and Wi-Fi.

It is important that technicians can configure and troubleshoot all types of network connections. There is a need to upgrade hardware and software solutions over time, and knowledge of any constraints or requirements when planning for upgrades is important. To offer a speedy response to customer support requests, the technician should be able to choose the correct tool or techniques, so a good understanding of the different configuration settings and menu options is important.

In order to be successful on the CompTIA A+ Core 2 (220-1102) certification exam, candidates must ensure they are familiar with the following objectives:

- 7.1 Identify basic features of Microsoft Windows editions
- 7.2 Given a scenario, use the appropriate Microsoft command-line tool
- 7.3 Given a scenario, use features and tools of the Microsoft Windows 10 operating system (OS)
- 7.4 Given a scenario, use the appropriate Microsoft Windows 10 Control Panel utility
- 7.5 Given a scenario, use the appropriate Windows settings
- 7.6 Given a scenario, configure Microsoft Windows networking features on a client/desktop
- 7.7 Given a scenario, apply application installation and configuration concepts
- 7.8 Explain common OS types and their purposes
- 7.9 Given a scenario, perform OS installations and upgrades in a diverse OS environment

- 7.10 Identify common features and tools of the macOS/desktop OS
- 7.11 Identify common features and tools of the Linux client/desktop OS

The rest of this chapter is committed to practice. For each of the concepts defined above, you will be given a series of questions designed to test your knowledge of each Core 2 exam objective as defined by the official certification exam guidance for this domain. These questions will test the candidate's knowledge of how to troubleshoot and configure common operating systems.

# Practice Exam Questions

## 7.1 Identify basic features of Microsoft Windows editions

1.  A user receives a new laptop computer that runs Windows 10. Upon first use, they are prompted to provide a password prior to the regular login prompt. What feature would likely cause this prompt?

    A.  Password-protected BIOS

    B.  Windows Privacy and Security

    C.  Windows Accessibility

    D.  BitLocker Drive Encryption

2.  A senior manager is insisting that their personal laptop be joined to the company's domain so that they can use their preferred operating system and hardware. Which operating systems would NOT be supported for this role? (Choose two.)

    A.  Windows 10 Home

    B.  Windows 8.1 Pro

    C.  Windows 10 Pro

    D.  ChromeOS

3.  A technician is attempting to enable BitLocker Drive Encryption on company laptops, but the option is only available for some of the laptops. Which versions of the Windows operating system support BitLocker Drive Encryption? (Choose two.)

    A.  Windows 10 Pro

    B.  Windows 10 Home

    C.  Windows 7 Pro

    D.  Windows 10 Enterprise

    E.  macOS

4.  A small company is looking to upgrade all company workstations from Windows 8.1 Pro to the equivalent Windows 10 edition. The systems are managed, and all conform to the company's baseline image. The company would like to use the least administrative effort to make this transition, migrating all applications and user data at the same time. Which of the following would be the best solution?

    A.  In-place upgrade

    B.  Fresh installation from a central server

    C.  Fresh installation from optical media

    D.  Fresh installation from USB media

5.  A technician is responding to a support ticket from a manager who cannot enable BitLocker on their personal computer while working from home. What is the MOST likely cause of this problem?

    A.  The system only has 2GB of RAM installed

    B.  The system is running Windows Home edition

    C.  The system is running a 32-bit edition of Windows

    D.  The system has a 128GB hard drive

6.  A service desk technician is tasked with connecting remotely to a Windows desktop computer. The technician needs to change configuration settings using a secure connection. It is important that the user must be logged off during this process. Which of the following tools would the technician MOST likely use?

    A.  RDP

    B.  Virtual network computing

    C.  Microsoft Remote Assistance

    D.  SFTP

7.  A company is proposing in-place upgrades for all the current Windows platforms that are running on a 32-bit OS. If these are performed, what would the memory limitation of the 32-bit OS be?

    A.  16MB

    B.  2048GB

    C.  4GB

    D.  128GB

8.  A deskside support technician has shown the marketing manager how to use BitLocker To Go. The technician MOST LIKELY encrypted which of the following?

    A.  A DVD-RW disk

    B.  A network drive

    C.  An internal disk drive

    D.  A USB drive

9.  A technician plans to install the latest version of the Windows OS on a user's device. The user insists all of their data files and configuration settings are retained during this process. Which of the following installation types should the technician use?

    A.  Network installation

    B.  Clean install

    C.  In-place upgrade

    D.  Image deployment

10. A home user has raised a support ticket requesting remote assistance for a problem they are experiencing with a locally installed application. When a technician attempts to connect to the remote system using RDP, there is a connection error. What is the MOST LIKELY reason for the error?

    A.  The system only has 2GB of RAM installed

    B.  The system is running a Windows Home edition

    C.  The system is running a 32-bit edition of Windows

    D.  The system is running a Windows Pro edition

## 7.2 Given a scenario, use the appropriate Microsoft command-line tool

1.  A network engineer must troubleshoot a section of a business network in which marketing users cannot access printers, e-mail, or websites. The network infrastructure equipment appears to be working correctly, so the engineer is looking to eliminate misconfigured user workstations as a possible cause of the problem. Which command-line tool would provide the best information regarding workstation configuration?

    A.  ping localhost

    B.  ipconfig /all

    C.  netstat -a

    D.  hostname

2.  An administrator is responsible for the operating system migration of 300 Windows users. As part of the migration, the administrator must save the end-users' data to a temporary shared drive. The data must retain all security permissions and support hidden files. Which of the following commands will achieve this result by default?

    A.  robocopy

    B.  copy

    C.  xcopy

    D.  cp

3.  A technician is troubleshooting network connectivity and receives the following output:

    Server: UnKnown

```
Address:  10.10.0.1
Non-authoritative answer:
Name:     www.google.com
Addresses:  2a00:1450:4009:81e::2004
            142.250.187.196
```

```
 1      <1 ms       *          <1 ms   WIN2022-DC [10.10.0.1]
 2       *          *           *      Request timed out.
 3       3 ms      1 ms        1 ms    172.17.48.1
 4       3 ms      3 ms        3 ms    192.168.0.1
 5       6 ms      6 ms        6 ms    151.231.252.44
 6      16 ms     72 ms       16 ms    2.120.11.144
 7      15 ms     14 ms      109 ms    72.14.219.96
 8      17 ms      *           *       216.239.40.71
 9      16 ms     16 ms       16 ms    142.251.54.35
10      17 ms     18 ms       17 ms    lhr25s33-in-f4.1e100.net
[142.250.187.196]
```

    Which of the following tools is the technician MOST LIKELY using? (Choose two.)

    A.  ping

    B.  ipconfig

    C.  netstat

    D.  nslookup

    E.  tracert

    F.  nbstat

4.  A support ticket is raised by a senior manager having computer-related problems while working from home on their personal Windows 10 computer. They are attempting to access e-mail prior to attending an important business event. The support technician is unable to access the system using remote desktop, so, as a workaround, they use a third-party desktop sharing application. The technician identifies a solution to the manager's problem and proposes that they make configuration changes using Group Policy Editor (gpedit.msc). However, when they attempt to run the tool, they find it is not available on the manager's computer. What is the most likely reason that these tools have not been present on the manager's computer?

    A.  The computer is running Linux

    B.  The computer is running Windows 10 Enterprise

    C.  The computer is running Windows 10 Home

    D.  The computer has a corrupt registry

5.  A customer powers on their laptop and discovers that, though their device displays the normal Windows desktop, they are unable to access any network-based resources. Which of the following tools should be used at the command line to troubleshoot this scenario?

    A.  ping

    B.  msconfig

    C.  nbtstat

    D.  nslookup

6.  A network technician investigates an ongoing incident in which a desktop computer makes a connection to an IP address across the network. The technician needs to resolve the computer's name associated with the IP address. Which of the following commands should the network technician use?

    A.  gpresult

    B.  ipconfig

    C.  nslookup

    D.  net user

7.  A malware infection has spread across a company's network via several USB storage devices. The support team must identify a method to prevent users from using storage devices that connect to USB ports. The team has been notified that this must be done quickly with minimum disruption to users. Which of the following is the BEST way for the support team to address this requirement?

    A.  Push a group policy to all users

    B.  Assign a local security policy

    C.  Create a network login script

    D.  Update the company AUP

8.  A support technician has added a Windows 10 workstation to the domain companydomain.com. The technician needs to verify that the workstation has received security policies from the domain. Which command will confirm whether the policies have been effective?

    A.  ipconfig /all

    B.  netstat -e

    C.  gpresult /Z

    D.  nslookup -query=a server1.companydomain.com

9.  A technician is using a command-line interface to perform tasks on a Windows 10 computer. The technician needs to determine which ports have active TCP connections to local or remote hosts. Which of the following commands should the technician use?

    A.  netstat -p TCP

    B.  net use -p TCP

    C.  nslookup -p TCP

    D.  netstat -p UDP

10. An administrator has tested a new Group Policy Object (GPO) and now wants to deploy it into the production environment. After deployment, the finance users do not appear to be receiving the new GPO. The administrator thinks the problem may be related to other GPOs that have been deployed at the same time. Which of the following command-line tools would be MOST USEFUL for the administrator to verify which GPOs are being deployed to the accounting department?

A. nbtstat

B. gpresult

C. nslookup

D. gpupdate

E. tasklist

11. A technician is creating a logon script that needs to automatically assign a drive mapping to a public folder shared on server1. The new drive letter on the user's workstation will be allocated the P drive letter. Which of the following commands will achieve the desired result?

A. net use P: \\server1\public

B. tracert \\server1\public local drive P:

C. net use \\P = Server\public

D. tracert P: \\server1\public

12. After a malware incident, a Windows system displays evidence of operating system files that have been modified. Anti-malware definitions were updated, and a full scan was performed. What needs to be performed next to verify the integrity of the Windows operating system files?

A. chkdsk /scan

B. SFC /SCANNOW

C. diskpart> RESCAN

D. netstat -s

13. An administrator has created a new group policy and deployed it into the production environment. The administrator would now like to verify that the new group policy settings have been downloaded and are now enforced on user workstations. Which of the following commands will allow the administrator to verify that the group policy is working?

    A.  shutdown -r

    B.  dcdiag

    C.  gpresult

    D.  gpmc.msc

    E.  gpupdate

## 7.3 Given a scenario, use features and tools of the Microsoft Windows 10 operating system (OS)

1.  Prior to beginning an online certification exam, a user must run an agent to manage the online exam. The agent reports that an application named "Dell Diagnostics" is preventing the online exam from starting. How can the user quickly identify the background application and end the task?

    A.  Go to Task Manager | Processes and End task

    B.  Go to Task Manager | Startup and disable the startup process

    C.  Go to Task Manager | Performance and End task

    D.  Run Registry Editor and modify Computer\HKEY_CURRENT_USER

2.  A technician is working on a computer when the PC suddenly experiences a Windows blue screen and restarts, apparently normally. To resolve the issue, the technician needs to determine which error message was displayed during the blue screen event. Which of the following should the technician use to help troubleshoot the issue?

    A.  sfc

    B.  msconfig

    C.  regedit32

    D.  eventvwr

    E.  msinfo32

3.  A recently terminated employee had made several undocumented changes to a manager's laptop computer. These changes are preventing Office 365 applications from receiving updates in a timely manner and have halted the automated disk defragmentation service. In order to ensure these services run automatically, which tool will BEST remediate the problems?

    A.  Task Scheduler (taskschd.msc)

    B.  Device Manager (devmgmt.msc)

    C.  Performance Monitor (perfmon.msc)

    D.  Certificate Manager (certmgr.msc)

4.  Ann, a payroll manager, has complained of poor system performance on her company laptop computer. Applications are running slowly during certain parts of the day and occasionally in the evening, when she stays late to finish a task. The support technician allocated the ticket would like to monitor Ann's computer in an effort to identify the problem. Which of the following tools should the technician use to BEST analyze the computer's behavior?

    A.  Computer Management

    B.  Event Viewer

    C.  Performance Monitor

    D.  Task Manager

5.  An employee returns from a six-month assignment working with a business partner. A computer technician would like to check whether the hardware vendor's BIOS updates were installed on the employee's laptop during the six-month period. Which tool would BEST display this information?

    A.  System Information (msinfo32.exe)

    B.  Resource Monitor (resmon.exe)

    C.  System Configuration (msconfig.exe)

    D.  Registry Editor (regedit.exe)

6.  A service desk technician is allocated a ticket when a user's Windows workstation is running slowly. The computer boots up slowly and has long delays when executing large files. After checking the local hard disk, it appears to be near capacity. The technician needs to free up space and optimize access times for large files. Which two commands will BEST address this requirement? (Choose two.)

    A.  Boot into safe mode

    B.  Reboot the computer

    C.  Defragment the hard drive

    D.  Install device drivers

    E.  Run Disk Cleanup

7.  Due to a misconfigured workstation build template, workstations used by the sales team have a very small amount of storage space available. Technicians would like to view the currently allocated space for the main operating system drive and, if possible, extend the size of the drive. What graphical-based tool would be BEST for this task?

    A.  Diskpart

    B.  Disk Management

    C.  Device Manager

    D.  Disk Cleanup

8.  A support technician is troubleshooting a helpdesk ticket raised by a sales executive. Applications that load on Windows startup are resulting in a wait time of nearly five minutes before the user is able to use the computer. What can be done to help the user avoid this long wait time?

    A.  Use the System Configuration | Startup options to disable startup applications

    B.  Delete entries listed under the registry key

    C.  HKEY_LOCAL_MACHINE\SOFTWARE\Microsoft\Windows\CurrentVersion\Run

    D.  Use Task Manager to disable all startup tasks currently set as enabled, then reboot the computer to ensure the issue has been resolved

    E.  Open Task Manager | Startup and identify applications with High start-up impact. Disable these apps causing excessive boot times on startup.

9.  A user from the human resources department raises a support ticket. The reason for the ticket is their desktop computer has been running slowly. The user reports that there have been no changes made to the PC. Which of the following tools should the support technician use to determine the cause of the speed reduction?

    A.  Task Scheduler

    B.  Windows Memory Diagnostic

    C.  The Performance tab in Task Manager

    D.  Disk Defragmenter

10. A department manager was accidentally assigned privileges that allowed them to make several unauthorized changes to their company laptop. One of the changes made was to add additional certificates to their laptop's Trusted Root Certificate Authorities store. The company is a government contractor, and these new certificates are not trusted as they do not meet government compliance regulations. How can a support technician ensure these certificate authorities will not be trusted by applications run on the manager's laptop?

    A.  Remove the certificates from the Trusted Root Certificate Authorities store using certmgr.msc on the laptop

    B.  Remove the certificates from the Trusted Root Certificate Authorities store using regedit.msc on the laptop

    C.  Remove the certificates from the Trusted Root Certificate Authorities store using devmgmt.msc on the laptop

    D.  Request the external certificate authorities put all of their certificates on a certificate revocation list (CRL)

## 7.4 Given a scenario, use the appropriate Microsoft Windows 10 Control Panel utility

1.  A support technician is helping a user to solve a printing problem on their desktop computer. To test for a possible fix, it is necessary for the technician to disable the printer. Which of the following tools should the technician use to do this?

    A.  Devices and Printers

    B.  Sync Center

    C.  Device Manger

    D.  Power Options

2. A user calls the service desk after discovering they are unable to open a JPEG file in their pictures folder. When the user double-clicks on the file, instead of being able to view the picture, a command prompt window flashes up for a few seconds and then disappears. A technician views the file and sees the following:

```
Name            Date modified Type           Size
Sunshine.jpg    22/10/2020    Application     78KB
```

Which of the following Windows Control Panel utilities should the technician use to resolve this issue?

A. Default Programs

B. Display Settings

C. Device Manager

D. Internet Options

3. Technicians must ensure that all users' web browser traffic is forwarded to the new proxy server. Select the Control Panel utility that will allow the relevant settings to be configured.

A. Network and Sharing Centre | Change Adapter Settings

B. Internet Options | Connections

C. Device Manager

D. Windows Defender Firewall | Advanced Settings

4. A support technician is resolving a support issue for a visually impaired user who is having issues with default colors and screen resolution. Which of the following utilities should the technician use?

A. Device Manager

B. System

C. Ease of Access Center

D. Programs and Features

5. A support technician installs a new webcam and downloads the drivers from the manufacturer's site, but the webcam fails to operate as expected. Which of the following options will BEST allow the technician to troubleshoot problems associated with the newly installed hardware?

A. Services

B. Device Manager

C. Event Viewer

D. Programs and Features

6.  A project manager allowed a colleague to use their computer. Afterward, they notice that webpages are not being displayed as intended in the web browser. A technician troubleshoots the issue and discovers that many settings have been changed from their defaults. The technician must find a way to reset the web browser back to its default settings. Which Control Panel utility should the technician use?

    A.  System

    B.  Programs and Features

    C.  Network and Sharing Center

    D.  Internet Options

7.  A technician needs to manually set a temporary IP address for five workstations in a branch office due to the DHCP server failing. Where will the technician find the controls to manage manual IP address assignment?

    A.  Network and Sharing Center

    B.  Sync Center

    C.  User Account Control

    D.  Credential Manager

8.  A service provider supports a small organization with less than ten users. The organization is informed by their Internet Service Provider (ISP) that the email server has been changed to a different DNS name. A technician needs to visit the small organization to update configurations for all the local users. What Control Panel utility will allow the technician to make the changes?

    A.  Internet Options

    B.  Windows Defender Firewall

    C.  User Accounts

    D.  Mail

9.  A research scientist user wants to connect a Windows 10 laptop computer to an external desktop monitor, keyboard, and mouse. When the scientist shuts the lid, the system shuts down. How can the system be configured to remain powered up whenever the lid is closed?

    A.  Control Panel | Power | Do nothing

    B.  Control Panel | Power | Sleep

    C.  Control Panel | Power | Hibernate

    D.  Control Panel | Power | Shut down

10. A user responsible for creating rich digital media has installed an additional sound card into their tower computer system. However, the audio output still uses the default built-in hardware. How can the user ensure the default playback device is configured for the new sound card?

    A. Device Manager | Audio inputs and outputs

    B. Control Panel | Sound

    C. Devices and Printers

    D. Speech Recognition

## 7.5 Given a scenario, use the appropriate Windows settings

1. A legal firm has recently installed a new word-processing application on all user desktops. Some users have raised support tickets, complaining that they do not get what they expect when trying to input special characters. Where should the support technician go to remediate this problem?

    A. Settings | Time & language

    B. Settings | Accessibility

    C. Settings | Personalization

    D. Settings | Apps

2. A support technician has been tasked with configuring a multiple-display setup for several members of the marketing team. After connecting all appropriate power and display cables, where should the technician go to configure the displays?

    A. Settings | Time & language

    B. Settings | Personalization

    C. Settings | System

    D. Settings | Bluetooth & devices

3. A sales manager has returned from a company event and complains that their laptop computer is displaying warning messages about a lack of disk space. The manager saved a lot of new data on the local storage and was required to install some software during the event. A technician must now try to fix the problem. Where should they go NEXT to support the user?

    A. Settings | Time & language

    B. Settings | Personalization

    C. Settings | System

    D. Control Panel | File History

4. A new company policy is being implemented and, prior to this policy being pushed out company-wide, the security settings must be configured and tested. One of the policy requirements is that when the screensaver locks the screen, a password must be used to unlock the screen. Where can this setting be accessed?

   A. Settings | Personalization | Lock screen

   B. Settings | Screen Timeout settings

   C. Control Panel | User Accounts

   D. Settings | Privacy & security | Lock screen

5. A company would like to use BitLocker to secure all Windows mobile devices, which will be centrally managed through group policy. In the pilot phase, a small number of laptops will be manually configured with this security feature. To do this, the Device Encryption settings will need to be accessed through which of the following paths?

   A. Settings | System

   B. Settings | Apps

   C. Settings | Privacy & security

   D. Settings | Network & internet

6. A small publishing company would like to configure all devices to connect through a newly purchased proxy server before accessing internet resources. Which Settings menu option will allow technicians to access the proxy server settings?

   A. Settings | System

   B. Settings | Apps

   C. Settings | Privacy & security

   D. Settings | Network & internet

7. A research and design company has a Corporate Owned Personally Enabled (COPE) policy in place. The Acceptable Use Policy (AUP) allows users to access personal email accounts, as well as their business email. Where can these settings be accessed?

   A. Control Panel | Internet Options

   B. Settings | Apps

   C. Settings | Privacy & security

   D. Settings | Accounts

8.  A company is testing a new gaming application and seeks to gauge customer feedback by recording the customer experience during gaming sessions. What Windows settings would allow them to record customer reactions and feedback during a game?

    A.  Settings | Gaming | Captures

    B.  Control Panel | Autoplay

    C.  Settings | Apps | Video Playback

    D.  Control Panel | Sync Center

## 7.6 Given a scenario, configure Microsoft Windows networking features on a client/desktop

1.  A network technician must add a new workstation to the Windows domain. What Windows settings would be used to switch from workgroup configuration to a domain-joined configuration?

    A.  Settings | Accounts | Sign-in Options

    B.  Control Panel | Region Settings

    C.  Settings | System | About | Domain or Workgroup

    D.  Control Panel | Credential Manager | Domain or Workgroup

2.  A user contacts the service desk and reports that they cannot access any network resources. A support technician asks the user to open Command Prompt and type in IPCONFIG /ALL. The resulting output contains the 169.254.23.66 IP address. What is this address type and what is most likely the problem on the network?

    A.  Private IPv4 address

    B.  Automatic Private IP Addressing (APIPA)

    C.  IPv6 link-local address

    D.  DHCP service failure

    E.  Active Directory service failure

    F.  DNS service failure

3.  A support ticket is raised by a user who is unable to share a newly installed departmental printer. The user has been assigned privileges to share folders and printers. The user is part of a workgroup NOT on the Windows domain. The user reports that email and internet browsing are working correctly. What setting is likely causing sharing error?

    A.  The user does not have permission to share the printer

    B.  The Network profile is set to public

    C.  The Network interface is disabled

    D.  The Network profile is set to private

4.  What Windows feature can be configured to prevent P2P file-sharing applications from being used by members of the sales department?

    A.  Windows Defender Firewall

    B.  Windows Virus & threat protection

    C.  Windows Secure Boot

    D.  Windows BitLocker Drive Encryption

5.  A user raises a support ticket after being prevented from adding an exception to Windows Defender Firewall. The user has an application launcher that they are attempting to run from their Downloads folder. Which type of user account allows for the modification of firewall rules?

    A.  Guest Account

    B.  Power Users

    C.  Administrator

    D.  Standard users

6.  A technician is troubleshooting a user's workstation that has no network connectivity. After confirming that the current IP address is set to 169.254.44.89, what is the next action that the technician should take?

    A.  Attempt to obtain an IP address using ipconfig /flushdns

    B.  Attempt to obtain an IP address using ipconfig /all

    C.  Attempt to obtain an IP address using ipconfig /renew

    D.  Attempt to obtain an IP address using ipconfig /flushdhcp

7.  A company has recently switched to a remote workforce model. The company supports many users in remote locations with expensive cellular and satellite connections. In order to minimize the costs for these links, the company would like to restrict monthly data usage. Which TWO configuration options will BEST allow the organization to restrict data use?

    A.  Settings | System | Storage settings

    B.  Advanced Network Settings | Data usage

    C.  Advanced Network Settings | Network Interface | Metered Connection – On

    D.  Advanced Network Settings | Advanced Sharing

    E.  Advanced Network Settings | Network Interface | Flight Mode – On

8.  A business unit has had a new network printer installed and directly connected to the Local Area Network (LAN) switch, and a technician must now configure several workstations to connect directly to the network printer. When adding a printer on the client workstations, which of the following options will allow the technician to connect the network printer?

    A.  Select a shared printer by name

    B.  Add a printer using an IP address or hostname

    C.  Add a Bluetooth or wireless discoverable printer

    D.  Connect directly with a USB cable

## 7.7 Given a scenario, apply application installation and configuration concepts

1.  A technician is supporting a customer who has a Windows 10 x86 computer with 4GB of RAM. The customer needs to increase the available memory to 16GB RAM in order to install an engineering application. What should the technician recommend to the customer in order to meet this requirement?

    A.  Install Ubuntu Linux

    B.  Install a larger SSD

    C.  Use a 64-bit architecture

    D.  Install 16GB DDR4 RAM

2.  Several members of the engineering design team have raised service tickets due to latency issues and poor performance when using a Computer-Aided Design (CAD) application. A hardware scan of the workstations reveals the following:

    - 64GB DDR4 Memory

    - 2GB Integrated Graphics

    - 1TB SSD HDD

    - Intel XEON 3.4GHZ 16-Core CPU

    What change can the engineers make that would be most beneficial when using the CAD application?

    A.  Increase memory

    B.  Install dedicated graphics cards

    C.  Install faster CPUs

    D.  Install faster HDDs

3.  A marketing team is using a Customer Relationship Manager (CRM) system on their 32-bit Windows 8.1 workstations. After upgrading the workstations to Windows 11 64-bit edition, the team wants to use the same CRM application. Which of the following restrictions will they encounter when using a 32-bit application on a 64-bit OS?

    A.  32-bit applications will be restricted to 32GB of RAM

    B.  32-bit applications do not support multi-threading

    C.  32-bit applications will be restricted to 4GB of RAM

    D.  32-bit applications do not support multi-tasking

4.  Following the upgrade of a customer's Windows 8 operating system to Windows 10, an application now fails to launch. An error message is displayed, stating that the application was written for Windows 8 and is incompatible with the current operating system. What can a support technician offer as a quick fix for this problem?

    A.  Contact the application vendor to investigate whether an updated version can be purchased

    B.  Set the application compatibility setting to Windows 8

    C.  Boot Windows into safe mode to run the application

    D.  Set the application compatibility setting to Windows 7

5. A software development company has designed a Computer-Aided Design (CAD) application at great expense. They need a control to ensure that each copy of the application will only run from a licensed workstation. What would be the MOST effective way to protect the application from theft?

    A. Make each customer agree to strict licensing requirements during installation

    B. Deploy an external hardware token for each copy of the application

    C. Make each customer sign an Acceptable Use Policy (AUP)

    D. Only sell the application to trustworthy customers

## 7.8 Explain common OS types and their purposes

1. An engineer needs to format a USB storage device in preparation to copy 20GB of data from an Ubuntu Linux server to a Windows system. Which of the following filesystems will the engineer MOST likely use?

    A. FAT32

    B. ext4

    C. NTFS

    D. exFAT

2. A recent risk assessment has highlighted a security issue, wherein legacy equipment has a 32-bit edition of Windows XP as its embedded OS. The company does not receive any quality or security updates for this operating system. What term would BEST describe this operating system?

    A. End of Life (EOL)

    B. Incompatible operating system

    C. 32-bit operating system

    D. Vendor-supported operating system

3. A school is looking to invest in easy-to-support technology for student workstations. The chosen devices will run a lightweight operating system based on a browser interface. What would be the BEST choice to meet these requirements?

    A. Linux

    B. macOS

    C. ChromeOS

    D. Windows

4.  A company wants to streamline its customer support after a recent inventory assessment reported that four different operating systems were in use by servers, workstations, and mobile devices. To compound the issue, there were also five different versions of Android OS and three different versions of iOS in use. The company would like to choose a single operating system to support servers, workstations, and handheld devices. Which of the following is the BEST choice?

    A.  Linux

    B.  iOS

    C.  Windows

    D.  ChromeOS

5.  After installing the most recent version of Red Hat Linux on a datacenter server, additional storage is added. The new hard drive must be formatted with a filesystem that supports 40TB of storage, and it is also anticipated that the storage will need to be regularly defragmented. Which of the following is the BEST choice of filesystem?

    A.  FAT32

    B.  ext3

    C.  NTFS

    D.  ext4

6.  A marketing company is looking to deploy smartphones to their workforce. The smartphone must support an operating system based on Linux, as developers will create applications for the company and have experience with Linux operating systems. Which of the following Os's would be the BEST choice for this?

    A.  iOS

    B.  SUSE Linux

    C.  Android OS

    D.  Windows mobile

## 7.9 Given a scenario, perform OS installations and upgrades in a diverse OS environment

1.  A support engineer is tasked with upgrading multiple desktop computers to Windows 10. However, they are only able to obtain a single copy of the installation media, and so they propose that they perform the upgrade over the network. Which of the following boot methods allows such an upgrade?

    A.  SSD

    B.  Optical drive

    C.  Flash drive

    D.  PXE

2.  A pharmaceutical company needs to deploy 500 new Windows 11 desktops in the most efficient way. The process needs to be automated so that the technicians' time spent on this installation is minimized. What installation would be the BEST choice?

    A.  Remote network installation

    B.  Repair installation

    C.  Clean installation

    D.  Unattended installation

3.  During a manual installation of Windows 11 x64 on a brand-new desktop computer, a technician must select a partitioning scheme for the 12TB hard disk drive. Which partition format would make the best use of the available storage?

    A.  ext4

    B.  MBR

    C.  GPT

    D.  APFS

4.  A technician is helping a remote customer upgrade their Windows workstation to the latest edition. The customer would like to retain all their applications and settings. Which option will upgrade the system and meet the customer's requirements?

    A.  Clean install

    B.  Repair install

    C.  Unattended install

    D.  In-place upgrade

5.  Which was the first Microsoft Windows operating system with a mandatory requirement for feature upgrades?

    A.  Windows 11

    B.  Windows 8.1

    C.  Windows 10

    D.  Windows 7

6.  A large multinational manufacturer has a user base of 6,000 Windows desktops and would like to create a baseline configuration so that all desktops have identical features and applications. What would be the BEST solution for this organization?

    A.  Upgrade

    B.  Clean install

    C.  Image deployment

    D.  Repair installation

7.  An installation team is deploying new images using pxe boot. In order to minimize the load on the deployment server, they are deploying images to only 30 workstations simultaneously. There is a possibility that this process may cause bottlenecks. What should the team most closely monitor?

    A.  Impact on users

    B.  Impact on the network segment

    C.  Impact on the DHCP scope

    D.  Impact on workstations

8.  A technician is helping the company upgrade a mixture of laptops and desktops to run Windows 11. In order to support larger volume sizes and multiple partitions, it has been decided that hard drives will be configured using GPT partitioning. In order to support Windows 11 and GPT disks, what MINIMUM hardware specifications must be in place? (Choose two.)

    A.  32GB RAM

    B.  UEFI

    C.  TPM 2.0

    D.  LEGACY BIOS

    E.  8-core CPU

9.  A Windows desktop computer fails to boot following a power loss and unexpected system shutdown. What should the technician try FIRST to see if the system can be recovered?

    A.  Unattended installation

    B.  Repair installation

    C.  Image deployment installation

    D.  Remote installation

10. Technicians are preparing to upgrade departmental workstations to the latest Windows OS. In order to avoid problems during the upgrade, they would like to see a report listing potential missing hardware features that may prevent an upgrade.

    A.  Microsoft Windows HCL (hardware compatibility list)

    B.  Microsoft Windows PC Health Check App

    C.  Microsoft Windows System Information

    D.  Microsoft Windows Task Manager

## 7.10 Identify common features and tools of the macOS/desktop OS

1.  Several users in the publishing department would like to have access to Skype, as this is the standard tool within the organization for conducting meetings and making calls with colleagues. The users in the publishing department all use macOS and cannot find the Skype application in the Apple App Store, but it is available as a download from the official Microsoft site. What file format should the users select to ensure the Skype application can be installed on their macOS computers?

    A.  MSI

    B.  EXE

    C.  DMG

    D.  APK

2.  A support technician is helping a user to restore deleted files from a recent backup. The user's workstation runs on macOS, and the user needs to take a look through the files on the backup before restoring some of the files. Which macOS utility will be MOST useful for this task?

    A.  Keychain

    B.  Finder

    C.  Mission Control

    D.  Explorer

3.  A user raises a support ticket as they are unsure how to create automated backups onto an external hard disk that they have purchased. The client workstation is running the latest version of macOS. What tool or application would be the BEST choice for scheduling automatic backups onto the drive?

    A.  File History

    B.  Time Machine

    C.  Windows Backup

    D.  Mission Control

4.  A technician is providing support to the user of a macOS computer on which the e-mail application is unresponsive. What feature will allow the technician to view a list of currently active applications and shut down the unresponsive application?

    A.  Force Quit menu

    B.  Task Manager

    C.  Task List

    D.  Control Panel

5.  A research department recently purchased MacBook computers for departmental users. Due to highly sensitive data being stored on these computers, management is asking for additional security for locally stored content. What feature would be a good choice to secure the local data drive?

    A.  iCloud

    B.  Keychain

    C.  FileVault

    D.  BitLocker

6.  macOS is based upon what source code?

    A.  Linux

    B.  Android

    C.  Unix

    D.  ChromeOS

7.  A user visits several different internet sites where a user account and password must be entered to access the site. The user would like to automate this process so that, when they sign in to their macOS computer, they will not need to enter additional passwords to access these sites. What macOS feature will allow the use and management of multiple credentials?

    A.  Mission Control

    B.  Spotlight

    C.  Keychain

    D.  Dock

8.  A technician has been asked to uninstall a large application that is no longer used on a manager's MacBook Pro. How can they uninstall the application?

    A.  Use Finder to locate the application and delete the application folder

    B.  Use Mission Control to locate the application and delete the application window

    C.  Use the App Store to remove the unwanted application

    D.  Use Finder to locate the application and move it to Trash

9.  A marketing manager raises a support request when their macOS laptop fails to boot, displaying the following error message:

    ```
    No bootable device - insert boot disk and press any key
    ```

    What should the technician do FIRST?

    A.  Access the Recovery menu by holding Command + R during boot and choose the Disk Utility

    B.  Access the Recovery menu by holding Command + R during boot and choose Reinstall macOS

    C.  Access the Recovery menu by booting from DVD installation media and choose the Disk Utility

    D.  Boot into safe mode using Command + R during the boot and choose Restore from the Time Machine Backup

10. After installing a number of applications on a user's MacBook Pro, the technician deletes a number of DMG and PKG files from the downloads folder. Upon running Activity Monitor, there does not appear to be much free disk space. What can the technician do to free up disk space?

    A.  Use the Trash application to permanently delete the files

    B.  Use the Recycle Bin application to permanently delete the files

    C.  Use the Disk Cleaner application to identify unwanted files

    D.  Use Disk Utility to split the hard drive into separate partitions

11. A user would like to customize the list of available utilities and applications that they see after successfully logging on to their MacBook Pro. What feature should they customize?

    A. Mission Control

    B. Dock

    C. Start menu

    D. Toolbar

12. A technician must perform a number of tasks to configure a macOS workstation before assigning it to a user. They need to configure network settings, set up a printer, and configure backups. Which folder will host these configuration utilities?

    A. Mission Control

    B. System Preferences

    C. Dock

    D. Disk Utilities

13. A user wants to use multiple desktops on their macOS workstation. Which of the following methods will allow the user to switch between desktops? (Choose two.)

    A. Control + right or left arrow keys

    B. Select the desktop from the Dock using the mouse or trackpad

    C. Enter Mission Control and choose the desired desktop using the mouse or trackpad

    D. Command + spacebar

## 7.11 Identify common features and tools of the Linux client/ desktop OS

1. A technician is assisting the HR manager in protecting a number of sensitive files that had been saved in the HR documents folder. The technician is able to see the following output:

```
-rw-r----- 1 mark HumanResources 0 Jan 9 14:37 Employee-Conduct
-rw-r----- 1 mark HumanResources 0 Jan 9 14:37 Employee-Details
-rw-r----- 1 mark HumanResources 0 Jan 9 14:36 Employee-Health
-rw-r----- 1 mark Sales          0 Jan 9 14:37 Employee-Reports
```

    A. Which command did the technician use to view the output, and which command would BEST secure sensitive file(s)? (There are TWO answers.)

    B. dir /L

    C. sudo chown :HumanResources Employee-Reports

D.  ls -l

E.  sudo chmod 664 Employee-Reports

F.  pwd

G.  sudo mv Employee-Reports ../Sales

2.  A technician must log into the Linux print server and restart the print service. What command-line syntax will they use if they want to make use of root privileges during the session?

A.  pwd

B.  grep

C.  samba

D.  sudo

3.  A technician is investigating user complaints of latency when accessing applications on the Ubuntu Linux server. The technician reviews the following output in an attempt to see what might be causing this latency:

```
Tasks: 140 total,    1 running, 139 sleeping,    0 stopped,    0 zombie
%Cpu(s):   4.0 us,   2.6 sy,   0.0 ni, 93.4 id,   0.0 wa,   0.0 hi,   0.0 si,   0.0 st
MiB Mem :   3930.4 total,    2531.8 free,    643.7 used,    754.9 buff/cache
MiB Swap:    975.0 total,     975.0 free,      0.0 used.   3041.8 avail Mem

  PID USER      PR  NI    VIRT    RES    SHR S  %CPU  %MEM     TIME+ COMMAND
 3841 root      20   0  404048  44664  34388 S   3.0   1.1   0:03.42 xfce4-taskmanag
  534 root      20   0  372876 137032  53220 S   2.3   3.4   0:12.53 Xorg
   12 root      20   0       0      0      0 S   0.3   0.0   0:00.27 ksoftirqd/0
 3473 root      20   0       0      0      0 I   0.3   0.0   0:00.45 kworker/0:0-events
 3633 root      20   0  351168  28412  20912 S   0.3   0.7   0:00.39 panel-13-cpugra
 3864 root      20   0  405764  82144  63056 S   0.3   2.0   0:00.46 qterminal
 3878 root      20   0   10244   3708   3096 R   0.3   0.1   0:00.24 top
    1 root      20   0  164388  10780   7988 S   0.0   0.3   0:01.50 systemd
    2 root      20   0       0      0      0 S   0.0   0.0   0:00.01 kthreadd
    3 root       0 -20       0      0      0 I   0.0   0.0   0:00.00 rcu_gp
    4 root       0 -20       0      0      0 I   0.0   0.0   0:00.00 rcu_par_gp
    6 root       0 -20       0      0      0 I   0.0   0.0   0:00.00 kworker/0:0H-events_highpri
    9 root       0 -20       0      0      0 I   0.0   0.0   0:00.00 mm_percpu_wq
   10 root      20   0       0      0      0 S   0.0   0.0   0:00.00 rcu_tasks_rude_
   11 root      20   0       0      0      0 S   0.0   0.0   0:00.00 rcu_tasks_trace
   13 root      20   0       0      0      0 I   0.0   0.0   0:00.24 rcu_sched
   14 root      rt   0       0      0      0 S   0.0   0.0   0:00.38 migration/0
   15 root      20   0       0      0      0 S   0.0   0.0   0:00.00 cpuhp/0
   17 root      20   0       0      0      0 S   0.0   0.0   0:00.00 kdevtmpfs
   18 root       0 -20       0      0      0 I   0.0   0.0   0:00.00 netns
```

Figure 7.1: Linux performance data example

What command did the technician use to view this performance data?

A. nano

B. dig

C. top

D. ps

4. What command can be used to delete a file or folder on a Linux operating system?

A. chmod

B. man

C. df

D. rm

5. A developer is worried that they may be running short of available disk space on their local system. They run a command at the prompt that results in the following output:

```
Filesystem    1K-blocks    Used         Available    Use%    Mounted
on
/dev/sda1     263174212    230887666    32286546     87%     /
```

What Linux command have they used?

A. ps

B. top

C. df

D. ip

6. A technician provides support to a remote user who is operating on an Ubuntu Linux workstation with NO graphical interface. The technician needs to access a terminal session securely as the system contains sensitive intellectual property. They will need to use a number of command-line tools during the session. What will allow the technician to perform this task?

A. RDP (Remote Desktop Protocol)

B. SSH (secure shell)

C. telnet (teletype network)

D. cp (copy command)

7. What is the purpose of the man command when it precedes a command-line interface (CLI) command in Linux?

   A. It elevates the users' privileges so they can perform administrative tasks

   B. It automatically assigns the manager privilege to the command

   C. It displays help in the form of a manual

   D. It enters maintenance mode for the command

8. A department would like their Windows 10-based workstations to be able to access shared files on an Ubuntu Linux server using mapped drives. What service would allow for this functionality?

   A. Install the telnet service on the Ubuntu server

   B. Install the samba service on the Windows 10 workstations

   C. Install Windows File and Print Sharing on the Ubuntu server

   D. Install samba service on the Ubuntu server

9. Which command allows an administrator to download and install new application packages on a Red Hat Linux workstation?

   A. grep

   B. ps

   C. yum

   D. dig

10. The Human Resources manager is searching the HR folder for a file called Employee-Details. Once found, they need to search the file for information regarding Joe Smith. What TWO commands were used to generate the following output?

    ```
    -rw-r--r-- 1 mark HumanResources 263 Jan  9 18:24 Employee-
    Details
    Joe Smith   6 Beacon Drive, Edinburgh EH1 4DL   0131 789765
    ```

    A. ls -l Employee-Details

    B. dir /L Employee-Details

    C. cat "Joe Smith" Employee-Details

    D. grep "Joe Smith" Employee-Details

11. A technician is troubleshooting a networking issue on an Ubuntu Linux workstation. The technician issues commands in the terminal window, resulting in the following output:

```
eth0: <BROADCAST,MULTICAST,UP,LOWER_UP> mtu 1500 qdisc mq state
UP group default qlen 1000
link/ether 00:15:5d:30:49:57 brd ff:ff:ff:ff:ff:ff
inet 172.22.64.215/20 brd 172.22.79.255 scope global eth0
inet6 fe80::215:5dff:fe30:4957/64 scope link

ANSWER SECTION:
www.google.com.          0        IN        A        142.250.114.104
www.google.com.          0        IN        A        142.250.114.106
www.google.com.          0        IN        A        142.250.114.99
www.google.com.          0        IN        A        142.250.114.147
www.google.com.          0        IN        A        142.250.114.103
www.google.com.          0        IN        A        142.250.114.105
;; Query time: 130 msec
```

What TWO Linux network commands were used to generate the output?

A. ip address

B. ipconfig

C. nslookup

D. dig

E. tracert

F. ping

12. A developer raises a support ticket as they cannot access a file shared from a colleague's Red Hat Linux workstation. What command would be BEST to assign permissions for the file?

A. grep

B. chmod

C. ip address

D. pwd

# 8

# Security

## Introduction

This chapter will test an exam candidate's knowledge of security concepts, procedures, and security best practices. Threats and threat actors are constantly changing, and security professionals must understand how to recognize threats and mitigate them in different ways. Common environments that need to be secured include wireless networks, **small office/home office (SOHO)** networks, enterprise networks, and situations where securing remote access is crucial. Mobile devices and support for IoT also present many challenges for security professionals. It is important to understand the threats posed by social engineering, often referred to as hacking humans (where users are targeted). To mitigate these threats, it is important to recognize the correct controls that need to be enabled and to understand the correct response to specific threats.

In order to be successful in the CompTIA A+ Core 2 (220-1102) certification exam, candidates must be familiar with the following objectives:

- 8.1 Summarize various security measures and their purposes
- 8.2 Compare and contrast wireless security protocols and authentication methods
- 8.3 Given a scenario, detect, remove, and prevent malware using the appropriate tools and methods
- 8.4 Explain common social-engineering attacks, threats, and vulnerabilities
- 8.5 Given a scenario, manage and configure basic security settings in the Microsoft Windows OS
- 8.6 Given a scenario, configure a workstation to meet best practices for security
- 8.7 Explain common methods for securing mobile and embedded devices
- 8.8 Given a scenario, use common data destruction and disposal methods
- 8.9 Given a scenario, configure appropriate security settings on small office/home office (SOHO) wireless and wired networks
- 8.10 Given a scenario, install and configure browsers and relevant security settings

The rest of this chapter is committed to practice. For each of the previously defined concepts, you will be given a series of questions designed to test your knowledge of each core 2 objective as defined by the official certification exam guidance for this domain. These questions will test the candidate's knowledge of how to implement security best practices within an organization.

## Practice Exam Questions

### 8.1 Summarize various security measures and their purposes

1. What is the purpose of a motion sensor in a security system?

    A. To detect the presence of unauthorized individuals or objects

    B. To control the temperature of the surrounding environment

    C. To amplify the sound of nearby movements

    D. To adjust the brightness of the lighting system

2. A CISO is proposing to use an app on company-deployed smartphones as a soft token. What is the purpose of a soft token?

    A. Generating secure passwords

    B. Authenticating user identity

    C. Encrypting data

    D. Blocking malicious websites

3. A call center manager is proposing to support an initiative where workers will be able to work from home. The security team is discussing methods that will allow the use of personal equipment and the control and management of employees' personal devices. Which of the following controls allows the team to manage this infrastructure and ensure users are given guidance to support this initiative? (Choose two.)

    A. Fingerprint scanner

    B. Multifactor authentication (MFA)

    C. BYOD policy

    D. Equipment locks

    E. MDM policy

    F. Time-based login policies

4.  A chief information security manager (CISO) is reviewing the security controls that will best prevent a user from gaining unauthorized physical access to the server room. What two controls would best address this requirement?

    A.  Access control vestibule

    B.  Alarm

    C.  Video surveillance

    D.  Bollards

    E.  Motion sensors

    F.  Door locks

5.  A cloud service provider (CSP) has recently added a number of security controls in response to a recent security audit. These controls have required the installation of perimeter fencing and security gates and additional guards to be employed to secure all external entry points. The audit also highlighted the lack of detective controls, within the CSP data center, in the event the perimeter security is breached. What detective controls would BEST address this requirement? (Choose two.)

    A.  Access control vestibule

    B.  Badge reader

    C.  Video surveillance

    D.  Equipment locks

    E.  Motion sensors

    F.  Door locks

6.  A security team must design controls to ensure the business will be compliant with stringent requirements regarding safeguarding customer payment card details. Servers hosting customer card payment details will be physically secured in a server room. Access to the server room needs to be controlled using two-factor authentication (2FA). Currently, administrators access the server room using a fingerprint reader. What could be used in addition to fingerprints to support two-factor access control?

    A.  Smart cards

    B.  Retina scanner

    C.  Palmprint scanner

    D.  Motion detector

7. A security team is evaluating additional security controls to ensure physical equipment, including storage devices, cannot be removed by authorized members of staff from the internal data center. What control would allow security guards to be alerted if there is an attempt to remove equipment from the data center?

   A. Access control vestibule

   B. Video surveillance

   C. Equipment locks

   D. Lighting

   E. Magnetometers

8. A network administrator onboards a new user who has joined the sales team as a junior sales executive. They have created a unique account for the user and added the user to a security group with limited access rights. What best describes why this process would be adopted?

   A. To adhere to the principle of least privilege

   B. To enforce access control lists (ACLs)

   C. To ensure the user is using multifactor authentication (MFA)

   D. To support the use of organizational units

9. When a user logs in to the Windows domain, an automated process is run that assigns the user a default storage location on a Windows server. The user is able to access this network link through the explorer interface. What describes this feature and how the system automates the creation of the link? (Choose two.)

   A. Use of a login script

   B. Management of security groups

   C. Multifactor authentication

   D. Use of home folders

   E. Organizational units

10. When a user needs to access company assets from a laptop computer, they must have access to an app on their mobile phone. The app provides a time-based one-time password (TOTP) that must be provided along with a log-in ID and password. What best describes the technology used? (Choose two.)

    A. Principle of least privilege

    B. Multifactor authentication (MFA)

    C. Short Message Service (SMS)

    D. Voice call verification

    E. Use of an authenticator application

11. When a user authenticates their Active Directory account from any workstation, they can access all their common folders (Desktop, Documents, Pictures, and more). The folders contain all the up-to-date content that they saved. What two Windows features allow for centralized storage of user data and transparent network access to this data?

    A. Login script

    B. Group Policy settings

    C. Organizational units

    D. Home folder

    E. Folder redirection

12. A bank needs to ensure customers can provide an additional authentication factor when authorizing payments during online banking. The bank intends to support this using a second out-of-band mobile phone authentication. What 2FA methods require the user to have access to a mobile phone? (Choose two.)

    A. Email verification link

    B. Short Message Service (SMS)

    C. Voice call verification

    D. Use of a hard token

13. Which of the following is true about Active Directory security groups?

    A. Security groups are used to assign permissions to shared resources

    B. Security groups are used to organize user accounts

    C. Security groups are used for email distribution lists

    D. Security groups are used to control network connectivity

14. An administrator is creating an Active Directory (AD) organizational unit (OU) for the new research department. What is the primary purpose of an OU in Active Directory?

    A.  It determines the physical location of a user or computer object

    B.  It defines the security policies for a domain

    C.  It groups related objects for easier administration

    D.  It provides the domain name resolution services

## 8.2 Compare and contrast wireless security protocols and authentication methods

1.  A security consultant is advising a small business on the subject of securing the Wi-Fi network when giving access to customers. The small business only has access to a wireless router provided by the internet service provider (ISP). The business intends to print a code on the bottom of till receipts to allow customers to access the Wi-Fi. Which wireless standard offers the highest levels of security when a customer needs to access the Wi-Fi using a supplied passcode/passkey?

    A.  Wi-Fi Protected Access 2 (WPA2)

    B.  Wi-Fi Protected Access 3 (WPA3)

    C.  Temporal Key Integrity Protocol (TKIP)

    D.  Advanced Encryption Standard (AES)

2.  A security team is planning for the deployment of Wi-Fi for internal business units. It is anticipated that over 50% of the workforce will need secure access to Wi-Fi. Management is insisting that all users should use unique domain credentials to authenticate onto the network. What service can be deployed to ensure user authentication requests are securely passed back to the Active Directory?

    A.  WPS

    B.  WEP Open

    C.  RADIUS

    D.  WPA-PSK

3.  A technician is configuring a wireless LAN and must ensure that the configuration of the Wi-Fi router supports the latest encryption standards. What configuration choice would BEST protect confidential data sent over Wi-Fi?

    A.  WEP

    B.  WPA2-TKIP

    C.  WPA2-AES

    D.  WPA Open

## 8.3 Given a scenario, detect, remove, and prevent malware using the appropriate tools and methods

1.  What do boot sector viruses target?

    A.  Files stored on external hard drives

    B.  The master boot record or boot sector of a computer

    C.  Network routers and switches

    D.  User passwords and login credentials

2.  What is the primary purpose of a keylogger?

    A.  To mine cryptocurrencies

    B.  To delete files and disrupt system operations

    C.  To track user activities and collect sensitive information

    D.  To capture and record keystrokes on a computer

3.  What are the typical signs that a ransomware attack is taking place?

    A.  An attacker is exploiting software vulnerabilities

    B.  An attacker is tracking user activities and collecting sensitive information

    C.  An attacker is encrypting files and demanding a ransom for their release

    D.  An attacker is hijacking a computer's boot process

4.  Technicians are investigating an issue with a sales department laptop computer. Windows Defender Security features are turned off and when the technicians attempt to re-enable the features, the settings are reversed. What type of malware may be the cause of the issue?

    A.  Trojan

    B.  Rootkit

    C.  Virus

    D.  Spyware

    E.  Ransomware

5.  Security staff are preparing a set of automated actions to assist the service desk when dealing with malware incidents. They propose to create a number of playbooks to assist the team. One scenario requires the entire hard drive to be erased and the OS to be re-installed. What malware type would require this action?

    A.  Trojan

    B.  Rootkit

    C.  Virus

    D.  Spyware

6.  A user calls the service desk, complaining that after opening a file sent by a co-worker, they can no longer access any local folders. In addition, they see pop-up messages displaying a telephone number and requests to make payments to fix the problem. What has likely caused this issue on the user's computer?

    A.  Trojan

    B.  Rootkit

    C.  Virus

    D.  Spyware

    E.  Ransomware

7.  After installing a number of technical preventative controls on the company network, in order to reduce malware incidents, there has been a 90% reduction in infected systems. The controls consist of spam filters, content inspection, and endpoint detection and response (EDR). In addition to these technical controls, what would be most effective in further reducing malware incidents?

    A.  User education regarding rootkits

    B.  User education regarding viruses

    C.  User education regarding common threats

    D.  User education regarding spyware

8. A user calls the service desk after receiving a number of messages in the Windows 10 action center. The messages appear to be non-malicious and are being generated by the web browser. What action would be the BEST to remediate this issue?

   A. Disable the web browser

   B. Perform a full anti-virus scan

   C. Block all outgoing traffic on ports 80 and 443

   D. Delete and re-install the OS

9. A recent spate of spam emails has targeted the finance team. The emails appear to originate from genuine suppliers and often contain links to reset login details. What course of action will BEST help to reduce these incidents?

   A. Software firewalls

   B. Anti-phishing training

   C. User education regarding common threats

   D. OS re-installation

10. After installing a new video driver from an unofficial third-party internet site, a user's workstation is exhibiting strange behavior. The workstation is running slowly, and the user reports no other changes have been made apart from the updated driver. What action will allow a technician to BEST determine whether the driver is the cause of the behavior?

    A. Reboot the workstation into recovery mode, select Troubleshoot\Advanced options\Startup settings, and choose to enable Safe Mode

    B. Perform a full anti-virus scan

    C. Ensure anti-malware is updated

    D. Configure Windows Firewall to block all outgoing connections

11. A company has recently seen a high number of user accounts compromised. The accounts belong to the engineering team, which hot desks using a limited number of engineering workstations. Despite the user passwords being reset, the problem persists. What is the MOST likely reason for the accounts being compromised?

    A. Remote access trojan

    B. Rootkit replacing key OS files

    C. Hardware keyloggers on the engineering workstations

    D. Cryptominers stealing user credentials

12. A number of users recently returned from a marketing event with digital promotional materials provided on USB media. The service desk received a number of calls from the users complaining that applications are slow to load and their workstations are unacceptably slow. After investigation, it appears that CPU/GPU activity is running at 100%. What type of malware is MOST likely affecting the users?

A.  Spyware

B.  Cryptominers

C.  Keyloggers

D.  Boot sector virus

## 8.4 Explain common social-engineering attacks, threats, and vulnerabilities

1.  A chief information officer (CIO) receives an email from the chief executive officer (CEO) requesting confidential information to be supplied. The email appears to originate from a personal email address that the CIO does not recognize. What type of attack is this likely to be?

A.  Phishing

B.  Dumpster diving

C.  Shoulder surfing

D.  Whaling

2.  A user is picking up printed documents from the centralized office printer. Despite the large number of other users in the crowded print room, after a wait in line, the user is able to successfully type in their password to pull down the print job. Later, the user is warned of a suspicious login using the same credentials. What social engineering event likely took place?

A.  Phishing

B.  Vishing

C.  Shoulder surfing

D.  Whaling

3.  A team of contractors arrives on site, wearing shirts and jackets with the logo of a well-known support contractor. The contractors say they are responding to error messages that have been received from the bank's critical servers in the data center. There is no record of a support call being generated. What is the likely vector of attack?

    A.  Tailgating

    B.  Impersonation

    C.  Dumpster diving

    D.  Evil twin

4.  A user raises a support ticket complaining about slow Wi-Fi speeds, local mapped drives, and printers not being available. On several occasions, the user has been asked for credentials when connected to internet sites. The user suspects that their online accounts may have been compromised. What is the likely threat vector?

    A.  Tailgating

    B.  Impersonation

    C.  Dumpster diving

    D.  Evil twin

5.  A courier wearing a high-visibility jacket carrying a parcel follows an employee into an unmanned reception area. Later, it is discovered that laptop computers and a tablet have been reported as missing or stolen. What was the likely cause of this security breach?

    A.  Tailgating

    B.  Impersonation

    C.  Dumpster diving

    D.  Evil twin

6.  An online retailer receives multiple complaints that customers cannot access the site. Upon investigation, engineers discover thousands of remote connections to the site's web servers. The connections do not appear to be genuine customers logging in to the site. What is the likely threat?

    A.  Distributed denial of service (DDoS)

    B.  Denial of service (DoS)

    C.  Zero-day attack

    D.  Spoofing

7.  A user is attempting to log in to their online banking site, but the web browser reports an error regarding the website certificate. The URL in the browser does not appear to be the normal URL that the user was expecting. What type of attack is likely occurring?

    A.  On-path attack

    B.  Insider threat

    C.  Structured Query Language (SQL) injection

    D.  Cross-site scripting (XSS)

8.  A security engineer is investigating logs on the customer-facing web application server. One of the entries is causing the engineer concern. The following string is logged:

    ```
    <script>alert('http://malwaresite.com/javascriptcookiestealer.
    com')</script>
    ```

    What type of attack has likely occurred?

    A.  Spoofing

    B.  Structured Query Language (SQL) injection

    C.  Cross-site scripting (XSS)

    D.  Zero-day attack

9.  An attacker is able to target a vulnerability present on a web server where there is no available patch or update. What type of threat does this describe?

    A.  Insider threat

    B.  Structured Query Language (SQL) injection

    C.  Cross-site scripting (XSS)

    D.  Zero-day attack

10. An attacker is able to log on to a website, despite the fact that the attacker has not been assigned valid credentials. The logs indicate that the attacker was able to access the site using the first account stored in a table on the database server. The following log entry was recorded around the time of the incident:

    ```
    SELECT * FROM Users WHERE Username=foo' OR '1' = '1' AND
    Password='pass' OR '1' = '1'
    ```

    What type of attack has occurred?

    A.  Brute-force attack

    B.  Dictionary attack

    C.  Structured Query Language (SQL) injection

    D.  Cross-site scripting (XSS)

## 8.5 Given a scenario, manage and configure basic security settings in the Microsoft Windows OS

1.  An administrator is tasked with configuring permissions for the marketing folder on a user's Windows 10 laptop. The permissions should allow the marketing team to have read permissions on the folder. What should the administrator configure to allow marketing users network access to the folder?

    A.  Set NTFS permissions to read for the marketing group

    B.  Choose to share the folder and give the marketing group read network access

    C.  Select the folder attributes and ensure read-only is checked

    D.  Set NTFS permissions to modify for the marketing group

2.  A help desk receives a call from a home user who would like to synchronize their preferences, themes, and browser shortcuts when signing in to different Windows devices. Currently, the user has a unique local account configured on each device. The user would also prefer to have a single account for all devices. What feature would satisfy the user's request?

    A.  Have the user create a Microsoft account and enable this on each device

    B.  Create a local account on the current device and copy the account to all devices

    C.  Have the user sign on with the default guest account on each device

    D.  Have the user sign in to the Edge browser and enable synchronization options

3.  A standard user is assigned a second privileged account that can be used to reset other users' passwords when requested. The user has access to the Active Directory Users and Computers (ADUC) console. What would be the recommended best security practice when considering the use of the two accounts? (Choose two.)

    A.  Always sign in to the workstation using a standard user account

    B.  Use the run as administrator option when using the privileged account

    C.  Always sign in to the workstation using the privileged user account

    D.  Use the run as standard user option when using the privileged account

4.  A user has requested to store sensitive information on a removable USB drive. Company policy states that all removable storage must support data encryption and all data must be encrypted at rest. What Windows feature can be used to meet the company policy?

    A.  Pretty Good Privacy (PGP)

    B.  BitLocker to Go

    C.  Extensible File Allocation Table (exFAT) filesystem

    D.  User Account Control (UAC)

5. A finance manager has raised a support ticket. They would like to protect sensitive files stored on Windows 10 workstations. The files contain customer details and are stored in a single folder. The files must be encrypted to meet security best practices. What can a support technician configure to protect the folder?

   A. Enable Encrypting File System (EFS) for the folder

   B. Enable BitLocker Drive Encryption for the folder

   C. Enable BitLocker to Go on the folder

   D. Ensure NTFS permissions are set to read for the finance tea

6. A technician is attempting to manually set an IP address on a server's network interface card. They are prompted with a security dialog box, asking whether they approve of the application making changes to the computer. What has likely required this extra verification?

   A. Windows Defender anti-virus

   B. User Account Control (UAC)

   C. Multifactor authentication (MFA)

   D. Windows Defender Firewall

7. A technician has quarantined a user's Windows 10 laptop after an unknown process was found running on the system. The process is identified as malicious and is documented on many anti-virus vendor sites. The user has been using the laptop on a network with no internet access for 2 months. What should the technician do next?

   A. Update Windows Defender definition files and run a full anti-virus scan

   B. Manually remove the malicious file and return the laptop to the user

   C. Use a system restore to revert to the last restore point

   D. Wipe the system and perform a fresh Windows installation

8. A recently installed database application has been configured and tested on a departmental server. The departmental users cannot connect to the application across the network. A technician performs a port scan on the server and observes the following output:

```
Nmap scan report for 192.168.0.22
Host is up (0.000086s latency).
Not shown: 994 closed ports
PORT      STATE     SERVICE
135/tcp   open      msrpc
139/tcp   open      netbios-ssn
445/tcp   open      microsoft-ds
514/tcp   open      shell
3306/tcp  filtered  mysql
```

What should the technician do next to allow users to access the database application?

A.  Deactivate the Windows Defender firewall on the server

B.  Activate the Windows Defender firewall on the users' workstations

C.  Add a firewall rule to allow inbound traffic to port 3306 on the server

D.  Re-install the database application on the server and perform a system restart

## 8.6 Given a scenario, configure a workstation to meet best practices for security

1.  A senior manager who is attending a conference needs to ensure that confidential data stored on a laptop computer is secured when the laptop is shut down. What will best secure the data at rest?

A.  BitLocker full disk encryption

B.  Use Pretty Good Privacy (PGP) to encrypt the system files

C.  Restrict login times

D.  Use timeout/screen lock

2.  An administrator must ensure that user accounts are added to groups, giving only the necessary privileges needed to carry out assigned tasks. What best practice will ensure that users do not become over-privileged?

A.  Ensure all users are members of the Power Users group only

B.  Implement least privilege policies

C.  Ensure guest accounts are disabled

D.  Rename the default administrator account

3.  Which of the following is NOT a recommended practice for creating a strong password?

A.  Using a combination of uppercase and lowercase letters

B.  Including personal information such as your name or birthdate

C.  Incorporating special characters and numbers

D.  Making it at least eight characters long

4.  A technician has disabled support for Wake-on-LAN (WoL) network support. This is a requirement for all company laptop computers. The technician is concerned that users will simply turn this feature back on. What is the most effective way to block this action?

    A.  Enable Unified Extensible Firmware Interface (UEFI) passwords

    B.  Ensure user passwords have complexity requirements set

    C.  Ensure user passwords have expiration requirements set

    D.  Ensure user passwords have length requirements

5.  A CISO is preparing guidance for company employees on the use of password managers. What is the purpose of a password manager?

    A.  To generate secure passwords

    B.  To store and organize passwords

    C.  To encrypt your passwords

    D.  All of the above

6.  An administrator must ensure that contract personnel employed in the payroll team will only be able to log in to the network when other members of staff are present. What would be the most effective way to ensure this is enforced?

    A.  Restrict user permissions outside of core business hour

    B.  Restrict login times for contractors to core business hours

    C.  Disable guest accounts on all contractors' workstations

    D.  Ensure contractors' accounts are locked out after three failed attempts

7.  During a security awareness briefing, users are given examples of password attacks. Which of the following is a common method for "brute-forcing" passwords?

    A.  Guessing common passwords or phrases

    B.  Exploiting software vulnerabilities

    C.  Intercepting network traffic

    D.  Repeatedly trying different combinations of characters

8.  An administrator is concerned that an attacker can gain access to a user's account by using a dictionary attack at the login prompt. What security setting would be the most effective?

    A.  Enforce a minimum password length of 10 characters

    B.  Restrict login times for contractors to core business hours

    C.  Disable guest accounts on all workstations

    D.  Ensure accounts are locked out after three failed attempts

9.  A senior manager raises a support ticket after encountering a problem during an important presentation. The manager inserted a memory card, to access the presentation material, and a movie file began to play. What can a support technician do to resolve the ticket?

    A.  Configure autoplay settings for memory cards

    B.  Block access to external media

    C.  Configure autoplay settings for removable drives

    D.  Ensure Windows Movie Player is blocked from playing

10. Which of the following is the best practice for maintaining password security?

    A.  Sharing passwords with trusted family members or friends

    B.  Using the same password across multiple accounts

    C.  Changing passwords frequently

    D.  Writing down passwords on a piece of paper and keeping it in a visible place

11. A CISO must ensure the company is compliant with recommended best security practices. The CISO has noticed that on occasion, users' laptops are displaying personally identifiable information (PII) and intellectual property (IP) when users are not at their desks. What would be the most effective control to secure the workstations?

    A.  Use a timeout to automatically enable screen locks

    B.  Have all users read and sign an acceptable use policy (AUP)

    C.  Have all users lock their laptops in a secure location whenever they leave their desks

    D.  Use cable locks to secure the laptops to desks

12. A service desk operator takes a call from a user who suspects that their password has been compromised. What would be the operator's best recommended action for the user?

   A. Continue using the same password but monitor account activity closely

   B. Immediately change the password for the affected account

   C. Delete the account and create a new one

   D. Do nothing and hope for the best

## 8.7 Explain common methods for securing mobile and embedded devices

1. An administrator is following best practices by ensuring that company-issued mobile devices have preventative controls enabled to ensure the privacy of stored data, in the event of the loss or theft of the devices. What two settings will be most effective?

   A. Restrictive firewall settings

   B. Always-on VPN connection

   C. Screen lock with a password with a minimum of 10 characters

   D. BYOD acceptable use policy

   E. Full device encryption (FDE)

2. Which of the following statements accurately describes a security concern specific to bring your own device (BYOD)?

   A. BYOD devices have limited compatibility with corporate applications

   B. COBO devices may compromise employee privacy and personal data

   C. BYOD increases the risk of unauthorized data access through lost or stolen devices

   D. COBO devices are more susceptible to phishing attacks and social engineering

3. Which network location type in Windows Defender Firewall offers the highest level of security?

   A. Home

   B. Public

   C. Domain

   D. Work

4. An international bank issues smartphones to some employees and allows the use of personal devices for other staff members. It is important that audio and video recordings can be restricted when devices are taken into restricted areas. What would allow mobile devices to be managed in this way? (Choose two.)

    A. MDM

    B. BYOD

    C. Geofencing

    D. Screen locks

    E. Device encryption

5. An organization needs to store data on a mobile device that will include PII and proprietary information. The organization has already implemented FDE and screen locks. In order to add another layer of security, there is a requirement for users to authenticate using biometrics. Which of the following could be used to satisfy the organizational requirements? (Choose two.)

    A. Facial recognition

    B. PIN codes

    C. Fingerprint

    D. Pattern

    E. Swipe

6. What is a major security concern when considering the deployment of IoT devices, when used in building automation systems?

    A. Zigbee protocol

    B. Resilient mesh networks

    C. Location services

    D. Default accounts

## 8.8 Given a scenario, use common data destruction and disposal methods

1. A CISO is developing a company policy to ensure the correct procedures are followed when data is removed from storage. To ensure that there are no data remnants on magnetic media, what data destruction will be BEST?

   A. Erasing

   B. Standard formatting

   C. Degaussing

   D. Wiping

2. A technician has been tasked with rendering hard disk drives unusable as they have been used to store company intellectual property (IP). It is important the drives cannot be reused and must contain no data remnants. The technician has no access to specialist equipment. What would the best solution be?

   A. Shredding

   B. Standard formatting

   C. Degaussing

   D. Drilling

3. A government agency is working with a third-party data destruction specialist. It is important that the agency has a full audit trail for all data that is in use and for data that is to be removed. What documentation should the vendor provide to the government agency?

   A. Certification of destruction

   B. Non-disclosure agreement (NDA)

   C. Certification of incinerating

   D. Service-level agreement

4. A manager must ensure that paper-based documentation is rendered unreadable. The documents contain data classified as secret. What two methods, when used together, would ensure classified documents are rendered unreadable?

   A. Shredding

   B. Degaussing

   C. Incinerating

   D. Erasing

## 8.9 Given a scenario, configure appropriate security settings on small office/home office (SOHO) wireless and wired networks

1.  A network technician is following a checklist that involves updating firmware on all company SOHO routers. What is the purpose of firmware updates on a SOHO router?

    A.  To improve router performance and stability

    B.  To add new features and functionalities

    C.  To fix security vulnerabilities and bugs

    D.  All of the above

2.  A technician is helping a user to configure their home router. The wireless router is new and has not been configured. In the first instance, the technician wants to configure the network interface with the correct IP address supplied by the internet service provider (ISP). What configuration option should they choose?

    A.  Create Dynamic Host Configuration Protocol (DHCP) reservations

    B.  Configure the static wide-area network (WAN) IP

    C.  Enable Universal Plug and Play (UPnP)

    D.  Configure a screened subnet

3.  A home user is having difficulty connecting their PlayStation gaming system to the internet gaming service. The user thinks that the router may be blocking the gaming system from accessing the internet service. What feature would allow the user to access the internet gaming service?

    A.  Disable content filtering on the router

    B.  Disable Dynamic Host Configuration Protocol (DHCP) on the router

    C.  Enable Universal Plug and Play (UPnP) on the router

    D.  Deploy a screened subnet

4.  A small print shop wants to host an FTP server to allow customers to upload documents that can then be printed as part of the service. The intention is to use a computer that has access to the internet. The print shop has a SOHO wireless router only. What feature will allow this service to be securely hosted? (Choose two.)

    A.  Configure IP filtering to protect the customer-facing FTP server

    B.  Configure a screened subnet to place the customer-facing computer

    C.  Configure firmware updates on the router

    D.  Configure port forwarding to route traffic from the internet to the FTP server

5.  A technician is helping a user to configure their Wi-Fi home router. The wireless router is new and has not been configured. The technician wants to secure the device against the threat of unauthorized connections. What two settings would be most effective? (Choose two.)

    A.  Disabling the SSID broadcast

    B.  Enabling a screened subnet

    C.  Enabling guest access

    D.  Changing default passwords

6.  A sales outlet in a shopping mall is experiencing latency on the wireless network. Staff are complaining that when they are demonstrating features on phones and tablets, the devices appear very slow to display pages. A technician notices that there are many other wireless networks in close proximity. What may offer a solution for a better-quality wireless signal?

    A.  Disabling SSID broadcast

    B.  Encryption settings

    C.  Disabling guest access

    D.  Changing channels

7.  A network technician is assisting a coffee shop with establishing a wireless network for customers to use. The shop intends to print a passkey onto sales receipts so that customers can access free Wi-Fi. The technician is asked to secure the network so that only legitimate customers can securely use the network. What security setting would be best for these requirements?

    A.  Enable WPA3-SAE

    B.  Enable WEP-PSK

    C.  Enable WPA2-TKIP

    D.  Enable WPA2-AES

## 8.10 Given a scenario, install and configure browsers and relevant security settings

1.  A technician is advising a customer who requires assistance with the installation of a web browser. For ease of use, the user would prefer to download and install a browser that did not come installed with the default OS. What two pieces of advice can the technician offer the user to ensure a safe installation?

    A.  Make sure to download the browser from trusted sources

    B.  After download, check that the file size is identical to the file size on the vendor site

    C.  Make sure to download a browser with a password manager

    D.  After download, check that the hash value is identical to the value published on the vendor site

2.  A company would like to allow users to view websites that are not automatically translated into the user's native language. Presently, users are complaining that they need to copy and paste the content into the word processing application to perform translation. What can the company do to best help the users?

    A.  Add a language translator as a browser extension

    B.  Install a new browser that supports language translation

    C.  Ensure the browser supports HTML5

    D.  Add support for additional languages to the Windows settings menu

3.  A support desk operator has been assigned a support ticket raised by a user who complains that web pages take too long to load and seem to display a lot of advertising content within the pages. What will be the best solution to speed up the user's browser when displaying web pages?

    A.  Enable a pop-up blocker

    B.  Clear the browsing data cache

    C.  Enable private-browsing mode

    D.  Enable an ad blocker

4.  A customer asks a support technician how can they be sure that the banking website can be trusted. They have been told that fake sites can be made to resemble genuine sites. What ensures that a website can be trusted?

    A.  The site will display a padlock when connecting using HTTPS

    B.  Ensure there is a trusted certificate when connecting using HTTP

    C.  The site will display a security rating when connecting using HTTPS

    D.  Ensure to always connect using private-browsing mode

# Software Troubleshooting

## Introduction

In order to successfully pass the A+ certification exam, the candidate must understand the best practice approach used to perform effective software troubleshooting.

When troubleshooting desktop environments, a solid understanding of the Windows OS is a key requirement. A technician must be able to interpret system messages and respond to common errors and events using the correct techniques. Desktop computers are still a mainstay of the modern office environment, and the correct troubleshooting methods should be observed when supporting users on these platforms.

A technician must understand the correct proactive approach to ensure systems are kept optimized and malware free. This includes the timely deployment of OS patches and OS updates.

A thorough understanding of supporting software applications on mobile OSs is also very important.

In order to be successful on the CompTIA A+ Core 2 (220-1102) certification exam, candidates must ensure they are familiar with the following objectives:

- 9.1 Given a scenario, troubleshoot common Windows OS problems
- 9.2 Given a scenario, troubleshoot common personal computer (PC) security issues
- 9.3 Given a scenario, use best practice procedures for malware removal
- 9.4 Given a scenario, troubleshoot common mobile OS and application issues
- 9.5 Given a scenario, troubleshoot common mobile OS and application security issues

The rest of this chapter is committed to practice. For each of the previously defined concepts, you will be given a series of questions designed to test your knowledge of each core two objective as defined by the official certification exam guidance for this domain. These questions will assess the candidate's knowledge of how to support and troubleshoot software applications.

# Practice Exam Questions

## 9.1 Given a scenario, troubleshoot common Windows OS problems

1. Which of the following is a common cause of a blue screen of death (BSOD) error in Windows?

    A. Outdated device drivers

    B. Overclocked CPU

    C. Insufficient disk space

    D. Incorrect BIOS settings

2. Which of the following actions can help resolve a blue screen of death (BSOD) error caused by faulty RAM?

    A. Cleaning the computer's cooling fans

    B. Updating the anti-virus software

    C. Replacing the RAM modules

    D. Re-installing the operating system

3. What is the purpose of the STOP error code displayed on a blue screen of death (BSOD)?

    A. To indicate the severity of the error

    B. To identify the specific cause of the error

    C. To inform the user about available system updates

    D. To provide instructions for recovering data

4. A user raises a support ticket as their Windows computer consistently shuts down after a few minutes of use, and there is no error message displayed. Which of the following is the MOST probable cause of this issue?

    A. Power supply failure

    B. Overheating

    C. Virus or malware infection

    D. Faulty motherboard

5.  A user calls the service desk as they have an error that states a Windows service is not starting. Which of the following is the most likely reason for a Windows service not starting?

    A.  Insufficient disk space

    B.  Outdated device drivers

    C.  Incorrect service configuration

    D.  Incompatible software installation

6.  A technician is responding to a user support ticket. The user is experiencing error messages relating to low memory availability. Which of the following actions can help resolve low-memory warnings in Windows? (Choose two.)

    A.  Closing unnecessary applications

    B.  Deleting temporary files

    C.  Adding more RAM to the system

    D.  Upgrading the processor

7.  Which of the following warnings is most likely to indicate system instability on a Windows computer?

    A.  "The system has detected a critical error and will shut down in 1 minute."

    B.  "Your anti-virus software has expired. Please renew your subscription."

    C.  "A new update is available for your web browser. Click here to install."

    D.  "Low disk space. Free up some space to optimize system performance."

8.  A technician is troubleshooting a Windows desktop computer, which displays the error message "No OS found" during startup. What is the most likely cause?

    A.  The Windows operating system is missing or corrupted

    B.  The hard drive is not properly connected or has failed

    C.  The computer's BIOS settings are incorrect

    D.  The computer is infected with a virus

9.  A user reports slow profile load times when logging in to a Windows computer. Which of the following could be the cause?

    A.  Insufficient system resources

    B.  Corrupted user profile

    C.  Network connectivity issues

    D.  Outdated device drivers

10. Which of the following factors can contribute to time drift issues in Windows?

   A.  Incorrect time zone settings

   B.  Malware infection

   C.  Hardware clock malfunction

   D.  Power outage

11. Which of the following methods should be used to restart a service using the Windows Services management console?

   A.  Right-clicking the service and selecting "Stop" and then "Start"

   B.  Right-clicking the service and selecting "Restart"

   C.  Double-clicking the service and selecting "Restart" from the toolbar

   D.  Right-clicking the service and selecting "Pause" and then "Resume"

12. Which of the following statements is true regarding the impact of a reboot on an unresponsive application?

   A.  Rebooting the system resets all running applications to the default configuration settings

   B.  Rebooting the system has no effect on unresponsive applications

   C.  Rebooting the system may force the closure of the unresponsive application

   D.  Rebooting the system automatically repairs any issues with unresponsive applications

13. If an application crashes immediately upon launch, what should be checked first?

   A.  System requirements of the application

   B.  Available disk space on the computer

   C.  Anti-virus software settings

   D.  Compatibility mode settings

14. After a recent operating system update, a user's computer fails to boot and displays a "boot device not found" error message. Which of the following is the most likely cause of the failure?

   A.  Corrupted boot loader

   B.  Overheating CPU

   C.  Insufficient hard drive space

   D.  Incorrect BIOS settings

15. A user's computer is frequently experiencing blue screen of death (BSOD) errors after installing a new anti-virus software. Which of the following actions should be taken to troubleshoot the issue?

    A.  Uninstall the anti-virus software

    B.  Upgrade the computer's RAM

    C.  Re-install the operating system

    D.  Replace the graphics card

16. A user's computer is repeatedly prompted to install the latest operating system update but encounters errors during the installation process. Which of the following steps can be taken to address the OS update failures?

    A.  Clear temporary files and retry the update

    B.  Install a different web browser

    C.  Upgrade the computer's power supply

    D.  Increase the screen resolution

17. Which of the following is important to perform if a technician needs to roll back unsuccessful updates?

    A.  Re-install the latest updates

    B.  Disable automatic updates

    C.  Create a system restore point

    D.  Increase system resources

18. What troubleshooting step should a technician take when a Windows computer fails to boot and displays a blue screen of death (BSOD)?

    A.  Restart the computer and try again

    B.  Use System Restore to roll back to a previous working state

    C.  Re-install all third-party applications

    D.  Update the computer's BIOS

19. When should a computer technician consider running a Windows System File Checker?

    A.  When encountering hardware driver issues

    B.  After installing new software updates

    C.  When experiencing frequent application crashes

    D.  Before performing disk defragmentation

20. What command is used to initiate a Windows System File Checker from Command Prompt?

    A.  sfc /scanfile

    B.  sfc /verifyonly

    C.  sfc /scannow

    D.  sfc /restorehealth

21. When might a technician consider using Windows reimaging as a troubleshooting step?

    A.  When a specific software application is not launching properly

    B.  When the computer's internet connection is unstable

    C.  When the computer experiences frequent crashes and blue screen errors

    D.  When the computer's display resolution needs adjustment

## 9.2 Given a scenario, troubleshoot common personal computer (PC) security issues

1.  A user is unable to access the network from their personal computer (PC). Which of the following steps should a service desk technician take to troubleshoot this issue?

    A.  Check the physical network connections and cables

    B.  Update the anti-virus software

    C.  Re-install the operating system (OS)

    D.  Increase the PC's RAM

2.  A user frequently receives desktop alerts warning about potential security threats, but these alerts are false positives. Which of the following steps should the technician take to address this issue?

    A.  Update the anti-virus software

    B.  Adjust the settings of the firewall

    C.  Run a full system scan using an anti-virus program

    D.  Exclude the false positive files from anti-virus scans

3.  A user reports that their personal files have been altered or are missing/renamed on their PC. Which of the following security issues is most likely responsible for this?

    A.  Phishing attack

    B.  Ransomware infection

    C.  Rootkit installation

    D.  Unauthorized access by a network intruder

4.  A user raises a service ticket as they are experiencing unwanted notifications within the operating system (OS) of their PC. Which of the following steps should a technician take to troubleshoot this issue?

    A.  Disable startup programs

    B.  Update the BIOS

    C.  Re-install the OS

    D.  Clean the registry using a registry cleaner tool

5.  A user is encountering failures when attempting to install updates for their operating system (OS) on their PC. Which of the following steps should the technician take to resolve this issue?

    A.  Disable the anti-virus software temporarily

    B.  Restart the PC and try installing the updates again

    C.  Re-install the OS from scratch

    D.  Clear the browser cache and try again

6.  Which of the following browser-related symptoms is typically associated with adware or malware infections?

    A.  Random/frequent popups

    B.  Certificate warnings

    C.  Redirection

    D.  Slow internet speed

7.  What is the most likely cause of receiving repeated certificate warnings when accessing secure websites?

    A.  Outdated browser

    B.  Firewall blocking secure connections

    C.  Expired security certificate

    D.  DNS cache poisoning

8.  Which browser-related symptom is commonly associated with browser hijacking?

    A.  Random/frequent popups

    B.  Certificate warnings

    C.  Redirection

    D.  Slow internet speed

## 9.3 Given a scenario, use best practice procedures for malware removal

1.  A user's computer is exhibiting slow performance, frequent pop-up advertisements, and unexpected system restarts. Upon investigation, you suspect the presence of malware. What is the best practice procedure to remove the malware from the computer?

    A.  Disconnect the computer from the network, perform a full system scan using updated anti-malware software, and remove any detected malware

    B.  Manually delete suspicious files and folders from the computer, then restart it to check for any further issues

    C.  Re-install the operating system to ensure the complete removal of all malware

    D.  Ignore the issue as it may be a temporary glitch in the system

2.  Which of the following is the recommended practice for updating anti-malware software?

    A.  Disable automatic updates to prevent interruption during important tasks

    B.  Update the software manually only when prompted by the operating system

    C.  Configure the software to update automatically and regularly

    D.  Uninstall and re-install the software to ensure the latest version is installed

3.  Why is it important to investigate and verify malware symptoms before proceeding with the removal process?

    A.  It helps to determine the cost of the malware removal process

    B.  It allows for more accurate identification and selection of appropriate removal techniques.

    C.  It helps in estimating the time required to remove the malware

    D.  It ensures the end user is educated about the potential risks of malware

4.  A technician must follow best practice procedures to BEST prevent future malware infections. Which best practice should be followed?

    A.  Regularly update anti-virus software

    B.  Disable the system's user account control (UAC) feature

    C.  Share user credentials with trusted colleagues

    D.  Enable all browser extensions and plugins by default

5. Why is it necessary to quarantine infected systems during the malware removal process?

   A. To prevent the malware from spreading to other systems

   B. To disable System Restore in Windows

   C. To create a restore point for future use

   D. To schedule scans and run updates

6. What is the purpose of disabling System Restore in Windows during malware removal?

   A. To prevent the malware from spreading to other systems

   B. To remove any infected restore points

   C. To ensure the malware cannot re-infect the system after removal

   D. To speed up the malware removal process

7. What happens when System Restore is disabled during malware removal?

   A. The malware is immediately deleted from the system

   B. All existing restore points are deleted

   C. The malware is isolated and prevented from executing

   D. The system becomes immune to further malware infections

8. Why is it important to educate the end user as part of the malware removal process?

   A. To shift the responsibility of malware removal to the end user

   B. To enhance the end user's technical skills

   C. To minimize the risk of re-infection and prevent future malware incidents

   D. To create a sense of panic and urgency among end users

9. Which of the following is a potential benefit of educating the end user about malware removal?

   A. Decreased user productivity

   B. Increased reliance on IT support

   C. Improved incident response time

   D. Increased likelihood of data breaches

10. What is one potential consequence of neglecting to educate the end user about malware removal?

    A. Increased IT budget allocation

    B. Decreased system performance

    C. Higher incidence of successful malware attacks

    D. Decreased network bandwidth

## 9.4 Given a scenario, troubleshoot common mobile OS and application issues

1. Sara's smartphone battery drains quickly even though she does not use it extensively. Which of the following could be a possible cause of the issue?

    A. Background app refresh

    B. Low screen brightness

    C. Mobile data usage

    D. Overcharging the device

2. David is preparing to use AirDrop to wirelessly share files, photos, and more between Apple devices. Which of the following statements accurately describes AirDrop?

    A. AirDrop only works when both devices are connected to the same Wi-Fi network

    B. AirDrop can only be used to transfer files between iPhones

    C. AirDrop requires Bluetooth and Wi-Fi to be enabled on both devices

    D. AirDrop can transfer files between Apple devices and non-Apple devices

3. A user's smartphone suddenly becomes unresponsive and does not respond to touch inputs. Which of the following troubleshooting steps should be attempted first?

    A. Perform a soft reset on the device

    B. Clear the cache of all installed applications

    C. Re-install the mobile operating system

    D. Remove the battery and reinsert it

4. Which of the following is a common symptom of a malware-infected mobile device?

    A. Frequent battery drain

    B. Improved device performance

    C. Enhanced battery life

    D. App icons rearranging automatically

5.  Which of the following technologies enables contactless data exchange between two devices in close proximity?

    A.  Near-field communication (NFC)

    B.  Bluetooth

    C.  Wi-Fi

    D.  GPS

6.  A user reports that the screen of their mobile device does not autorotate. Which of the following troubleshooting steps should be performed first to resolve the issue?

    A.  Restart the device

    B.  Check the screen rotation settings

    C.  Update the mobile operating system

    D.  Perform a factory reset

7.  A user reports that their mobile device randomly reboots while they are using an application. Which of the following troubleshooting steps should be performed first to address this issue?

    A.  Clear the cache and data of the application

    B.  Update the operating system to the latest version

    C.  Re-install the application

    D.  Factory reset the mobile device

8.  A user reports that their mobile device is running out of storage space and is unable to install new applications. Which of the following actions would be the MOST appropriate troubleshooting step to resolve the issue?

    A.  Clear the device cache

    B.  Uninstall unnecessary applications

    C.  Perform a factory reset

    D.  Upgrade the device's operating system

9.  A user's mobile device battery drains quickly, even when not in use. Which of the following actions should be taken to troubleshoot this issue? (Choose two.)

    A.  Enable battery optimization settings

    B.  Close background applications

    C.  Replace the device battery

    D.  Disable push email notifications

10. A user reports that their mobile device's touchscreen is unresponsive. Which of the following troubleshooting steps should be performed FIRST to address the issue?

    A. Restart the device

    B. Calibrate the touchscreen

    C. Update the device's firmware

    D. Clean the touchscreen

11. A mobile device user complains about frequent app crashes. Which of the following actions should be taken to troubleshoot this problem?

    A. Clear the app cache

    B. Uninstall and re-install the app

    C. Update the device's operating system

    D. Restart the device

12. A mobile device user is experiencing slow performance when launching apps and navigating the interface. Which of the following steps should be taken to troubleshoot this problem?

    A. Clear app cache and data

    B. Perform a factory reset

    C. Install a performance optimization app

    D. Upgrade the device's memory (RAM)

13. A mobile device user reports that their device frequently loses Wi-Fi connectivity. Which of the following steps should be taken to troubleshoot this issue? (Choose two.)

    A. Forget and reconnect to the Wi-Fi network

    B. Reset the device's network settings

    C. Replace the device's Wi-Fi antenna

    D. Update the device's firmware

14. A user's mobile device frequently displays the message "Insufficient storage available." Which of the following troubleshooting steps would BEST resolve this issue?

    A. Clear the app cache

    B. Move apps and data to an external storage device

    C. Delete unnecessary files and applications

    D. Upgrade the device's storage capacity

15. A mobile device user complains about frequent device reboots and freezes. Which of the following actions should be taken to troubleshoot this problem? (Choose two.)

    A. Update the device's firmware

    B. Perform a factory reset

    C. Replace the device's battery

    D. Disable unnecessary background processes

## 9.5 Given a scenario, troubleshoot common mobile OS and application security issues

1. Which of the following best describes an APK file?

    A. A file format used to store music files on mobile devices

    B. An executable file containing an Android application

    C. A compressed file format used to store images on iOS devices

    D. A system file responsible for managing network connections

2. What does enabling developer mode on a mobile device allow you to do?

    A. Access advanced system settings and debugging features

    B. Install applications from unofficial sources

    C. Extend battery life by optimizing system performance

    D. Increase the device's screen resolution

3. What is the primary purpose of rooting an Android device?

    A. To remove malicious applications

    B. To enhance device security

    C. To gain administrative access and control over the operating system

    D. To extend battery life and improve performance

4. What is the term used to describe the process of bypassing software restrictions on an iOS device?

    A. Jailbreaking

    B. Bootlegging

    C. Application spoofing

    D. Malicious application

5.  Which of the following terms refers to a pirated or unauthorized copy of a mobile application?

    A.  APK file

    B.  Developer mode

    C.  Bootleg application

    D.  Root access

6.  Which of the following symptoms is commonly associated with a mobile device experiencing high network traffic?

    A.  Sluggish response time

    B.  Limited internet connectivity

    C.  High number of ads

    D.  Fake security warnings

7.  Which symptom is commonly observed when a mobile device reaches its data usage limit?

    A.  No internet connectivity

    B.  Unexpected application behavior

    C.  Leaked personal files/data

    D.  Sluggish response time

8.  Which of the following is a common symptom of a compromised mobile operating system or application?

    A.  Slow device performance and frequent crashes

    B.  Improved battery life and faster processing speed

    C.  Enhanced security features and increased app compatibility

    D.  Smooth user interface and seamless multitasking

9.  Which of the following can suggest a security issue with mobile applications?

    A.  Excessive battery usage

    B.  Regular software updates

    C.  Limited app permissions

    D.  Encrypted data storage

10. Which of the following is a common symptom of a mobile OS vulnerability?

    A.  Unexpected app crashes

    B.  Enhanced device performance

    C.  Improved battery life

    D.  Seamless network connectivity

11. Which of the following is a common security issue with mobile devices?

    A.  Weak network signal strength

    B.  Strong device encryption

    C.  Regular backups of data

    D.  Unauthorized app installations

12. Which of the following is a common symptom of a mobile application security breach?

    A.  Unwanted pop-up advertisements

    B.  Enhanced app functionality

    C.  Increased device storage capacity

    D.  Improved user experience

13. Which of the following is a common indication of a security issue associated with mobile operating systems?

    A.  Excessive RAM utilization

    B.  Prompt security updates

    C.  Secure boot process

    D.  Encrypted user data

14. Which of the following is a common symptom of a mobile application vulnerability?

    A.  Application crashes upon launch

    B.  Faster battery charging

    C.  Enhanced network connectivity

    D.  Increased app compatibility

15. Which of the following is a common security issue with mobile operating systems?

    A.  Frequent app updates

    B.  Encrypted device backups

    C.  Outdated software versions

    D.  Optimized power-saving features

16. Which of the following is a common symptom of a compromised mobile application?

    A.  Unexpected data usage

    B.  Improved device performance

    C.  Enhanced battery longevity

    D.  Seamless app integration

# 10

# Operational Procedures

## Instructions to Unlock the Free Practice Resources

To access the free online content that comes with the book, you'll need to unlock it first. Unlocking **takes less than 10 minutes**, **can be done from any device**, and **needs to be done only once**. Follow these 5 easy steps to complete the process:

## STEP 1

Open the link `https://packt.link/core12unlock` OR scan the following QR code:

Figure 10.1: QR code for page that lets you unlock this book's free online content

Either of those links will lead to the following page:

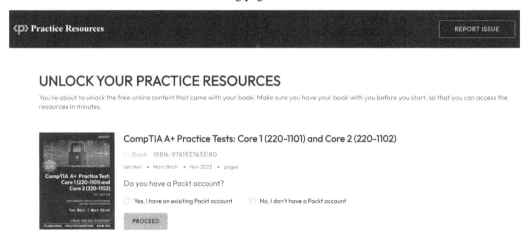

Figure 10.2: Unlock page for Core1 and 2 Online Practice Resources

## STEP 2

If you already have a Packt account, select the option "**Yes, I have an existing Packt account**".

If not, select the option "**No, I don't have a Packt account**".

If you don't have a Packt account, you'll be prompted to create a new Packt account on the next page. It's free and takes just a minute to create.

Click **Proceed** after selecting one of those options.

> **Forgot your password?**
>
> If you have a Packt account but have forgotten your password, you can reset it from this link before proceeding to the next step. You can reset your password here
>
> `https://www.packtpub.com/forget-password.`

## STEP 3

After you've created your account or logged in to an existing one, you'll be directed to the following page:

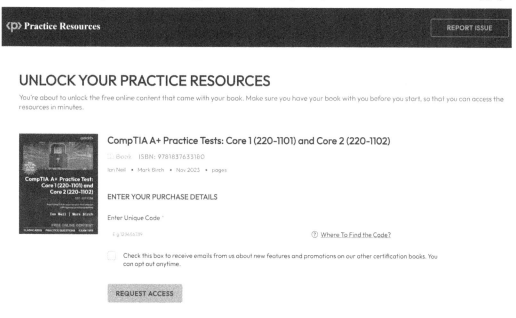

Figure 10.3: Enter your unique sign-up code to unlock the resources.

## STEP 4

Enter the following unique code:

*ECZ1532*

**Optional**: You may choose to opt into promotions regarding other certification books. We don't spam, only send the best deals, and it's easy to opt out at any time.

Click **Request Access**.

## STEP 5

If the code you entered is correct, you'll see a button that says, "**OPEN PRACTICE RESOURCES**".

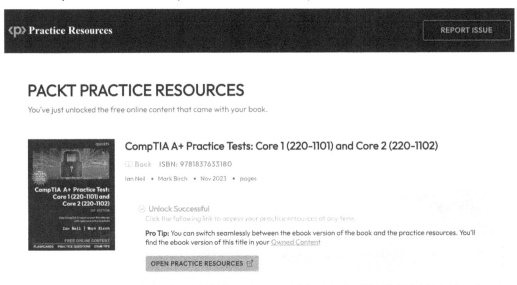

Figure 10.4: Page that shows up when you've successfully unlocked the free online content.

Click the **OPEN PRACTICE RESOURCES** link to start using your free online content. You'll be redirected to the Dashboard that looks similar to the following screenshot.

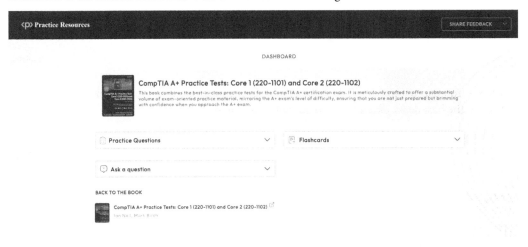

Figure 10.5: Dashboard page upon successful unlock of practice resources.

Refer to the *Practice Resources – A Quick Tour* section of the *Preface* for a quick tour of these Practice Resources.

> **Bookmark this link**
>
> Now that you've unlocked the resources, you can come back to them anytime by visiting this link: `https://packt.link/comptiacore12practice`.
>
> Or by scanning the following QR code:
>
>
>
> Figure 10.6: QR code for your free practice resources

## Troubleshooting Tips

If you're facing issues unlocking, here are 3 things you can do:

1. Double-check your unique code. All unique codes in our books are case sensitive and your code needs to match exactly as it is shown in *STEP 5*.

2. If that doesn't work, use the "**Report Issue**" button located at the top-right corner of the page.

3. If you're not able to open the unlock page at all, write to `customercare@packt.com` and mention the name of the book.

# Introduction

As a support technician, you play a crucial role in ensuring the smooth operation of computer systems and providing efficient technical support to end users. This chapter focuses on operational procedures. A vital aspect of your role involves following established protocols and best practices to maintain a productive and secure computing environment.

In this chapter, you will face questions on the key objectives outlined in CompTIA A+ Core 2 (220-1102) domain 4: Operational Procedures. These objectives are designed to equip you with the necessary knowledge and skills to perform your duties effectively and contribute to the overall success of your organization.

By mastering these operational procedures, you will enhance your effectiveness as a helpdesk technician and improve user satisfaction.

In order to be successful on the CompTIA A+ Core 2 (220-1102) certification exam, candidates must ensure they are familiar with the following objectives:

- 10.1 Given a scenario, implement best practices associated with documentation and support systems information management

- 10.2 Explain basic change-management best practices

- 10.3 Given a scenario, implement workstation backup and recovery methods

- 10.4 Given a scenario, use common safety procedures

- 10.5 Summarize environmental impacts and local environmental controls

- 10.6 Explain the importance of prohibited content/activity and privacy, licensing, and policy concepts

- 10.7 Given a scenario, use proper communication techniques and professionalism

- 10.8 Identify the basics of scripting

- 10.9 Given a scenario, use remote access technologies

The rest of this chapter is dedicated to practice. For each of the concepts defined above, you will be given a series of questions designed to test your knowledge of each core objective as defined by the official certification exam guidance for this domain. These questions will assess the candidate's knowledge of how to implement operational procedures.

# Practice Exam Questions

## 10.1 Given a scenario, implement best practices associated with documentation and support systems information management

1.  A company is implementing regulatory compliance requirements for its documentation and support systems. It wants to ensure that users are informed about the organization's policies and procedures before accessing the system. Which of the following best practices should it implement?

    A.  Password complexity rules

    B.  Network segmentation

    C.  Splash screens

    D.  Incident reports

2.  A helpdesk team is responsible for documenting and reporting any incidents that occur during their support activities. Which of the following documents should they use to record detailed information about each incident?

    A.  Knowledge base articles

    B.  Splash screens

    C.  Incident reports

    D.  Service-level agreements

3.  Which of the following is an example of a best practice for complying with regulatory requirements related to incident reporting?

    A.  Implementing splash screens on all company devices

    B.  Conducting regular vulnerability assessments

    C.  Encrypting sensitive customer data during transit

    D.  Training employees on data handling and privacy policies

4.  Which of the following is an example of documentation that should be included in a support system information management plan?

    A.  Network diagrams

    B.  Software licenses

    C.  Customer contact information

    D.  User passwords

5.  In the context of support system information management, which of the following is the purpose of a knowledge base?

    A.  To store customer feedback

    B.  To track hardware inventory

    C.  To centralize troubleshooting guides

    D.  To schedule technician appointments

6.  When documenting a support request, which of the following details should be included?

    A.  Customer's favorite color

    B.  Date and time of the request

    C.  Technician's lunch preferences

    D.  Weather conditions in the area

7.  Which of the following is the best practice for managing support system documentation?

    A.  Storing documents in multiple physical locations

    B.  Sharing sensitive information via email

    C.  Regularly updating and reviewing documentation

    D.  Printing documentation only when necessary

8.  Which of the following is an example of a ticketing system used in support systems?

    A.  Microsoft Office Suite

    B.  ServiceNow

    C.  Adobe Photoshop

    D.  Google Chrome

9.  What is the primary purpose of a service level agreement (SLA) in support system documentation?

    A.  To outline the technician's work schedule

    B.  To establish pricing for support services

    C.  To define response and resolution times

    D.  To determine the customer's preferred contact method

10. Which of the following should be included in a support system knowledge base article?

    A.  Sales promotional material

    B.  Personal opinions of support technicians

    C.  Tested solutions to known issues

    D.  Company's financial reports

11. Which of the following is a common method of organizing and categorizing support system documentation?

    A.  Alphabetical order

    B.  Reverse chronological order

    C.  Color-coded labels

    D.  Random arrangement

12. Which of the following is an example of a customer relationship management (CRM) system used in support systems?

    A.  Salesforce

    B.  Dropbox

    C.  Microsoft Word

    D.  Spotify

13. In support system documentation, what is the purpose of creating an inventory list?

    A.  To track technician attendance records

    B.  To monitor customer satisfaction ratings

    C.  To keep an inventory of spare parts and equipment

    D.  To schedule routine maintenance tasks

14. Which of the following statements best describes an acceptable use policy (AUP) in relation to documentation and support systems information management?

    A.  An AUP outlines the procedures for creating backups of critical data

    B.  An AUP establishes guidelines for the appropriate use of computer systems and networks

    C.  An AUP specifies the steps to troubleshoot and resolve hardware-related issues

    D.  An AUP defines the process for documenting software license agreements

## 10.2 Explain basic change-management best practices

15. A company is updating operational procedures and will adopt change management. Which of the following best describes a basic change-management best practice?

    A.  Implementing changes without proper planning

    B.  Communicating changes only after they have been implemented

    C.  Documenting changes thoroughly

    D.  Ignoring user feedback

16. Which of the following is a key element of change management?

    A.  Minimizing user involvement

    B.  Avoiding communication with stakeholders

    C.  Assessing and managing risks

    D.  Rushing the implementation process

17. Which of the following is a recommended practice for managing user resistance during change implementation?

    A.  Ignoring user concerns

    B.  Providing clear communication and training

    C.  Limiting user access to system documentation

    D.  Implementing changes abruptly without prior notice

18. Which of the following best describes the purpose of a change advisory board (CAB)?

    A.  Approving all changes without review

    B.  Monitoring the progress of change implementation

    C.  Evaluating and prioritizing proposed changes

    D.  Limiting user involvement in the change process

19. Which of the following is a common risk associated with change management?

    A.  Improved system performance

    B.  Increased user satisfaction

    C.  Temporary service disruptions

    D.  Enhanced security measures

20. Which of the following is an example of a change management best practice for software deployments?

    A.  Skipping the testing phase

    B.  Performing regular backups

    C.  Implementing changes during peak hours

    D.  Avoiding user communication

21. Which of the following is an example of a change management best practice for hardware replacements?

    A.  Ignoring user feedback

    B.  Conducting a thorough inventory assessment

    C.  Implementing changes without testing

    D.  Excluding stakeholders from the process

22. Which of the following best describes the purpose of a rollback plan in change management?

    A.  Preventing any changes from being implemented

    B.  Documenting the reasons for change implementation

    C.  Identifying potential issues and their resolutions

    D.  Excluding user feedback during the change process

23. Which of the following is a recommended practice for managing change-related risks?

    A.  Avoiding risk assessment altogether

    B.  Implementing changes without backup plans

    C.  Conducting regular risk assessments

    D.  Ignoring risk mitigation strategies

24. Which of the following is a key consideration when communicating changes to users during change management?

    A. Providing vague and general information

    B. Overemphasizing the negative aspects of the changes

    C. Tailoring the message to the target audience

    D. Delaying communication until after the changes are implemented

## 10.3 Given a scenario, implement workstation backup and recovery methods

25. Which workstation backup method involves creating a copy of all user data and settings at a specific point in time?

    A. Full backup

    B. Differential backup

    C. Incremental backup

    D. Selective backup

26. Which workstation recovery method involves using a backup of the entire workstation's hard drive to restore the system to its previous state?

    A. Bare-metal recovery

    B. Cloud-based recovery

    C. File-level recovery

    D. Incremental recovery

27. Which backup storage medium provides the fastest transfer rates but is also the most expensive option for workstation backup?

    A. Tape drive

    B. External hard drive

    C. Network-attached storage (NAS)

    D. Cloud storage

28. Which workstation backup method only backs up data that has changed since the last backup, regardless of whether it was a full or incremental backup?

    A.  Differential backup

    B.  Incremental backup

    C.  Synthetic backup

    D.  Continuous backup

29. Which backup rotation scheme involves using a set of backup media and cycling through them on a daily basis, overwriting the oldest backup when the set is full?

    A.  Grandfather-father-son

    B.  Tower of Hanoi

    C.  Back up to disk

    D.  Back up to tape

30. Which workstation backup method provides the fastest recovery time when compared to other backup methods?

    A.  Incremental backup

    B.  Differential backup

    C.  Snapshot backup

    D.  Full backup

31. Which backup method ensures data redundancy by creating multiple copies of backups on different backup media?

    A.  Mirroring

    B.  Replication

    C.  Archiving

    D.  Versioning

32. Which backup method provides the highest level of data protection by storing multiple copies of backups across different geographical locations?

    A.  Cloud-based backup

    B.  Tape backup

    C.  Disk-to-disk backup

    D.  Offsite backup

33. Which workstation backup method captures an exact copy of the workstation's operating system, applications, and data, allowing for quick restoration to a functional state?

   A.  Image backup

   B.  File-level backup

   C.  Incremental backup

   D.  Differential backup

34. Which workstation backup method involves automatically backing up data in real time as changes occur, ensuring minimal data loss in the event of a failure?

   A.  Continuous backup

   B.  Synchronization backup

   C.  Manual backup

   D.  Snapshot backup

## 10.4 Given a scenario, use common safety procedures

35. Which of the following is a common safety procedure when working on computer hardware?

   A.  Wear an ESD wrist strap

   B.  Disconnect the power supply without turning it off

   C.  Handle circuit boards with bare hands

   D.  Stand on a wet surface

36. When working on computer equipment, which of the following safety precautions should be taken?

   A.  Use compressed air to clean debris from fans and heatsinks

   B.  Use a magnetized screwdriver to secure components

   C.  Store liquids near the computer to easily access them

   D.  Place the computer on an unstable surface

37. Which of the following safety measures should be followed when handling computer cables?

   A.  Pull the cable from a distance to disconnect it

   B.  Bend the cable sharply to fit it in tight spaces

   C.  Secure cables using cable ties or clips

   D.  Leave cables loose and tangled

38. What safety precaution should be taken before opening a computer case?

    A. Ensure the computer is turned off and unplugged

    B. Wear gloves to protect against static electricity

    C. Use a metal tool to open the case

    D. Keep the case on a soft, cushioned surface

39. What should be done to prevent injuries while working with computer hardware?

    A. Follow ergonomic practices

    B. Wear heavy jewelry and accessories

    C. Use damaged tools if no others are available

    D. Skip breaks and work for long periods without rest

40. Which safety measure should be taken when cleaning the inside of a computer?

    A. Use an antistatic vacuum cleaner

    B. Spray cleaning solution directly onto components

    C. Clean the computer while it is still powered on

    D. Use a dry cloth to wipe the motherboard

41. Which safety precaution should be taken when disposing of old computer equipment?

    A. Recycle the equipment according to local regulations

    B. Disassemble the equipment without protective gear

    C. Throw the equipment in regular household waste

    D. Store the equipment in a humid environment

42. Which of the following safety precautions should be followed when working with high-voltage equipment?

    A. Wear insulated gloves and safety glasses

    B. Work alone to minimize distractions

    C. Use a metal ladder when working at heights

    D. Use equipment with damaged cords

43. What should be done if a chemical spill occurs in the vicinity of computer equipment?

    A.  Shut down the equipment immediately

    B.  Use a vacuum cleaner to remove the spill

    C.  Follow proper procedures for chemical cleanup

    D.  Ignore the spill and continue working

44. What safety measures should be taken when installing or replacing computer hardware components?

    A.  Use proper lifting techniques for heavy components

    B.  Use excessive force when inserting connectors

    C.  Install components in an unventilated area

    D.  Install components without grounding yourself

## 10.5 Summarize environmental impacts and local environmental controls

45. Which of the following describes the purpose of material safety data sheets (MSDSs) in relation to handling and disposal of hazardous materials?

    A.  To provide guidelines for safe transportation of hazardous materials

    B.  To document the potential hazards and precautions for using a specific material

    C.  To outline the proper procedures for recycling electronic waste

    D.  To certify the quality and durability of protective equipment

46. What is the primary purpose of reviewing material safety data sheets (MSDSs) before handling or disposing of hazardous materials?

    A.  To assess the financial cost associated with the materials

    B.  To determine the expiration date of the materials

    C.  To understand the potential health and safety risks

    D.  To identify potential sources of the materials

47. Proper battery disposal is essential to protect the environment and prevent hazardous materials from contaminating landfills. Which of the following statements accurately describes the correct way to dispose of used batteries?

    A.  Place used batteries in the regular trash bin

    B.  Take the batteries to a nearby electronics store for disposal

    C.  Recycle used batteries at designated recycling centers or facilities

    D.  Bury the batteries in the backyard to decompose naturally

48. When disposing of toner cartridges from printers and copiers, what is the recommended method to ensure proper disposal?

    A.  Place the toner cartridges in any nearby recycling bin for regular waste collection

    B.  Throw the toner cartridges in the trash as they are not considered hazardous waste

    C.  Return the used toner cartridges to the manufacturer or a designated recycling program

    D.  Burn the toner cartridges to reduce waste volume before disposing of them

49. When disposing of other electronic devices and assets, which of the following methods should you avoid to ensure data security and prevent environmental damage? (Choose all that apply.)

    A.  Selling the devices to an unknown individual or entity

    B.  Donating the devices to a local charity or non-profit organization

    C.  Erasing all the data from the devices before recycling or disposal

    D.  Disassembling the devices and disposing of their parts separately

50. What environmental factors should be considered to maintain optimal equipment performance and longevity?

    A.  Temperature, humidity, and proper ventilation

    B.  Noise level, cable management, and power supply

    C.  Lighting conditions, firewall settings, and antivirus software

    D.  Backup systems, network security, and data encryption

51. What device is designed to protect electronic equipment from power surges, under-voltage events, and power failures?

    A.  Uninterruptible Power Supply (UPS)

    B.  Power over Ethernet (PoE)

    C.  Network-Attached Storage (NAS)

    D.  Wireless Access Point (WAP)

52. Which device is used to suppress power surges and voltage spikes?

    A.  Surge protector

    B.  Uninterruptible Power Supply (UPS)

    C.  Power inverter

    D.  Power strip

53. What is the purpose of using a battery backup system?

    A.  To provide backup power during outages

    B.  To increase network bandwidth

    C.  To protect against electromagnetic interference

    D.  To prevent power surges

54. What is a recommended practice for location/equipment placement to ensure optimal computer performance?

    A.  Placing the computer on an uneven surface

    B.  Locating the computer near direct sunlight

    C.  Positioning the computer away from electrical interference

    D.  Stacking multiple computers on top of each other

55. A technician must choose the best method suitable for dust cleanup in a computer system. Which of these is the recommended solution?

    A.  Blowing compressed air directly into the components

    B.  Using a dry cloth to wipe the components

    C.  Applying water or liquid cleaning agents on the components

    D.  Utilizing a vacuum designed for electronics

## 10.6 Explain the importance of prohibited content/activity and privacy, licensing, and policy concepts

56. Which concept ensures the integrity and preservation of data during an incident response in relation to prohibited content/activity?

    A.  Chain of custody

    B.  Incident escalation

    C.  Password recovery

    D.  Data compression

57. When encountering prohibited content/activity during an incident response, which action should be taken?

    A.  Inform management or law enforcement, if necessary

    B.  Continue the investigation without involving anyone else

    C.  Delete the prohibited content/activity immediately

    D.  Perform a system reboot

58. What is the purpose of making a copy of a drive during an incident response?

    A.  To preserve data integrity and evidence

    B.  To speed up the incident resolution process

    C.  To minimize the impact on system performance

    D.  To reduce the risk of future incidents

59. Which concept involves documenting the handling and transfer of evidence during an incident response?

    A.  Chain of custody

    B.  Incident containment

    C.  Data classification

    D.  System hardening

60. What is the purpose of documenting an incident during an incident response?

    A.  To provide a reference for future incidents

    B.  To inform management of ongoing activities

    C.  To facilitate collaboration with other teams

    D.  To create a detailed record for analysis and accountability

61. Which concept defines the terms and conditions under which software can be used by an individual or organization?

    A.  Privacy policy

    B.  Open source license

    C.  End-user license agreement (EULA)

    D.  Digital rights management (DRM)

62. What distinguishes a personal use license from a corporate use license?

    A.  Personal use licenses require individual registration, while corporate use licenses allow multiple users

    B.  Personal use licenses have shorter validity periods compared to corporate use licenses

    C.  Personal use licenses have fewer restrictions on usage compared to corporate use licenses

    D.  Personal use licenses are free, while corporate use licenses require a fee

63. Which licensing concept ensures that users comply with the terms of the software license and prevents unauthorized copying or distribution?

    A.  Open source license

    B.  Valid license

    C.  Non-expired license

    D.  Digital rights management (DRM)

64. What is the purpose of licensing/digital rights management (DRM)/the end-user license agreement (EULA) in relation to prohibited content/activity?

    A.  They facilitate the sharing of prohibited content/activity

    B.  They prevent the use of prohibited content/activity

    C.  They monitor and report the use of prohibited content/activity

    D.  They establish penalties for the use of prohibited content/activity

65. Which type of license allows users to view, modify, and distribute the source code of software?

    A.  Privacy policy

    B.  Open source license

    C.  End-user license agreement (EULA)

    D.  Digital rights management (DRM)

66. Which of the following best describes regulated data in the context of privacy and policy concepts?

    A. Data that is subject to government regulations and restrictions

    B. Data that is freely accessible to the public

    C. Data that is stored without any encryption or security measures

    D. Data that is shared among employees within an organization

67. Which type of data is considered as personally identifiable information (PII)?

    A. Social media posts and comments

    B. Names and addresses of individuals

    C. Publicly available company information

    D. Non-sensitive email communication

68. Which of the following describes a key concern when handling credit card transactions?

    A. Ensuring data availability

    B. Securing cardholder data

    C. Maintaining accurate financial records

    D. Maximizing transaction speed

69. Which of the following is an example of personal government-issued information?

    A. Social media account usernames

    B. Driver's license number

    C. Wi-Fi network passwords

    D. Home address

70. Which of the following best describes data retention requirements?

    A. The amount of time it takes to process data

    B. The policies and procedures for storing and managing data

    C. The frequency at which data is backed up

    D. The speed of data transmission over a network

## 10.7 Given a scenario, use proper communication techniques and professionalism

71. When service desk personnel are communicating with customers, which communication technique demonstrates professionalism and empathy?

    A.  Interrupting the customer to provide quick solutions

    B.  Using technical jargon to establish expertise

    C.  Active listening and paraphrasing the customer's concerns

    D.  Offering discounts or freebies to resolve the issue

72. Which of the following is an example of non-verbal communication that reflects professionalism?

    A.  Maintaining eye contact and nodding in agreement

    B.  Checking personal emails on a mobile device

    C.  Speaking softly to avoid disrupting others

    D.  Using slang terms and informal language

73. In a business email, which of the following is the most appropriate way to address the recipient?

    A.  Hey [Recipient's First Name],

    B.  Dear [Recipient's First Name],

    C.  To whom it may concern,

    D.  Hi there,

74. Which of the following communication methods is most suitable for conveying complex technical information to a non-technical audience?

    A.  Using technical terms and acronyms extensively

    B.  Providing detailed written documentation only

    C.  Utilizing visual aids, diagrams, and illustrations

    D.  Speaking rapidly to ensure all information is covered

75. Which of the following is an example of appropriate use of professional language in customer communication?

    A.  "Your computer is totally messed up"

    B.  "Your device is experiencing some technical difficulties"

    C.  "Your machine is acting weird"

    D.  "Your PC is broken"

76. When speaking with a customer, which of the following is a professional way to handle a disagreement or conflict?

    A.  Raising your voice to assert dominance

    B.  Blaming the customer for the issue

    C.  Offering alternative solutions and compromises

    D.  Ignoring the customer's concerns

77. Which of the following is an example of appropriate professional behavior when interacting with colleagues?

    A.  Gossiping about other team members

    B.  Taking credit for others' work

    C.  Actively listening and respecting others' opinions

    D.  Criticizing colleagues in public forums

78. Which of the following communication methods is best suited for delivering sensitive or confidential information?

    A.  Public announcement during a team meeting

    B.  Sending a mass email to all employees

    C.  Holding individual face-to-face meetings

    D.  Posting the information on a public bulletin board

79. Which of the following is an example of maintaining professionalism in a virtual meeting?

    A.  Eating a meal while on camera

    B.  Keeping the microphone on mute when not speaking

    C.  Using informal language and abbreviations in chat messages

    D.  Sharing irrelevant personal anecdotes

80. When communicating with customers, which of the following is a professional approach to managing their expectations?

    A.  Overpromising to ensure customer satisfaction

    B.  Setting realistic expectations and providing updates

    C.  Ignoring customer requests to avoid conflicts

    D.  Redirecting customers to a different support channel

81. Which of the following actions should a technician take to deal appropriately with a customer's confidential and private materials stored on a desktop computer?

    A.  Regularly share the customer's data with colleagues for collaborative purposes

    B.  Encrypt the customer's sensitive files and folders using strong encryption algorithms

    C.  Upload the customer's confidential data to a cloud storage service for backup

    D.  Dispose of the customer's computer without securely wiping the hard drive

82. When dealing with a customer's confidential materials on a printer, which of the following steps should a technician take to maintain security?

    A.  Share the printer's access credentials with other technicians for easier troubleshooting

    B.  Disable logging features on the printer to prevent potential privacy breaches

    C.  Implement access controls on the printer to restrict unauthorized usage

    D.  Print the customer's confidential documents in a public area for quick access

83. A technician is helping a customer secure their desktop computer. The technician must implement best practices to protect the customer's confidential materials. Which offers the best solution?

    A.  Create a shared user account with unrestricted access for the customer and their colleagues

    B.  Regularly perform data backups without verifying the integrity and confidentiality of the backup media

    C.  Implement strong password policies and enable full disk encryption for the customer's desktop

    D.  Store the customer's confidential files in publicly accessible folders for easier collaboration

## 10.8 Identify the basics of scripting

84. A developer must identify the scripting language used by the web development community. Which scripting language will be the best choice?

    A.  Python

    B.  Bash

    C.  JavaScript

    D.  PowerShell

85. Which scripting language is commonly used for task automation in Windows environments?

    A.  Python

    B.  Bash

    C.  JavaScript

    D.  PowerShell

86. Which scripting language is commonly used for system administration tasks in Unix-like operating systems?

    A.  Python

    B.  Bash

    C.  JavaScript

    D.  PowerShell

87. Which scripting language is known for its versatility and can be used for a wide range of tasks, including web development, automation, and data analysis?

    A.  Python

    B.  Bash

    C.  JavaScript

    D.  PowerShell

88. Which scripting language is commonly used for client-side scripting in web browsers?

    A.  Python

    B.  Bash

    C.  JavaScript

    D.  PowerShell

89. What are some potential risks associated with using scripts that need to be considered to avoid unintentionally introducing malware, inadvertently changing system settings, and causing browser or system crashes due to mishandling of resources?

    A.  Inadequate error handling

    B.  Insufficient debugging tools

    C.  Lack of version control

    D.  Incompatible scripting languages

90. Which precaution should be taken to prevent unintentionally introducing malware when using scripts?

    A.  Regularly update antivirus software

    B.  Implement input validation and sanitization

    C.  Disable the firewall temporarily

    D.  Increase user privileges

91. What can cause browser or system crashes due to mishandling of resources when using scripts?

    A.  Excessive memory usage

    B.  Frequent disk read/write operations

    C.  Incompatible browser extensions

    D.  Network connectivity issues

92. Which of the following actions poses a risk of unintentionally introducing malware into a system when using scripts?

    A.  Using reputable script repositories

    B.  Regularly updating the script interpreter

    C.  Downloading scripts from untrusted sources

    D.  Running scripts in a sandbox environment

93. What can be a consequence of inadvertently changing system settings when executing scripts on a computer?

    A.  Improved system performance

    B.  Enhanced user experience

    C.  Increased security measures

    D.  System instability or malfunction

94. To prevent browser or system crashes due to mishandling of resources in scripts, what should be done?

    A.  Increase script execution speed

    B.  Avoid error handling in scripts

    C.  Optimize resource usage in scripts

    D.  Disable browser extensions

## 10.9 Given a scenario, use remote access technologies

95. A technician needs to troubleshoot a user's computer remotely. The user is running a Windows operating system and is connected to the same network as the technician. Which remote access technology should the technician use in this scenario?

    A.  Microsoft Remote Assistance (MSRA)

    B.  Virtual Network Computing (VNC)

    C.  Remote Desktop Protocol (RDP)

    D.  Secure Shell (SSH)

96. In a scenario where an IT technician needs to remotely monitor and manage multiple devices in a network, which remote access technology would be most suitable?

    A.  Virtual private network (VPN)

    B.  Remote Desktop Protocol (RDP)

    C.  Telnet

    D.  Remote monitoring and management (RMM)

97. Which remote access technology allows users to access their office computer from a remote location?

    A.  Virtual private network (VPN)

    B.  Remote Desktop Protocol (RDP)

    C.  Telnet

    D.  Secure Shell (SSH)

98. In a scenario where a user needs to remotely access a Windows server, which remote access technology would be most suitable?

    A.  Remote Desktop Protocol (RDP)

    B.  File Transfer Protocol (FTP)

    C.  Telnet

    D.  Secure Shell (SSH)

99. A user wants to remotely connect to a Linux server using a command-line interface. Which remote access technology would be most appropriate?

    A.  Telnet

    B.  Remote Desktop Protocol (RDP)

    C.  Secure Shell (SSH)

    D.  Virtual private network (VPN)

100. In a scenario where a user wants to remotely access their home network from a remote network, which remote access technology would be the most appropriate?

    A.  Virtual private network (VPN)

    B.  Remote Desktop Protocol (RDP)

    C.  Telnet

    D.  Secure Shell (SSH)

101. Which remote access technology commonly uses port 3389 by default?

    A.  Remote Desktop Protocol (RDP)

    B.  File Transfer Protocol (FTP)

    C.  Telnet

    D.  Secure Shell (SSH)

102. In a scenario where a user wants to remotely access a Mac computer from another Mac, which built-in remote access technology can be used?

    A.  Apple Remote Desktop

    B.  Virtual Network Computing (VNC)

    C.  Remote Desktop Protocol (RDP)

    D.  Secure Shell (SSH)

103. Which remote access technology allows users to access their office network resources securely over the internet?

    A.  Virtual private network (VPN)

    B.  Remote Desktop Protocol (RDP)

    C.  Telnet

    D.  Secure Shell (SSH)

# Mock Exam: Core 2 (220-1102)

The final chapter is intended to provide the candidate with a realistic mock exam comprising 93 questions. The official CompTIA A+ Core 2 (220-1102) certification exam allows for 90 minutes to complete all questions. This mock exam is intended to cover all the following CompTIA certification objectives:

- Install, configure, and maintain computer equipment, mobile devices, and software for end users

- Service components based on customer requirements

- Understand networking basics and apply basic cybersecurity methods to mitigate threats

- Properly and safely diagnose, resolve, and document common hardware and software issues

- Apply troubleshooting skills and provide customer support using appropriate communication skills

- Understand the basics of scripting, cloud technologies, virtualization, and multi-OS deployments in corporate environments

To get an accurate measurement of your knowledge, it is recommended that you give yourself 90 minutes to complete all 90 questions (or break it down into blocks of 30 questions per 30 minutes).

## Mock Exam Questions

1. You are troubleshooting a smartphone that is exhibiting unusual behavior, such as slow performance, excessive data usage, and unexpected pop-up ads. You suspect it may be infected with malware. What is the most appropriate first step to take in addressing this issue?

   A. Perform a factory reset on the smartphone

   B. Download a popular antivirus app and run a full scan

   C. Disconnect the smartphone from the internet

   D. Update the smartphone's operating system and all apps

2.  Management within a banking organization is reviewing change management documentation. The team needs to understand the correct steps used within the process. When a change has been approved, what is the next step?

    A.  End user acceptance

    B.  Conduct risk analysis

    C.  Communicate the change to stakeholders

    D.  Perform sandbox testing

3.  A user reports encountering sporadic, seemingly non-malicious advertisement notifications within the Windows 10 Action Center. These notifications suggest that the advertisements originate from a web browser. What is the MOST effective solution for a technician to implement?

    A.  Deactivate the browser's ability to send notifications to the Action Center

    B.  Perform a comprehensive antivirus scan on the computer

    C.  Turn off all notifications within the Action Center

    D.  Transfer specific site notifications from the Allowed category to Block

4.  What action should the systems administrator take to minimize the number of help desk tickets submitted, as reported by the manager regarding staff members frequently forgetting passwords for their mobile devices and applications?

    A.  Enable multifactor authentication

    B.  Raise the failed login threshold

    C.  Eliminate complex password requirements

    D.  Implement a single sign-on system with biometrics

5.  A service desk technician is responding to a service ticket that appears to indicate the presence of a rootkit. In order to resolve the suspected rootkit installation, which of the following options would be the MOST effective?

    A.  Updating applications

    B.  Utilizing anti-malware software

    C.  Reinstalling the operating system

    D.  Restoring files

6.  A technician is asked to re-deploy unused wireless access points for the new warehouse. The devices have been in storage since 2015. The technician must ensure they are configured with the most secure wireless network settings. Bearing in mind the age of the equipment, which configuration will provide the technician with the most secure implementation?

    A.  WPA3 with AES-128

    B.  WPA2 with AES

    C.  WPA3 with AES-256

    D.  WPA2 with TKIP

7.  A call center technician receives a call from a home user seeking guidance on updating Windows. They would like to ensure that they are running the latest Windows edition when it is made available to customers. What is the appropriate course of action for the technician to take?

    A.  Suggest that the user consider using a different system if they are unable to complete updates

    B.  Instruct the user to send their password via text to the technician

    C.  Guide the user to click on the Search field, type "Check for Updates," and then press the Enter key

    D.  Suggest the user waits for an upcoming, automatic patch

8.  When a customer contacts a technician to report an issue, what practice should the technician employ to ensure the service ticket is correctly associated with the user?

    A.  Verify the customer's identity then issue a unique ticket

    B.  Assign a random ticket number to maintain customer privacy

    C.  Use the technician's personal identification as the ticket reference

    D.  Create a generic ticket without associating it with any user

9.  The service desk for a large financial institution has raised support tickets after several members of staff returned to the workplace, after months of working remotely from home. When the users attempt to connect to the wired network, they encounter login errors. What is the most likely cause of the login issue for the users, considering that the network uses 802.1X with EAP-TLS for wired network authentication?

    A.  The OS may need the latest security updates

    B.  An important service has not started

    C.  Application crash

    D.  The client certificates may have expired

10. A user wants to exclude certain folders from the Windows search feature to improve search results. Which of the following steps should they follow?

    A.  Disable Windows Search Service in Services.msc

    B.  Add the folders to the "Excluded Folders" list in the Windows search settings

    C.  Delete the folders from the hard drive

    D.  Reinstall the Windows operating system

11. When the "cat ssh_config" command is executed on a Linux terminal, which of the following outcomes should be anticipated?

    A.  The original "ssh_config" file will be replaced with a new blank document

    B.  The contents of the "ssh_config" file will be displayed

    C.  The lines of text in the "ssh_config" file will be sorted in alphabetical order

    D.  The contents of the "ssh_config" file will be copied to another file named " ssh_config"

12. In order to preserve evidence for potential litigation, what is the MOST likely action an incident handler will take?

    A.  Apply encryption to the files

    B.  Create duplicates of any affected hard drives

    C.  Reach out to the cyber insurance company

    D.  Notify law enforcement authorities

13. Important business data must be backed up to meet industry regulations, a technician is seeking the most suitable backup method. The requirement is to regularly modify only a few files while considering limited storage space. Which backup methods should the technician choose?

    A.  Full backups

    B.  Incremental backups

    C.  Cloud-based backups

    D.  Tape rotation

14. Why would a support technician set their mobile to silent before visiting a customer?

    A.  To avoid disrupting the customer's environment

    B.  To conserve battery life during the visit

    C.  To prevent incoming calls from being recorded

    D.  To enable location tracking for service records

15. A technician must identify a solution to copy a large number of files, which may take several hours. In the past, they have experienced interrupted connections and network disruptions. If the network connection between the source and destination machines is unstable or experiences a temporary interruption, what will allow the file copying process to recover?

    A.  System File Checker (sfc)

    B.  Check Disk (chkdsk)

    C.  Git Clone (git clone)

    D.  Robocopy

16. A technician, working for a large regional bank, is configuring a new tape backup system. After installing the system in the server room, which backup types will need to be completed FIRST?

    A.  Copy backup

    B.  Mirror backup

    C.  Differential backup

    D.  Full backup

17. A user is experiencing frequent popups on their web browser. What will offer the BEST solution to remediate this problem? (Choose two.)

    A.  Install a reputable ad blocker extension

    B.  Update the browser to the latest version

    C.  Disable the computer's firewall

    D.  Ignore the popups; they are harmless

    E.  Download and run a registry cleaner tool

    F.  Reset the computer to factory settings

18. When installing new software on a macOS computer, which of the following file extensions is most commonly used by technicians?

    A.  .pkg

    B.  .bat

    C.  .msi

    D.  .dmg

19. A user reports that their smartphone is overheating when not being used, and newly launched applications frequently crash. Which actions will BEST resolve these issues with minimal impact on the user? (Choose two.)

    A.  Clear the app cache and data, update the apps, and ensure proper ventilation

    B.  Perform a factory reset and install a third-party cooling app

    C.  Disable automatic updates and limit app background processes

    D.  Buy a new smartphone with better hardware capabilities

    E.  Ignore the issues, as they are common with older smartphones

    F.  Close down unneeded applications

20. A user's desktop computer was automatically rebooted overnight, and now the system will no longer run some of the Windows applications. What is the recommended action to fix the problem?

    A.  Perform a System Restore to a previous working state

    B.  Reinstall Windows

    C.  Delete the affected applications and reinstall them

    D.  Ignore the issue; it will resolve itself eventually

21. What option from the list below can be utilized to establish secure physical access to a data center?

    A.  Perimeter barrier

    B.  Intrusion detection system

    C.  Proximity card reader

    D.  Surveillance camera

22. A user notifies a technician about a sluggish computer performance. Which of the following tools can assist the technician in identifying the underlying cause of the issue?

    A.  System Optimizer

    B.  Performance Monitor

    C.  Registry Editor

    D.  Task Scheduler

23. An open source software build is downloaded from the GitHub repository. Prior to installing the software image, a technician encounters the following string:

   A.  7d3bb8e188cd9154e99b7ea8db38a24181efb2d1

   B.  Which option MOST accurately describes the intended use of this string?

   C.  Checksum for verification of download integrity

   D.  Encryption key

   E.  Product license key

   F.  Network port number

24. A user has installed unapproved utilities and applications on a mobile phone. The company has recently deployed MDM tools and would like to prevent users from sideloading unapproved applications. What two MDM policies will prevent future users from sideloading unapproved applications?

   A.  App whitelisting

   B.  Enforce application store restrictions

   C.  Enable USB debugging control

   D.  Implement full device encryption

   E.  Enable remote wipe

   F.  Implement geofencing

25. A technician is experiencing problems while trying to add a sales manager's personal laptop to the company's Active Directory domain. What is the most probable reason why a technician is unable to join a Windows 10 laptop computer to an Active Directory domain?

   A.  The computer processor is an AMD version

   B.  The laptop is equipped with Windows 10 Home edition

   C.  The laptop does not have a touchscreen

   D.  The laptop is connected to a docking station

26. An engineering firm is considering implementing the latest version of its computer-aided design (CAD) software, which includes a feature requiring backups of all CAD files to be stored externally in the software vendor's data center. Which of the following is MOST likely to raise concerns for the IT manager?

    A.  Comprehensive compatibility testing with all system types and accessories must be conducted for the updated software

    B.  Adequate budget allocation for additional staff hours during the installation of updates needs to be ensured

    C.  Network utilization is expected to significantly increase due to the larger size of CAD files being backed up

    D.  The local hard drives may become overloaded due to the size of the update and installation files

27. A company employee receives a phone call from an individual falsely claiming to represent a mortgage company. Which of the following best describes this incident?

    A.  Social engineering

    B.  Phishing

    C.  Impersonation

    D.  Identity theft

28. Following an overnight network breach, security logs reveal that a dictionary attack successfully breached a single user's account after 400 attempts. Which of the following measures would be the MOST effective in mitigating this specific threat?

    A.  Two-factor authentication

    B.  Intrusion detection system

    C.  Password complexity requirements

    D.  Network segmentation

    E.  Account lockout

29. A payroll manager has created a file on a shared drive and wants to protect it from accidental deletion by other team members. Which of the following applications should the technician recommend to assist the manager in hiding the file?

    A.  Disk Cleanup

    B.  Task Scheduler

    C.  File Properties

    D.  Control Panel

30. After dedicating several hours to troubleshooting a computer problem for the company's Chief Executive Officer (CEO), the technician is now pressed for time to resolve the issue promptly. What should the technician do as the next step?

    A.  Engage in further research to address the problem

    B.  Restart the diagnostic process from the beginning

    C.  Notify the CEO that the repair may take a few weeks

    D.  Escalate the support ticket to higher-level technicians

31. While configuring a Small Office/Home Office (SOHO) device, a technician needs to ensure that the server maintains a consistent IP address at all times, following the company's policy against static IP addresses. Which of the following options should the technician choose to achieve this requirement?

    A.  IP address reservation via DHCP

    B.  Network address translation (NAT)

    C.  Dynamic Name System (DNS) record

    D.  Virtual private network (VPN) configuration

32. A research scientist needs access to a specialist application that is only supported on a Linux OS. The scientist currently only has access to a Windows OS. The scientist needs to work in a remote laboratory with no access to external networks during the day. What offers the BEST solution for the scientist to access the specialist application?

    A.  Pay for a remote desktop utilizing a Linux OS

    B.  Install the Linux application within the supported Windows Linux subsystem

    C.  Install Linux as the primary OS and purchase a second computer to handle the Windows application

    D.  Enable the Windows Hyper-V client and install the Linux OS and the Linux application

33. Several desktop computers are to be upgraded in order to support a new software installation. The system upgrades will involve replacing the processor and increasing the memory in the desktop computers. Which of the following should be done to ensure no damage occurs during this upgrade process?

    A.  Ground yourself by using an anti-static wrist strap before handling any components

    B.  Upgrade the processor first, then add the memory modules afterward

    C.  Keep the computers powered on while making the upgrades

    D.  Skip the anti-static precautions as they are not necessary for desktop upgrades

34. A customer calls the service desk as they would like to activate speech recognition on their Windows 10 Home PC. Which Windows Settings tool should the user utilize to enable this feature?

    A.  Regional Settings

    B.  Accessibility

    C.  Appearance

    D.  Privacy

35. A recent security audit within a company has identified the widespread use of several unauthorized software applications on employee's work desktops, employees are engaged in social media activities using these installed applications. These activities are against the company's policies. In light of this violation, which of the following should be modified to reflect this new requirement?

    A.  EMM

    B.  SLA

    C.  DLP

    D.  AUP

36. A departmental manager is proposing to upgrade the design team's workstations with 32 GB of RAM. The plan is also to upgrade the OS from 32-bit to 64-bit. What will be the major benefit of the move to a 64-bit OS?

    A.  A 64-bit OS can utilize more RAM efficiently, allowing applications to access larger amounts of memory

    B.  A 64-bit OS provides faster processing speeds than a 32-bit OS

    C.  A 64-bit OS improves graphics performance and rendering capabilities

    D.  A 64-bit OS enhances network connectivity and data transfer rates

37. What is the most probable cause of an issue where a user cannot log in to the domain with a desktop PC, while a laptop PC on the same network functions properly, and a technician is unable to access the secure intranet site for troubleshooting tools?

    A.  Network connectivity issues

    B.  Incorrect domain credentials

    C.  Browser compatibility problems

    D.  Firewall restrictions

38. A network technician is deploying a new desktop computer into a SOHO environment. The computer must be configured so that the user can share folders with other Windows users on the network. Which of the following configurations should the technician implement to accomplish this objective?

    A. Set the network configuration to private

    B. Establish a proxy server connection

    C. Assign the user with network administrator privileges

    D. Create a shortcut to the shared drive's public documents

39. In order to resize a partition on the internal storage drive of a computer running macOS, which tool should a technician utilize for this task?

    A. Activity Monitor

    B. Disk Utility

    C. Time Machine

    D. Terminal

40. A development company has a high staff turnover. They would like to identify the most efficient way to use Microsoft Windows 10 features to install a fresh Windows OS when a laptop is re-purposed for a new member of staff. Which of the following is the most suitable?

    A. Manually reinstall Windows 10 from installation media

    B. Use Windows 10's Reset This PC feature

    C. Clone the laptop's hard drive

    D. Use Windows 10 System Restore

41. While using in-flight Wi-Fi on an iPhone to watch a movie, an executive received unexpected pictures without any prior contact history. To effectively address this issue, which of the following actions should the executive take?

    A. Configure AirDrop to exclusively accept transfers from known contacts

    B. Disable all wireless systems entirely throughout the flight

    C. Cease using iMessage and opt for secure communication applications

    D. Restrict messages and calls to saved contacts only

42. A high-street jewelry store needs to improve its physical security measures after a spate of ram-raids have hit similar businesses. To improve building security and prevent vehicles from driving into the premises while not impacting pedestrian access, which of the following options is MOST effective?

    A.  Security personnel

    B.  Protective barriers

    C.  Motion detection systems

    D.  Controlled entryway

43. A small retail store has recently set up a wireless network, but they are encountering interference from other wireless networks within proximity of the store. Which of the following actions would be MOST effective in resolving the interference with the LEAST disruption?

    A.  Choosing a wireless frequency that is not currently being used

    B.  Replacing the wireless equipment with Ethernet cables and switches

    C.  Regular power cycling of the equipment

    D.  Renaming the access point

44. Given the Chief Financial Officer's concerns about maintaining access to sensitive, legacy, unmaintained personally identifiable information (PII) on a workstation in the event of a ransomware outbreak, and considering the regulatory requirement to retain this data for an extended period, which of the following backup methods would be the MOST suitable?

    A.  Daily, incremental backup that is securely stored on an external hard drive

    B.  Regular snapshots taken and stored on a network-attached storage (NAS) device

    C.  A complete backup of the data that is transferred to an offline, encrypted tape storage

    D.  Weekly, differential backups that are securely transmitted to an offsite backup service

45. When a doctor needs to briefly leave their workstation, which of the following methods is the most effective for quickly securing the workstation?

    A.  Implementing a key combination to lock the computer upon departure

    B.  Verifying the absence of unauthorized individuals in the vicinity

    C.  Setting up a screensaver to automatically lock the computer after approximately 30 minutes of inactivity

    D.  Powering off the monitor to prevent unauthorized access to displayed information

46. Which of the following options would a technician utilize to enable automatic application boot-up upon logging into a conference room computer? (Choose two.)

    A. Windows Explorer

    B. Startup Folder

    C. System Overview

    D. Programs and Features

    E. Task Scheduler

    F. Device Manager

47. A systems administrator needs to reset a user's password due to the user forgetting it. After creating the new password, the systems administrator wants to implement additional security measures to protect the user's account. Which of the following actions should the systems administrator take?

    A. Enable password change requirement at the next login

    B. Prohibit the user from changing the password

    C. Deactivate the user's account

    D. Set a password with no expiration date

48. A home user downloaded free software from an online gaming site. While installing the downloaded software, the user was prompted to read through a long document with legal phrases and terminology. In order to complete the download, the user was prompted to agree to the terms of use set out within the document. What is being presented to the user in this scenario?

    A. Service level agreement (SLA)

    B. Non-disclosure agreement (NDA)

    C. End user license agreement (EULA)

    D. Memorandum of understanding (MOU)

49. After a regulatory audit, an administrator is tasked with adding more security to the authentication process. The audit recommends deploying multi-factor authentication (MFA). Which method would best address this requirement?

    A. Voice recognition and facial recognition

    B. Username and password

    C. One-time password (OTP) and fingerprint scan

    D. Password and PIN

50. When configuring a new laptop for an employee who frequently travels, which security practice would be most effective in ensuring data protection?

    A. Implementing PIN-based login for authentication

    B. Enforcing quarterly password changes for enhanced security

    C. Enabling hard drive encryption to safeguard sensitive information

    D. Utilizing a physical laptop lock for theft prevention

51. A university professor who is unable to connect to the staff network submits a help desk ticket. The assigned help desk technician inquires about whether any recent changes have been made. The professor reports that due to the college vacation, there is a large amount of construction activity in the surrounding offices. The help desk technician proceeds to ping the user's desktop, which does not respond. Which of the following is the MOST likely cause of this issue?

    A. The DHCP server is offline

    B. The firewall is blocking network access

    C. The user's account is locked

    D. The network cable has become disconnected

52. A sales manager has been unable to access a website and has submitted a help desk ticket. The website that is causing the problem for the manager has been verified to be online. Which of the following troubleshooting steps will MOST likely resolve the issue?

    A. Deleting the browser history

    B. Clearing the DNS cache

    C. Flushing the ARP cache

    D. Enabling JavaScript in the browser

53. Which method should the support technician choose to perform a local Windows 8.1 to Windows 10 upgrade, migrating files and user preferences while ensuring that each system is upgraded individually?

    A. Master image

    B. Fresh install

    C. In-place upgrade

    D. Windows Deployment Services (WDS)

54. A recent security audit highlighted a high risk of data loss from lost or stolen laptops. To mitigate this risk for Windows laptop users while minimizing the impact on user experience, which of the following measures would be the most effective?

    A. Implementing full disk encryption

    B. Enforcing regular laptop backups

    C. Implementing biometric authentication

    D. Enforcing mandatory laptop tracking software

55. A technician has been tasked with configuring a new wireless router for the payroll office. They must ensure optimal security is configured. Which of the following security measures should the technician implement to achieve the highest level of wireless network protection?

    A. Wi-Fi Protected Setup (WPS)

    B. Temporal Key Integrity Protocol (TKIP)

    C. Wi-Fi Protected Access 3 (WPA3)

    D. Wired Equivalent Privacy (WEP)

    E. Media Access Control (MAC) filtering

56. A support technician installed an antivirus application on a user's home computer. The user later reports that the computer has been running slowly, with the hard drive activity light constantly solid. What should be the FIRST step to address this issue?

    A. Check Services in Control Panel to identify any overutilization of system resources

    B. Monitor performance using Performance Monitor to analyze resource utilization

    C. Run System File Checker to verify the integrity of Windows files for any modifications

    D. Review Event Viewer logs to identify any errors or issues

57. A customer services representative asks a professional to fix a laptop problem. The representative complains that the browser redirects to several pages and programs open without being activated. Which of the following is the MOST LIKELY cause?

    A. Keylogger

    B. Cryptominers

    C. Virus

    D. Malware

58. A technician is dealing with frequent micro power outages in their area of operation. These outages are typically brief, with the longest occurrence lasting up to five minutes. Which of the following options should the technician employ to effectively address this issue and minimize its impact?

    A.   Surge suppressor

    B.   Battery backup

    C.   CMOS battery

    D.   Generator backup

    E.   Uninterruptible power supply (UPS)

59. A marketing team leader is helping a new starter get acquainted with their iMac desktop computer. Which graphical user interface (GUI) and file manager is typically set as the default in macOS for managing files and folders?

    A.   Disk Utility

    B.   Finder

    C.   Dock

    D.   FileVault

60. A publishing company supports a mixed desktop environment, containing many older versions of the Microsoft Windows OS. In order to ensure the compatibility of removable media, which of the following filesystem formats would be the BEST choice?

    A.   APFS

    B.   ext4

    C.   CDFS

    D.   FAT32

61. After performing a System Restore on a Windows workstation that was affected by malware, the technician notices that the malware is still detected. Which of the following BEST explains why the system still has malware?

    A.   The antivirus protection and host firewall were disabled by a system patch

    B.   The system updates did not include the latest anti-malware definitions

    C.   The malware compromised the System Restore process

    D.   The malware was installed before the creation of the System Restore point

62. While working at a local office, a technician discovers that multiple copies of home edition software are installed on computers. Which of the following is the MOST likely violation in this scenario?

    A. End user license agreement (EULA)

    B. Personally identifiable information (PII)

    C. Digital rights management (DRM)

    D. Open source agreement

63. When preserving data from a hard drive for forensic analysis, which two options should be given the MOST consideration?

    A. Licensing agreements

    B. Chain of custody

    C. Incident management documentation

    D. Data integrity

    E. Material safety data sheet

    F. Retention requirements

64. When a technician needs to remotely connect to a Linux desktop for troubleshooting assistance, which of the following tools is the most likely choice, considering the requirement for a tool natively designed for Linux?

    A. SSH

    B. VNC

    C. Remote Desktop Protocol (RDP)

    D. TeamViewer

65. During a hotel stay, a guest wants to connect to the hotel Wi-Fi network but notices that several SSIDs have extremely similar names. What social engineering attack is most likely being attempted in this scenario?

    A. Evil twin

    B. Impersonation

    C. Insider threat

    D. Whaling

66. After installing Windows 10 on a workstation, a technician notices that the system is only utilizing 3.5 GB of the installed 8 GB RAM. What is the MOST probable reason for this discrepancy?

    A.  The system is missing critical updates

    B.  The system is operating on a 32-bit operating system

    C.  The system's RAM modules are malfunctioning

    D.  The system requires updates to its BIOS

67. A computer on a corporate network has been infected with malware. What is the most effective method for restoring the computer to operational status?

    A.  Scanning the system with a Linux live disk, flashing the BIOS, and then returning the computer to service

    B.  Flashing the BIOS, reformatting the drive, and then reinstalling the OS

    C.  Degaussing the hard drive, flashing the BIOS, and then reinstalling the OS

    D.  Reinstalling the OS, flashing the BIOS, and then scanning with on-premises antivirus

68. A user reports that all the desktop icons on their newly issued PC have become unusually large after a recent software patch deployment. Which of the following actions would be the most effective in resolving this issue?

    A.  Rolling back video card drivers

    B.  Restoring the PC to factory settings

    C.  Repairing the Windows profile

    D.  Reinstalling the Windows OS

69. A bank must implement operational controls after recommendations were made by a third-party audit. The bank must implement change management best practices for all its information systems. The implementation team must understand what term is used to describe the range or boundaries of a change. Which of the following is the correct term?

    A.  Impact

    B.  Purpose

    C.  Analysis

    D.  Scope

70. A user encounters connection issues when attempting to use a third-party USB adapter. Which of the following tools should a technician employ to address this problem?

    A. taskschd.msc

    B. eventvwr.msc

    C. devmgmt.msc

    D. diskmgmt.msc

71. Upon investigating, a technician uncovers that user input has been surreptitiously captured by a malicious actor. Considering the circumstances, which of the following malware types is the MOST probable cause for this occurrence?

    A. Cryptominers

    B. Rootkit

    C. Spear phishing

    D. Keylogger

72. An asset disposal company needs to ensure potential customers that sensitive data will be rendered uncoverable when it is sent for destruction. When it comes to the physical destruction of SSDs containing sensitive information, which method is considered the most effective?

    A. Overwriting

    B. Formatting

    C. Physical destruction

    D. Deleting

73. A software development company would like to support a hybrid OS environment. How can they easily access shared filesystems and printers between Windows and Linux systems?

    A. yum

    B. CIFS

    C. Samba

    D. chmod

74. A pharmaceutical company needs to ensure all new employees are correctly onboarded, which of the following documents must be signed by the employee before being granted login access to the network?

    A.  MSDS

    B.  EULA

    C.  UAC

    D.  AUP

75. Following a failed update, an application is no longer launching and displays the error message "Application needs to be repaired." To address this concern in Windows 10, which of the following utilities should a technician utilize?

    A.  Device Manager

    B.  Administrator Tools

    C.  Programs and Features

    D.  Recovery

76. Which protocol can a technician utilize to establish a secure tunnel that conceals IP addresses and ensures enhanced security for network traffic?

    A.  DNS

    B.  IPS

    C.  VPN

    D.  SSH

77. While troubleshooting an issue with a computer that contains sensitive information, a technician determines that the computer needs to be taken off-site for repair. What should the technician do NEXT?

    A.  Remove the hard disk drive (HDD) and then send the computer for repair

    B.  Check corporate policies for guidance

    C.  Delete the sensitive information before the computer leaves the buildin

    D.  Get authorization from the manager

78. When creating a comprehensive inventory of a company's IT hardware, which documentation management method should a technician employ?

    A. Checklist for new user setup

    B. User information

    C. Asset tags and IDs

    D. Procurement life cycle

79. A user receives a call from someone who claims to be from the user's bank and requests information to ensure the user's account is safe. Which of the following social engineering attacks is the user experiencing?

    A. Phishing

    B. Smishing

    C. Whaling

    D. Vishing

80. In order to manually set an IP address on a computer running macOS, which of the following commands should a technician use?

    A. ipconfig

    B. ifconfig

    C. arpa

    D. ping

81. What is the term used to indicate that a vendor no longer supports a product, including the discontinuation of patches and updates?

    A. AUP

    B. EULA

    C. EOL

    D. UAC

82. A large online retailer must support wireless networks in all of its main warehouse facilities, where there is a mixture of older wireless access points using WPA2 and newer equipment supporting WPA3. Which of the following is an advantage of continuing to support WPA2 instead of WPA3?

    A.  A higher level of security

    B.  Greater backward compatibility

    C.  Improved resistance to brute-force attacks

    D.  Support for larger device networks

83. You are troubleshooting a Windows 10 computer that is experiencing slow performance. Task Manager shows high disk usage, but no specific application is consuming a significant amount of resources. Which of the following steps should you take first?

    A.  Run a full antivirus scan

    B.  Update the graphics card driver

    C.  Increase the virtual memory (pagefile) siz

    D.  Clear the browser cache.

84. You are setting up a new wireless network for a small office. Which wireless encryption method provides the highest level of security?

    A.  Wired Equivalent Privacy (WEP)

    B.  Wi-Fi Protected Access (WPA)

    C.  Wi-Fi Protected Access 2 (WPA2)

    D.  Wi-Fi Protected Setup (WPS)

85. A customer's computer is displaying a "No bootable device found" error during startup. Which of the following should you check first?

    A.  Boot sequence in BIOS

    B.  RAM modules

    C.  Graphics card drivers

    D.  Internet connectivity

86. A user's smartphone is not connecting to the company's Wi-Fi network. Other devices are connecting without issues. What should you check first?

    A. Bluetooth settings

    B. Network password

    C. Cellular data usage

    D. App updates

87. You are setting up a new email account for a user in Microsoft Outlook. Which protocol should you use if you want the email to be accessible from multiple devices and keep emails synchronized across them?

    A. Post Office Protocol 3 (POP3)

    B. Simple Mail Transfer Protocol (SMTP)

    C. Internet Message Access Protocol (IMAP)

    D. Hypertext Transfer Protocol (HTTP)

88. You receive a report from a mobile device user complaining about sluggish response time and an unusually high number of ads appearing while using various applications on their Android device. What is the most likely security issue causing these symptoms?

    A. Developer mode enabled

    B. Bootleg/malicious application

    C. Limited internet connectivity

    D. Unexpected application behavior

89. A user's Android device suddenly displays fake security warnings, even when not using any particular application. What security issue is most likely causing this problem?

    A. Android package (APK) source

    B. Data-usage limit notification

    C. Root access/jailbreak

    D. Application spoofing

90. A mobile device user reports that they are unable to connect to the internet, even though they have a stable Wi-Fi connection. What could be the security concern causing this issue?

    A.  Developer mode enabled

    B.  Limited internet connectivity

    C.  High network traffic

    D.  Leaked personal files/data

91. A user's Android device frequently displays unexpected application behavior, such as apps crashing or freezing. What is the most likely security issue?

    A.  High network traffic

    B.  No internet connectivity

    C.  Security concerns related to the Android package (APK) source

    D.  Root access/jailbreak

92. A mobile device user keeps receiving fake security warnings and notices a high number of ads, even when not using any applications. What is the most likely security issue?

    A.  Limited internet connectivity

    B.  Unexpected application behavior

    C.  Developer mode enabled

    D.  Bootleg/malicious application

93. A user's mobile device constantly exceeds its data usage limit, despite not using data-intensive applications. What is the most likely security issue?

    A.  High network traffic

    B.  Data-usage limit notification

    C.  Root access/jailbreak

    D.  Application spoofing

# Solutions

## Chapter 1: Mobile Devices

### 1.1 Given a scenario, install and configure laptop hardware and components

1.  The correct answer is **A**. The biometric reader should be set up on each laptop or desktop for only the user of that device. In the accounts department, only one person should have access to each device. All other answers are incorrect. Some users in accounts may deal with more sensitive data, and it is therefore inadvisable to give everyone access to their laptop/desktop. Employees from other departments should not be permitted access to any account's devices. Guests are people from other companies and should not be given access to any company resources.

2.  The correct answer is **B**. RAM is volatile, and you will need to wear an electrostatic discharge strap to protect the RAM against any static electricity. All other answers are incorrect. DDR RAM is for desktops, and SODIMMs are used by laptops. You would only check the power voltage if you had power problems. Operating system updates have no relationship to RAM upgrades.

3.  The correct answer is **D**. When the laptop is used at work, the power lead will likely be plugged into the power socket and draw power from the mains. Therefore, the most likely source of the problem in this scenario is the battery. All other answers are incorrect. If the device works correctly when plugged into the mains, the problem is unlikely to be the power adapter. If the operating system is corrupt, the laptop will still power up but display a blue screen of death. If the system fan is used as a cooling device aiding airflow, its failure would cause the computer to overheat and then crash, not prevent it from booting up.

4.  The correct answer is **D**. A Small Outline Dual In-Line Memory Module (SODIMM) is smaller and thinner so that it fits into a laptop that has restricted space. All other answers are incorrect. A Dual In-Line Memory Module (DIMM) is normally known as a RAM stick and is about double the size of a SODIMM, and is used for desktop computers, workstations, and servers. Double Data Rate 3 (DDR3) RAM is larger than a SODIMM commonly used in computers, though you can now get SODIMM versions. Synchronous Dynamic Random Access Memory (SDRAM) is larger than a SODIMM and is used in desktop computers.

5.  The correct answers are **B**, **C**, **D**, and **E**. When installing a Solid-State Drive (SSD) into a laptop, you must first shut the system down, then disconnect the power cable and remove the battery. You must then ground yourself by wearing an Electrostatic Discharge (ESD) wrist strap to protect the components against the static electricity in your body. The remaining answer choice is incorrect. Clearing your desk would be nice, but it is not a safety precaution.

6.  The correct answers are **B** and **C**. The iPhone 10 uses Touch ID, and iPhone 11 uses Face ID. All other answers are incorrect. iPhones cannot use fingerprint or vein ID, the latter of which is another name for a palm scan.

7.  The correct answer is **C**. When the battery has come to the end of its life, it will not fully charge nor retain charge for very long. It will also have a tendency to overheat. All other answers are incorrect. The digitizer is the glass on the front of the phone that is used by the touchscreen and would not make the phone hot, even if it were broken. If the cable were faulty, there would be no charge, but the phone would not be hot either. When an iPhone battery is set to low power mode, less power is used and the phone should therefore be cooler.

8.  The correct answer is **B**. A DHCP client will only get an Automatic Private IP Address (APIPA) if it cannot obtain an IP address from the DHCP server. This could be because of network issues contacting the DHCP server or because the server has run out of IP addresses. All other answers are incorrect. DNS is used for hostname-to-IP-address name resolution. NETBIOS is a legacy Microsoft name resolution protocol. If they were using a static IP address, then DHCP Enabled would be set to No.

9.  All answer choices are correct. The first stage is to make a full backup of the HDD, just in case anything goes wrong. You'll thereafter remove any redundant data that you are not going to migrate, resize the data partition so it is less than the size of the SSD, clone the old HDD partition, shut down the laptop and remove the old HDD, install and initialize the SSD, and finally, restore the cloned data onto the SSD.

10. The correct answer is **D**. A 13.56-MHz frequency is used by RFID applications. This includes Near-Field Communication (NFC), which is a scanner type used in door access and card payment systems. All other answers are incorrect. Biometrics would not use the phone as an interface. You would simply use your fingerprint or facial recognition to gain access. Certificates are used for encryption and not as an access control. Open Authentication (OAuth) is used for internet-based authentication only.

11. The correct answer is **B**. Most Solid-State Drives (SSDs) come in a 2.5-inch standard form factor. All other answers are incorrect. 3.5 inches is the size of a converter to place an SSD into a computer. 5.25 and 8 inches were the sizes of the first floppy disks.

12. The correct answer is **C**. He should first confirm the power rating of the charger, which is most likely too low to charge the phone and therefore the most probable cause of the issue. All other answers are incorrect. Deleting unwanted apps will reduce resources used by the phone but will not prevent it from charging. Putting the phone back to its factory setting will not fix a power issue. Setting the battery to low power mode will use less battery once the phone has been charged but will do nothing to resolve the current problem.

13. The correct answers are **A** and **D**. The easiest of the available options is a Bluetooth-enabled keyboard to connect to an Android tablet. You can also use a USB-C connector, which you would then connect to either DVI or, preferably, HDMI. All other answers are incorrect. No tablet has an Ethernet connection as these devices are too thin. Lightning cables are used only by Apple phones and tablets.

14. The correct answer is **A**. Near-Field Communication (NFC) is commonly used for card payments. All other answers are incorrect. Tethering is the process of creating a personal hotspot. A digitizer provides touchscreen technology. Dedicated VPN software creates a VPN.

## 1.2 Compare and contrast the display components of mobile devices

1. The correct answer is **D**. The digitizer is a piece of glass that enables touchscreen technology. All other answers are incorrect. The inverter converts DC to AC power. Vertical Alignment (VA) supports a contrast ratio of 2000:1. The backlight controls the brightness of an LCD monitor.

2. The correct answer is **D**. The gyroscope is used by the phone to rotate the screen as you twist your phone around. All other answers are incorrect. The bezel is the border between the phone's frames and the screen. The digitizer is a layer of glass that enables touchscreen functionality. The accelerometer tracks the motion of the phone and adjusts the screen size.

3. The correct answer is **C**. Since the webcam is not showing an image, it is likely to be a setup issue. In this case, reinstalling the webcam is the best solution. All other answers are incorrect. Rebooting the computer will not resolve an image issue. Purchasing a new webcam is unnecessary. Plugging the webcam into another port is unlikely to resolve an image issue.

4. The correct answer is **C**. An inverter converts DC power to AC power. All other answers are incorrect. An inverter does not convert AC to DC power. A digitizer is a piece of glass that provides touchscreen functionality. A backlight increases readability in low-light conditions.

5. The correct answer is **A**. Twisted Nematic (TN) displays use crystals that twist or untwist depending on the voltage level. It supports fast response time in relation to other TFT displays. All other answers are incorrect. Modern IPS displays have similar response times to TN, but the crystals rotate rather than twist. VA panels are prone to blurring and ghosting. A Cathode Ray Tube (CRT) has a display that is prone to screen burn-in and ghosting due to non-uniform use of the screen.

6. The correct answer is **C**. In Windows, if the microphone is not working properly, you should go to Privacy, select Microphone, then ensure the Allow apps to access your microphone feature is turned on. All other answers are incorrect. Rebooting the laptop is unlikely to resolve the issue. Getting an up-to-date driver is unlikely to resolve the issue if you have not enabled access for apps to the microphone. Purchasing additional voice recognition software will not resolve the issue if voice recognition is not enabled in the privacy settings.

7. The correct answer is **C**. An LCD monitor gets its brightness from a backlight, so if it fails, the screen may be very dim or even black. All other answers are incorrect. The backlight failing has no relationship to the brightness settings. You can have the brightness set to its highest setting, but if the backlight is malfunctioning, the screen will still be dim. A digitizer is used in touchscreen technology, and a legacy LCD monitor will not be touchscreen. If the VGA cable were broken, the screen would be black.

8. The correct answer is **D**. The digitizer is a thin layer of glass that converts analog touch into digital signals, and in this scenario, the most likely reason for the black areas is that the digitizer is broken. All other answers are incorrect. The Liquid Contact Indicators (LCIs) on an iPhone are normally white or silver, and if the phone has suffered water damage, these will be red. Look at the side of the phone with a lighted magnifying glass to view this. Inverters are used by older laptops to convert DC power from the motherboard to AC power. If the brightness of the phone were too low, it would be uniform across the entire screen and would not appear as dark patches.

9. The correct answer is **D**. In-Plane Switching (IPS) uses crystals that rotate rather than twist. This means that it produces better color definition with a wider range of viewing angles, making it suitable for both gaming and graphic design. All other answers are incorrect. LEDs can be used for low-budget gaming but not for graphic design. LCDs deliver less color accuracy than LED displays, which makes them a poor choice. CRTs are a legacy display technology and are not suitable for either gaming or graphic design.

10. The correct answer is **B**. Vertical Alignment (VA) uses crystals that tilt rather than twist or rotate and supports a wider color gamut and a contrast ratio of 2000:1 or 3000:1. However, the viewing angles are not as good as In-Plane Switching (IPS), making it more prone to blurring and ghosting. All other answers are incorrect. OLED could be described as having an infinite contrast ratio and can support 1,000,000:1. IPS can only support a contrast ratio of up to 1200:1. VGA has an aspect ratio of 4:3.

11. The correct answer is **C**. In an Organic Light-Emitting Diode (OLED) display, each pixel is produced by a separate LED. This screen therefore does not require a separate backlight. OLEDs are used in modern TVs, smartphones, monitors, and tablets. All other answers are incorrect. A Cathode Ray Tube (CRT) is a legacy display and uses a backlight. Liquid Crystal Displays (LCDs) use a fluorescent backlight. Light-Emitting Diode (LED) displays also use various backlight configurations.

12. The correct answer is **D**. When users have connected dual monitors and there is no image, they will need to adjust the display settings by going to Settings, Home, Display, Multiple Displays, and then selecting Extend these displays. This will enable dual monitors. All other answers are incorrect. If they choose the Duplicate these displays option, the image will be the same on both screens. They cannot create a dual-monitor setup using the Projecting to this PC option.

13. The correct answers are **A** and **D**. The iPhone must be within 10 meters of the speaker, and Bluetooth must be enabled in user Settings. All other answers are incorrect. There is no Bluetooth option under General settings, and 20 meters is out of the range of Bluetooth devices.

14. The correct answer is **C**. The wireless antenna is normally located on the bezel on the top of the laptop. All other answers are incorrect. There are no interface cards on the front or the rear of a laptop; they are normally on the sides. If the wireless antenna were on the base, there would be no signal.

15. The correct answer is **A**. The digitizer is a piece of glass that sits over the phone screen and enables touchscreen functionality. When you can see the icons perfectly but cannot open them, this most likely means that the digitizer is broken and will need to be replaced. All other answers are incorrect. If there was no power, the screen would be black. A broken CPU would mean that each app would respond but would be much slower than normal. "All of the above" is not the correct solution as some answers are incompatible.

16. The correct answers are **B** and **C**. The touchpad (sometimes known as the trackpad) can be used instead of a mouse. If it is unresponsive, the first step is to remove an external mouse. If that does not work, then you need a driver update. All other answers are incorrect. Rebooting the laptop will not resolve this issue. A gyroscope is used by phones and tablets to rotate their screens when you change the orientation of the device.

## 1.3 Given a scenario, set up and configure accessories and ports of mobile devices

1. The correct answer is **D**. The charger for iPhone 10 uses a Lightning cable. All other answers are incorrect. USB-A is used by computers, TVs, and gaming consoles. USB-B is used by printers, and USB-C is used by Android phones and most other new devices, such as game controllers and earbud cases.

2. The correct answers are **A** and **C**. A legacy laptop will not have a USB 3.0 port. It could also be that the USB slot is the wrong form factor. All other answers are incorrect. It is very unlikely that the USB drive being upside down is the source of the problem, as any user would try it both ways around, thereby easily resolving the issue. It is unlikely that damage has been caused to the end of a USB drive as it is very robust. It would be more likely to be the case that is damaged.

3. The correct answer is **B**. The Samsung Galaxy uses a USB-C connector. All other answers are incorrect. No phones use a normal USB connector. Micro USBs are used for small devices such as power banks, headphones, and gaming controllers. Mini USB ports were used to transfer data from early smartphones and PDAs.

4. The correct answer is **A**. When a cable cannot be fully inserted into a charging port, the most likely reason is a build-up of lint or another foreign object that is lodged in the port. The best way to remove the lint is to give it a good blast of compressed air. All other answers are incorrect. You should not blow into the port as your breath contains moisture that could damage the electrical components. You should never use WD-40 as it is a liquid and spraying electrical components is an electrical hazard. When it dries it leaves an oily residue. You could also use a toothpick for this job, but using a metal object such as a pin or needle risks causing an electrical short circuit that could damage the phone.

5.   The correct answers are **B** and **C**. Before using any Bluetooth product, you must first enable Bluetooth on the phone, then pair both devices. All other answers are incorrect. There is no need to install drivers on a smartphone that has built-in Bluetooth capability. Until the devices are paired, any music you play will come through the phone speakers and not the earbuds.

6.   The correct answers are **A**, **D**, and **E**. A docking station is a sophisticated port replicator and, when combined with DisplayPort, can provide keyboard and mouse, speaker, and dual-monitor functionality. All other answers are incorrect. Wi-Fi normally comes built in, but if the laptop is older, you may need to purchase a Wi-Fi card. Laptops usually come with Ethernet ports, but for older models, you will need to purchase a network card.

7.   The correct answer is **C**. Using a smartphone to create a personal hotspot is the fastest way to get internet access on their laptop. All other answers are incorrect. Traveling 10 miles might mean missing the conference call due to traffic and the user would be overheard by other Starbucks customers even if they did make it in time. Connecting an Ethernet cable directly to a wireless router that has no connectivity is not a solution. Rebooting the wireless router is not going to obtain an internet connection.

8.   The correct answer is **B**. Port replicators can be plugged into the back of a laptop to give the user a variety of additional ports. All other answers are incorrect. A KVM switch is used for the keyboard, mouse, and monitor when there are multiple monitors or computers attached. A dual monitor will only give you a second monitor; it will not fulfill the other requirements. A hub is an internal device that is used to connect multiple computers.

9.   The correct answers are **A**, **C**, and **D**. When you are having problems with the touchscreen, and it shows any erratic behavior, the first thing you should do is check that the screen is not damaged. Then, check that it is clean. After that, you should recalibrate the screen. The remaining answer is incorrect. The touch pen battery life has nothing to do with erratic cursor behavior. If the battery were running low, the touch pen would simply become unresponsive.

10.  The correct answer is **C**. The micro USB connection was replaced by the USB-C cable. All other answers are incorrect. Serial cables are legacy cables that used an RS232 port. Lightning cables are used by Apple devices only. Parallel cables are old cables used by printers and have since been replaced by USB.

11.  The correct answer is **C**. The iPhone 14 uses a USB-C charger. All other answers are incorrect. The charger for iPhone 11 uses a Lightning cable, while iPhone 12 and 13 models come with a Lightning-to-USB-C connector. USB-A is used by computers, TV, and gaming consoles. USB-B is used by printers, and USB-C is used by Android phones and most new devices, such as game controllers and earbud cases.

12.  The correct answer is **D**. Serial devices that use the nine-pin RS-232 hardware port include legacy mice, printers, and modems. All other answers are incorrect. RJ45 is used by Ethernet cables. RJ11 was used to connect a modem to a telephone line. Parallel connections are used by legacy printers.

13. The correct answers are **A** and **C**. Web cameras can only provide input to one type of software at a time. If the webcam privacy setting is not set to Allow apps to access this camera, then the webcam will not work. All other answers are incorrect. It is unlikely that plugging the webcam into another port will resolve the issue as it worked yesterday. Purchasing another webcam will not resolve the issue of software clashes or enable the camera setting to allow apps to use the camera.

14. The correct answer is **B**. Windows devices have features such as sensitivity and touch mode for touchscreens. You can adjust the touchscreen settings and calibrate the screen under the computer settings. All other answers are incorrect. When setting up the touchscreen, a digitizer is installed. At the time of this installation, the technician must ensure that there are no air bubbles. However, as the screen was working previously (i.e., after its initial installation), air bubbles beneath the glass are not likely to be the current problem. The display settings affect the screen, not the touchscreen itself. A touchscreen only needs between 0.1 and 2 watts; it is a very low-power aspect of the device.

15. The correct answer is **C**. When a webcam stops functioning, the first thing to try is to unplug it and then plug it back in. If that fails to work, then you should uninstall it completely and reinstall the webcam software and any latest updates from the manufacturer's website. All other answers are incorrect. When an update is applied to an operating system, it is likely that the computer has already been rebooted as part of the update, so doing so again is unlikely to help. It is most likely that there is nothing wrong with the webcam, and the user may not have enough time to go to the shops, make a purchase, and set it up before the Zoom conference commences. There is no need to update the operating system as this has already been done and is the root cause of this issue.

16. The correct answer is **C**. NFC is used for card payment types where the card must be within four inches of the reader and so would be the source of the problem described. All other answers are incorrect. Bluetooth is too insecure for financial transactions. Wireless is not used by contactless cards. Infrared requires a line of sight between two devices and has no security; therefore, it is not used for financial transactions.

17. The correct answers are **B**, **C**, and **E**. When a cell phone gets hot, it may be due to excessive use, such as being used as a Wi-Fi hotspot for a long time. Phones also overheat when the battery is nearing the end of its lifespan, at which point it also fails to charge fully and can lose charge very quickly. Having too many applications open at the same time forces the CPU to work harder than normal and, especially in the case of outdated applications, can also increase the phone's temperature. All other answers are incorrect. A cracked screen does not make the phone hot but may prevent the screen from responding. A cheap charging cable will prevent the phone's battery from being charged.

18. The correct answer is **A**. Apple introduced the reversible Lightning cable in 2012 to replace the Apple 30-pin connector. All other answers are incorrect. 20-pin and 25-pin connectors do not exist. Most of Android phones use the USB-C connector.

## 1.4 Given a scenario, configure basic mobile-device network connectivity and application support

1.  The correct answer is **B**. Most companies have a data cap on their mobile devices and wireless routers that need to be topped up once the limit has been reached. All other answers are incorrect. Network coverage must be available in the area as the salesperson was able to watch a movie online the previous evening. MDM solutions test updates prior to releasing them. Companies are highly unlikely to miss mobile phone payments as they are critical to business operations.

2.  The correct answer is **B**. A password is "something you know" and a fingerprint is "something you are". This is an example of two-factor authentication. All other answers are incorrect. A retina and fingerprint are both "something you are", a password and PIN are both "something you know", and gait and swiping a card are both "something you do".

3.  The correct answer is A. If a SIM card is not installed in a new smartphone, the user will not be able to make any calls or get access to mobile data. All other answers are incorrect. You cannot turn on mobile data without a SIM card. The film protecting the screen does not affect call functionality or mobile data. Activating Bluetooth does not affect calls or mobile data.

4.  The correct answer is **B**. The easiest way to pair an Apple Watch with an iPhone is to use the Apple Watch app. This is done by aligning the watch face with your phone camera, just as you would scan a QR code. All other answers are incorrect. Although you can manually set up pairing by entering a six-digit passcode, it is not the easiest method. You cannot pair devices manually using a four-digit passcode; it needs to be six digits. The four-digit code is only used to access the Apple Watch itself.

5.  The correct answer is **C**. When a calendar application is not updating, it is normally down to the password not being updated. Updating the corporate password should resolve the issue. All other answers are incorrect. The remaining battery has no impact on the calendar application. Rebooting the phone will not have any impact on the phone app. Remotely wiping the phone will not help in this scenario as doing so will revert the device to its factory settings.

6.  The correct answer is **B**. A Global System for Mobile Communication-based phone has a removable SIM that can be inserted into another handset with the same network provider. All other answers are incorrect. Global System for Mobile Communication can work with cellular, wireless, and satellite communications, so all other answers that use the word "only" are false.

7.  The correct answer is **C**. MDM solutions allow you to enforce policies and send updates to smartphones. Remotely wiping devices will revert them to factory settings. All other answers are incorrect. WPA2 PSK means connecting to a wireless network using a password. Disabling Bluetooth will only prevent Bluetooth devices from being used. Using a VPN on company phones only secures a remote session from the phone. It does not prevent access to the local data on the phone.

8.  The correct answers are **B** and **C**. MAM solutions are used to set policies for apps that can process corporate data and prevent the transfer of corporate data to personal devices. All other answers are incorrect. Mobile Device Management (MDM) is responsible for patching mobile devices and remotely wiping them when they are lost or stolen to prevent data compromise.

9.  The correct answer is **B**. Samsung Galaxy users use Google Drive as their backup location. All other answers are incorrect. Gmail is the Google email application. Knox containers are used by Samsung to separate personal and business data on their phones. Office 365 is a Microsoft product.

10. The correct answer is **D**. When a user downloads and installs an app from the Apple App Store, they need their Apple ID and password. If the installation fails, they will need to reset the password. All other answers are incorrect. A Hotmail account is used to access Microsoft products. A Gmail account is used to access Google products. The iPhone passcode is used to access the iPhone itself.

11. The correct answer is **D**. Satellite communication devices connect to satellites above the earth and can communicate in areas where no cell phone masts exist. All other answers are incorrect. Digital Subscriber Line (DSL) requires the use of a splitter to enable phone and internet to be used at the same time. A hotspot connects to a wireless or cellular provider and cannot be used in this case.

12. The correct answer is **C**. If the weather app is left running constantly, it will drain the iPhone battery. They need to both turn off severe weather notifications and modify the location permissions so that they can manually enter the location for which they want to get results. All other answers are incorrect. The location services While Using Your App will still drain the battery. Turning off location services does not affect the weather app. It merely prevents the user from getting notifications when they enter a different country. A local wireless network connection merely provides internet and would not drain the battery. Purchasing a new battery will not resolve this issue.

13. The correct answer is **B**. When the phone is set to power conservation mode, the battery will only charge 50-60%. Smartphones may enter low power mode if the battery is being drained too quickly, and GPS will not work when the phone is in low power mode. Switching this off would correct the issue. All other answers are incorrect. Enabling Bluetooth only allows Bluetooth devices to connect to the phone. Cleaning the touchscreen does not affect GPS. GPS does not use Wi-Fi settings.

14. The correct answer is **C**. If the agent turns off location services, they will prevent the phone's GPS location from being advertised. All other answers are incorrect. You cannot set location services to pause, nor can you delete them.

15. The correct answer is **D**. Your iPhone is backed up to iCloud. All other answers are incorrect. Microsoft uses Office 365, and Google uses Google Drive. Apple uses neither. Boot Camp is an Apple product, but its purpose is to host third-party operating systems.

16. The correct answer is **A**. In Windows 10, the tile turns blue when Bluetooth is switched on. All other answers are incorrect. The tile is gray when it is switched off. The Bluetooth tile will never appear white or green in Windows 10.

17. The correct answer is **D**. Data Loss Prevention (DLP) prevents someone from sending an email containing PII and sensitive information. It blocks data if it finds a pattern match. All other answers are incorrect. A legal hold prevents users from deleting emails from a mailbox. MailTips warn you of events such as a large distribution group being chosen prior to dispatching an email. A firewall is used to block traffic coming into or going out of your company's networks.

18. The correct answer is **C**. GSM phones have removable SIM cards that can be used in another handset from the same provider, whereas CDMA phones have no SIM cards as the provider has a built-in handset. All other options are incorrect.

19. The correct answer is **B**. The Preferred Roaming List (PRL) is a database held on your mobile telephone. This is used when your phone connects to the tower. The salesperson will need to install a PRL update to enable roaming data on their smartphone. All other answers are incorrect. A firmware update will not update the PRL database on your phone. Turning on location services just advertises the location of your phone. Restarting the smartphone will not work in this situation.

20. The correct answer is **C**. The user will need to go to Settings, then Mobile Data, to enable a 4G data connection. All other answers are incorrect. Wi-Fi calling only allows you to communicate from remote locations as long are there is an internet connection over Wi-Fi.

21. The correct answers are **A**, **C**, **D**, and **E**. Following a 14-day free trial, a Google Workspace subscription starts at $5.75 per user and allows access to many applications, at least 30 GB of storage, and video meetings with up to 100 users. All other answers are incorrect. You cannot create virtual machines, and a live.com email address is for Microsoft products.

22. The correct answer is **B**. A legal hold means that a mailbox has no mailbox limit, and any deleted emails are retained in a purges folder. This prevents a user under investigation from deleting emails. All other answers are incorrect. If they set a backup at a certain time each day, they will not capture any emails that have been removed from the deleted items folder. A forensic toolkit is used to extract data from a computer and will not be able to extract emails that have been deleted from the deleted items container. Chain of custody refers to the bagging, tagging, and signing over of evidence to anyone handling the data to prove to the judge that it is the original evidence.

23. The correct answers are **B**, **C**, and **D**. If you are wearing a headset, go into Zoom, then Audio Settings | Microphone | Test mic. When testing a Bluetooth connection, if you are wearing earbuds, then go to your phone and play some music. If you hear music, then you are connected. If you are wearing a headset, you can go into Zoom, and under Audio Settings, you can go to Speaker | Test speaker. All other answers are incorrect. There are no options under Video Settings to test speakers or microphones as it deals only with the camera and video. A Bluetooth connection is only shown in blue when you are using a Windows 10 laptop and not earbuds.

# Chapter 2: Networking

## 2.1 Compare and contrast TCP and UDP ports, protocols, and their purposes

1.  The correct answer is **B**. Secure Shell (SSH) is used for secure remote access. All other answers are incorrect. Telnet provides unsecure remote access, RDP uses port 3389 and is a secure remote access protocol that can only be used to connect to Microsoft desktops/servers, and SNMP 161 is unsecure and provides status and reports on network devices.

2.  The correct answer is **B**. Hypertext Protocol Secure (HTTPS) is used when establishing a secure session on a web server. All other answers are incorrect. TFTP is unsecure and is used to transfer configuration files. HTTP is used to make an unsecure session on a web server. SSH is used for secure remote access.

3.  The correct answer is **A**. Post Office Protocol (POP) is a legacy mail client that stores emails locally and uses port 110. All other answers are incorrect. IMAP is a mail client that provides diaries and calendars, allows you to create multiple folders, has a permanent connection to the mail server, and uses TCP port 143; SMTP is used to transfer email between mail servers and uses TCP port 25.

4.  The correct answer is **C**. Server Message Block (SMB) uses port 445 for file and print sharing in a Windows environment. However, it is internal only and cannot be used on the internet. All other answers are incorrect. NETBIOS (ports 137-139) is used for legacy name registration and resolution by Microsoft. 67/68 are used by DHCP to automatically assign IP addresses. 389 is used by LDAP that is used to manage directory services by querying and updating X500 directory objects.

5.  The correct answer is **B**. Port 995 is the standard port used by Secure Post Office Protocol (SPOP). All other answers are incorrect. Unsecure POP uses 110. Secure IMAP uses 993. Unsecure IMAP uses 143.

6.  The correct answer is **C**. User Datagram Protocol (UDP) is connectionless and can be used to stream video and audio. All other answers are incorrect. TCP is connection-orientated and far too slow for audio or streaming video. RDP is used for secure remote access to Windows servers/desktops. TFTP is a connectionless fast transfer of data. Normally, it is used by network devices to obtain configuration files.

7.  The correct answer is **D**. Simple Network Management Protocol (SNMP) v3 is secure and uses UDP port 162. All other answers are incorrect. SNMP uses UDP port 161 but is insecure. Port 389 is used by LDAP to create, manage, and search directory services. POP (the unsecure mail client) uses TCP port 110.

8.  The correct answer is **B**. File Transfer Protocol (FTP) port 21 is unsecure and transfers data in clear text. All other answers are incorrect. TFTP is a UDP version of FTP. SSH is a secure method of remote administration. FTPS is a secure version of FTP.

9.  The correct answers are **B** and **D**. Hypertext Transfer Protocol (HTTP) uses port 80 and Hypertext Transfer Protocol Secure (HTTPS) uses port 443. All other answers are incorrect. Port 23 is used by Telnet. Port 110 is used by POP. Port 445 is used by SMB.

10. The correct answer is **D**. The correct sequence for the Transmission Control Protocol (TCP) three-way handshake is SYN, then SYN-ACK, and, finally, ACK. The sequences in all the other answers are incorrect.

11. The correct answer is **D**. Simple Mail Transfer Protocol (SMTP) uses port 25. All other answers are incorrect. FTP uses port 21. SFTP, SSH, and SCP all use port 22. Telnet uses port 23.

12. The correct answer is **A**. Port 993 is the standard port used by secure Internet Mail Access Protocol (IMAP). All other answers are incorrect. Unsecure POP uses 110. Secure POP uses 995. Unsecure IMAP uses 143.

13. The correct answer is **C**. Telnet is an insecure remote access protocol. All other answers are incorrect. SSL is an encryption-based protocol designed for securing connections between web clients and servers. SSH is a secure remote access protocol than can replace Telnet. RDP is a secure access protocol for Windows operating systems.

## 2.2 Compare and contrast common networking hardware

1.  The correct answers are **B** and **C**. The back of the patch panel is where wires are terminated at the IDC using a punch-down tool, and the front has prewired RJ45 ports. All other answers are false.

2.  The correct answer is **C**. An SDN allows the rapid provisioning and deprovisioning of networks in a virtual environment. All other answers are incorrect. A WAN is a network over a large geographical area. A LAN is a network that is secure and doesn't extend beyond close proximity, for example, a building or even just a single floor of the building. A SAN comprises fast redundant disks.

3.  The correct answer is **D**. A UTM solution can perform multiple security functions. All other answers are incorrect. A stateless firewall can only perform basic packet filtering. A host-based firewall can only protect a desktop or laptop, blocking and allowing certain types of traffic. A stateful firewall can provide deep inspection of traffic to assess the verbs in use. For example, in HTTP traffic, the GET verb can be allowed while the PUT or POST verbs can be blocked.

4.  The correct answer is **B**. The ONT converts optical signals to electrical signals. All other answers are incorrect. FTTC is where a telecom provider runs fiber cables to multiple customers. ONT does not convert electrical signals to optical signals. The reverse is true. An optical line terminal (OLT) is located in a street cabinet, and the ONT is on the customer's premises.

5.  The correct answer is **A**. Power over Ethernet (POE) allows a device to pull its power from the switch. All other answers are incorrect. Thunderbolt can be used as a display interface, similar to HDMI or a display port. A managed switch is an enterprise switch that has 28 or 48 ports and can be configured by a web or command-line interface. A shielded twisted pair cable has the wires wrapped in foil for more protection and to limit EMI.

6.  The correct answer is **A**. A broadcast domain refers to the number of people that you can broadcast to. If you create a Virtual Local Area Network (VLAN) on a managed switch, you can reduce its size. All other answers are incorrect. A load balancer sends an incoming client request to the least utilized of a number of web servers performing the same function. A router joins multiple networks together. A hub is a slow device that connects multiple hosts together.

7.  The correct answer is **A**. A Storage Area Network (SAN) is a set of fast redundant disks used by virtual servers for storage to host the server's virtual machines. All other answers are incorrect. A PAN is a personal area network normally used by Bluetooth devices and smartphones. A cluster uses a quorum disk that is shared by two servers, one of which is active and the other passive and waiting for the active server to fail. RAID 0 is a setup involving an array of disks as a stripe set for faster reads. However, if one disk fails, then it takes down the whole RAID 0 configuration. It does not provide fault tolerance or redundancy.

8.  The correct answer is **C**. Installing power injectors allows you to connect your POE device to a non-POE switch. All other answers are incorrect. A UPS is used to allow a server to shut down gracefully following a complete loss of power. A generator is an alternative power source following a complete loss of power. The purchase of two POE-capable switches is not cost effective.

9.  The correct answer is **D**. An unmanaged switch is taken out of the box and plugged in. All other answers are incorrect. A managed switch is an enterprise switch that has 28 or 48 ports and can be configured by a web or command-line interface. An aggregate switch is used to aggregate data from multiple switches and forward it to a core switch. A power diode switch is used for lights.

10. The correct answer is **D**. A hub is an internal legacy device that was implemented to connect hosts using 10BASE-T Ethernet cabling. All other answers are incorrect. A load balancer receives client requests and sends them to the least utilized host. These servers all perform the same job function. A switch is a more modern device that connects hosts but, unlike the hub, can send the traffic to one particular host and is therefore a faster replacement for the hub. A router is a device that connects networks together.

11. The correct answer is **C**. A firewall and router control access by an access control rule (ACL). When installed, only one rule is set up: the last rule, deny. When traffic arrives at the firewall and there is no allow rule, the last rule of deny will be applied. This is known as implicit deny. All other answers are incorrect. No allow rule means the document will be blocked. The document will be blocked at the network level and therefore will never get as far as the host. Explicit deny occurs when a deny rule has been set up on the firewall.

12. All statements are true.

13. The correct answers are **A**, **C**, and **D**. The application layer applies business logic to prioritize traffic. The control layer contains routing information and is inserted between the application and infrastructure layer and uses a virtual device known as the SDN controller. The infrastructure layer handles the routing and switching of traffic. All other answers are incorrect. The transport layer uses TCP or UDP for the delivery of packets. The data link layer provides error control and framing, moving from the physical layer to the network layer. The physical layer defines the connection and transmission types, such as Ethernet, wireless, or token ring.

14. The correct answer is **B**. Cat 5 cable is a type of Ethernet cable that uses an RJ45 connector. All other answers are incorrect. A BNC connector uses a coax cable. An RJ11 connector is used to connect a modem to a telephone line. A Cat 3 cable runs at 10Mbps while Cat 5 runs at 100Mbps.

15. The correct answer is **B**. 802.3at (POE+) allows powered devices to draw up to about 25W. All other answers are incorrect. 802.11 is a wireless standard. 802.3af allows powered devices to draw up to about 13W. 802.3bt (POE++ or 4PPOE) allows powered devices to draw up to 51W (type 3) or 71W (type 4).

16. The correct answers are **B** and **D**. Asymmetrical Digital Subscriber Line (ADSL) has a faster download than upload speed, and symmetric DSL has the same upload and download speed. All other answers are false.

## 2.3 Compare and contrast protocols for wireless networking

1. The correct answers are **A**, **C**, **D**, and **E**. Only Wi-Fi 5 is incorrect. Wi-Fi 6 (802.11ax), 802.11 b and g, and Wi-Fi 4 (802.11n) all operate on 2.4GHz. Wi-Fi 5 (802.11ac) operates at 5GHz.

2. The correct answer is **D**. Wi-Fi 6 (802.11ax) operates in both the 2.4GHz and 5GHz ranges, thus creating more available channels. Wi-Fi 6 chipsets support a total of 12 channels, eight in the 5GHz and four in the 2.4GHz range. All other answers are incorrect. 802.11b supports 2.4GHz. 802.11g supports 2.4GHz, and 802.11a supports 5GHz.

3. The correct answer is **D**. The user should go to Settings on the smartphone, enable Bluetooth, then pair the device. All other answers are incorrect.

4. The correct answer is **B**. Long-range fixed wireless can be used as a bridge to connect two wireless networks and can be either licensed or unlicensed. All other answers are incorrect. GPS is used to determine your latitude and longitude using orbital satellites. Unlicensed wireless networks use a public frequency and interference is a risk. Licensed wireless networks are those for which exclusive rights are purchased to a given frequency band within a given geographical area from the relevant regulator.

5. The correct answer is **C**. Near-Field Communication (NFC) is used for short-range contactless payments. All other answers are incorrect. Bluetooth is used to connect devices wirelessly and share data. RFID is used to tag high-value items to prevent them from being stolen. Tethering is the protocol whereby your phone is used to create an internet connection for a laptop or desktop using a data cable.

6.  The correct answer is **A**. 802.11a is 5GHz only. All other answers are incorrect. 802.11b and 802.11g are 2.4GHz only. 802.11n uses both 2.4 and 5GHz, known as Multiple Input Multiple Output (MIMO). It can multiplex signal streams from 2-3 separate antennas.

7.  The correct answers are **A** and **C**. 2.4GHz is both slower and covers a greater distance than 5GHz. All other answers are incorrect.

8.  The correct answer is **B**. 802.11ax goes up to 3.5GBps. All other answers are incorrect. 802.11c goes up to 866 Mbps. 802.11a runs at 54 Mbps. 802.11b runs at 11Mbps.

9.  The correct answer is **A**. Both 802.11b and 802.11g work on a frequency of 2.4GHz. All other answers are more modern than 802.11g and are therefore not backward compatible.

10. The correct answers are **B** and **C**. 5GHz is less effective at propagating through solid surfaces, supports more individual channels, and suffers less congestion than 2.4GHz. All other answers are incorrect. 2.4GHz can penetrate solid surfaces much better than 5GHz but supports fewer channels and therefore suffers more congestion.

11. The correct answer is **D**. 802.11n uses both 2.4 and 5GHz, which is known as Multiple Input Multiple Output (MIMO). It can multiplex signal streams from 2-3 separate antennas. All other answers are incorrect. 802.11a is 5GHz only. 802.11b and 802.11g are 2.4GHz only.

## 2.4 Summarize services provided by networked hosts

1.  The correct answer is **C**. The Dynamic Host Configuration Protocol (DHCP) server allocates an IP address to each host, and this should be checked first. All other answers are incorrect. A domain controller authenticates hosts. A DNS server provides name resolution and would be an issue if you could not access websites. A mail server provides users with access to email.

2.  The correct answer is **D**. When you have network connectivity but cannot access any websites, it means that you cannot access a DNS server. All other answers are incorrect. If you have an internet connection, then your log-on has been successful. If you have an internet connection, then your IP address is valid. There is no need to check the web server location as it will not change.

3.  The correct answer is **B**. A proxy server can do webpage caching. All other answers are incorrect. File servers store documents. UTM firewalls can provide content filtering, URL filtering, and malware inspection. Web servers host websites but cannot cache the pages.

4.  The correct answer is **C**. A SCADA network is an industrial control system that can be used in the production of oil or gas. All other answers are incorrect. There is no such network as a production network. A local area network is not used in the production of oil or gas but rather hosts many users and devices. A Metropolitan Area Network (MAN) is a network within a city used by either the police, ambulance, or fire services.

5.  The correct answers are **A** and **C**. IoT devices need access to the internet and often fall into the category of home automation. Alexa is used by many households to find out facts or play music. A smart meter can tell you the amount of energy that you use and at the same time update your energy supplier. All other answers are incorrect. Neither alarm clocks nor headsets require internet access.

6.  The correct answers are **A**, **C**, and **D**. A spam gateway prevents spam from entering your network using SPF, DKIM, and DMARC. It also uses DLP to prevent PII and other sensitive information from leaving your network and filters incoming messages to users' mailboxes. However, an organization will never send out spam through a spam gateway.

7.  The correct answer is **B**. A load balancer can deal with a high volume of web traffic and route it to the least-utilized host. Installing one ensures that all web servers are utilized efficiently. All other answers are incorrect. A cluster is two servers sharing a quorum disk to provide high availability. A proxy server filters outgoing traffic and caches webpages. A DNS server provides hostname-to-IP-address name resolution.

8.  The correct answer is **D**. A mail server uses Simple Mail Transfer Protocol (SMTP) to transfer email using port 25. All other answers are incorrect. DNS servers use port 53. DHCP servers use ports 67/68. Proxy servers use port 8080.

9.  The correct answer is **B**. A web server hosts websites, each of which has a home page through which customers can access applications and information about a product or service. All other answers are incorrect. A file server is an internal service that hosts data. A mail server contains mailboxes. A RADIUS server, also known as an AAA server, provides authentication from supplicants.

10. The correct answer is **B**. \\server1\data is a UNC path used to connect either to a file or print service. Since the name of the share is data, it will be a file share. All other answers are incorrect. A print server allows someone to send documents to a printer. A syslog server centralized log files from multiple servers. A proxy server caches website pages and controls outbound traffic via URL and content filters.

11. The correct answer is **D**. A RADIUS server is an AAA server that provides authentication, authorization, and accounting without needing to hold a copy of the directory services. Supplicant is another name for devices such as VPN servers, switches, and access points. All other answers are incorrect. A syslog server centralizes log files from multiple sources. A DNS server provides hostname-to-IP-address resolution. A proxy server caches webpages and handles URL and content filtering.

12. The correct answer is **C**. It is likely that the driver for the operating system is not on the installation media. Therefore, we need to download the up-to-date driver from the manufacturer's website. All other answers are incorrect.

13. The correct answer is **A**. A syslog server is also known as a log collector and centralizes log files from multiple servers. All other answers are incorrect. A file server hosts documents that are to be accessed by members of the domain. A domain controller authenticates users within a domain.

14. The correct answer is **D**. IoT devices have default passwords that can be found on search engines. Because the device is connected to the internet, a hacker could use these publicly available passwords and gain access to your home network. Therefore, the first thing the user should do is reset the default password to something more secure. All other answers are incorrect. Some IoT devices have no means of updating and this is not the main priority. If you disconnect an IoT device from the internet, it will not function as it is an internet-connected device. Reading the user manual is important but not as important as your home security.

## 2.5 Given a scenario, install and configure basic wired/wireless small office/home office (SOHO) networks

1. The correct answer is **B**. A static address is set up manually, and a server or printer IP address should never change. All other answers are incorrect. Dynamic addresses are allocated by DHCP. These addresses could continually change, and users will have difficulty connecting to it. APIPA cannot be set up as they are allocated when a fault has been detected. Servers can be allocated either a public or private IP address, but static is more relevant.

2. The correct answer is **A**. Private IP addresses can only be used in an internal network. All other answers are incorrect. Private IP addresses can be used in networks with up to 16,777,214 hosts. Every IPv4 address has a network ID and a host ID.

3. The correct answer is **A**. 131.107.1.1 is a Class B public IP address. All other answers are incorrect. 192.168.1.1 is a private IP address. 169.254.1.223 is an APIPA that is allocated. You cannot get an IP address from DHCP. 172.16.5.14 and 10.10.15.6 are private IP addresses. IP addresses starting 10.172 and 192 are private IP addresses and can only be used internally. 169.254.x.x is an APIPA and cannot be used externally. Any other IP address ranges than these are public and can be used on the internet.

4. The correct answer is **B**. Class B addresses use the first two octets for the network ID. Therefore, the subnet mask is 255.255.0.0. All other answers are incorrect. 255.0.0.0 is the default subnet mask for a Class A address. 255.255.255.0 is the default subnet mask for a Class C address. 169.254.1.1 is an APIPA address, and you cannot access valid addresses from DHCP servers. With this address, you cannot communicate with others on the network.

5. The correct answer is **D**. A home network is more likely to have a Wireless Access Point (WAP) as a home router. All other answers are incorrect. Hubs join multiple hosts together but very slowly. A router is an enterprise product that joins networks together and is normally used in enterprise settings. Switches join multiple internal hosts together more quickly than a hub.

6.  The correct answer is **C**. 212.15.1.2 is a valid IPv4 address. All other answers are incorrect. 10.1.1.0 cannot be used for a host as it ends in 0, indicating that it is a network address. Any address starting with 255 is a subnet mask and cannot be used for a host. 12.1.1.255 cannot be used as a host as it ends in 255, indicating that it is the broadcast address.

7.  The correct answer is **D**. A Windows server that uses both IPv4 and IPv6 addresses is known as dual stack. All other answers are incorrect.

8.  The correct answers are **A** and **D**. A desktop may be allocated a 169.254.x.x address either because it is an Automated Private IP Address (APIPA) assigned due to a duplicate IP address or (most commonly) it is unable to get network connectivity to the DHCP server. All other answers are incorrect. A DNS server is used for hostname-to-IP-address resolution. A domain controller is used for authentication.

9.  The correct answer is **B**. The default gateway is missing, and this prevents the user from leaving the internal network. A default gateway is required to access the internet. All other answers are incorrect. If the gateway was present, then DNS might be an issue with the same scenario, but this is not the case. 132.24.0.1 is a public Class B address and therefore can get onto the internet. You would need to run ipconfig /all to determine whether the IP address is dynamic or static.

10. The correct answer is **A**. An IPv4 address has 4 octets of 8, making it a 32-bit addressing schema. All other answers are incorrect.

11. The correct answer is **D**. 2001:0dC8:0000:0000:0abc:0000:def0:2311 is an IPv6 address. All other answers are incorrect. 10.1.1.1 is a private IPv4 address. B4-2E-99-C0-75-45 is a MAC address. 169.254.1.5 is an APIPA address used to contact the DHCP server or results from a duplicate IP address being allocated.

12. The correct answer is **C**. If you cannot access the internet, it is most likely to be the router's gateway or a DNS problem. All other answers are incorrect. NETBIOS is a legacy naming convention. Server Message Block (SMB) traffic is a communication protocol that allows access to file shares and printers. SMTP is used to transfer mail between mail servers.

13. The correct answer is **D**. When you shorten an IPv6 address, you remove the leading zeros. Therefore, 0dc8 becomes dc8. Then you look at the third and fourth octets, which are 0000:0000. This can be replaced by ::. You know there are 8 octets, so when you count six remaining, you know 0000:0000 is missing. You then take 0abc and remove the leading zero, leaving abc. The sixth octet is 0000, but you cannot use :: again, so you reduce it to :0:. Thus, the shortened IPv6 address becomes 2001:dC8::abc:0:def0:2311. All other answers are incorrect.

14. The correct answer is **C**. 126.1.1.1 is a public IPv4 address. All other answers are incorrect. The IPv4 addresses 10.10.10.1, 172.16.1.3, and 192.168 are all private. Any addresses starting with 10, 172.16-172.31, or 192.168 are private and cannot be used externally.

15. The correct answer is **D**. An IPv6 address has 64 bits for the network ID and 64 bits for the interface ID, making it a 128-bit addressing schema. All other answers are incorrect. IPv4 uses 32-bit addressing.

## 2.6 Compare and contrast common network configuration concepts

1.  The correct answer is **A**. It is most likely that the financial director has an APIPA, and that is why they cannot connect to anyone else. Check to see whether the DHCP server has allocated an IP address. All other answers are incorrect. Simple Network Management Protocol (SNMP) monitors the status of and creates reports on network devices. RADIUS is an AAA server that controls access to the network, but the administrator is already on the network. A DNS server translates host names to IP addresses.

2.  The correct answer is **B**. The address above is an IPv6 address and needs an AAA record. All other answers are incorrect. An A record is used for an IPv4 host. An MX record is used by a mail server. A TXT record is used for any free-form record such as an SPF record.

3.  The correct answer is **C**. A Microsoft Dynamic Host Configuration Protocol (DHCP) server has a default lease duration of 8 days. All other answers are incorrect.

4.  The correct answer is **A**. An MX record is used for mail servers. All other answers are incorrect. An A record is used for an IPv4 host. An AAA record is used for an IPv6 host. SRV records are used to find services such as domain controllers.

5.  The correct answer is **C**. A Local Area Network (LAN) is an internal secure network. All other answers are incorrect. A Wide Area Network (WAN) spans multiple geographical locations. A Metropolitan Area Network (MAN) is used by the police, ambulance, and fire services in a city. CAN refers to a campus area network used in academic institutions.

6.  The correct answer is **D**. With DomainKeys Identified Mail (DKIM), an organization uploads a public key as a TXT record. The authenticity of the originating servers of incoming messages can be verified using this key. All other answers are incorrect. SPF uses a TXT record to indicate that a host from a particular domain is allowed to send mail. A syslog centralizes the log files from many servers.

7.  The correct answer is **D**. With a DHCP reservation, an IP address is reserved for a host as identified by their MAC address. All other answers are incorrect. A DHCP scope refers to the addresses that a DHCP server can allocate for a particular subnet. IP address lease durations cannot be customized; everyone gets the same lease duration. If a client has a static address that is manually configured, the host will not send out a DHCPDISCOVER packet to try and obtain an address from DHCP.

8.  The correct answer is **A**. A Virtual Local Area Network (VLAN) is normally used for departmental isolation or isolation within a LAN. All other answers are incorrect. A proxy server controls access from the internal network to an external network. A firewall is used to control access between the internal and external networks. A router joins multiple external networks together.

9. The correct answer is **C**. DMARC can validate incoming email messages and has the ability to detect and prevent email spoofing. Therefore, any emails arriving from an illegitimate source can be blocked. All other answers are incorrect. A content filter is used by a proxy server or UTM firewall to prevent anyone from accessing a website (such as a gambling site) that has inappropriate content. A proxy server controls outgoing requests and has the ability to cache website content. It can also carry out URL or content filtering by blocking access to websites hosting inappropriate content.

10. The correct answer is **A**. A Dynamic Host Configuration Protocol (DHCP) scope is a range of IP addresses that can be allocated to a subnet. All other answers are incorrect. In a DHCP reservation, the same IP address can be allocated to the same host as identified by their MAC address. A DHCP lease refers to the limited time that a host is allocated an IP address. A DHCP superscope allows two or more scopes to be used as if they were a single scope to increase the number of IP addresses in a subnet.

11. The correct answer is **A**. 131.122.14.12 is an IPv4 address and therefore uses an A record. All other answers are incorrect. An AAA record is used for an IPv6 host. An MX record is used for mail servers. A Sender Policy Framework (SPF) record is used to prove the authenticity of mail servers to prevent spam.

12. The correct answer is **B**. The DHCP handshake sequence is DISCOVER, OFFER, REQUEST, ACK (normally known as DORA). The host sends a DHCPDISCOVER broadcast packet to find a DHCP server. The DHCP server replies with DHCPOFFER containing an IP address along with other configuration, such as the DNS server and the default gateway. The client then replies with DHCPREQUEST to accept the offer. The DHCP server then sends a DHCPACK packet confirming the allocation of the IP address with a lease time of 8 days, normally. All other answers are incorrect.

13. The correct answer is **D**. A Virtual Private Network (VPN) creates a secure tunnel between an external location and the corporate network. All other answers are incorrect. A WAN is an external network (e.g., the internet). SSL is a method of encrypting data in transit, normally via a web browser. DHCP dynamically allocates IP addresses to hosts.

14. The correct answers are **B**, **C**, and **D**. Each company should have one SPF record in the DNS as a TXT file that identifies the hosts that are authorized to send mail. DKIM uses cryptographic keys to verify that the mail server sending the email is authorized to do so. DMARC detects and protects against email spoofing. The remaining answer is incorrect. A stateless firewall is a very basic packet-filtering firewall.

## 2.7 Compare and contrast internet connection types, network types, and their features

1.  The correct answer is **C**. The internet is a Wide Area Network (WAN), due to the large geographical area it covers. All other answers are incorrect. A Metropolitan Area Network (MAN) (such as one used by police) is a network that covers a city. A Personal Area Network (PAN) is used by a single person, for example, Bluetooth. A Local Area Network (LAN) LAN is a network confined to a single location (this could be an entire building or even a single room) connected by one or more switches.

2.  The correct answer is **B**. Satellite phones are the only method that are able to communicate in remote areas. All other answers are incorrect. A cable modem would not work as there are no cables to connect to. GPS is used for navigation, and only works via satellite. There would not be any wireless access point up a mountain in a remote location.

3.  The correct answer is **A**. Fiber-optic cabling works on light pulses, is immune to EMI, and is very secure. All other answers are incorrect. Coax has many layers that protect against emitting EMI, but, as a hacker could attach a vampire tap and connect to the cable, it is not secure. It is also very slow. Because of the foil layers, STP can reduce EMI but is not as fast as fiber. 10-BASE-T is a legacy Ethernet-cable version and can be UTP or STP. However, it is quite slow (10Mbps).

4.  The correct answer is **C**. An iPhone 11 is a smartphone that uses cellular communication (hence the term "cellphone"). All other answers are incorrect. DSL is used to provide internet in a SOHO. An iPhone 11 can use a wireless connection, but this is not the main connection type. An iPhone is not a satellite communication device.

5.  The correct answers are B and C. A WISP connects customers and service providers using long-range fixed wireless technology. All other answers are incorrect. A WISP does not manufacture modem wireless access points nor monitor bandwidth.

6.  The correct answer is **A**. A Wide Area Network (WAN) is an unsecure network over a large geographical area. All other answers are incorrect. A LAN is a secure fast network with its users all in close proximity, such as a single floor in a building. A DMZ is a boundary network that sits between the LAN and the WAN. As two of these statements are false, "All of the above" is also incorrect.

7.  The correct answer is **B**. A Dynamic Host Configuration Protocol (DHCP) server automatically assigns IP addresses on machine startup. It allows an administrator to create a reservation based on the user's MAC address, ensuring that this particular host gets the IP address to be monitored. All other answers are incorrect. SMTP is used for email and not IP addresses. SSL refers to secure data in transit via a web browser. A DNS server is used to perform hostname-to-IP-address name resolution.

8.  The correct answer is **C**. A Wireless Local Area Network (WLAN) is used to connect multiple devices wirelessly. All other answers are incorrect. A PAN is one individual network connecting two devices together, such as the Bluetooth connection between a user's earbuds and a smartphone. A WAN is a network over a large geographical area.

9. The correct answer is **A**. A Digital Subscriber Line (DSL) uses telephone lines as a communication channel. All other answers are incorrect. Satellite communication is not reliant on telephones. Neither fiber nor cable modems use telephone lines either.

## 2.8 Given a scenario, use networking tools

1. The correct answer is **D**. A loopback plug is used to test a network card or switch port. If you get a solid LED, this then tells you that the port or network card can send and receive data. All other answers are incorrect. Pliers would cut through the cable and are better used to firmly grip objects. A cable stripper scores the jacket of a cable and makes it easy to remove. A punch-down tool is used to terminate wires in the back of the patch panel to the IDC.

2. The correct answer is **C**. A cable stripper scores the jacket of a cable and makes it easy to remove. All other answers are incorrect. A crimping tool is used to connect an RJ45 plug to a cable. Pliers would cut through the cable and are better used to firmly grip objects. A loopback plug is used to test network cards and switch ports to confirm whether they can send and receive data.

3. The correct answer is **A**. A punch-down tool is used to push wires into the IDC. All other answers are incorrect. A crimping tool is used to connect an RJ45 plug to a cable. A cable stripper is used to score the jacket so that it can easily be removed. A cable tester can be attached to both ends of a cable to test the permanent link.

4. The correct answer is **D**. A toner probe can trace an RJ45 cable to the patch panel. All other answers are incorrect. A crimping tool is used to connect the RJ45 connector to an Ethernet cable. A punch-down tool is used to fix each conductor into an IDC. An OTDR is used to analyze faults in a fiber cable.

5. The correct answer is **A**. A network tap allows you to divert network traffic to a secondary device for analysis. All other answers are incorrect. A loopback plug is used to test a network card or switch port. A spectrum analyzer analyzes the input signal against a frequency range within a wireless network. A toner probe can trace an RJ45 cable to the patch panel.

6. The correct answer is **C**. A crimping tool is used to seal the RJ45 into either a T568A or B layout. All other answers are incorrect. A punch-down tool is used to terminate wire pairs into the IDC blocks. A cable stripper is used to score the outer jacket from a cable just enough to allow it to be removed to expose the cable. Pliers are used to firmly grip an object.

7. The correct answer is **A**. A Wi-Fi analyzer is a piece of software that can be installed on a laptop. It will detect any other wireless access points in the vicinity and record the signal strength of the different networks using each channel. All other answers are incorrect. A protocol analyzer will collect packets traveling across the network. A bandwidth monitor measures the available bandwidth on a network. RFID detects objects by using tags, commonly used on high-value items in shops.

8. The correct answer is **B**. A cable tester is connected to each end of a cable and tests each wire in turn and a successful connection will show an LED light. All other answers are incorrect. A loopback plug is used to test a network card or switch port. A bandwidth monitor measures the available bandwidth on a network. An OTDR is used to test fiber-optic cables for faults.

# Chapter 3: Hardware

## 3.1 Explain basic cable types and their connectors, features, and purposes

1.  The correct answer is **A**. Copper cables are subject to signal attenuation, which refers to the loss of signal strength over distance. Copper cables can be susceptible to electromagnetic interference. This will reduce speed but is not the main limitation. Bandwidth limitation primarily affects the overall capacity of the network but does not directly impact the speed of data transmission. Insulation-related issues are more likely to cause signal quality problems rather than limiting the speed of data transmission.

2.  The correct answer is **A**. An Optical Time Domain Reflectometer (OTDR) is a tool used for troubleshooting and testing fiber optic cables. It sends light pulses into the cable and measures the reflections to identify any issues, such as breaks or signal loss. Wire cutters are used for cutting wires and not troubleshooting fiber optic cables. An Ethernet cable tester is used to verify the connectivity and quality of Ethernet cables. A multimeter is used for measuring voltage, current, and resistance in electrical circuits.

3.  The correct answer is **A**. ST connectors are typically used with single-mode fiber cables. Their key benefit is low signal loss, not high data rates. Multi-mode fiber is used for high data rates. They use an ST connector that has a bayonet-style design, and they are easy to install. For high-density networks, LC (Lucent Connector) connectors are commonly used. LC connectors are small form factor connectors that offer high-density connectivity while maintaining excellent performance. Coaxial cables are compatible with various connectors and devices, making them versatile for different applications. They can be easily connected to devices such as TVs, modems, routers, antennas, and video cameras.

4.  The correct answer is **A**. Cat 5 cables are designed for Ethernet networking and have a maximum distance limitation of 100 meters. All other options are beyond the 100 m limitation.

5.  The correct answer is **A**. A punch-down tool is used to connect wires to the demarc securely. A wire stripper removes insulation from wires. A cable tester verifies cable connectivity and quality but is not specifically used for adding lines to the demarc. A crimping tool is used to attach connectors to cables, but not specifically for adding lines to the demarc.

6.  The correct answer is **A**. RJ11 connectors are used for telephony applications to connect telephone handsets to wall jacks. RJ11 connectors are not typically used for connecting computers to routers. Printers are usually connected to computers using USB cables, not RJ11 connectors. Connecting a TV to a cable box typically involves HDMI or coaxial cables, not RJ11 connectors.

7.  The correct answer is **A**. Cat 5 cables can support a maximum data transmission speed of 100 Mbps. Cat 5e can run at 1 Gbps. Cat 6 runs at 1 Gbps and Cat 8 runs at 40 Gbps.

8.  The correct answer is **A**. Thunderbolt cables are commonly used in Apple's macOS systems for high-speed data transfer and device connectivity. Windows is commonly associated with a wireless or Ethernet connection. Linux is associated with Ethernet cables. Android uses micro-USB or USB-C connections.

9.  The correct answer is **A**. A crimping tool is commonly used to create an RJ45 cable. It is used to attach the RJ45 connectors to the ends of Ethernet cables, ensuring secure and reliable connections. A wire stripper removes insulation from wires. A punch-down tool is used to connect wires to the demarc. A multimeter is used for measuring voltage, current, and resistance in electrical circuits.

10. The correct answer is **A**. Lightning to USB cables are commonly used for charging iPhones and other Apple devices. Printers usually require specific printer cables or USB cables with different connectors. A crossover cable is used to transfer data between two computers. Display cables, such as HDMI or DisplayPort cables, are typically used for connecting monitors to laptops or other devices.

11. The correct answer is **A**. A crossover cable where we are connecting two similar devices (e.g., a computer to a computer or a switch to a switch). Straight-through cables typically have the same wiring scheme (either T568A or T568B) on both ends, not a combination of both. Coaxial cables typically use BNC (Bayonet Neill–Concelman) or F-type connectors. BNC connectors are commonly used in professional video and networking applications, while F-type connectors are predominantly used in television and consumer audio/video systems. Fiber optic cables use different connectors, such as SC, ST, or FC connectors.

12. The correct answer is **A**. USB offers a speed of 12 Mbps, while USB 2 offers a speed of 480 Mbps. They do not have the same speed: USB (USB 1.1) has a lower speed of 12 Mbps, while USB 2.0 offers a higher speed of 480 Mbps. USB and USB 2 are specific versions of the USB standard with defined speeds.

13. The correct answer is **A**. Plenum-grade cables have fire-resistant properties to meet the stringent safety regulations in air-handling spaces. Plenum-grade cables are not primarily designed for outdoor use. While plenum-grade cables can support high-speed data transfer, it is not their primary use case. While plenum-grade cables can be used for long-distance connections, their main advantage lies in specific environments rather than distance capabilities.

14. The correct answer is **A**. The metallic shielding around STP cables helps prevent EMI from interfering with the transmitted signals. STP cables are not specifically designed for outdoor use. STP cables can support lengths of up to 100 meters (328 feet) for Ethernet applications, making them unsuitable for long distances. You would never use STP cables in a low electromagnetic interference (EMI) environment.

15. The correct answer is **C**. F-type connectors are a type of coaxial connector commonly used for cable television (CATV) and other video or audio applications. Ethernet network connections use an RJ45 cable. Fiber optic networks typically use different types of connectors, such as SC or LC connectors. Wi-Fi devices, such as routers and access points, use integrated antennas or external antenna connectors to establish wireless connections with other devices.

16. The correct answer is **A**. Wire cutters are used to strip the outer sheath of the cable, then we insert the cable into an RJ45 connector and use the crimper to terminate Ethernet cables with RJ45 connectors. All other options are wrong.

17. The correct answer is **B**. LC connectors are known for their small form factor and high density, making them commonly used in data centers and other environments where space is a concern. While SC connectors are widely used in fiber optic networks, they do not provide a higher density compared to LC connectors. ST connectors are older and larger connectors, not known for their high density. FC connectors, similar to ST connectors, are larger and not known for their high density. They are primarily used in specialized applications, such as high-power or industrial settings.

18. The correct answer is **C**. eSATA (External Serial Advanced Technology Attachment) is specifically designed for connecting external storage devices, such as hard drives, to a computer at speeds of 6 Gbps. USB 2.0 (Universal Serial Bus 2.0) has a maximum data transfer speed of 480 Mbps. HDMI (High-Definition Multimedia Interface) is primarily used for connecting audio-visual devices, such as monitors and TVs, and not storage. VGA (Video Graphics Array) is an older interface primarily used for connecting monitors or projectors for video display.

19. The correct answer is **A**. DisplayPort supports simultaneous video and audio transmission over a single cable, making it convenient for connecting monitors with audio capabilities. DisplayPort does not work with a wide range of older display devices. DisplayPort could be more expensive than other interfaces.

## 3.2 Install the appropriate RAM given a scenario

1. The correct answer is **B**. The primary purpose of virtual RAM is to improve system performance by extending the available memory. It allows the computer to use a portion of the hard drive or SSD as additional RAM when the physical RAM becomes insufficient. Virtual RAM's purpose is not to provide additional storage for files and documents. Virtual RAM serves as an extension of the available memory, rather than a backup solution. Virtual RAM has nothing to do with CPU and GPU.

2. The correct answer is **A**. The primary reason for using DDR RAM in computer systems is its improved data transfer rates. DDR RAM enables data transfer on both the rising and falling edges of the clock signal, effectively doubling the transfer rate compared to earlier memory technologies. This boost in speed enhances system performance and responsiveness. DDR RAM is not used for increasing storage capacity in computer systems. DDR RAM is not used for power efficiency; the main reason is increased data transfer rates. DDR RAM can contribute to reducing latency to some extent; its primary purpose is to enhance data transfer rates.

3.  The correct answer is **D**. SODIMM RAM (Small Outline Dual Inline Memory Module) is the type of memory module commonly used in laptops and small form factor computers due to its compact size. DIMM RAM (Dual Inline Memory Module) is a larger form factor memory module typically used in desktop computers. RIMM RAM (Rambus Inline Memory Module) is an older memory module type that was used in high-end workstations or servers that demanded high-speed memory access and data transfer rates. MicroDIMM RAM is a smaller variant of DIMM RAM commonly found in specialized or niche devices.

4.  The correct answer is **C**. ECC RAM is designed to detect and correct memory errors, improving data integrity. ECC RAM is not specifically designed to provide faster data transfer between the CPU and RAM. Its main focus is error detection and correction rather than improving transfer speeds. ECC RAM does not enhance graphics processing capabilities. ECC RAM does not increase the storage capacity of RAM.

5.  The correct answer is **B**. The primary benefit of using dual-channel RAM is faster data transfer rates. It utilizes two differently colored memory slots, allowing for parallel data access and improving overall system performance. Typically, a black slot and a contrasting color such as blue, gray, or white, depending on the manufacturer. Dual-channel RAM does not directly increase the storage capacity of the RAM. Dual-channel RAM does not directly improve graphics performance. Dual-channel RAM does not specifically lower power consumption.

6.  The correct answer is **C**. The primary advantage of using quad-channel RAM is improved data transfer rates. It utilizes four memory channels simultaneously, allowing for increased bandwidth and faster data transfer between the RAM and the CPU. Quad-channel RAM does not have any effect on storage. While quad-channel RAM can offer some benefits for multitasking scenarios, it is not its primary advantage. Memory latency is more influenced by factors such as memory speed and timings.

7.  The correct answer is **A**. DDR2 goes from 400 to 1,066 MHz, DDR3 goes from 800 to 2,133 Mhz, and DDR4 goes from 2,133 to 3,200 MHz. All other options are wrong.

8.  The correct answer is **D**. The combination of an SSD, Intel Core i7 CPU, and 16 GB DDR4 RAM is the best choice for a gaming PC due to faster storage access, high-performance processing capabilities, and ample memory capacity. SSD, Intel Core i5, 8 GB DDR4, offers a good balance, but a higher-end CPU such as the Intel Core i7 is preferred for gaming. 16 GB of DDR4 RAM provides a more comfortable gaming experience. An SSD is preferred over an HDD for faster loading times, while AMD Ryzen 3 CPUs and DDR3 RAM are less powerful options compared to the others for gaming purposes.

## 3.3 Given a scenario, select and install storage devices

1.  The correct answer is **C**. The primary advantage of installing an M.2 hard drive directly on the motherboard without cables is the simpler and more secure connection. It eliminates the need for extra cables and reduces clutter within the system. Faster data transfer rates are not the main advantage. The IDE is an older interface used for traditional hard drives and optical drives, and it does not apply to M.2 drives. Increased storage capacity is not the primary advantage of installing M.2 drives without cables.

2.  The correct answer is **B**. 1 TB NVMe SSDs offer significantly faster data transfer rates compared to traditional hard drives, such as SATA SSDs or HDDs. They provide improved performance, lower latency, and faster access times, making them the optimal choice for maximizing speed. eSATA is not used as a hard drive but it is used for external storage. A USB 3.0 flash drive will not be used as a hard drive but is slower than NVMe SSD. A 1 TB SATA SSD is not as fast as an NVMe SSD.

3.  The correct answer is **A**. Slower rotational speeds of 5,400 rpm result in slower data access and transfer rates due to the increased time taken by the read/write head to locate and access data on the spinning disk. 7,200 rpm, 10,000 rpm, and 15,000 rpm are all faster than 5,400 rpm.

4.  The correct answer is **A**. Flash drives, commonly known as USB drives are used for portable storage due to their convenience and ease of use. Memory cards are also used for portable data storage. Optical drives are used for reading or writing optical disks. Hard disk drives are used internally in the system.

5.  The correct answer is **A**. When selecting a motherboard for a specific CPU, a critical consideration is ensuring socket compatibility. The CPU socket on the motherboard must match the socket type of the CPU for proper physical and electrical connections. Memory type support is important but not critical, but it will tell you how much and what type of memory the motherboard supports. Expansion slot availability is important for adding additional components, but it is not critical. Form factor compatibility ensures that the motherboard fits into the computer case, but it is not the main factor when choosing a motherboard for a specific CPU.

6.  The correct answer is **C**. Optical drives, such as CDs or DVDs, are used for reading or writing optical disks. Flash drives use solid-state memory and do not rely on laser technology for reading and writing data. Memory cards, such as SD or microSD cards, also do not use laser technology for data storage. SSDs use flash memory technology for data storage and do not require laser technology for data access.

7.  The correct answer is **A**. A SATA cable has a small, L-shaped connector at one end and a flat connector at the other end. A wide, rectangular connector at both ends would be an IDE cable. An audio/video cable would be a round, barrel-shaped connector at one end and a flat connector at the other end. A triangular-shaped connector at one end could be a DisplayPort cable or an HDMI cable.

8.  The correct answer is **D**. HDDs with 15,000 rpm are used in specialized enterprise environments requiring high-performance storage due to their faster data access and transfer rates. However, they may generate more heat and noise compared to HDDs with lower rotational speeds, such as 5,400 rpm, 7,200 rpm, or 10,000 rpm.

9.  The correct answer is **C**. RAID 5 uses a minimum of three drives, which distributes data and parity across the drives, providing both data redundancy and increased storage capacity. RAID 0 does not provide data redundancy and would not be suitable for ensuring data protection in this case. RAID 1, which mirrors the data across the drives only uses two drives. RAID 10, which combines striping and mirroring, would require a minimum of four drives to implement.

10. The correct answer is **A**. PCIe is commonly used for connecting high-speed graphics cards in computer hardware. It provides a high-bandwidth interface that enables fast communication between the graphics card and the motherboard. This allows for optimal performance and rendering of complex graphics, resulting in enhanced gaming experiences and improved graphics-intensive applications. All other options are incorrect.

11. The correct answers are **A** and **D**. RAID 6 uses a minimum of four drives, which distributes data and parity across the drives, providing both data redundancy and increased storage capacity. RAID 10 also uses a minimum of four drives, which combines striping and mirroring, providing both data redundancy and increased storage capacity. RAID 0 does not provide data redundancy and would not be suitable for ensuring data protection in this case. RAID 5 requires a minimum of three drives.

12. The correct answer is **B**. RAID 1, also known as mirroring, duplicates the data across the two drives, providing redundancy in case one drive fails and the other drive takes over. RAID 0, also known as striping, does not provide data redundancy. RAID 5 needs a minimum of three drives and RAID 10 a minimum of four drives.

13. The correct answer is **B**. Memory cards, such as SD or microSD cards, can be used for data storage. Flash drives can be used in digital cameras and smartphones, but memory cards are a much better option. Optical drives are not used in digital cameras and smartphones. SSDs are used in various devices, including computers and laptops, but are not used as expansion storage in digital cameras and smartphones.

14. The correct answer is **B**. M.2 NVMe SSDs provide the fastest data access speeds for laptops. They utilize the NVMe interface and offer significantly faster performance compared to other SSD options. 2.5" SAS HDDs provide high reliability and integrity and are not the best choice for achieving the fastest data access. IDE HDDs are slow legacy hard drives. mSATA SSDs offer faster data access but are slower than M.2 NVMe SSDs.

15. The correct answer is **A**. The main difference between a 2.5" SSD and a 3.5" SSD is their physical form factor and size. A 2.5" SSD is smaller and commonly used in laptops and small form factor desktops, while a 3.5" SSD is larger and typically intended for use in traditional desktop computers. This size difference affects their compatibility with drive bays and installation methods. Both 2.5" and 3.5" SSDs typically operate with the same power. The data transfer speed of an SSD is not directly related to its physical size. 2.5" and 3.5" SSDs determine their compatibility with different drive bays, but this is not the key difference between them. The form factor primarily affects their physical dimensions and installation options.

## 3.4 Given a scenario, install and configure motherboards, central processing units (CPUs), and add-on cards

1. The correct answer is **C**. NVMe SSDs require a specific NVMe-compatible motherboard with an M.2 slot. All other options are incorrect.

2. The correct answer is **B**. x86 architecture, also known as 32-bit processors, has a maximum addressable memory limit of 4 GB. 2 GB is incorrect as it underestimates the maximum RAM capacity. x64 architecture, also known as 64-bit processors can address memory higher than 4 GB.

3. The correct answer is **A**. In the BIOS settings, ensure that the desired operating system is set as the first boot option. All other options are incorrect as they are unrelated to boot option troubleshooting.

4. The correct answer is **D**. Heat sinks and fans are essential components in desktop computers to dissipate heat generated by the CPU. As the CPU performs computations, it generates heat, and if not properly managed, it can lead to overheating. Heat sinks are designed to absorb and disperse the heat away from the CPU, while fans provide airflow to carry the heat away from the heat sink. Heat sinks and fans do not focus on power consumption, speed of data transfer, or EMI.

5. The correct answer is **A**. The ITX form factor is commonly chosen when building a compact and portable gaming PC. The small size of ITX motherboards allows for a more compact system build, making it easier to transport and suitable for LAN parties or gaming on the go. Other options are not ideal scenarios for using an ITX form factor. They typically require motherboards with more expansion slots and connectivity options.

6. The correct answer is **A**. The primary advantage of liquid cooling over air cooling is improved thermal efficiency. Liquid cooling systems, such as all-in-one (AIO) coolers or custom loops, are designed to effectively dissipate heat from the components, resulting in lower temperatures compared to air cooling. This enhanced thermal efficiency allows for better overclocking potential and overall improved performance of the system. All other options are incorrect.

7. The correct answer is **C**. Performing a TPM reset clears the previous encryption key stored in the TPM and establishes a fresh secure connection with the upgraded hardware, allowing the system to boot and regain access to the stored data. Disabling the TPM functionality in the BIOS may prevent the system from accessing the encrypted key required to decrypt the data. Reverting to the previous hardware configuration might not be practical or necessary, and it does not address the issue of the TPM encryption key.

8. The correct answer is **A**. A clicking noise during computer bootup may indicate a failing hard drive with mechanical issues such as a malfunctioning read/write head or a failing spindle motor. Promptly backing up the data and replacing the failing hard drive is crucial to prevent data loss. An overheating CPU can cause the computer to shut down. A loose power cable might result in power loss. A malfunctioning graphics card is not related to a clicking noise.

9. The correct answer is **A**. The 8-pin EPS connector is commonly used to provide dedicated power to the CPU on a desktop motherboard. It ensures stable and sufficient power delivery to meet the high power demands of modern CPUs. The 4-pin Molex connector is commonly used for connecting fans and cooling devices. The 6-pin PCIe connector is used to provide supplementary power to PCIe expansion cards, such as graphics cards. The 24-pin ATX connector is the primary power connector for the motherboard.

10. The correct answer is **A**. Operating a disk infrastructure in a degraded state increases the risk of data loss. When one or more disks in the infrastructure are degraded or experiencing issues, the system relies on the remaining disks to maintain data integrity. All other options are wrong.

11. The correct answer is **A**. If the CPU fan fails to function properly, it can result in inadequate cooling of the CPU. As a consequence, the CPU may overheat, which can lead to system instability, unexpected shutdowns, or even permanent damage to the CPU. Proper cooling is essential for maintaining the CPU's optimal temperature and ensuring its reliable operation. The CPU's performance may decrease but it is not the primary reason. All other options are incorrect.

12. The correct answer is **A**. A continuous beep from a computer typically indicates a RAM failure or a compatibility issue. If the CPU is not properly seated in its socket, you may encounter an error such as a "CPU Fan Error" or a "No POST" (Power-On Self-Test) error. Power-related issues will result in experiencing intermittent power loss, sudden shutdowns, or power failure.

13. The correct answer is **A**. The main difference between AT and ATX motherboards is their size and form factor. Other options that are differences but not the main difference are AT is considered legacy where motherboards are larger in size, while ATX motherboards are smaller and more commonly used in modern computer systems. ATX motherboards introduced improvements such as better component placement, standardized I/O ports, and improved power management. AT uses a single power supply whereas ATX uses a 20/24-pin connector. ATX supports more expansion slots compared to AT. ATX supports DDR4 RAM while AT supports the older DDR3 RAM.

14. The correct answer is **D**. When a heat sink is not working optimally, it is recommended to check for dust accumulation and clean the heat sink, as dust can obstruct airflow. Additionally, replacing the thermal paste between the CPU and heat sink helps ensure efficient heat transfer. Finally, ensuring proper contact between the CPU and heat sink is crucial for effective heat dissipation.

15. The correct answer is **A**. The technician should use the BitLocker Drive Encryption tool to unlock and access the encrypted USB drive. By entering the decryption key or password in the BitLocker Drive Encryption settings, the drive can be unlocked, allowing authorized access to the files stored on it while ensuring data security. Disk Clean-up is a tool used to free up disk space by removing unnecessary files. Windows Defender Firewall is responsible for network traffic filtering and protection against unauthorized access. Task Scheduler is used to automate tasks and launch programs at specified times or events.

16. The correct answer is **A**. To prevent unauthorized booting from a CD, implement secure boot. Secure boot ensures that only trusted and digitally signed operating systems can be booted, preventing the use of unauthorized live CDs. All other options are important security measures but they do not directly address the specific scenario of booting from a live Linux CD.

17. The correct answer is **A**. Use a power supply with a higher wattage. If plugging in a device causes the power to the PC to go down, it indicates that the current power supply is not providing enough wattage to support the additional power demands of the device. By upgrading to a power supply with a higher wattage, you can ensure that your PC has sufficient power to handle the device and other components without experiencing power interruptions. All other options are incorrect.

18. The correct answer is **A**. When a CPU runs hot due to worn thermal paste, it can lead to system instability and crashes. High temperatures can cause the CPU to perform slowly and trigger thermal protection mechanisms, resulting in system instability and unexpected shutdowns to prevent damage from excessive heat. Other options are potential concerns associated with high CPU temperatures; they are not directly caused by worn thermal paste.

19. The correct answer is **A**. Increasing the RAM capacity improves the system performance when using multiple applications simultaneously. RAM acts as temporary storage for active applications, enabling efficient management and access to data. More RAM allows applications to operate without frequent data swapping, enhancing system responsiveness. Close unnecessary background processes and applications will not improve performance drastically. Installing a faster SSD (Solid-State Drive) can enhance storage performance and application loading times but may not specifically address multitasking performance. Increasing the CPU clock speed can improve application performance, but it may not be the most efficient solution when dealing with multiple applications simultaneously, as it may lead to increased heat generation and power consumption.

20. The correct answer is **B**. The Molex connector is primarily used for connecting fans and cooling devices. It provides power to the fans and allows for speed control and monitoring. All other options are incorrect.

21. The correct answer is **A**. In a degraded state, one or more disks in the RAID array have failed or are experiencing issues, and the system operates with reduced redundancy and performance until the faulty disks are replaced. None of the other options can work in a degraded state.

22. The correct answer is **D**. When some keys on the keyboard do not work and there is no physical damage, a potential cause could be a misconfiguration in the BIOS settings. Incorrect BIOS settings related to the keyboard can result in non-functional keys. Checking and adjusting the keyboard settings in the BIOS settings can help resolve the issue and restore the functionality of the affected keys. While software compatibility issues, incorrect keyboard layout settings, or outdated keyboard drivers can also cause keyboard problems, in this scenario, the BIOS settings are most likely.

23. The correct answer is **A**. The boot password acts as a security measure, ensuring that only authorized users can make changes to the BIOS configuration and protecting sensitive system settings from unauthorized modification. All other options are incorrect.

24. The correct answer is **A**. HSMs securely store and manage cryptographic keys, providing a high level of security for sensitive information such as encryption keys, certificates, and digital signatures. All other options and incorrect.

25. The correct answer is **A**. The purpose of multithreading in computer systems is to increase parallel processing and improve performance. Multithreading enables the execution of multiple threads or tasks simultaneously, allowing for better utilization of CPU resources and faster completion of tasks. All other options are incorrect.

26. The correct answer is **B**. To enable virtualization in your system, you need to access the BIOS settings and enable the "Virtualization Technology," "Intel VT-x" (for Intel processors), or "AMD-V" (for AMD processors) option. This setting allows the CPU to support virtualization instructions. Updating the BIOS firmware may also be necessary to ensure compatibility and access to the latest features, but is not the main reason. Hardware or installed drivers are not the main reasons virtualization will not run.

27. The correct answer is **A**. Advanced risk computing, such as Intel's Advanced RISC Machines (ARM) architecture and multicore processors, offers improved performance and efficiency compared to traditional computing architectures. The use of advanced instruction sets and parallel processing allows for faster execution of tasks and more efficient resource utilization. All other options are incorrect.

28. The correct answer is **A**. Intel architecture plays a crucial role in enabling high-performance computing applications. With features such as advanced instruction sets, cache hierarchy, and integrated memory controllers, Intel processors provide the performance and capabilities required for demanding computational tasks. All other options are incorrect.

29. The correct answer is **A**. Multicore processors offer increased parallel processing capabilities by integrating multiple CPU cores on a single chip. This allows for the simultaneous execution of multiple threads and tasks, resulting in improved performance and faster task completion times. All other options are incorrect.

30. The correct answer is **B**. Intel Core M processors are specifically designed for ultra-thin notebooks, tablets, and 2-in-1 detachable devices. All other options are incorrect.

## 3.5 Given a scenario, install or replace the appropriate power supply

1.  The correct answer is **A**. Modular power supplies allow you to detach and connect only the necessary cables, minimizing cable mess inside the computer case. This improves airflow and facilitates easier maintenance and upgrades. All other options are incorrect.

2.  The correct answer is **A**. Installing dual power supplies with separate power sources ensures an uninterrupted power supply by providing redundant backup in the event of a power failure. Redundant power supplies do not affect storage capacity. Redundant power supplies do not enhance CPU performance. Redundant power supplies do not improve network connectivity.

3.  The correct answer is **A**. 3.3V: Orange or yellow (typically used in motherboards, network cards, and certain digital circuits); 5V: Red (commonly used in USB ports, power supplies, and various peripherals); 12V: Yellow or blue (frequently employed in power supplies, SATA connectors, and fans). All other options are wrong.

4.  The correct answer is **A**. ATX motherboards commonly use a 20-pin or 24-pin power connector, which supplies power to the motherboard and its components. These motherboards are widely used in desktop computers and provide various expansion slots and features to accommodate different hardware configurations. Mini-ITX (Information Technology eXtended) motherboards are compact and designed for small form factor systems. Micro-ATX motherboards are a smaller form factor variant of ATX motherboards. ITX (Information Technology eXtended) motherboards, including both Mini-ITX and Nano-ITX variants, are designed for ultra-compact systems.

5.  The correct answer is **A**. The main benefit of a modular power supply is the ability to customize cable management. With modular power supplies, you can connect only the necessary cables, resulting in a cleaner and more organized system. This improves airflow, enhances aesthetics, and simplifies maintenance and upgrades. High efficiency is not the primary advantage of modular power supplies. Modular power supplies do not impact cooling performance. Modular power supplies do not provide increased power output.

6.  The correct answer is **A**. In North America, the standard voltage for electrical devices is in the range of 110-120 VAC (Volts AC). This voltage range is commonly used for residential and commercial applications in North America and are designed to deliver power within this range. On the other hand, in Europe and many other regions around the world, the standard voltage for electrical devices is in the range of 220-240 VAC. All other options are wrong.

7.  The correct answer is **A**. Redundant power supplies ensure uninterrupted power flow by utilizing backup power sources or UPS systems during outages, minimizing downtime, and preserving productivity in the office. Redundant power supplies do not increase the number of power outlets. Redundant power supplies have nothing to do with office furniture. Backup generators can provide power during outages. They are not considered redundant power supply systems.

8.  The correct answer is **B**. For a typical desktop computer, a power supply with a wattage rating of around 500 W is often sufficient. This should provide enough power to support the CPU, graphics card, storage drives, and other peripherals commonly found in a standard desktop setup. 300 W will not give you enough power. 750 W/1,000 W will pull more power than the standard desktop and be used by a gaming machine.

## 3.6 Given a scenario, deploy and configure multifunction devices/ printers and settings

1.  The correct answer is **B**. The carbon paper is not aligned properly in the printer, causing the first page to print lighter. The alignment of the carbon paper in dot matrix printers is crucial for accurate and consistent printing. If the carbon paper is not aligned properly, it can result in lighter print on the first page while the subsequent pages may still be legible. All other options are incorrect.

2.  The correct answer is **D**. The primary corona wire charges the photosensitive drum uniformly during the charging stage. This prepares the drum for the subsequent stages of the printing process. All other options are incorrect.

3.  The correct answer is **A**. Laser printers utilize a laser beam or LED light source to create an electrostatic image on a photosensitive drum. They also use toner. Dot matrix printers create images by using a series of pins that strike an inked ribbon, producing dot patterns on the paper. Thermal printers use heat to activate special heat-sensitive paper, resulting in the formation of images or text. Impact printers create images by physically striking an inked ribbon against the paper, typically using a series of pins or hammers.

4.  The correct answer is **A**. Configuring the MFD with the IP address of an SMTP server. To use the scan-to-email functionality, the MFD needs to be set up with the IP address of an SMTP (Simple Mail Transfer Protocol) server. This server is responsible for accepting the scanned document as an attachment and delivering it as an email. Authentication may also be required by the SMTP server to ensure secure and authorized access for sending the email. All other options are incorrect.

5.  The correct answer is **C**. Print servers enable print sharing among multiple computers, allowing them to connect and send print jobs to a shared printer, improving printing efficiency and simplifying printer management. Devices can download print drivers from the print server. All other options are incorrect.

6.  The correct answer is **A**. Implementing user authentication and access control measures ensures that only authorized individuals have permission to use the printer. This can be achieved through various methods, such as requiring user login credentials or using access cards/badges to authenticate users before allowing them to print. All other options are incorrect.

7. The correct answer is **B**. Dot matrix printers create images by using a series of pins that strike an inked ribbon, producing dot patterns on the paper. Laser printers utilize a laser beam or LED light source to create an electrostatic image on a photosensitive drum. Thermal printers use heat to activate special heat-sensitive paper, resulting in the formation of images or text. Impact printers create images by physically striking an inked ribbon against the paper, typically using a series of pins or hammers.

8. The correct answer is **A**. The charging stage involves applying a uniform charge to the photosensitive drum using a corona wire. This prepares the drum for the next step in the printing process. In the exposing stage, a laser beam or LED light source is used to selectively discharge the charged areas on the drum, creating an electrostatic image of the printed content. During the developing stage, toner particles are attracted to the areas of the drum that have been discharged, forming a visible image on the drum's surface. The transferring stage involves transferring the toner image from the drum onto the paper or another media. An electric field is applied to pull the toner from the drum onto the paper, resulting in the image being transferred. In the fusing stage, heat and pressure are applied to melt and bond the toner particles onto the paper, creating a permanent image. This is typically done using a fuser assembly that contains heated rollers. After each printing cycle, the cleaning stage ensures that any residual toner or debris is removed from the drum surface. This is important to maintain print quality and prevent contamination of subsequent printouts.

9. The correct answer is **C**. Thermal printers use heat to activate special heat-sensitive paper, resulting in the formation of images or text. Laser printers utilize a laser beam or LED light source to create an electrostatic image on a photosensitive drum. They also use toner. Dot matrix printers create images by using a series of pins that strike an inked ribbon, producing dot patterns on the paper. Impact printers create images by physically striking an inked ribbon against the paper, typically using a series of pins or hammers.

10. The correct answers are **A** and **B**. Poor print quality can be caused by low ink or toner levels, which can result in faded or streaky prints. Additionally, using low-quality paper can also affect print quality, leading to smudges, bleeding ink, or a lack of sharpness in the prints. It is important to ensure both ink/toner levels and paper quality are adequate for the desired print results. The printer driver needing an update would not directly cause poor print quality. Incorrect printer settings may affect print quality, but they are not the primary cause.

11. The correct answer is **A**. The toner on the paper is fused and melted into the fibers through heat and pressure during the fusing stage. This ensures that the toner becomes permanently bonded to the paper and produces a durable printout. All other options are incorrect.

12. The correct answers are **A** and **B**. The issue could be due to the top paper tray having run out of paper and documents are now being printed on more expensive labels. Additionally, selecting the wrong paper tray from the printer settings or in the print dialog can also cause the documents to be printed on labels instead of paper. The printer driver needing an update would not directly cause the issue of printing on labels instead of paper. Low ink or toner levels would not cause the issue of printing on labels instead of paper.

13. The correct answer is **A**. Enable DHCP reservation. By enabling DHCP reservation, you can assign a specific IP address to the printer based on its MAC address, ensuring it always receives the same IP when connecting to the network. A static IP address does not use DHCP. Restarting the router has nothing to do with DHCP. A USB cable has nothing to do with obtaining an IP address.

14. The correct answer is **A**. Configuring the MFD with the path to a suitably configured file server and shared folder. To utilize the scan-to-folder functionality using SMB, the MFD needs to be set up with the network path to a properly configured file server and shared folder. Each user must also have the necessary write permissions on the shared folder to save the scanned documents. All other options are incorrect.

15. The correct answer is **A**. Uploading the scan as a file to a document storage and sharing account in the cloud. When using the scan-to-cloud feature, the scanned document is uploaded and saved as a file on a cloud-based document storage and sharing account, such as OneDrive or Dropbox. All other options are incorrect.

16. The correct answer is **A**. Enabling printing only when authorized users insert a PIN ensures that users are at the printer and therefore prevents print jobs from being sent to the printer and forgotten about. All other options are incorrect.

## 3.7 Given a scenario, install and replace the printer consumables

1. The correct answer is **C**. The charging stage in a laser printer is performed by the corona wire. The corona wire is a thin wire located close to the photosensitive drum. It applies a uniform charge to the drum, preparing it for the subsequent stages of the printing process. All other options are incorrect.

2. The correct answer is **A**. The type A USB connector is the most common and recognizable USB connector type. It is typically used for connecting printers and other peripheral devices to a computer. The type B USB connector is less common and often used for connecting devices such as scanners. The type C USB connector is a newer, more versatile connector that is becoming increasingly popular. However, it is not the standard connector used for printers. The micro-USB connector is a smaller version of the type B connector and is commonly used for mobile devices, but not typically used for printers.

3. The correct answer is **B**. The wrong paper orientation is selected in the printer settings; the printed document will come out with the incorrect orientation. The printer driver is responsible for the communication between the computer and the printer, but it does not determine the paper orientation. Low ink or toner levels would not affect the paper orientation. The paper size being incorrect would result in printing on the wrong size paper, not necessarily the wrong paper orientation.

4.  The correct answer is **B**. Installing the latest printer driver compatible with Windows 10 is crucial for proper functionality. The printer driver acts as a bridge between the printer hardware and the operating system, allowing the computer to understand and send print commands to the printer. All other options may be important, but they are not the most important reasons to ensure functionality.

5.  The correct answer is **B**. The printers are connected to a central print server that handles wireless print jobs. In a network with multiple printers, a central print server is typically used to manage and distribute print jobs wirelessly. This server acts as an intermediary between the devices sending the print jobs and the printers themselves, ensuring efficient and organized printing across multiple devices. Setting up separate Wi-Fi networks for each printer would be impractical and inefficient. While printers may have unique IP addresses, they typically communicate with devices through a central print server or network protocols rather than direct communication. Wireless printing eliminates the need for physical connections such as USB cables.

6.  The correct answer is **B**. Stereolithography (SLA) is a 3D printing technology that uses liquid resin materials cured by a laser to build objects layer by layer. SLA printers offer high-resolution, detailed prints, making them a popular choice for applications requiring fine details. Fused Deposition Modeling (FDM) is a 3D printing technology that uses thermoplastic filaments, not liquid resin materials. Selective Laser Sintering (SLS) uses powdered materials, typically plastics or metals, to create 3D objects. It does not involve the use of liquid resin materials. Digital Light Processing (DLP) is another 3D printing technology that uses liquid resin materials cured by a light source, typically a digital projector. DLP operates similarly to SLA but with a different light source.

7.  The correct answers are **A**, **B**, **C**, **D**, and **E**. They are all correct. Connect the printer to a computer acting as the print server. This computer will manage the print jobs and allow other computers to connect to the shared printer. Install printer drivers on each computer. This ensures that the computers can communicate with the printer and send print jobs. Enable printer sharing in the printer's properties on the print server computer. This allows other computers on the network to access and use the shared printer. Access the network settings on client computers and select the shared printer. This allows the client computers to connect to the shared printer and send print jobs to it. Test the print-sharing functionality by sending a print job from a client computer. This ensures that the print-sharing setup is working correctly.

8.  The correct answer is **B**. Printer Control Language (PCL) is commonly used for printing text-based documents without complex formatting, such as simple word processing documents or basic office documents. PCL provides efficient and reliable printing capabilities for these types of documents. PostScript or printer-specific image enhancement technologies ensure accurate color reproduction and precise image rendering. All other options are incorrect.

9.  The correct answers are **A**, **B**, and **E**. Removing all protective tapes and packaging materials is essential to ensure that the print device is ready for use and to prevent any obstructions or damage during operation. Leave the device unboxed and powered off for a few hours to reduce risks of condensation forming within an appliance that has moved from a cold storage/transport environment to a warmer installation environment. Print devices are heavy, so make sure you use safe lifting techniques. It may require two persons to lift it safely.

10. The correct answers are **A** and **C**. Heating the extruder to a specific temperature is a common step in replacing filament in a 3D printer. By heating the extruder, the filament becomes soft and can be manually removed, allowing for easy replacement with a new filament. Pull as much of the old filament out as possible, then push the new filament through.

11. The correct answer is **A**. Fused Deposition Modeling (FDM) is a 3D printing technology that uses filament materials, typically thermoplastics such as ABS or PLA. The filament is melted and extruded through a nozzle to build objects layer by layer. Stereolithography (SLA) uses liquid resin materials, not filament materials, for 3D printing. Selective Laser Sintering (SLS) involves the use of powdered materials, such as plastics or metals, rather than filaments. Digital Light Processing (DLP) also uses liquid resin materials, similar to SLA, but with a different light source for curing. It does not use filament materials.

12. The correct answer is **B**. The printer creates its own Wi-Fi network for devices to connect and print wirelessly. Wi-Fi direct is a technology that allows devices to establish a direct wireless connection with each other, bypassing the need for a traditional Wi-Fi network. In the case of Wi-Fi direct printing, the printer acts as a Wi-Fi access point and creates its own network. Devices can then connect to this network and send print jobs wirelessly to the printer. Wi-Fi direct printing does not require an existing Wi-Fi network for connectivity. Wi-Fi direct printing does not use cables. Wi-Fi direct and Bluetooth are separate wireless technologies, therefore Bluetooth cannot be used.

13. The correct answer is **A**. A printer maintenance kit usually contains a new fuser assembly, which is the main component of the kit. Additionally, it includes a transfer/secondary charge roller and paper transport rollers for each tray, which consist of pickup rollers and a new separation pad. These components are essential for maintaining the proper functioning of the printer. Other items such as toner cartridges, ink cartridges, printheads, and additional paper trays are not typically included in a maintenance kit. All other options are incorrect.

14. The correct answer is **A**. PostScript is a page description language that excels at rendering complex graphics and images. It provides advanced capabilities for accurately representing graphical elements, including vector graphics, gradients, and shading. Printer Control Language (PCL) is commonly used for printing text-based documents without complex formatting, such as simple word processing documents or basic office documents.

# Chapter 4: Virtualization and Cloud Computing

## 4.1 Summarize cloud computing concepts

1. The correct answer is **B**. Infrastructure as a Service (IaaS) is a cloud computing service model in which a Cloud Service Provider (CSP) provides the hardware but nothing else. This is ideal when you want to move desktop computers to the cloud. To do this, you would install the operating system, configure it, and patch it. All other answers are incorrect. Software as a Service (SaaS) is a model in which a vendor creates an application, such as Salesforce, and companies lease the application. Security as a Service (SECaaS) is a model in which companies provide cloud identity management services through an external source. An example of this is Okta, which can provide SAML tokens. Monitoring as a Service (MaaS) is a model in which a cloud service provider monitors your network and servers for you.

2. The correct answer is **A**. With a hybrid cloud, a company has employees working in both on-premises and cloud infrastructures. It is the only cloud model that retains on-premises data centers. All other answers are incorrect. A private cloud is a single-tenant model as it is the only entity hosted in that cloud. It can also be hosted on the company's infrastructure. A community cloud is a type of model in which companies from the same industry share resources. Public cloud models use a multi-tenant infrastructure as the CSP hosts many different companies on the same servers.

3. The correct answer is **C**. Infrastructure as a Service (IaaS) provides companies with hardware, but they need to install operating systems, configure them, and patch them. All other answers are incorrect. Platform as a Service (PaaS) provides developers with the tools to create their own customized software. Software as a Service (SaaS) provides common applications on a subscription basis. Disaster Recovery as a Service (DRaaS) is needed when a massive disaster happens, such as a tornado or tsunami.

4. The correct answer is **B**. Software as a Service (SaaS) provides ready-made software. An example of this is Microsoft 365 (M365), which comes equipped with various applications, including Outlook for email, as well as optional add-in applications such as GoldMine and Salesforce. All other answers are incorrect. Platform as a Service (PaaS) provides developers with the tools to create their own customized software. Infrastructure as a Service (IaaS) provides companies with hardware, but they need to install operating systems, configure them, and patch them. Monitoring as a Service (MaaS) is a type of service in which a cloud service provider monitors your network for you.

5. The correct answer is **D**. A private cloud is single-tenant and ensures you have total control over all assets, including the storage and management of proprietary data. All other answers are incorrect. A hybrid cloud is a mixture of on-premises and cloud storage, meaning that not all data would be migrated to the cloud as desired. A community cloud is utilized by a group of people from the same industry sharing resources to create customized applications. A public cloud is a multi-tenant model on which multiple companies share resources and would thus not allow a single company total control of data.

6. The correct answer is **C**. Metered utilization measures the resources that are being consumed by a customer so that they are only required to pay for what they use. All other answers are incorrect. Unlimited resources for free is not a cost-effective option and is not allowable by any cloud service, including metered utilization. There is no reserve pool of resources in the cloud as a CSP can increase or decrease resources at the drop of a hat. There is no restriction for critical resources; you can purchase as many resources as you require.

7. The correct answer is **C**. In a community cloud model, companies within the same industry (for example, a group of law firms or hospitals) share the cost of creating and sharing resources. Each industry has its own software requirements. A private cloud is a single tenant and does not share resources, thereby allowing greater control over stored data than other cloud models. A public cloud model has a multi-tenant infrastructure in which users do not share the cost of creating resources. In a hybrid cloud, a company will both retain an on-premises environment and store some assets in the cloud.

8. The correct answer is **B**. By using a Virtual Desktop Infrastructure (VDI), separate virtual desktops can be allocated to each consultant. VDI uses a pool of virtual desktops with the same configuration, thereby maintaining a consistent desktop. Since the processing of the data is done on the virtual desktop, it secures and protects it against theft. The consultants would need a very low-spec machine that runs a thin client (that is, one that uses only mouse clicks and keyboard strokes) to access it. The company therefore maintains total control of the data. All other answers are incorrect. Once data is downloaded onto a surface laptop (that is, a foreign machine), the company loses all control of the data. Terminal servers are legacy servers that used to be accessed by thin clients, but this technology is now redundant. IaaS only provides the hardware (for example, virtual desktops), but the company still needs to install the operating system and may not be able to provide a consistent desktop.

9. The correct answer is **C**. With Platform as a Service (PaaS), the Cloud Service Provider (CSP) provides the application so that companies can offer their own bespoke (that is, customized) applications, such as MySQL, PHP, Azure, Oracle Database, and Google App Engine, to name a few. All other answers are incorrect. For Software as a Service (SaaS), the vendor has already created an application, for example, Office 365, Salesforce, or GoldMine. Infrastructure as a Service (IaaS) is a cloud service in which the CSP provides the hardware, such as servers, computers, switches, and firewalls. The customer then installs the software, configures it, and patches it. The private cloud is a single-tenant cloud model and would not meet this company's requirements.

10. The correct answer is **D**. The public cloud model is known as multi-tenant as the CSP hosts many different companies on the same servers. All other answers are incorrect. The private cloud model is known as single-tenant as there is only one entity hosted in that cloud. As it ensures exclusive access to resources and is isolated from everyone else, this tenant has total control of their environment. In a community cloud model, companies from the same industry share resources. The hybrid cloud is where a company has infrastructure on-premises as well as in the cloud.

11. The correct answer is **B**. A private cloud model would be the most appropriate purchase for this law firm as it would allow them to isolate their data entirely from all other entities as the single tenant on their host server. All other answers are incorrect. Public cloud models are multi-tenant, and there is a risk of shared tenancy, meaning that another company hosted on the same server would be able to access their data. A hybrid cloud is a model in which a company has some employees on-premises and some working from the cloud, meaning that not all company data would be migrated to the cloud. On a community cloud, companies in the same industry share both costs and resources. Like the public cloud model, this means that the law firm would not retain full control over all their migrated data.

12. The correct answer is **C**. Shared resources means that the cloud provider has a pool of hardware that can be allocated to any of their customers. All other answers are incorrect. Dynamic resource allocation means that a computer or server can adjust the allocation of resources, such as CPU or RAM, according to business demands. There is no such thing as a backup pool. System sprawl means that the consumption of resources by servers exceeds the available resources in a host's virtual environment.

13. The correct answer is **B**. High availability means that a server experiences very little downtime (the five nines), and in fact, observes 99.999% uptime. All other answers are incorrect. VDI is a pool of virtual desktops. Clustering means that two servers share the same quorum disk, in which one is normally active and the other passive; that is, it is on standby waiting for the active server to fail so that it can take over. Shared resources are a pool of hardware resources in a cloud provider's data center that are allocated to any customer that requests additional resources.

14. The correct answer is **C**. Rapid elasticity would allow the toy company to instantly increase and decrease cloud resources according to demand. All other answers are incorrect. Clustering means that two servers share the same quorum disk, in which one is normally active and the other passive, meaning that it is on standby waiting for the active server to fail so that it can take over. Shared resources mean that a cloud provider has a pool of resources that they can allocate to different companies instantly. They are not reserved for any one person. Metered utilization means the CSP will produce a dashboard for a customer so that they can monitor the cost and consumption of resources, such as storage, CPU cores, and bandwidth.

15. The correct answer is **A**. A company could host a private cloud on its own network, ensuring that cloud data is still available if the internet goes down. All other answers are incorrect. A community cloud allows one or more entities to share the storage cost and resources. It is maintained by a CSP and accessed via the internet. With an SaaS, a company develops an application that is leased by companies and accessed via the internet. A public cloud uses a multi-tenant infrastructure in which access to the public cloud is accessed via the internet. None of these three would permit access to cloud data if there is no internet connection.

16. The correct answer is **B**. Virtual Desktop Infrastructure (VDI) is the provision of desktops. The cloud service that relates to this is Desktop as a Service (DaaS), in which the CSP offers VDI (that is, provides desktops). All other answers are incorrect. Software as a Service (SaaS) is where the vendor has already created an application (for example, Office 365, Salesforce, or GoldMine), which you use in its default format. With Platform as a Service (PaaS), the Cloud Service Provider (CSP) provides an application so that companies can provide their own bespoke (customized) applications, such as MySQL, PHP, Azure, Oracle Database, and Google App Engine, to name a few. Infrastructure as a Service (IaaS) is a type of service in which the CSP provides the hardware, such as servers, computers, switches, and firewalls. The customer then installs the software and configures and patches it.

17. The correct answer is **B**. The private cloud model is known as single-tenant as only one entity is hosted in that cloud. It can also be hosted on the company's infrastructure. All other answers are incorrect. In a hybrid cloud, a company has an on-premises environment as well as in the cloud. A community cloud hosts multiple companies from the same industry that share resources. Public cloud models are known as multi-tenant as the CSP hosts many different companies on the same servers.

18. The correct answer is **A** and **D**. Software as a Service (SaaS) is a type of cloud service in which a company develops an application and leases it on a pay-as-you-go model. Your employees can gain access to the application through a web browser. Office 365 provides a built-in email solution, and Spotify is a music platform. All other answers are incorrect. Azure developer tools are an example of Platform as a Service (PaaS) as these tools give you a developer environment where you can build your own mobile applications. Home Depot is an on-premises shop that sells DIY products.

19. The correct answer is **A**. Virtual Desktop Infrastructure (VDI) enables separate virtual desktops to be allocated to each consultant. VDI uses a pool of virtual desktops with the same configuration, thereby maintaining a consistent desktop. Since data processing is done on the virtual desktop, the data is protected against theft. This makes it secure. The consultants would need a very low-level spec machine that runs a thin client (that is, one that uses only mouse clicks and keyboard strokes) to access it. All other answers are incorrect. SaaS is a cloud service in which a company develops an application that is leased by companies and accessed via the internet. The company does not have full control of the desktops. A Virtual Private Network (VPN) is a solution that will create a tunnel across the internet; it does not provide desktops. Remote Desktop Protocol (RDP) is a Microsoft solution for providing remote connections for an administrator to a Windows desktop or server.

20. The correct answer is **D**. File synchronization is an automated advantage of cloud storage that allows the file to be shared across different devices, such as a smartphone and a tablet. All other answers are incorrect. Multiple users can simultaneously access the content. Resource exhaustion means that a computer is running out of resources such as CPU cores, RAM, or disk space. Dynamic resource allocation means that a host can be allocated resources as they are needed; it has nothing to do with cloud storage. File sharing is not an automated process; access to files is done through a mapped drive.

21. The correct answer is **B**. The virtual desktop is on a virtual host, and if there is no network connection, then the desktop cannot be accessed. All other answers are incorrect. In a VDI environment, nothing is copied to the local desktop. Snapshots are a much faster way to recover a guest's machine. A Citrix connection is very fast as it is a thin client, meaning it uses only mouse clicks and keyboard strokes; this makes it an advantage. Disaster recovery being provided by the cloud provider is also an advantage.

22. The correct answer is **D**. Infrastructure as a Service (IaaS) provides the hardware so that the company can move all 10 servers and 50 desktops to the cloud, though they will still need to install the operating system and configure and patch them. All other answers are incorrect. Platform as a Service (PaaS) provides developers with the tools to create their own customized software and mobile applications. Software as a Service (SaaS) provides ready-made software (for example, M365) or common applications such as GoldMine and Salesforce. Monitoring as a Service (MaaS) allows a cloud provider to continuously monitor your network and applications. None of these last three services would be appropriate for the migration described in the given scenario.

23. The correct answer is **B**. Rapid elasticity enables cloud resources to be instantly increased or decreased according to demand. All other answers are incorrect. Rapid deployment describes rapid elasticity but does not exist as a concept in this exam. A load balancer controls access to an array of web servers to give the client a faster browsing experience. Metered utilization means that the CSP will produce a dashboard for a customer through which they can monitor their consumption of resources such as storage, CPU cores, and bandwidth.

## 4.2 Summarize aspects of client-side virtualization

1. The correct answer is **A**. A Type 1 hypervisor runs on a bare-metal virtual platform. This means that there is no operating system. Examples of this are Microsoft's Hyper V, VMware's ESX Server, and Citrix's XenServer. All other answers are incorrect. Type 2 hypervisors run on software (Windows 10, for example). There are no Type 3 or 4 hypervisors.

2. The correct answer is **A**. A resource pool can be created with additional RAM and CPU cores, which can be allocated to a database resource pool so that the database servers can utilize them as described in this scenario. All other answers are incorrect. System sprawl means that server consumption exceeds host resources in a virtual environment. Network segmentation only divides your network; it does not manage resources. Metered utilization is used by the cloud to charge for the consumption of additional resources.

3. The correct answer is **D**. A Virtual Machine (VM) escape is a type of attack in which an attacker uses a guest virtual machine to attack either another guest virtual machine, the hypervisor, or the host. All other answers are incorrect. Pivoting is a type of attack in which an attacker gains access to a computer on a physical network and attacks another computer or server. VM sprawl means that an unmanaged virtual machine has been added to your virtual network. A snapshot is a backup of a whole virtual machine that can be rolled back when there is a problem with the virtual machine.

4.  The correct answer is **B**. Oracle VirtualBox runs on a type 2 hypervisor, meaning that it must sit on top of an operating system such as Windows 10. All other answers are incorrect. A type 1 hypervisor runs on a bare-metal virtual platform, meaning that there is no operating system. Examples of this include Microsoft's Hyper-V, VMware's ESX Server, and Citrix's XenServer. There are no type 3 or type 5 hypervisors.

5.  The correct answer is **B**, **D**, and **E**. A sandbox is a virtual machine that is used to isolate applications in order to safely test new software, examine applications that might contain malware, and ensure that application patches do not have an adverse effect on software. All other answers are incorrect. A sandbox does not contain sand; it has nothing to do with fires. It tests software but not hardware.

6.  The correct answer is **C** and **D**. It is possible to build a virtual machine and install a legacy operating system, followed by the legacy application. You can then install Hyper-V on a Windows 11 desktop and import the virtual machine, enabling the legacy application to run. All other answers are incorrect. The application was built for a Windows operating system and is therefore unlikely to run on a Linux operating system. A sandbox is an isolated virtual machine and could not be used to run the legacy application. A SQL server is a database server and should not have any other applications running on it.

7.  The correct answer is **A**. Second Level Address Translation (SLAT) improves the performance of virtual memory when multiple virtual machines (guest machines) are installed. All other answers are incorrect. SLAT is not related to networking or throttling the processor. It definitely does not stop virtual memory from being used.

8.  The correct answer is **D**. Cross-platform virtualization means that software applications are tested with multiple operating systems, with their own resource constraints, prior to release. All other answers are incorrect. Installing applications on different versions of hypervisors is not a description of cross-platform virtualization. You cannot network sandboxes as they are isolated virtual machines. If you test applications one at a time, you are using the same operating system, not cross-platform virtualization.

9.  The correct answer is **D**. Bridged networking is a method by which a virtual client using a type 2 hypervisor is connected to a host virtual machine's physical network card, allowing it to join the virtual network. Here's a reference you can go through: `https://packt.link/UosZ9`. All other answers are incorrect. A Network Address Translator (NAT) hides the internal network when internal users browse the internet. An attacker would join the LAN that the host resides on, not the host itself. A virtual private network is a network that allows guest virtual machines to have their own isolated network.

10. The correct answer is **B** and **E**. The easiest method to accomplish the professor's goal is to use Virtual Desktop Infrastructure (VDI), whereby each student's virtual machine can set its virtual desktop experience to non-permanent. This way, when the students log off, the image will revert to the original image without saving any changes. Another way to do this is to build virtual machines and create snapshots, which can then be reset between classes. All other answers are incorrect. Using a ghost image could take up to 45 minutes to reimage each desktop, which would not be an effective solution if there is insufficient time between classes. Taking a data backup will not resolve anything in this case. Implementing a system could take as long as using a ghost image.

11. The correct answer is **C**. Virtual machine sprawl is where an unmanaged virtual machine is placed on a virtual network. It poses a security risk as the unmanaged virtual machine may not be patched and an attacker could use it to gain access to your network. All other answers are incorrect. System sprawl occurs when servers overconsume host resources in a virtual environment. A sandbox is an isolated virtual machine used for testing applications and software patches and investigating malware.

12. The correct answer is **C**. Fiber Channel provides a very fast connection to a Storage Area Network (SAN) and is the best choice in this scenario. A SAN uses extremely fast disks that are already configured with built-in redundancy. All other answers are incorrect. RAID 0 is neither fault tolerant nor suitable for a virtual network, though it could be used for a proxy server's cache. A Local Area Network (LAN) is not a storage solution. RAID 5 is redundant, but Hard Disk Drives (HDDs) are too slow.

13. The correct answer is **B**. Isolation means that you separate a virtual machine from the guest or another virtual machine. Here's a reference you can go through: `https://packt.link/URHYE`. All other answers are incorrect. A DMZ is a physical network that sits between the Local Area Network (LAN) and the Wide Area Network (WAN). Docker is used to separate applications from your infrastructure and is particularly useful for developers creating software. A snapshot is a backup of a virtual machine that will allow you to revert to previous settings.

14. The correct answer is **A** and **C**. The problem described in this scenario is virtual machine sprawl, the process of deploying unmanaged virtual machines onto a network. The consultant will likely recommend a two-step solution. The first would be to deploy virtual machines using a template. This would ensure that a consistent baseline is maintained, and the image is patched. The second step is to use SolarWinds Virtualization Manager to prevent virtual machine sprawl, as it has built-in sprawl management capability. All other answers are incorrect. Installing anti-virus on unmanaged virtual machines would be futile. These unmanaged virtual machines might have more vulnerabilities than just anti-virus. Removing these unmanaged machines is a step forward, but it does not prevent reoccurrence.

15. The correct answer is **C**. Virtual Technology for Directed Inputs/Output (VT-d) allows the virtual machine to access the underlying hardware that resides on the host. All other answers are incorrect. When you are preparing to run a hypervisor, you will see an option to turn on Intel VT-d in your BIOS. Here's a reference you can go through: `https://packt.link/ POvT5`. Virtual Technology Extensions (VT-x) are used in x86 platforms to allow the virtual machine to access the hardware. A host machine using more than 4 GB of RAM (such as that described) is 64-bit and needs VT-d. Multi-cores allow better performance from the processors. Intel Graphics Virtual Technology (Intel GVT) provides near-native graphic performance on a virtual machine. Neither of these will resolve the current issue.

16. The correct answer is **B** and **C**. An Uninterruptible Power Supply (UPS) is similar to a battery in that it holds a charge and, in the event of a very short power outage, can supply power to the company's servers. If power loss exceeds a few seconds, a UPS can be used to shut down the virtual host gracefully. All other answers are incorrect. The UPS cannot keep the host running if there is a total power loss; that would require a generator. The UPS is a backup power supply and cannot be used to boot up computers, servers, or other devices.

17. The correct answer is **C**. One example of container virtualization is Docker. It only virtualizes the application layer and sits on top of the operating system. This makes writing applications and testing code much more efficient. All other answers are incorrect. A virtual machine backup is called a snapshot. A sandbox is used to test malware. A virtual machine escape occurs when the hypervisor, host, or guest virtual machines are attacked.

18. The correct answer is **D**. Application virtualization is a process by which you can run an application from a remote server, but it has the appearance of running locally. This is great when a virtual machine does not have enough resources to run the application locally. All other answers are incorrect. A sandbox is not a live environment. It is an isolated virtual machine that tests applications and software patches and investigates malware. Installing an application locally on the virtual machine is not how one performs application virtualization. A container such as Docker is used for application development and is not part of application virtualization.

# Chapter 5: Hardware and Network Troubleshooting

## 5.1 Given a scenario, apply the best-practice methodology to resolve the problem

1.  The correct answer is **C**. The first stage is to identify the problem with the printer and ignore any solution that a user gives you. After this, you will establish a possible cause, and then test the theory and implement a plan of action.

2.  The correct answer is **C**. The junior administrator has violated company policies. The standard operating procedure would state that any server updates should be done out of hours. They did not carry out patch management as that would be an enterprise solution. They just applied a single update to a single server. They did not communicate with users, which is a poor practice but not the main reason for the incident. Since there was no incident before they patched the server, it is not the troubleshooting process we need to look at; therefore, we can rule it out and establish a plan of action.

3.  The correct answers are **B** and **C**. The first task that the support technician has is to identify the problem. They will ask the user what they did before the problem occurred and ask whether they made any changes to their laptop, for example, an operating system update. After identifying the problem, they should then back up the data before making any changes. Searching the vendor's website is part of "establishing a plan of action," which comes later in this process.

4.  The correct answer is **C**. After the incident has been resolved, the system administrator should document the findings, actions, and outcome. All other options occur before the incident has been resolved.

5.  The correct answer is **A**. They have just established a theory of a possible cause. They think that the cause is a recent Windows update. The next stage would be to test the theory, followed by establishing a plan of action. The problem was identified as soon as they started investigating the problem.

## 5.2 Given a scenario, troubleshoot problems related to motherboards, RAM, CPU, and power

1.  The correct answers are **B** and **D**. When replacing RAM, you should always power down the server and wear an electromagnetic static wrist strap. This will prevent you from damaging the RAM. Putting a machine in standby mode or trying to hot-swap RAM is not a good idea, as either could damage the RAM.

2.  The correct answer is **B**. Continuous beeps means that the problem is with the RAM modules or the memory controller. A motherboard problem can be either no beeps or 1 long followed by 2 short beeps. A power supply problem would have no beeps. A video adapter error can be 1 long beep followed by either 2, 3, or 4 short beeps.

3.  The correct answer is **B**. Before upgrading the CPU on a server, you should consult the manufacturer's website to identify the socket type of the motherboard. Then, search to see whether that socket type can be upgraded to a faster CPU. Backing up the data, turning the power off, and wearing an electromagnetic static wrist strap should be done prior to the upgrade.

4.  The correct answers are **A** and **D**. After installing memory modules, if they are not detected, check the BIOS. If they are not seen in the BIOS, the computer cannot read them; therefore, reset the memory modules to see whether they can be detected. Rebooting the computer will not help and an electromagnetic static wrist strap should be worn but does not detect RAM.

5.  The correct answers are **A** and **D**. If maintenance was carried out, the storage adapter cable may have been plugged in with the wrong orientation. Although the technician can hear the fan spinning, the PSU might have a fault preventing the power good signal from being sent to the CPU. Both of these faults will prevent the computer from carrying out the Power-On Self-Test (POST). A motherboard problem can be either no beeps or 1 long followed by 2 short beeps. It is very unlikely that a computer technician will not attach a monitor when booting up a computer.

6.  The correct answer is **C**. The clock time on a computer uses the real-time clock that is part of the chipset to keep the time, date, and calendar accurate. The real-time clock is powered by the CMOS battery, and if the clock keeps losing time, then the battery needs to be replaced. The power from the cable to the computer does not affect the computer clock. The PSU does not power the real-time clock. Obtaining a BIOS update does not affect the real-time clock.

7.  The correct answer is **B**. A capacitor absorbs spikes in the direct current voltage and then can temporally store charge. If the capacitor is faulty, then it becomes swollen, and if it is not removed, it will blow and cause damage to the computer. The CMOS battery powers the real-time clock and not the capacitor. The capacitor does not store data; the hard drive stores data.

8.  The correct answer is **B**. Windows 10 stores keys and biometric data in the local TPM; therefore, if fingerprints are not recognized, we need to clear the TPM. Restoring a system image will not repair biometric errors. Updating the BIOS will not prevent a biometric fingerprint problem.

9.  The correct answer is **D**. The problem is a video adapter error. This can be 1 long beep, followed by either 2, 3, or 4 short beeps. A motherboard problem can be either no beeps or 1 long followed by 2 short beeps. It cannot be a normal post because there is an error; however, a normal post would be 1 short beep. A power supply problem would have no beeps.

10. The correct answers are **A**, **C**, and **D**. The first thing to check is that there is power to the wall socket. Then, replace the power cable with a known good cable. After that, plug a lamp into the power socket to ensure you get power. Changing memory will not help power issues. If there was a problem with the memory modules, a continuous beep would be heard.

11. The correct answers are **A** and **C**. This is known as the "blue screen of death" and can be caused by a serious fault – either a system memory fault, a corruption of the operating system, or a device driver fault. A motherboard problem can be either no beeps or 1 long followed by 2 short beeps. Continuous beeps mean that the problem is with the RAM modules or the memory controller.

12. The correct answers are **A**, **B**, **C**, and **D**. A burning smell might occur if the CPU fan has stopped working. This will cause the CPU to overheat and the system might reboot or crash. If the heatsink that cools the CPU is not fitted properly or the thermal paste is old, then this can also cause the CPU to overheat. If the PSU is overheating, you will smell burning. If the fan vents are clogged with dust, it will stop the fan from working and cause components to overheat and you will then smell burning.

13. The correct answer is **B**. A computer will perform sluggishly if there has been an incorrect configuration change. A keyboard or a mouse not plugged in will not affect a computer's performance. A computer without a CPU will not boot up.

14. The correct answers are **B** and **C**. On an inkjet printer, a grinding noise indicates that there is a fault in the carriage mechanism. On a hard drive, any grinding or clicking indicates a mechanical problem. A healthy hard drive makes a low-level noise. A motherboard problem can be either no beeps or 1 long followed by 2 short beeps. Continuous beeps mean that the problem is with the RAM modules or the memory controller.

15. The correct answer is **C**. The keyboard has dust or debris stuck under some of the keyboard keys. You should use compressed air to clean between the keys. You should never vacuum a keyboard as it could suck up any loose keys. If you use a wet cloth, you may damage the electronics underneath the keyboard. Equally, sticky keys are an accessibility feature to help disabled people use the keyboard.

## 5.3 Given a scenario, troubleshoot and diagnose problems with storage drives and RAID arrays

1. The correct answer is **C**. Redundant Array of Independent Disks (RAID) 5 uses a minimum of three disks and produces a fast read speed. With RAID 5, you can lose one disk and still retain your data. RAID 0 does not provide fault tolerance or redundancy. RAID 1 is called mirroring. It uses only 2 disks, but it does not have the fast read speed that RAID 5 has; it is redundant, and you can lose one disk. RAID 6 uses a minimum of four disks. It provides fault tolerance and redundancy, as you can lose 2 disks.

2. The correct answer is **D**. RAID 5 can function if only one drive fails. If you remove a healthy disk, then the RAID controller will detect a two-drive failure and you will lose all your data. Although the hardware RAID will show the failed disk in red, option C does not answer the question posed. There is a risk with RAID 5 of you removing a second disk from the array, resulting in data loss. Pulling a healthy disk out when searching for the SCSI ID will result in data loss.

3. The correct answer is **C**. SMART is a Self-Monitoring, Analysis, and Reporting Technology tool that monitors the health of hard drives. When an error states that an imminent failure has been detected, then the disk is beyond repair, and you need to replace the disk. All other options are not viable.

4.   The correct answer is **C**. If you cannot boot from a hard drive but can see the data by using recovery software, then you should back up the data. At any time, this disk could fail. Although recovery software can access the data, it does not mean that the disk is bootable; therefore, you cannot boot from it even if you install recovery software on it. Formatting the disk will remove the data, and if the disk is not very healthy, it will not function properly.

5.   The correct answer is **D**. They will turn on BitLocker on the USB drive and then unlock the disk. The USB drive can now be used. An encrypted USB drive cannot be viewed in Disk Management. Turning BitLocker on in the C drive will not make encrypted data on a USB readable. Converting the USB drive into NTFS will lose all data residing on the USB drive.

6.   The correct answer is **C**. The SMART monitoring is reporting errors that are not there; therefore, it is malfunctioning. Disk management is functioning as we can use it to see that all disks are in a healthy state. The filesystem for corporate computers should be NTFS as it provides security. If a disk was missing from the RAID 5 set, then disk management would indicate it was either missing or in a degraded state.

7.   The correct answer is **B**. When a computer has a solid orange light, it indicates there is a hardware or driver problem with the hard drive. If there is a problem with the computer memory, you will hear continuous beeps. If the processor has a problem, then the computer screen will be black. If SMART monitoring has been disabled, then there will be no warning when there is a hard drive error.

8.   The correct answer is **C**. The first thing we should do is run the system diagnostic program that was supplied with the computer. This should reveal the cause of the extended read/write times. Launching SMART monitoring is a good idea after the system diagnostic check so that you can be notified of imminent disk failure. Swapping out the disk is premature as the system diagnostic test may find that there is a minor error. Disabling SMART monitoring is never a good idea.

9.   The correct answers are **B** and **D**. When a disk is in a degraded state, that means that the disk has failed. In a RAID 5 set, one disk can fail and the data will still be available. You should immediately back up the data. You cannot format a disk in a degraded state as it has failed.

10.  The correct answer is **C**. When the disk that holds the operating system fails it will generate a "missing operating system" error. If there is a disk missing from a RAID set, the error will say that one of the disks is degraded. If the computer is undergoing a Windows update, it will boot and then notify you it is updating. If the CMOS battery is failing, then the date and time will be wrong.

11.  The correct answer is **B**. If you believe that your storage device's performance is degraded, check the input/output operations per second (IOPS) against the manufacturer's baseline. A solid orange light indicates that there is a hard drive failure. Disk management cannot measure the performance of a storage device. A flashing green light indicates that your hard drive is healthy.

## 5.4 Given a scenario, troubleshoot video, projector, and display issues

1. The correct answer is **D**. The bulb on a projector has a finite lifespan, and when is it nearing the end of its life, the bulb starts to dim. This is called a burned-out bulb. You might hear a popping sound when it fails completely. Inverters, digitizers, or display settings cannot help a burned-out bulb.

2. The correct answer is **A**. If the projector is displaying a "no signal" error, either the cable is not connected properly or it is faulty and needs replacing. At this stage, the computer is not using its bulb. If the computer's monitor is broken, it should still project the computer's desktop. At this stage, it is too early to extend the display setting as we are not getting any signal.

3. The correct answer is **C**. If the projector has a fuzzy image, then the lens needs to be rotated until the lens shows a clear picture. If the cable was defective, it would say "no signal." The laptop display has no control over a fuzzy image. If the projector bulb needed to be replaced, then the image would be very dim.

4. The correct answer is **B**. The High-bandwidth Digital Content Protection (HDCP) allows a content source (such as a DVD/Blu-ray disc) to disable itself if the display adapter and monitor and/or speaker system do not support HDCP and fail to authenticate themselves with the playback source. If the HDMI cable was faulty, then a "no signal" error would appear. The display setting does not need to be adjusted as there is output on the projector. If there was a problem with the DVD player, then there would be no sound.

5. The correct answers are **C** and **D**. If we get a "no source found" error after changing the cables to known good cables, we need to project from the laptop to the projector. If we run the displayswitch.exe command, then we have four options to project and we should choose duplicate or extend, then the laptop image will be on the computer screen. We can also complete this from the display settings on the laptop. Choose multiple displays and then choose "duplicate these displays" or "extend these displays." There is no need to replace the projector bulb as errors are being displayed. Since the cables have just been replaced, there is no need to check the HDMI cable connection.

6. The correct answers are **A** and **C**. When using a projector from a laptop, if the connectors are not connected securely at both ends, then the screen will flicker. Flickering, flashing images or bright spots around the edges indicate that the backlight is failing. Checking the display setting or rebooting the laptop will not solve anything as it is a hardware error that is causing the problem.

7. The correct answer is **C**. The HDMI-ARC allows the audio from the TV to be sent to an external sound system. If we don't use this port, then the soundbar will not receive any audio from the TV. It is unlikely that the soundbar does not have any power. A soundbar does not have volume control; the volume is controlled by the TV remote. Video resolution has nothing to do with sound.

8.  The correct answer is **C**. When a monitor shows either pink or purple discoloration, it is probably caused by a faulty or loose cable. Display burn-in shows a ghost image of the previous image on the screen. The color here covers the whole screen. A faulty graphics card will show a flickering screen but, in this instance, there is no flickering screen. A burned-out bulb will cause the screen to be dim.

9.  The correct answer is **B**. When the cursor keeps drifting, then you need to calibrate the screen to fix it. A discolored screen would be a video cable problem. There is no mention of a graphics driver update; therefore, rolling back the driver is not an option. Changing the screen resolution will not fix this problem; it will merely change the size of the screen.

10. The correct answers are **B** and **C**. The projector is overheating, which is why it is intermittently rebooting. We would first check that the fans are working, that no dust or obstruction is stopping the fan from working, and that the air vents are free from dust or obstruction. You might check that the power cable is plugged in properly, but you should not change the cable at this time. The projector display resolution is not the cause of a reboot.

11. The correct answer is **A**. Display burn-in is where the previous image remains on the screen or is shown as a ghost image. Dead pixels are where the screen may freeze, and black areas might be visible. A faulty cable would flicker. The laptop freezing could end up with a "no-signal" error.

12. The correct answer is **C**. Testing the output resolution is primarily done to ensure that the system's output is compatible with a variety of display devices. Display devices can have different resolutions and capabilities, and testing helps confirm that the system can adapt to and function properly with these devices. It ensures that the output is correctly scaled, aligned, and compatible, avoiding issues such as distorted images or cut-off content. The accuracy of color representation and optimization of image quality are secondary considerations, but the main focus is on compatibility with various display devices. It does not enhance system performance.

13. The correct answer is **C**. The display settings is the correct answer as the display settings often include options for touch-screen calibration and enabling touch input. The battery status is incorrect as the battery status does not have a direct impact on touch-screen functionality. The network connection is incorrect as the network connection does not affect touch-screen functionality. The keyboard settings is incorrect as keyboard settings do not directly relate to touch-screen functionality.

## 5.5 Given a scenario, troubleshoot common issues with mobile devices

1.  The correct answer is **B**. The CMOS battery is the correct answer as a faulty or depleted CMOS battery can cause issues with the computer's ability to retain BIOS settings, leading to POST errors. RAM modules will emit continuous beeping noises. Issues with the hard drive will typically result in boot errors or an inability to access data, but not directly affect the POST process. Graphics card issues may cause display-related problems, but they do not directly impact the POST process.

2. The correct answer is **C**. A PoE injector can supply power to the network device through the Ethernet cable, resolving the power-related problem. Checking cable connections can help resolve physical connectivity issues but will not provide power to the network device. Resetting network settings would not provide power to the device and may not address the power-related issue. Restarting a network device will not resolve the power issue.

3. The correct answer is **C**. The phone's battery is defective when the phone is getting excessively hot. Running resource-intensive apps may cause some heat, but excessive heat is more likely due to a defective battery. Exposure to direct sunlight can cause some heat, but it is unlikely to result in excessive heating. An outdated operating system can cause performance issues, but it is not directly related to excessive heat.

4. The correct answer is **D**. If your phone has liquid damage, you need a professional repair service to repair the phone. Turning on the phone when it has been exposed to liquid can potentially cause short circuits and further damage. Although using rice to absorb moisture is a common suggestion, it is not an effective solution for fully drying the internal components of a phone. Using a hairdryer can introduce heat, which may further damage the phone's internal components.

## 5.6 Given a scenario, troubleshoot and resolve printer issues

1. The correct answer is **A**. Duplex printing automatically prints on both sides of the paper. The printing speed of a printer does not necessarily affect paper usage. The type of paper used (recycled or not) does not directly impact the paper usage of a printer. A larger paper tray may reduce the frequency of paper refills but does not address the issue of excessive paper usage itself.

2. The correct answer is **C**. The printer's fuser unit is not functioning properly as it fused the text to the paper. Low-quality ink cartridges may affect the print quality, but they are unlikely to cause the printed text to not stick to the paper. Using incompatible paper might affect the print quality but will not be the cause of this problem. The printer's temperature settings are not adjustable but are based on the specific printing requirements.

3. The correct answer is **B**. The printer's duplex unit is not properly set up. You need to read the manufacturer's leaflet that comes with instructions on how to set it up. Firmware updates are unlikely to resolve a hardware-specific issue related to the duplex unit. The alignment of the paper tray does not directly affect the functioning of the duplex unit. Low ink levels will not affect the printer's ability to perform double-sided printing.

4. The correct answers are **B** and **C**. The printer's drum unit is damaged, or it has dirty feed rollers. Firmware updates generally do not directly relate to the print quality. Low ink levels may affect the print quality, but not marks on the paper.

5. The correct answer is **B**. The paper is too thick for the printer because printers have specific paper weight and thickness limitations, which is why it is failing to feed into the printer. If the paper tray was empty, the printer would not attempt to feed any paper in the first place. Low ink cartridges do not directly affect paper feeding in a printer. Outdated printer drivers can cause various issues, such as printing errors, but not issues with the paper feed.

6.  The correct answer is **C**. The most likely cause of a paper jam is any foreign objects or obstructions present in the paper path, such as small pieces of torn paper or debris. These can cause the paper to jam when it is fed through the printer. While an empty paper tray can prevent the printer from feeding paper, it will not cause a jam. While wrinkled or folded paper can cause paper-feed issues, this is not the most likely cause of a paper jam. Low ink cartridges do not directly cause paper jams.

7.  The correct answer is **C**. Implementing a login requirement for print jobs allows better control over print resources. Users must authenticate themselves before their print jobs are processed, reducing the likelihood of abandoned or unnecessary printouts, and thus minimizing paper waste. Loading a large stack of paper may lead to increased paper usage and the potential for unnecessary prints, depending on user behavior. While printing double-sided documents can help reduce paper waste, it does not specifically address the need for print job control. Manually feeding paper instead of utilizing paper trays may not be practical for larger print jobs, and it does not directly address the issue of print job control.

8.  The correct answer is **C**. The failure of air conditioning can lead to blank spots or missing text on thermal paper due to the print head overheating or improper contact with the paper. To resolve this issue, it is important to clean the print head to remove any dust or debris and ensure that the print head has proper contact with the paper for consistent printing. Overheating and damage to the print head do not address the specific issue of blank spots or missing text. The failure of air conditioning does not directly cause a decreased print speed or slower output in a thermal printer. Thermal printers do not use ink cartridges.

9.  The correct answer is **A**. A dirty air filter restricts airflow, causing the projector to overheat. To prevent damage, projectors power down automatically when overheating occurs. An insufficient power supply doesn't directly cause unexpected power downs during operation. A malfunctioning lamp can cause issues, but it's not the most likely cause of unexpected power-downs. A loose connection can cause problems, but it doesn't directly lead to unexpected power downs during operation.

10. The correct answer is **B**. Blank receipts may be printed due to paper feed issues or incorrect paper loading in the printer. Empty ink or toner cartridges can cause other printing issues, but they are not the most likely cause of blank receipts. Overheating of the print head is not directly associated with printing blank receipts. Outdated printer driver software can cause various issues, but it is not the most likely cause of blank receipts.

11. The correct answer is **D**. The ribbon in a dot matrix printer contains ink-soaked fabric or polymer material that strikes against the paper, forming characters or images through impact printing. Inkjet printers use liquid ink cartridges or tanks, not ribbons, to produce printed output. Laser printers use toner cartridges that contain powdered ink, not ribbons. Thermal printers use heat-sensitive paper and do not require ribbons.

12. The correct answer is **A**. When the ribbon becomes worn, it may not transfer ink properly to certain areas of the paper, leading to gaps and missing words in the output. Paper feed issues or misalignment results in skewed prints or paper jams rather than missing words. Overheating will generally affect the overall print quality or lead to other issues, but not specifically missing words. Outdated printer driver software can cause various printing issues, but it is not the most likely cause of missing words.

13. The correct answer is **A**. Excessive heat can damage the print head and lead to poor print quality. Cold print heads will not allow the ink to flow. Maintaining an optimal temperature is crucial to prevent both overheating and clogging problems. Increased temperature can slow down printing. Excessive heat can increase the risk of printer malfunctions but is not the most important factor.

14. The correct answer is **B**. Incorrect label alignment or positioning can cause gaps on printed labels. Gaps on printed labels are typically not related to low ink or toner levels. A paper jam will cause gaps on labels and outdated printer drivers or firmware can cause various printing problems, but gaps on labels are typically related to alignment or positioning.

15. The correct answer is **C**. If the drum is not properly cleaned or has physical damage, it can retain remnants of the previous image, causing a faint duplicate to appear on subsequent printouts. An insufficient fuser temperature typically causes issues such as toner smearing or incomplete bonding, but it does not directly relate to the appearance of a ghost image on the printed page. Low toner levels may result in faded or light printouts. A loose connection between the printer and the computer may lead to communication issues or prevent print jobs from being processed.

16. The correct answer is **D**. If the paper gets stuck to the fuser in a newly installed printer, it is best to contact the printer manufacturer or a technician for assistance. They can provide guidance specific to your printer model and help resolve the issue without causing further damage. Using tweezers or pliers could potentially damage the fuser or other printer components, so it is not recommended. If the paper gets stuck to the fuser in a newly installed printer, turn off the printer and allow it to cool down. Instead of removing the paper yourself, consult the printer's manual or contact the manufacturer for specific instructions. It can provide guidance or recommend contacting a technician to avoid potential damage. Ignoring the problem and continuing to print can lead to additional paper jams or even damage to the printer.

17. The correct answer is **D**. Using an incompatible (third-party) toner can lead to poor print quality and specifically cause lines to appear on copied pages. A clogged printer head can result in inconsistent or distorted prints on both copied and directly printed pages. An overheated fuser would generally affect both copied and directly printed pages, rather than only causing lines on copied pages. Damaged scanning glass would typically result in inconsistent or distorted images on both copied and directly printed pages.

18. The correct answer is **B**. Updating the printer drivers or firmware to the latest version can help resolve the issue. Low ink or toner levels will typically result in faded prints or incomplete text, rather than garbled text. Damaged printer cables or connections could potentially cause printing problems, but not garbled text. Incorrect printer settings or font compatibility can cause printing issues, but they are more likely due to outdated printer drivers or firmware.

19. The correct answer is **B**. Flatbed scanners are commonly used for digitizing a large number of printed documents efficiently and accurately. NFC devices are primarily used for card payments. While a digital camera can capture images, it is not the most suitable or efficient method for capturing electronic images of a large collection of historical handwritten documents. QR scanners are specifically designed for scanning QR codes.

20. The correct answer is **D**. Dust or debris on the imaging drum can cause a consistent line from top to bottom on every sheet. Cleaning the imaging drum using appropriate cleaning methods can often resolve the issue. Low ink or toner levels typically result in faded prints or incomplete text, rather than a consistent line from top to bottom. While a malfunctioning paper feed mechanism can cause various printing problems, it wouldn't cause a single line to be consistently printed from top to bottom on every sheet. A consistent line from top to bottom is not a common symptom of outdated drivers or firmware.

21. The correct answer is **B**. A grinding noise during printing is commonly associated with a paper jam or obstruction. Low ink or toner levels typically do not result in a grinding noise. A grinding noise is not typically related to driver or firmware issues. Network connectivity issues do not typically result in a grinding noise.

## 5.7 Given a scenario, troubleshoot problems with wired and wireless networks

1. The correct answer is **A**. Interference can disrupt the wireless signal and limit your ability to choose an optimal channel. Outdated firmware will not limit your ability to choose an optimal channel. Incorrect network configuration settings do not directly affect the ability to choose a specific channel for the router. Insufficient signal strength may lead to connectivity problems, but it does not directly affect the ability to choose a specific channel for the router.

2. The correct answer is **A**. Incorrectly entering a MAC address in the filter list can result in devices that should be blocked being able to connect to the network. Outdated firmware on the wireless router is not related to MAC filtering. Interference from neighboring wireless networks does not affect MAC filtering. Incompatible wireless encryption protocols are not directly related to the MAC filtering functionality.

3. The correct answer is **A**. The client should release its current IP address and request a new one from the network's DHCP server. It is unlikely that the network card has a driver problem. Changing the wireless channel on the router will not resolve the issue. Flushing the DNS cache will not resolve the issue.

4.  The correct answer is **A**. The licensed band is exclusively allocated to authorized users with specific licenses, ensuring controlled and interference-free operation. The licensed band requires authorization and is not available for unrestricted public use. The licensed band is not designated for temporary or experimental use; it is reserved for authorized users. The licensed band requires specific licenses; therefore, any unlicensed option is incorrect.

5.  The correct answer is **B**. Configure each router on different non-overlapping channels, each with its own IP address range, minimizing interference and optimizing performance. Channel bonding increases bandwidth but will increase interference and worsen latency issues. Since we want a wireless network, we will not be using cable connections. QoS can help manage network traffic, but it may not directly address latency issues.

6.  The correct answer is **A**. A VPN establishes a secure and encrypted connection between the remote device and the company LAN, ensuring data privacy and security during remote access. Enhancing the internet speed does not create a secure connection. Firewalls are separate security measures that control network traffic and protect against unauthorized access; they don't create a secure connection.

7.  The correct answer is **A**. Relocate the wireless router. Moving the router to a central location improves the signal coverage and reduces device interference and connection drops. Upgrading the bandwidth doesn't directly address the dropping connection issue. Completely disabling other devices may not be feasible in an office environment. Changing encryption enhances security, but it may not resolve the dropping connection problem directly.

8.  The correct answer is **A**. A Wi-Fi analyzer helps identify sources of signal interference, such as overlapping channels or nearby devices, aiding in troubleshooting wireless connectivity issues. A Wi-Fi analyzer's primary purpose is to identify and troubleshoot connectivity issues rather than directly increasing speed. Changing the Wi-Fi password is a security measure but is not directly related to troubleshooting connectivity issues. Expanding coverage requires additional hardware or configuration changes, which are beyond the scope of a Wi-Fi analyzer's capabilities for troubleshooting.

9.  The correct answer is **C**. Poor VoIP quality can occur when there is not enough available bandwidth to support voice data transmission, leading to audio quality issues. Outdated hardware is not directly linked to poor VoIP quality. A low battery will not affect poor VoIP quality.

## Chapter 6: Mock Exam: Core 1 (220-1101)

1.  The correct answer is **C**. M.2 allows faster data transfer rates compared to traditional hard drives. M.2 is a form factor that is commonly used for solid-state drives (SSDs) and offers faster data transfer speeds than traditional hard drives. M.2 supports both SATA and PCIe interfaces. Graphics cards typically use the PCIe form factor. M.2 can be used as a boot device.

2.  The correct answer is **A**. RAID 5 requires a minimum of three drives and distributes data and parity across multiple drives to provide fault tolerance. RAID 6 provides a higher level of fault tolerance with dual parity. RAID 0 offers increased read performance due to data striping without redundancy. RAID 5 does not require dedicated parity drives.

3.  The correct answer is **B**. Secure Digital (SD) is commonly used in digital cameras. SD cards are widely adopted and offer varying capacities for storing photos and videos. CompactFlash (CF) was popular in the past, but it has been largely replaced by SD cards. Memory Stick (MS) is primarily used by Sony devices. eXtreme Digital (xD) cards are less common and are used in older Olympus and Fujifilm cameras.

4.  The correct answer is **D**. ATX motherboards support dual-channel memory architecture. Dual-channel memory allows for increased memory bandwidth and improved system performance. ATX motherboards support both Intel and AMD processors. ATX motherboards typically have more expansion slots than microATX. Modern ATX motherboards use the 24-pin ATX power connector.

5.  The correct answer is **A**. Secure Boot is a security feature provided by UEFI. Secure Boot ensures that only trusted operating system bootloaders and drivers are loaded during system startup. Although a BIOS password is a security feature, it is not specific to UEFI. The CMOS clear jumper is not a security feature provided by UEFI. TPM is a separate hardware component that provides secure storage and cryptographic functions (such as encryption and digital signatures) to enhance overall system security.

6.  The correct answer is **B**. Enhanced audio quality and capabilities. An expansion sound card enhances the audio output of a computer by providing dedicated audio processing and additional audio ports. This results in better sound quality and the ability to support advanced audio features. An expansion sound card does not directly affect CPU performance. Cooling efficiency is related to cooling fans and heat sinks, not sound cards. An expansion sound card is not related to storage capacity.

7.  The correct answer is **C**. To regulate the temperature of components. Cooling fans are used to circulate air within a computer system, dissipating heat generated by components such as the CPU, GPU, and power supply. This helps prevent overheating and ensures optimal performance and longevity of the hardware. Display resolution is unrelated to cooling fans. Wireless connectivity is achieved through other components, such as network adapters. Cooling fans do not impact sound quality.

8. The correct answer is **C**. To dissipate heat from a component. A heat sink is a passive cooling device that absorbs and disperses heat generated by computer components, such as the CPU or GPU. It consists of a metal finned structure that increases the surface area available for heat transfer. Heat sinks are not involved in audio signal amplification. Heat sinks are not designed for storage purposes. Heat sinks do not impact network performance.

9. The correct answer is **C**. To connect peripheral devices. Motherboard connector headers are used to provide connection points for various peripheral devices, such as USB ports, audio jacks, front panel buttons and LEDs, and internal connectors for storage devices. System configuration settings are typically stored in the BIOS/UEFI. CPU power is typically supplied through the CPU power connector. Display output is controlled by the graphics card or integrated graphics, not connector headers.

10. The correct answer is **C**. Multisocket motherboards are designed to support more than one CPU, allowing multiprocessing configurations. This is commonly seen in server-grade motherboards or high-end workstation systems. All other options are incorrect.

11. The correct answer is **C**. PostScript printing is a page description language that provides advanced graphics capabilities and color management. It offers precise control over color reproduction, resulting in more accurate and consistent color representation in printed documents. Printing speed is determined by the printer's hardware capabilities and other factors, not specifically by PostScript. Print resolution is primarily determined by the printer's hardware and the input image quality. Printer security features are not directly associated with PostScript printing.

12. The correct answer is **A**. Duplexing refers to the ability to print on both sides of a sheet of paper. This feature significantly reduces paper consumption and waste by utilizing both sides of the paper, making it an environmentally friendly printing option. Printing speed is not directly affected by duplexing. Print quality is determined by other factors, such as resolution and ink/toner quality. Printer durability is unrelated to the duplexing feature.

13. The correct answer is **B**. Removing all protective films and covers before powering on. When unboxing a device, it is crucial to remove any protective films or covers to ensure proper functionality and prevent damage to the device. All other options are less important. Keeping the original packaging materials may not be necessary in all cases. The instruction manual provides important information for setup and operation. Inspecting the device for any visible damage is essential before plugging it in.

14. The correct answer is **C**. Adjusting the paper size and type for printing. Printer tray settings involve configuring the paper size, orientation, and type to ensure compatibility with the printing requirements. This ensures that the printer feeds the correct paper size and type from the designated tray. Changing color settings only relates to a color printer. You might not decide to connect your printer to a network. Aligning print heads is specific to inkjet printers.

15. The correct answer is **A**. When selecting a printer paper, it is important to consider the weight and thickness that is compatible with the printer. Different printers have specific requirements, and using the appropriate paper weight and thickness ensures optimal print quality and prevents paper jams. Color and texture are subjective preferences and do not directly affect print quality. Paper brand and manufacturer may vary, but quality can be determined by considering weight and thickness. Paper price and affordability do not directly impact print quality.

16. The correct answer is **B**. Aligning the print heads to ensure precise ink placement. Inkjet calibration refers to the process of aligning the print heads in an inkjet printer, which ensures accurate ink placement and improves print quality, especially for documents with fine details or images. Ink cartridge settings usually involve ink-level monitoring and replacement. Connection settings relate to printer connectivity, not calibration. Cleaning the inkjet carriage is a separate maintenance procedure.

17. The correct answer is **B**. Controlling the movement of the printhead assembly. The inkjet carriage belt is a crucial component in inkjet printers. It is responsible for controlling the movement of the printhead assembly across the paper during the printing process. The belt is attached to the printhead assembly and ensures precise and accurate positioning of the printhead as it moves back and forth across the paper. This movement is necessary for the printhead to deposit ink droplets onto the paper, resulting in the desired image or text. The ink transfer from the cartridge to the printhead is typically managed by the ink supply system. Paper feed and alignment are controlled by separate mechanisms, such as feed rollers and paper guides. Maintaining optimal ink flow and print quality is influenced by factors such as ink formulation, printhead maintenance, and calibration, but not directly by the inkjet carriage belt.

18. The correct answer is **C**. A firewall is designed to monitor and control incoming and outgoing network traffic based on predetermined security rules. It filters network packets, allowing or denying access based on factors such as source, destination, port, and protocol. Data encryption is not a function of a firewall. Virus scanning is typically performed by antivirus software. User authentication is usually handled by separate authentication systems.

19. The correct answer is **C**. Overclocking involves running a computer component, such as a CPU or GPU, at a higher clock speed than its default or rated speed. This is done to achieve higher performance and potentially improve system responsiveness in tasks that are heavily dependent on the overclocked component's performance. Overclocking can potentially shorten the component's lifespan due to increased heat and stress. Overclocking often leads to increased power consumption. Software compatibility is not directly related to overclocking.

20. The correct answer is **D**. Among the options, 802.11ac offers the highest data transfer rates. It operates on the 5 GHz frequency band and supports multiple spatial streams, providing faster wireless speeds compared to the older 802.11a, 802.11b, and 802.11g standards. All other options offer lower data transfer rates.

21. The correct answer is **D**. NAT is commonly used in networking to allow multiple devices on a private network to share a single public IP address. It translates the private IP addresses of devices on the local network to the public IP address assigned to the router, enabling communication with devices on the internet. Encryption is not the primary purpose of NAT. DNS (Domain Name System) is responsible for translating domain names into IP addresses. DHCP (Dynamic Host Configuration Protocol) is typically used to assign IP addresses on a network.

22. The correct answer is **C**. FTP port 21 is specifically designed for file transfers between a client and a server. It allows users to upload, download, and manage files on remote servers. IMAP port 143 is used by an email client. HTTP port 80 is used for web page retrieval. SMTP port 25 is used for email transmission between mail servers.

23. The correct answer is **A**. Secure Shell (SSH) provides secure remote access to a server and facilitates secure file transfers between systems. SNMP is used for network management. POP is used for email retrieval. NTP is used for time synchronization.

24. The correct answer is **D**. Telnet is used for insecure remote command-line access to a server. It allows users to log in and execute commands on a remote system. DNS is used for translating domain names into IP addresses. HTTP is used for web page retrieval. SNMP is used for network management.

25. The correct answer is **B**. Simple Mail Transfer Protocol (SMTP) is the standard protocol for sending email messages between mail servers. It handles the transmission of email from the sender's server to the recipient's server. FTP is used for file transfers. HTTP is used for web page retrieval. POP is used for email retrieval.

26. The correct answer is **A**. DNS is responsible for translating human-readable domain names into IP addresses. It allows users to access websites and services using domain names rather than remembering IP addresses. DHCP is used to assign IP addresses to devices on a network. HTTP is used for web page retrieval. SNMP is used for network management.

27. The correct answer is **D**. Dynamic Host Configuration Protocol (DHCP) is responsible for automatically assigning IP addresses, as well as other network configuration parameters, such as subnet masks, default gateways, and DNS server addresses, to devices on a network. SNMP is used for network management. DNS is responsible for translating domain names into IP addresses. HTTP is used for web page retrieval.

28. The correct answer is **A**. GPS is a satellite-based navigation system that enables mobile devices to determine their precise geographic location. It utilizes signals from a network of satellites to triangulate the device's position on Earth. Wi-Fi connectivity does not directly provide location information. Bluetooth technology is primarily used for short-range wireless communication. NFC is used for close-range communication between devices.

29. The correct answer is **B**. Cellular location services estimate the location of a mobile device by triangulating the signal strength from nearby cellular towers. By analyzing the signal strength and timing information, the network can approximate the device's location. Wi-Fi positioning uses Wi-Fi access points for location estimation. Bluetooth proximity detection is used for identifying nearby Bluetooth devices. GPS satellite tracking provides precise location information through satellite signals.

30. The correct answer is **C**. To manage and control mobile device configurations and applications. MDM and MAM solutions allow organizations to remotely manage and control mobile devices, including device configurations, application installations, security policies, and data access. Encryption is typically implemented separately from MDM/MAM. Physical device security is not the primary purpose of MDM/MAM solutions. Remote wipe functionality is one of the security features but not the sole purpose of MDM/MAM solutions.

31. The correct answer is **B**. IMAP is commonly used for corporate email configuration on mobile devices. It allows users to access and manage email messages stored on a mail server, offering features such as syncing across devices and server-side mailbox management. POP3 is used for email retrieval but does not offer advanced synchronization features. SMTP is used for email transmission between mail servers. LDAP is used for directory services.

32. The correct answer is **C**. To verify the identity of users with an additional authentication factor. Two-factor authentication (2FA) adds an extra layer of security by requiring users to provide two different authentication factors to verify their identity. Data encryption during transmission is not the primary purpose of 2FA. Secure physical access to devices is typically achieved through other means, such as biometric authentication or physical keys. The primary purpose of 2FA is to enhance identity verification, although it can indirectly help prevent unauthorized access to corporate applications.

33. The correct answer is **C**. To delete all data on the stolen device remotely. The remote wipe feature allows the owner of a stolen mobile phone to remotely erase all data stored on the device. This helps protect sensitive information from falling into the wrong hands. Remote wipe does not physically retrieve the stolen device. Tracking the location of the device is typically handled by other features, like GPS or cellular location services. Disabling network connectivity is not the primary purpose of remote wipe, although it may be an additional security measure in some cases.

34. The correct answer is **B**. Enabling Bluetooth on a device allows it to discover, pair, and establish wireless connections with other Bluetooth-enabled devices. This enables data transfer, audio streaming, and other forms of communication between devices. Bluetooth is not directly related to wireless internet connectivity. GPS navigation is unrelated to Bluetooth. Bluetooth typically consumes additional battery power.

35. The correct answer is **A**. To enable pairing on a Bluetooth device, the user typically needs to press a specific button or combination of buttons on the device. This action puts the device into a discoverable mode, allowing it to be detected and paired with other Bluetooth devices. All other options are incorrect.

36. The correct answer is **A**. To find a device for pairing in Bluetooth, the device performs a scan to discover nearby Bluetooth devices. A Wi-Fi network is unrelated to finding a device for Bluetooth pairing. Syncing data is a separate process and not directly related to finding a device for pairing. Enabling location services is unrelated to Bluetooth pairing.

37. The correct answer is **A**. Access the device's settings and toggle the data network option. Enabling or disabling the wireless/cellular data network on a mobile device typically involves accessing the device's settings and locating the option to enable or disable data connectivity. Activation or deactivation is usually managed by the user through the device settings. Restarting the device does not directly enable or disable the data network. Updating the operating system does not control the enable/disable functionality of the data network.

38. The correct answer is **B**. GSM (Global System for Mobile Communications) and CDMA (Code Division Multiple Access) are wireless/cellular technology standards used for voice and data communication. They define the protocols and technologies used by mobile networks. 3G and 4G are generations of wireless technologies, not specific standards. Bluetooth and Wi-Fi are different types of short-range wireless technologies. LTE and WiMAX are specific wireless standards, but not commonly used for voice communication.

39. The correct answer is **C**. Share the device's internet connection with other devices. The hotspot feature on a mobile device allows the user to share their device's cellular data network connection with other devices, such as smartphones, tablets, or laptops. This enables those devices to access the internet using the mobile device's data connection. Hotspot functionality does not necessarily imply creating a secure network. Hotspot usage is not specifically related to high-speed data connectivity in remote areas. Hotspot usage is separate from automatically connecting to public Wi-Fi networks.

40. The correct answer is **C**. To improve the device's call and data connection quality. Preferred Roaming List (PRL) updates on a mobile device involve updating the list of preferred networks and their associated settings. This helps improve the device's call and data connection quality, ensuring that it connects to the most suitable network when roaming. PRL updates are not specifically related to international roaming. Network security protocols are separate from PRL updates. PRL updates do not directly optimize battery usage during roaming; that is typically handled by other power management features on the device.

41. The correct answer is **D**. Public addresses are assigned to devices that are connected to the internet. These addresses are globally unique and routable on the internet, allowing devices to communicate with each other across different networks.

42. The correct answer is **A**. USB 2.0 supports a maximum data transfer rate of 480 megabits per second (Mbps). It is commonly used for connecting various peripherals such as keyboards, mice, printers, and external storage devices to computers. 1 Gbps, 5 Gbps, and 10 Gbps all represent the data transfer rate of Gigabit Ethernet.

43. The correct answer is **C**. USB 3.0, also known as USB 3.1 Gen 1, supports a maximum data transfer rate of 5 gigabits per second (Gbps). 1 Gbps, 5 Gbps, and 10 Gbps all represent the data transfer rate of Gigabit Ethernet.

44. The correct answer is **A**. A LAN is a network that covers a limited area, usually within a building or a campus. It allows for the sharing of resources and communication between devices within that local area. A WAN is a network that covers a large geographical area, such as the internet. A PAN is a network that is used to connect personal devices in close proximity, such as Bluetooth. A MAN is the police, ambulance, or fire brigade within a city.

45. The correct answer is **B**. A WAN is a network that spans a large geographical area and connects multiple LANs. It enables communication and data transfer between different locations, such as offices in different cities or countries. A LAN is a network confined to a small geographic area. A PAN is a network that is used for connecting personal devices in proximity such as Bluetooth. A MAN is the police, ambulance, or fire brigade within a city.

46. The correct answer is **B**. Fast Ethernet, also known as 100BASE-TX, supports a maximum data transfer rate of 100 megabits per second (Mbps). It is a common networking standard used for Ethernet connections in both residential and small to medium-sized business environments. 10 Mbps represents the data transfer rate of 10BASE-T, an older Ethernet standard. 1 Gbps, represents the data transfer rate of Gigabit Ethernet (1000BASE-T). 10 Gbps represents the data transfer rate of 10 Gigabit Ethernet (10GBASE-T).

47. The correct answer is **D**. 10 Gigabit Ethernet (10GBASE-T). 10 Gigabit Ethernet supports a maximum data transfer rate of 10 gigabits per second (Gbps). It is a high-speed Ethernet standard used in enterprise networks and data centers to provide faster connectivity for demanding applications and increased network bandwidth. 10BASE-T is an old Ethernet standard that supports a maximum data transfer rate of 10 Mbps. 100BASE-TX supports a maximum data transfer rate of 100 Mbps. Gigabit Ethernet (1000BASE-T) supports a maximum data transfer rate of 1 Gbps.

48. The correct answer is **B**. The Cat 5 cable supports a maximum data transfer rate of 100 Mbps. 10 Mbps represents the data transfer rate of older Ethernet standards such as 10BASE-T. The Cat 5e cable supports a maximum data transfer rate of 1 gigabit per second (Gbps). 10 Gbps is beyond the capabilities of the Cat 5 cable and is supported by newer standards such as Cat 6 and Cat 6a.

49. The correct answer is **A**. A Class A private address range is 10.0.0.0 – 10.255.255.255 and it can only be used internally as these packets will be dropped by the routers on the internet. 179.16.0.0 – 179.30.255.255 and 179.16.0.0 – 179.30.255.255 are public IP addresses. 169.254.0.0 – 169.254.255.255 is the Automatic Private IP Addressing (APIPA), which is a feature in network protocols, such as IPv4, that allows devices to automatically assign themselves an IP address when a DHCP (Dynamic Host Configuration Protocol) server is not available.

50. The correct answer is **C**. Devices using APIPA will assign themselves an IP address from the range 169.254.0.0 - 169.254.255.255, ensuring temporary connectivity within a local network. Option A is incorrect as APIPA addresses are not globally routable. It indicates that the computer cannot obtain an IP address from DHCP. Incorrect answers – APIPA addresses are not globally routable, nor do they assign public IP addresses. APIPA is used within a single network, not for communication between different private networks.

# Chapter 7: Operating Systems

## 7.1 Identify basic features of Microsoft Windows editions

1. The correct answer is **D**. BitLocker Drive Encryption requires an additional BitLocker password before the Windows OS is launched. If this is successfully entered, then the user will be presented with the regular login prompt next. A BIOS password requires a special key sequence, such as Ctrl + D, the purpose of which is to prevent a user from entering the BIOS/UEFI at startup. Windows Privacy and Security does not ask for a prompt before the OS launches. Windows Accessibility is typically used for the configuration of Windows settings to help users with audio or visual impairments.

2. The correct answer is **A, D**. Windows 10 Home is intended for personal use and does not offer support features for enterprise/business users. ChromeOS is a simple-to-use OS and does not allow domain join. All Windows Pro and Enterprise editions DO support domain join functionality.

3. The correct answer is **A, D**. Windows 10 Pro and Enterprise editions are intended for business use and support additional functionality, including security features. They therefore support BitLocker. Older versions of Windows require Enterprise (or Windows 7 Ultimate) licenses to access advanced security features. Windows Home editions do not have access to BitLocker. macOS offers File Vault as an alternative to Windows BitLocker.

4. The correct answer is **A**. Assuming there are no compatibility issues, an in-place upgrade will require the least administrative effort to migrate all user settings and applications. A fresh installation will not migrate the settings and applications. The user settings would need to be backed up separately, and applications would need to be reinstalled.

5. The correct answer is **B**. As the manager is using a personal computer, it is highly likely that the system was purchased from a retail store, where the default Windows OS edition will be Home. BitLocker Drive Encryption requires at least Windows Professional. Having only 2GB of memory would not prevent BitLocker from being enabled. The size of the hard drive would only be an issue if there is not sufficient space to create a small unencrypted partition (100MB). BitLocker is supported on 32-bit and 64-bit editions of Windows.

6. The correct answer is **A**. The Remote Desktop Protocol (RDP) establishes a connection that allows a remote user to take control of another console/desktop, logging any existing users off the device. Virtual Network Computing (VNC) and Remote Assistance (RA) allow remote sharing of a desktop, meaning that the user would be able to view the session. Secure File Transfer Protocol (SFTP) only allows the transfer of files, not any configuration changes.

7.  The correct answer is **C**. A limitation of installing a 32-bit Operating System (OS) is that 4GB of RAM is the maximum available to the system, even if the underlying hardware is 64-bit. There are some restrictions on the maximum amount of memory even if a 64-bit OS is installed. 64-bit Windows Pro and Enterprise support 2TB of RAM, while the 64-bit edition of Home supports 128GB.

8.  The correct answer is **D**. BitLocker To Go can be used on a supported Windows OS to encrypt removable media. BitLocker can be used to encrypt fixed drives on supported Windows OSs but cannot be used to encrypt optical media.

9.  The correct answer is **C**. An in-place upgrade is intended to migrate user settings and installed applications. A network installation deploys from a server-based image (i.e., image deployment) and will perform the equivalent of a clean install. A clean install will install a fresh version of Windows, overwriting all the user settings.

10. The correct answer is **B**. Windows Home editions are intended for the consumer market and do not have the same tools and utilities as those offered in the Pro/Enterprise versions. RDP is only offered as a host service on Home editions. This means you can connect to a Pro or Enterprise desktop, but they cannot connect to your desktop. RDP service memory dependency is the same as the OS, so 2GB RAM is acceptable. RDP is offered on both 32-bit and 64-bit platforms. Using Windows Pro would not in itself be the reason for a failed RDP connection.

## 7.2 Given a scenario, use the appropriate Microsoft command-line tool

1.  The correct answer is **B**. ipconfig /all will give comprehensive configuration details for the workstation network interface/s, showing the IP address, subnet mask, DHCP server, DNS settings, and more. ping is a useful utility but, in this case, will only ping the loopback address (127.0.0.1), giving no configuration information. netstat will show network connections and listening ports. It can also be used to display Ethernet statistics but will not show network card configuration settings. hostname is a command that will show only the workstation name.

2.  The correct answer is **A**. robocopy (robust copy) is designed to mirror large amounts of data. It supports the copying of additional attributes, including hidden files, and maintains folder permissions. It has been included in the Windows OS since Vista. The copy command is not designed as a bulk copying tool; it does not retain permissions. xcopy does not support hidden files or maintain folder permissions. The cp command is a Linux command (although it would meet the criteria requested).

3.  The correct answer is **D, E** . nslookup (Name Server Lookup) is used to send a query to a DNS server (i.e., Name Server). The output in the question is from nslookup www.google.com. tracert is the Windows trace route command. It displays the "hops" as packets are forwarded to the destination system. It is useful to identify bottlenecks where traffic is slowed down. ping is useful to perform connectivity tests but does not display the hops. ipconfig is used to show network card configuration settings. netstat is used to display the network connections and listening ports of the local computer. nbstat (NetBIOS statistics) is used to show NetBIOS-related information.

4.  The correct answer is **C**. RDP and Group Policy Editor (gpedit.msc) are both features that are only included in the Pro and Enterprise versions of Windows. The computer is not running Linux as the technician would have discovered this when installing third-party tools. Windows 10 Enterprise would have allowed for the functionality that the technician required. It is unlikely that a corrupt registry would have caused these two very specific problems without impacting other services on the user's computer.

5.  The correct answer is **A**. ping will allow a support technician to establish where the connectivity fails. The ping command can be used to test gateway access and remote (internet) connectivity. msconfig will display the configuration used during the boot process. nbtstat will not allow a technician to test connectivity on the network. nslookup will be useful if the technician is troubleshooting name resolution but would typically be used after ping.

6.  The correct answer is **C**. nslookup can resolve names to IP addresses (that is, forward lookups) and IP addresses to names (reverse lookups). DNS servers need to be configured with Pointer Records (PTR) and reverse lookup zones to support reverse lookups. gpresult allows a technician to troubleshoot Group Policy settings on the local machine. ipconfig is used to display local network configuration settings (it does not display remote workstation configuration settings). net user is a Windows command that's used to manage local user accounts.

7.  The correct answer is **A**. USB access must be stopped quickly on multiple workstations. A domain-based group policy would be the most effective way to push out this security setting. For an immediate update, the support team can run invoke-gpupdate remotely or use the Group Policy Management Console (GPMC) to update multiple workstations at the same time with minimal disruption. Local security policy changes would be time-consuming to implement. A login script would impact the users as they would all need to log out of their workstations and log back in for a login script to be effective. Acceptable Use Policy (AUP) is a policy describing expected behavior while using an organization's information system and does not guarantee users will comply with that expected behavior.

8.  The correct answer is **C**. gpresult will process and output the current group policy settings, and the level of detail can be determined by a command switch. /Z is super-verbose output (that is, the most detailed). ipconfig /all will not display group policy settings. netstat /e will display only Ethernet statistics for a local network interface. nslookup will use DNS to resolve registered names to Internet Protocol (IP) addresses.

9.  The correct answer is **A**. netstat -p TCP (-p for protocol) allows the display of current TCP or UDP connections. In this case, the desired output is TCP connections. Note that switches can be combined. If the required output was connections and listening ports, netstat -a -p tcp could be used. net use would not support this function as it is used to manage local user accounts. nslookup is not used to display connections and listening ports but rather for DNS lookups. netstat -p UDP would only display UDP ports (NOT TCP ports).

10. The correct answer is **B**. gpresult will display the current group policy that has been deployed to the workstation. nbtstat displays NetBIOS statistics (not group policy). nslookup is used to query a DNS server. gpupdate will process any new and existing group policy but will not display the resultant settings. tasklist is a Windows command roughly equivalent to the GUI Task Manager process tab.

11. The correct answer is **A**. net use allows temporary access to a shared folder (or, in this case, a persistent drive mapping to a shared folder). It is important to choose the correct syntax. The allocated drive letter p: must be defined before the \\server1\public location. tracert is not used to map drives. The syntax for the command is also incorrect. net use \\P will not work as the syntax is wrong.

12. The correct answer is **B**. SFC is the built-in Windows "system file" checker. It runs as a background process, but it can also be run on demand. /SCANNOW scans for the integrity of all protected system files and repairs files with errors when possible. As the malware in this instance has targeted Windows operating system files, this is the best tool. chkdsk is a tool that's used to repair disk errors, such as corrupt areas on the disk. diskpart is a command-line tool for managing disk volumes. It can create and format disks.

13. The correct answer is **C**. There are three group policy tools in this question, so it is important to read this question carefully, as the goal is for a technician to verify the group policy locally. gpresult is run at the command prompt of a workstation to display applied group policy settings. The Group Policy Management Console (gpmc.msc) is typically run remotely by administrators to manage and report group policy objects. gpupdate could be used to apply new settings but does not report. msconfig is used to troubleshoot the boot process. shutdown -r (restart) will not report on group policy settings, although it could be used as a troubleshooting step, as some settings may require a reboot.

## 7.3 Given a scenario, use features and tools of the Microsoft Windows 10 operating system (OS)

1.  The correct answer is **A**. Task Manager's Processes tab will display all running applications, background processes, and Windows processes. The unwanted application or process can be terminated using the End task option. The task cannot be ended from either the Startup or Performance tabs of Task Manager. Directly editing the registry should never be the first choice for ending a task as it may have unpredictable outcomes.

2.  The correct answer is **D**. The reason for the blue screen error will be logged in one of the event viewer logs, and if it was a hardware driver issue, it will be found in the Windows System log. SFC can be used to ensure Windows system files are validated but will not display the event details. msconfig can be used to troubleshoot the boot process and could be configured to boot into safe mode if there is an unstable driver. regedit is the registry editor, which is not useful in this case. msinfo32 (system information) can be useful as a support tool for gathering configuration information but will not store details about the blue screen event.

3.  The correct answer is **A**. Task Scheduler (taskschd.msc) is the tool for configuring background tasks. Any settings that have been changed can be seen here. Device Manager (devmgmt. msc) will allow a technician to troubleshoot hardware. Task Scheduler (taskschd.msc) and Performance Monitor (perfmon.msc) can be useful for identifying performance bottlenecks. Certificate Manager (certmgr.msc) is used to manage local user and computer certificates as well as trusted certificate authorities.

4.  The correct answer is **C**. Performance Monitor can be configured to run a schedule, capturing detailed performance data during specific times of the day. Computer Management allows a technician to use multiple administrative tools on a local or remote workstation (user and group management services). Event Viewer logs can be useful to identify faulting applications or drivers. Task Manager shows events in real time and would require the support technician to interactively monitor the computer (it is not as convenient as Performance Monitor).

5.  The correct answer is **A**. System Information (msinfo32.exe) will display a comprehensive inventory of hardware, software, drivers, and so on. Resource Monitor (resmon.exe) shows system and network performance data in real time. System Configuration (msconfig.exe) allows configuration of the boot process. Registry Editor (regedit.exe) will not be the easiest tool with which to find this information.

6.  The correct answer is **C, E**. Disk Cleanup will identify files that are not needed and can be removed, and by defragmenting the hard drive, the technician will optimize the file fragments for large files. The defrag will actually move data so that large files occupy sequential clusters on the drive surface (which is not necessary for SSD drives). Booting the computer in safe mode is not necessary as the system is not unstable, just underperforming. Rebooting the computer may be necessary when configuration changes or new drivers require it. There is no reason to install any device drivers as there are no reported issues with hardware drivers.

7.  The correct answer is **B**. Disk Management will allow a disk to be extended if there is unused free space. Diskpart would allow the disk to be extended; however, it runs at the command prompt and, thus, is not graphical. Device Manager displays information about controllers and disk drives but does not allow the disk to be resized. Disk Cleanup would not allow the disk partition to be re-sized.

8.  The correct answer is **E**. The recommended tool to identify poorly performing start-up applications and disable them is to use the Task Manager. Using the System Configuration | Startup options to disable startup applications is only supported on older versions of Windows. Directly editing registry keys is not usually the best approach, and in this case, you would not know which startup apps to disable. Manually disabling all startup tasks currently listed as enabled and rebooting to check for issue resolution at startup is not necessary, as the startup impact is measured by Windows and is better addressed by following the steps in answer E.

9.  The correct answer is **C**. The Task Manager's Performance tab will give the technician real-time information on the system's all-around performance and enable the technician to identify obvious bottlenecks. Task Scheduler will allow heavy load tasks to be rescheduled but won't show performance data. Windows Memory Diagnostic is a tool that performs a health check on physical memory (for example, to determine whether there are any cells on a RAM module that are corrupt). Disk Defragmenter could be run in response to high disk latency, but it will not show actual disk performance information.

10. The correct answer is **A**. certmgr.msc can be used to manage certificates for the computer, user, and system accounts. The Trusted Root Certificate Authorities store is populated with trusted root certificate authorities. This list can be modified manually or centrally using group policy. Removing the certificates from the store using regedit.msc is not a good choice, as this may lead to unpredictable results. Device Manager (devmgmt.msc) does not allow the management of certificates on the laptop. A certificate revocation list (CRL) is used by a certificate authority to publish certificates that they have issued but that are now compromised/untrusted, and this is not appropriate in this case.

## 7.4 Given a scenario, use the appropriate Microsoft Windows 10 Control Panel utility

1.  The correct answer is **C**. Device Manager must be used to disable a hardware device. Devices and Printers allows for the installation and management of printers but does not offer the option to disable them. Sync Center allows for the management of offline files. Power Options does not offer any options to control printers.

2.  The correct answer is **A**. It is likely that the file type has been associated with the wrong application and this is what is causing an error. The default settings would open the JPEG in the Photos app. This can be corrected using the Control Panel | Default Programs option. Display settings do not offer the option to change file associations. Device Manager does not contain the option to change file associations. Internet Options contains web browser settings only.

3.  The correct answer is **B**. By configuring the Connections tab, we can ensure all web browser traffic is forwarded to the proxy server. Network and Sharing Centre | Change Adapter Settings does not allow for proxy configuration. Windows Defender Firewall cannot be used to configure proxy settings. Device Manager is used to troubleshoot problems with hardware.

4.  The correct answer is **C**. Ease of Access Center allows the system to be optimized for a variety of different disabilities. For example, the system can be optimized for users who cannot use a mouse or keyboard, as well as for visually impaired users. Device Manager allows the configuration of extra hardware for users with disabilities, but not the optimization of the interface for the user. System and Programs and Features would each allow the installation of new software, not the optimization of default system features.

5.  The correct answer is **B**. If a device is not working after installing device drivers, the first place to look is Device Manager, which offers important information to aid in troubleshooting. The Services console and Event Viewer's System logs (which will report a failed driver) would be useful to troubleshoot background services that may have failed, but Device Manager offers more information. Programs and Features is useful if a problematic application needs to be repaired.

6.  The correct answer is **D**. Internet Options allows browser settings to be adjusted or reset to their defaults. System offers no browser-related settings. Programs and Features allows the browser to be uninstalled or repaired, but not for settings to be changed. Network and Sharing Center allows for troubleshooting network adapters and connections.

7.  The correct answer is **A**. Network and Sharing Center allows an IP address to be manually set. Sync Center is used primarily to manage the synchronization of offline files. User Account Control is used to manage security prompts when configuration changes are attempted. Credential Manager is used to store accounts and passwords that allow the signed-in user to access third-party sites without being prompted for additional credentials.

8.  The correct answer is **D**. This setting can be accessed using the Mail option in the Control Panel. Internet Options configures browser settings, Windows Defender Firewall allows for the configuration of network access through ports and protocols, and User Accounts is where the local user account database can be managed.

9.  The correct answer is **A**. When the lid is shut, the Do nothing option will ensure the system does not enable any power-saving settings preventing the function of external peripherals. Sleep, Hibernate, and Shut down each enable a power saving setting that will power the screen off.

10. The correct answer is **B**. Control Panel | Sound allows the user to view settings to change their preference for the hardware used for audio output, as there will now be two choices (the original and new hardware). Device Manager | Audio inputs and outputs is where drivers are updated and devices disabled. Devices and Printers allows new devices to be detected or removed (but not the choice of preferred audio playback device). Speech Recognition is not a setting that allows for the default playback device to be selected.

## 7.5 Given a scenario, use the appropriate Windows settings

1.  The correct answer is **A**. Selecting Settings | Time & Language allows the current language keyboard to be selected. If this is not done, then a user in the United States, for example, would press Shift + 2 and expect to see the @ symbol. But if the keyboard language was set to U.K., the character displayed would be ". Settings | Accessibility is primarily used to configure settings for users with a disability. Settings | Personalization is used to manage a user's Windows environment, which includes options such as theme and default colors. Settings | Apps controls Windows applications.

2.  The correct answer is **C**. Settings | System allows the configuration of multiple monitors through the Display settings. The other choices do not give access to the multiple display configuration settings.

3.  The correct answer is **C**. It is possible to access Storage settings from Settings | System. The disk space used is displayed along with options to free up disk space. The other options here do not give access to Storage settings to review storage usage.

4.  The correct answer is **A**. The screensaver settings can be configured from the Settings | Personalization | Lock screen options. All the other choices are either non-existent paths or do not offer the option to set a screen lock timeout.

5.  The correct answer is **C**. In an organization where group policy is centrally managed, the BitLocker settings will be configured by the organization. To access the controls directly, you would need to enter Settings, then Privacy & security. Note that additional operating system and hardware support is required to successfully enable BitLocker (OS version needs to be a minimum of Windows Professional and TPM hardware support is needed). None of the other choices offer the option to enable BitLocker Drive Encryption.

6.  The correct answer is **D**. A proxy server enables an organization to protect client browser sessions by restricting access to unsafe sites based on URI/URLs and employing content filtering. None of the other choices offer the option to select a proxy server.

7.  The correct answer is **D**. To access mailbox configuration options from the Settings menu, Accounts must be selected. Settings | Accounts allows a user to customize their preferences for a number of options (including email). None of the other choices give access to email options.

8.  The correct answer is **A**. A company can use the same features to provide visual and audio feedback during a gaming session that a user would use to record and share their own gaming sessions. These are accessed through Settings | Gaming | Captures. This feature must be accessed through gaming controls. The other options will not provide access to the required settings.

## 7.6 Given a scenario, configure Microsoft Windows networking features on a client/desktop

1.  The correct answer is **C**. A domain-joined computer will allow the enterprise to centrally manage settings through tools such as Group Policy. There are a number of ways to add a computer to the domain, including the PowerShell Add-Computer command. To access the function through the settings menu, you must first select the System feature. While there are other ways to add a computer to a domain (for example, PowerShell), the other menu options presented do not allow this action.

2.  The correct answer is **B, D**. If a DHCP server cannot be located when a host computer requests an IP address, then an APIPA address will be locally assigned to the interface. The same behavior will occur if a lease expires on a previously assigned IP address. 169.254.23.66 is not a private IP address. A private IP address is from a range reserved for internal use. Private ranges include 10.0.0.0, 172.16.0.0-172.31.0.0, and 192.168.0.0. IPv6 does not assign APIPA addresses. Instead, a locally assigned (that is, default) address is a link-local address in a 32-character hexadecimal format and always begins with FE80. Active Directory and DNS services are not responsible for allocating IP addresses.

3.  The correct answer is **B**. Windows Defender Firewall does not allow Windows file and print traffic while the firewall profile is set to Public (this is intended to add security when not using a trusted network). The private network profile will allow file and print traffic. The user has been assigned the requisite privileges so this should not be a problem. Other network services are working so there cannot be a problem with the network card.

4.  The correct answer is **A**. Windows Defender Firewall can be configured to block unwanted incoming and outgoing connections. This is the most effective way to prevent the use of a P2P file-sharing application. Windows Virus & threat protection will protect a Windows operating system from malware. There are legitimate P2P file-sharing applications that will be considered malware. Windows Secure Boot is designed to ensure a private key cannot be tampered with. Windows BitLocker Drive Encryption offers protection from unauthorized access to Windows hard disk drives.

5.  The correct answer is **C**. Only Administrator accounts can modify Windows Defender Firewall settings. Power Users is a group that is provided for backward compatibility and allows the same privileges as a Standard user. Guest Account has the least privileges of all accounts, and Standard users do not have privileges to change system configuration settings.

6.  The correct answer is **C**. The current IP address of 169.154.44.89 is an Automatic Private IP Address (APIPA), which is self-assigned by the client computer. This happens if the DHCP service is unable to respond to a client request. It is likely that there was a temporary service disruption. ipconfig /renew will indicate whether the DHCP service is available or if the issue needs to be escalated. ipconfig /all shows the current network configuration. ipconfig /flushdns is used to resolve DNS-related problems. ipconfig /flushdhcp is a non-existent option.

7.  The correct answer is **B, C**. In order to restrict data usage on a network interface, a limit must be set and the Metered Connection setting must be configured. System | Storage settings allows you to optimize the use of locally available storage devices, not network traffic. Advanced Network Settings | Advanced Sharing enables the configuration of network profiles used by Windows Defender Firewall. Network Interface | Flight Mode – On will disable Wi-Fi and Bluetooth.

8.  The correct answer is **B**. The configuration will need to include an IP address or hostname as the printer is connected directly to the network switch. Selecting a shared printer by name would only work if the printer was already installed and shared by an existing computer on the network. The other options would not give the desired result as the printer is not wireless or connected via USB.

## 7.7 Given a scenario, apply application installation and configuration concepts

1.  The correct answer is **C**. The x86 architecture describes a processor that has 32 registers. This architecture means that a maximum of 4GB of RAM can be accessed by the system. To access any additional RAM purchased would require the system to be upgraded to an x64-bit architecture. Installing Ubuntu Linux will not affect the amount of memory that can be accessed. Installing a larger hard drive will not help, and the addition of more RAM on the existing x86 architecture will not be effective.

2.  The correct answer is **B**. While the exact requirements of the CAD application are unknown and the base hardware seems reasonably sufficient, the exception to this is the graphics card. CAD applications place heavy demands on the graphics hardware and will benefit from dedicated hardware comprising a multi-core Graphics Processing Unit (GPU) and dedicated video RAM. As the existing hardware is of a high standard, there is no obvious requirement to upgrade anything but the integrated graphics.

3.  The correct answer is **C**. 32-bit applications are able to run on 64-bit Windows using a compatibility setting provided by the Windows on Windows (WOW) architecture. They will run in a similar fashion as they would on a native 32-bit host, with the same memory restrictions (4 GB RAM at most). Apart from the memory restrictions, all other functionalities will still be supported, including multi-tasking and multi-threading.

4.  The correct answer is **B**. In some cases, an application makes a call to the operating system to get the current version and checks to see if that matches its requirements. Often, the application fails simply because the value is not the same as its requirements when the application is told that the OS is Windows 10, but it expected Windows 8. A quick fix is to try and trick the application into believing it is running on Windows 8 by selecting that as the compatibility setting. Updating the application to the latest version may be a long-term option, but it doesn't offer a quick fix. Safe mode is used to troubleshoot faulting drivers and services but is unlikely to offer a solution to the technician's current problem.

5.  The correct answer is **B**. A hardware token can store a unique key that is used to authorize the launch of the CAD software. Where the value of a single license may run into several thousand dollars, this is an effective way to ensure the software is not fraudulently used. None of the other options fully protect the developers from unscrupulous users.

## 7.8 Explain common OS types and their purposes

1.  The correct answer is **A**. The technician must find a filesystem compatible with both operating systems. FAT32 is compatible with many common operating systems, including Linux, macOS, and Windows. ext4 is used on Linux. NTFS and exFAT do not have the same wide support as FAT32 and may not be readable by some Linux operating systems.

2.  The correct answer is **A**. An End of Life (EOL) operating system no longer receives updates or security patches from the vendor. The issue is not an incompatible operating system as it still works on the hardware platform. The issue raised here is more about security and reliability issues; the fact that it is a 32-bit OS is not significant. A vendor may offer extended support for important customers (usually requiring the customer to pay for this extended support). In this instance, extended support is not being offered.

3.  The correct answer is **C**. ChromeOS is a lightweight OS based on the popular Chrome browser. There are many examples of versions of minimalist OSs, such as Windows IoT and Linux Lite, while Apple is rumored to be testing a Lite version of macOS for iPads. None of these are based on a browser-based interface, however.

4.  The correct answer is **C**. Windows offers the best solution to standardize all servers, workstations, and mobile devices across a single vendor OS. Windows Server offers centralized datacenter services, Windows 11 Enterprise can be used for managed desktops, and Windows Mobile can be employed for handheld devices. Linux is used to deliver datacenter services and is a very capable server-based platform. There are also user-friendly desktop editions such as Ubuntu/Red Hat, but these editions are not supported on smartphones or tablets. iOS is the Apple operating system used on the iPhone and iPad. ChromeOS is desktop only.

5.  The correct answer is **D**. Linux operating systems use the Extended Filesystem (ext), the first edition of which was created around 1992 and supported storage limits of 2GB. ext2 was followed by ext3 in 2001, which supported a maximum partition size of 16TB. ext4 was introduced around 2008 and supports a maximum partition size of 1EB (1,000,000 TB). The ext4 filesystem also supports online defragmentation, which is important to maintain efficient file access. FAT32 is not used as a core filesystem on Linux. It is intended for removable media and has a maximum volume size of 32GB. ext3 will not support online defragmentation or the volume size required. NTFS is a Windows filesystem.

6. The correct answer is **C**. Android is an open source (that is, royalty free) operating system developed by Google. It was initially released in 2008 and, in 2023, is currently on version 13 (codename Tiramisu). Android OS is based on a Linux kernel and supports many of the security features used in mainstream Linux distributions. iOS is a proprietary Apple-based mobile operating system originally used exclusively on Apple hardware, specifically the code base for iPhones, iPods, and iPads. SUSE Linux is not used on mobile devices or smartphones; it is primarily deployed on datacenter servers. Windows Mobile uses a modified version of the Windows desktop OS.

## 7.9 Given a scenario, perform OS installations and upgrades in a diverse OS environment

1. The correct answer is **D**. Pre-Boot Execution Environment (PXE) allows a computer to boot from the Network Interface Card (NIC) and access services on the network. In this case, the technician could use the media to create a Windows Deployment Server and perform the upgrades from a central location. Booting from a Solid State Drive (SSD) does not meet the requirements of installing over the network. Optical drives and flash drives can be used to install a single image but do not solve the problem of upgrading multiple computers across the network.

2. The correct answer is **D**. An unattended installation allows a central deployment image to be made available alongside an automated setup file (or unattended script). Once the installation is started, the technician can leave it to complete on its own. A remote network installation does not meet the requirements for an automated installation. A repair installation allows for a faulting computer to be reimaged back to a standard build configuration. A clean installation does not describe an automated process.

3. The correct answer is **C**. The GUID Partition Table (GPT) disk format allows partition sizes of up to 18 EB (that is, 18.8 million TB). A GPT drive can also contain as many as 128 separate partitions. ext4 is not supported on Windows; it is used on Linux filesystems. Master Boot Record (MBR) partitions are limited to a maximum size of 2TB and support a maximum of four partitions per disk. Apple File System (APFS) is not supported natively on Windows computers.

4. The correct answer is **D**. An in-place upgrade will allow the customer to keep all supported applications and retain their settings. It is important to check that in-place upgrades are supported for the version of Windows they are currently using. A clean install will not retain applications or settings. A repair installation will reset the image back to default for the current build of Windows on the customer's system and is intended as a troubleshooting option. An unattended install does not necessarily mean that an upgrade will be selected.

5. The correct answer is **C**. Windows 10 was the first Windows operating system to support feature upgrades (Windows 11 also supports feature upgrades). Typically released every six months, feature upgrades include additional features and functionality. In previous releases of Windows, new features and functionality were delivered with service packs or interim releases, such as the upgrade of Windows 8.0 to 8.1. Windows 7 and Windows 8.1 do not support feature upgrades.

6. The correct answer is **C**. An image deployment allows for a customized build of the operating system (along with any required applications) to be created. The image can be hosted on a Windows Deployment Server, and all new installations will use the standard centralized image. An upgrade will retain current applications and settings (some existing desktop computers may have different applications installed and be configured differently). Clean installations do not always ensure the same settings will be applied. A repair installation is used to set a Windows computer back up on a standard image as a troubleshooting step.

7. The correct answer is **B**. When installing images from a central server across the network, it is expected that the overall traffic on the network segment will increase. It is important that any unacceptable load on the network is identified. The impact on users will only be a concern if the network is overwhelmed with additional traffic. DHCP will need to provide IP addresses to 30 workstations at a time (during the build), so this should not add any great burden to the DHCP server. The impact on production workstations will only be a negative concern if the network is experiencing unacceptable volumes of additional traffic during the build process.

8. The correct answer is **B, C**. Unified Extensible Firmware Interface (UEFI) replaces the original Binary Input Output System (BIOS) seen in computer systems since the original 1980s PC systems. UEFI is needed to support GPT disks. Windows 11 installation requires the presence of a Trusted Platform Module (TPM) to support some of the security features now standard in the operating system. Windows 11 requires 4GB RAM and a 1GHz 64-bit processor in addition to TPM 2.0 and UEFI support.

9. The correct answer is **B**. A repair installation allows for boot issues, such as missing or corrupt startup files, to be fixed. The technician will be presented with the Advanced Options menu if Windows cannot boot and the Automatic Repair function has failed. This menu provides options including System Restore, System Image Recovery (if you have a backup), or to run a Startup Repair. Unattended, image deployment, and remote installations are not intended as troubleshooting steps.

10. The correct answer is **B**. The Windows PC Health Check App is a free Microsoft download and allows a Windows computer to be assessed prior to an upgrade. Following this assessment, the app will provide you with a list of system requirements for the given upgrade and state whether or not these are met by the system in question. While the other options do provide useful information for technicians, they do not present an easy-to-read upgrade report.

## 7.10 Identify common features and tools of the macOS/ desktop OS

1. The correct answer is **C**. The standard file extensions for a Mac installation file is DMG (from **D**isk i**Ma**Ge) and replaces the much older IMG file format. MSI and EXE file formats are used by Windows computers. APK files are Android Package files and are used to deploy applications on devices running the Android operating system.

2. The correct answer is **B**. The Mac Finder application allows the user to view files on all supported media. Keychain is used to support single sign-on (SSO) and allows transparent authentication across multiple sites. Mission Control is used to switch between different workspaces on a Mac. Explorer is a Windows feature.

3. The correct answer is **B**. The Mac feature used to back up and restore data files is Time Machine. File History and Windows Backup are features supported only on Windows operating systems. Mission Control is not used to back up or restore files.

4. The correct answer is **A**. The Force Quit menu allows unresponsive applications to be terminated. Task Manager, Task List, and Control Panel are all features available only on Windows computers.

5. The correct answer is **C**. FileVault allows a Mac hard drive to be encrypted using 128-bit or 256-bit Advanced Encryption Standard (AES). Once the feature has been enabled, the user must supply their password before the system can boot up. If no password is provided, then the disk will remain encrypted. iCloud is used to synchronize data from Apple devices to cloud-based storage. Keychain is used to manage multiple identities when accessing different sites. BitLocker is a disk encryption technology used on Windows operating systems.

6. The correct answer is **C**. The Mac operating system (beginning with Mac OS X in 1996) was developed as a custom operating system based on Berkeley Software Distribution (BSD) Unix. macOS is not based on Linux, Android, or ChromeOS.

7. The correct answer is **C**. The Keychain feature allows a user to store passwords and account information that can then be used to reduce the number of passwords that a user would otherwise need to remember. Mission Control is used to switch between applications and desktops. Spotlight is used for system-wide searches (such as searching for an application, email, or files) on a macOS machine. Dock is used to quickly navigate to applications and features.

8. The correct answer is **A**. The easiest way for this task to be accomplished is to locate the application and delete the application folder. None of the other options will give the desired result.

9. The correct answer is **A**. In the event that a Mac computer fails to boot, it is likely that one or more critical files on the hard disk are missing or damaged. To access the Recovery menu, Command + R must be pressed during the boot process. The recovery options can then be accessed to attempt to fix the error. Do not attempt to reinstall the operating system until all other options have been attempted. Important data files could be lost if they have not been backed up. The Recovery menu cannot be accessed by booting the computer from a DVD, not to mention that most modern Macs do not include a DVD drive. Safe mode is a feature of the Windows operating system.

10. The correct answer is **A**. To permanently delete the files and free up disk space, the Trash application should be emptied. Recycle Bin and Disk Cleaner are Windows features. Separating a disk into separate partitions with Disk Utility will not increase the available disk space.

11. The correct answer is **B**. The Dock is normally displayed at the bottom of the screen and is a convenient place through which to access features, applications, folders, and files. The Dock will display recently used applications by default but can be customized by dragging an item onto the Dock to create a persistent link. Mission Control allows users to switch between different workspaces. The Start menu is a Microsoft Windows feature. Toolbars are used to access features within an application.

12. The correct answer is **B**. System Preferences allows the configuration and customization of all common configuration preferences. Mission Control allows users to switch between different workspaces. Dock offers easy access to applications and files. Disk Utility is a system tool that handles disk-specific tasks on Mac computers.

13. The correct answer is **A, C**. To avoid an overly cluttered desktop due to a large number of running applications, it is possible for a Mac user to create additional desktops. These desktops are known as spaces. The user can switch between them either by using Control + right or left arrow keys or by adding and/or selecting another desktop in Mission Control. Desktops (or spaces) cannot be accessed directly from the Dock. Command + spacebar is used to call up the Spotlight search function.

## 7.11 Identify common features and tools of the Linux client/ desktop OS

1. The correct answer is **B, C**. To list files in a directory, the ls (list) command with the -l switch (for long listing) would be used to show all permissions for the contents of the directory. To show all possible options for the ls command, ls --help would be used. sudo + chown would allow the ownership of the Employee-Reports file to be changed from sales group ownership to the HumanResources group. Looking at the other permissions that have been allocated, it seems likely that the sales group has incorrectly been given group ownership of the file. dir is a Windows command and would show the same output. sudo + chown would allow the ownership of a file to be changed. sudo + chmod would reset permissions on a file or directory. pwd (present working directory) will show the directory where commands are currently being processed. sudo + mv will move a file to a different location.

2. The correct answer is **D**. Using the sudo command, a user can access the privileges of the superuser account. They will be prompted to type their own user password. It is also possible to switch user to an account that's alive with the su command. For more information on both these commands, use the given command along with --help switch. pwd displays the present working directory. grep is used to search for text strings. Samba is an interoperability suite that allows Windows platforms to access shared files from a Linux computer.

3.  The correct answer is **C**. The Linux top command shows real-time active processes. PID is the Process ID number, USER is the owner of the task, PR and NI show the priority of the task, and VIRT and RES show memory usage. Other important values are %CPU, which shows CPU usage, and %MEM, which shows the memory being used per process. nano is a text editor on Linux systems. dig is used to send DNS queries to a Name Server. ps is used to list running processes on a Linux system but does not display the details of resources being used to the same extent as the top command.

4.  The correct answer is **D**. The rm command (also known as the remove command) is used to delete files and directories from a Linux system. The command supports additional switches, such as -r (recursive), that allow for directories to be deleted along with files. Type rm --help to see all options. chmod allows for permissions on files and directories to be changed. man is used to display the manual for a command (for example man rm will display verbose information for the remove command). df is the disk-free command and displays filesystem information.

5.  The correct answer is **C**. The output from df shows the developer how much unused space remains on the storage location (hard disk). ps and top display the running processes. ip is used to configure settings for network interfaces.

6.  The correct answer is **B**. SSH (secure shell) will allow the technician to access a remote terminal session using a secure link. SSH uses symmetric encryption to protect the confidentiality of any data transferred. RDP is used on the Windows operating system to access the desktop of a Windows host. telnet is not secure; a malicious user may be able to intercept the network traffic and access details of the data. The cp command can be used to copy files between different Linux hosts but is not secure.

7.  The correct answer is **C**. The man command displays help in the form of a manual, usually offering much more detail than the corresponding --help command when typed after the CLI command. The other explanations are false.

8.  The correct answer is **D**. Installing the samba service on the Linux Ubuntu server will allow Windows computers to use native services and applications to access files and printers on the Linux server in the same way that they connect to other Windows computers. Windows uses a Microsoft protocol called Server Message Block (SMB), also known as Common Internet File System (CIFS) to access shared content across a network. samba supports the same protocols. telnet is used to access the CLI of a remote system but does not allow files to be transferred between systems. Windows 10 workstations do not run the samba service, as they already support the network protocols needed to create a persistent connection to shared resources using a mapped drive. Windows File and Print Sharing is native to Windows operating systems and cannot be installed on Linux systems.

9. The correct answer is **C**. A package management system allows for the installation, update, and removal of software packages. There are two common package management systems supported on Linux operating systems. Red Hat Linux supports yum. To install a package called application1, the following command could be used: sudo yum install application1. Ubuntu Linux uses a packager named apt. The remaining CLI tools are not used to install applications.

10. The correct answer is **A, D**. The first command, ls -l, will display the "long" listing for the Employee-Details file. The grep command searches for patterns in any line of text. Therefore, the second command will display any lines that have the pattern Joe Smith within the Employee-Details file. dir /L is a Windows command (although many Linux distributions do support a number of native Windows commands). /L is not supported when run from a Linux CLI. The Linux cat (concatenate) command cannot be used to search for a pattern of characters but could be used to display the contents of the Employee-Details file.

11. The correct answer is **A, D**. The Linux ip (Internet Protocol) command queries a network object. ip route will show the computer's default gateway, and in this case, ip address will show the configuration settings for all network interfaces. The second command, dig (Domain Internet Groper), is used to retrieve records from DNS servers. dig www.google.com was used to display the records for IP addresses registered against the domain name www.google.com. ipconfig, nslookup, and tracert are networking commands supported only on Windows operating systems (not Linux). ping is used to test connectivity between hosts on a network.

12. The correct answer is **B**. The chmod (change and modify) command allows the permissions to be reset. grep is used to search for patterns in lines of text. ip address displays the network configuration. pwd displays the current directory where commands are being run.

# Chapter 8: Security

## 8.1 Summarize various security measures and their purposes

1.  The correct answer is **A**. Motion sensors are primarily designed to detect any movement within their range. They are commonly used in security systems to identify the presence of unauthorized individuals or objects, trigger an alarm, or activate other security measures. Option B describes HVAC systems. Option C describes audio detection. Option D describes a photosensor.

2.  The correct answer is **B**. Soft tokens are software-based security tokens that generate one-time passwords (OTPs) to authenticate the user's identity during the login process. They are commonly used in logical security systems to provide an additional layer of security. Soft tokens generate unique passwords that are valid for a short period of time, ensuring that only authorized users can access sensitive information or perform specific actions. Option A, generating secure passwords, is incorrect because soft tokens are not primarily used for password generation. They are focused on the authentication aspect rather than password creation. Option C, encrypting data, is incorrect because soft tokens do not directly handle data encryption. Their primary function is to authenticate the user's identity, not to encrypt data. Option D, blocking malicious websites, is incorrect because soft tokens are not designed to block or prevent access to websites. They are specifically used for user authentication and cannot block malicious websites.

3.  The correct answer is **C, E**. A BYOD policy allows for standards and guidelines to be addressed for the use of personal equipment to access business systems. Mobile device management (MDM) allows the team to manage and configure a wide range of mobile devices. Options A, B, and F are designed to enhance security during the authentication process. Option D is designed to physically secure hardware.

4.  The correct answer is **A, F**. Physical controls are designed to prevent unauthorized access to facilities and information systems. An access control vestibule forces a user to enter a small space (designed for only one person), with interlocking doors to enforce security. The user must provide authentication before being allowed access through the second door. Door locks prevent unauthorized users from gaining access. Alarms, video surveillance, and motion sensors would allow intrusion to be detected but would not prevent unauthorized access to the server room. Bollards would help prevent intrusion using motor vehicles to ram or crash through perimeter fencing or guard posts.

5.  The correct answer is **C, E**. Detective controls would allow the security staff to be aware of breaches that evaded the physical security controls. This is referred to as defense in depth. Video surveillance and motion sensors would allow a security team to detect unauthorized intrusion. Access control vestibule, badge reader, equipment locks, and door locks are all considered preventative controls.

6.  The correct answer is **A**. To support two-factor authentication (2FA), you cannot choose another factor from the same group. A smart card is a physical device; it is something you have. Retina scanners and palmprint scanners are both considered biometrics, or something you are. They are in the same category as a fingerprint reader. A motion detector is not a method of authentication.

7.  The correct answer is **E**. Magnetometers are devices that can detect concealed metallic objects. This technology can be deployed at access points to the data center. Equipment can also be tagged in order to sound an alert on the magnetometer. An access control vestibule is designed to ensure only authorized personnel have access to a facility. In this case, we need additional controls. Video surveillance may not identify equipment that could be concealed (under a jacket or other clothing). Lighting is used to ensure video surveillance is effective. Equipment locks would be a good choice, but in this case, the requirement is for detective control (alerts).

8.  The correct answer is **A**. Adding a user to a group with security restrictions would adhere to the principle of least privilege. ACLs are used to ensure access is only given to the correct user or group. When combined with security groups, it will ensure only the correct security group has access to data. Adding a user to a group with restrictions is not part of MFA. An organizational unit (OU) is an administrative control that is useful when applying Group Policy settings to different business units.

9.  The correct answer is **A, D**. Home folders give each user a unique storage location, hosted on a central server. Home folders are assigned using login scripts. Option B, management of security groups, is not normally performed when a user logs in to the system. Option C, multifactor authentication, is designed to secure authentication by using two or more factors. Option E, organizational units, is used to manage objects within Active Directory services.

10. The correct answer is **B, E**. MFA requires the use of two or more authentication factors when logging on to their user account. There are three main groups: something you know, something you have, and someone you are. In this case, the user used something they knew (password) and a hardware token to generate TOTP HMACs (hash-based message authentication code). This would be considered something you have. Option A is associated with good account management. Options C and D are valid for MFA but are not being described in this instance.

11. The correct answer is **B, E**. Group Policy is used to ensure the user settings are updated on any workstation that the user accesses. The specific Group Policy configuration will be found under User Configuration\Administrative Templates\System\Folder Redirection. Login scripts are not used to configure folder redirection. Organizational units can be used to target particular users with settings, but do not actually push out configuration settings. A home folder is a default folder assigned to a user through a login script.

12. The correct answer is **B, C**. Voice call verification requires a user to take a call from a phone (including a mobile), and SMS messages require the user to validate a code sent to their mobile device. An email verification link can be received without access to a mobile phone. A hard token refers to a specific security device, such as a USB security key or an RSA key fob.

13. The correct answer is **A**. Active Directory security groups are primarily used to assign permissions to shared resources such as files, folders, printers, and other network resources. By assigning users or other groups to a security group, you can easily manage access control to various resources within the network. This option is correct because it accurately describes the main purpose of security groups in Active Directory. Option B is incorrect because while security groups can help organize user accounts, their primary purpose is to manage access control and permissions. Option C is incorrect because email distribution lists are typically implemented using distribution groups in Active Directory, not security groups. Option D is incorrect because controlling network connectivity is usually achieved through network security mechanisms such as firewalls and network access control lists (ACLs), rather than Active Directory security groups.

14. The correct answer is **C**. An organizational unit (OU) is a container within an Active Directory domain that can be used to group related objects such as users, computers, and other OUs. The primary purpose of an OU is to organize and manage these objects in a logical hierarchy that reflects the organizational structure. An OU helps in applying group policies, permissions, and administrative tasks to a specific set of objects. Option A is incorrect because the physical location is typically determined by attributes such as IP address or network subnet. Option B is incorrect because security policies are defined at the domain or group level, not at the OU level. Option D is incorrect because domain name resolution services are provided by the Domain Name System (DNS), not by OUs.

## 8.2 Compare and contrast wireless security protocols and authentication methods

1. The correct answer is **B**. Wi-Fi Protected Access 3 (WPA3) uses a secure handshaking process called simultaneous authentication of equals (SAE). This replaces the previous method, called preshared key (PSK). WPA2 uses an older security standard based on PSK. Temporal Key Integrity Protocol (TKIP) was designed to increase security when using WPA and RC4 encryption. Advanced Encryption Standard (AES) is the default encryption strength used to protect wireless data.

2. The correct answer is **C**. Remote Authentication Dial-In User Service (RADIUS) is also referred to as an authentication, authorization, and accounting (AAA) service. RADIUS servers allow the Wi-Fi controller to forward authentication requests from client devices. These authentication requests will then be forwarded to directory services. WPS allows a device to be paired with a Wi-Fi router without the need to share a key or password. WEP Open does not require an account or password (anyone can connect). WPA-PSK does not use Active Directory accounts.

3. The correct answer is **C**. WPA2-AES offers the highest levels of security. It uses AES 128-bit encryption. Wired Equivalent Privacy (WEP) was used prior to WPA and is no longer used. It is over 20 years old and crucially, it is not secure. WPA2-TKIP uses the older RC4 encryption algorithm. Open Wi-Fi networks do not use encryption.

## 8.3 Given a scenario, detect, remove, and prevent malware using the appropriate tools and methods

1.  The correct answer is **B**. Boot sector viruses infect the master boot record (MBR) or the boot sector of a computer system's hard drive. When the infected computer starts up, the virus becomes active and can spread to other parts of the system. Option A is not correct as this type of drive is not used to boot the OS. Option C, network routers and switches, is not targeted by boot sector viruses. Option D would more likely be associated with social engineering or password attacks.

2.  The correct answer is **D**. Keyloggers are able to record every keystroke made by a user on a targeted system. Attackers use it to steal login credentials, sensitive information, and payment card numbers. Options A, B, and C describe other types of malware or attacks, making them incorrect.

3.  The correct answer is **C**. Ransomware is malware that encrypts a victim's data files, making them inaccessible. This is then followed by a demand for payment in order to receive the decryption key. Options A, B, and D describe other types of attacks, making them incorrect.

4.  The correct answer is **B** . A rootkit will replace a privileged OS executable and is then able to block and disrupt OS processes. When a privileged account is used to configure OS functions or services, the rootkit can override these actions. Option A, trojan, doesn't typically focus on manipulating or reversing system settings like what's described in the scenario. While option C, viruses, can cause harm to a computer system, including disrupting its normal operation, it doesn't commonly target security settings such as Windows Defender. Viruses tend to focus more on replicating and spreading. While option D, spyware, can disable security features to facilitate its covert activities, the primary goal of spyware is data collection rather than actively manipulating system settings. Option E, ransomware, is more concerned with encrypting files and extorting money from the victim.

5.  The correct answer is **B** . Rootkits are difficult to remove as they will replace key system files and block attempts to remove malicious files. Completely wiping or erasing the hard drive will ensure no malicious files remain. Trojans, viruses, and spyware will not need the OS drive to be wiped and re-installed. An effective anti-malware suite should detect and remove these malicious files and processes.

6.  The correct answer is **E**. Ransomware demands a payment be made to access the data. Ransomware typically forces the user or organization to make a payment as important personal or business has been encrypted by the attacker. A trojan is installed along with a useful application. It is hidden within the application. A rootkit will replace a privileged OS executable and is then able to block and disrupt OS processes. A virus is malware that is typically introduced by a user clicking on an email attachment. Spyware will run in the background, stealing user information, including passwords.

7. The correct answer is **C**. As there is no specific malware type mentioned, the best approach is to roll out user awareness training to cover a broad range of threats. All other options only cover a specific single threat type.

8. The correct answer is **B**. As the web browser is the source of the incident and has access to websites, it makes sense to ensure the activity is not malicious. If the activity is harmless, then the anti-virus scan can confirm this. Disabling the web browser will be very disruptive and does not resolve the issue. Blocking ports 80 and 443 will be very disruptive as all web traffic is now blocked. Re-installing the OS is very disruptive and should only be used as a last resort.

9. The correct answer is **B**. Links sent in email messages are phishing attacks. In this case, specific training to counter this type of attack is the best solution. A firewall will not block content embedded with an email message. User education regarding common threats will not be as effective as specific training to counter phishing attacks. OS re-installation is not an option as the OS has not been compromised.

10. The correct answer is **A**. Windows Safe Mode will allow the system to be launched using a minimal set of drivers. If the newly installed video driver is corrupt or malfunctioning, then Safe Mode should launch into a stable desktop environment. An anti-virus scan using the latest definition files may reveal whether malicious code is present. However, in this case, there is the possibility that the driver is corrupt or not compatible. Windows Firewall can be used to block both incoming and outgoing network connections, but not verify whether the driver is stable.

11. The correct answer is **C**. As the compromised accounts are associated with a specific number of workstations, the hardware could have been the vector of attack. As the accounts have had passwords reset, this would not be effective as the keylogger will reveal the new passwords. Remote access trojan will allow an attacker to maintain command and control access to workstations and can be used to steal information. A rootkit is designed to intercept calls to system services. Cryptominers use CPU/GPU cycles to mine cryptocurrency.

12. The correct answer is **B**. Malicious cryptominers may be downloaded using a web browser or as a mobile app. The software will steal the resources of the computer to generate new cryptocurrency. This will target the central processing unit (CPU) and the graphical processing unit (GPU) found on advanced graphics cards. Spyware will be used to gather private information from a user or organization. It may slow the computer down but does not target the CPU/GPU specifically. Keyloggers will record all keystrokes entered and store them in a log file. A boot sector virus will replace the OS boot files, launching malware during the boot process.

## 8.4 Explain common social-engineering attacks, threats, and vulnerabilities

1.  The correct answer is **D**. When a single individual is targeted and that individual has a senior management position, they are considered a big fish. So, whaling is based on phishing, but it is a targeted attack against the big fish (a user in a senior position). Phishing is not correct in this case. Option B refers to stealing documents from dumpsters or trash cans that can contain useful intelligence. Option C refers to when somebody tries to catch a user typing a password or PIN code.

2.  The correct answer is **C**. Shoulder surfing is likely to take place in congested spaces when an attacker can be in close proximity to observe a user typing a password. Options A and D typically use an email link to coerce a user into sharing confidential data. Option B refers to eliciting information from a voice call.

3.  The correct answer is **B**. As the contractors have turned up unannounced, this could represent a threat. In this case, they are using impersonation by wearing clothing that gives them the appearance of genuine support contractors. Option A would be when an unauthorized person is able to follow closely behind a valid user through a physical control, such as a locked door controlled by an RFID badge. Option C refers to stealing documents from dumpsters. Option D refers to the placement of malicious Wi-Fi access points.

4.  The correct answer is **D**. An evil twin refers to a deceptive and malicious wireless network that is designed to resemble a legitimate network. It is essentially a rogue access point that appears to be a trusted Wi-Fi network but is set up by an attacker with the intention of intercepting sensitive information or conducting other malicious activities. As the access point is not connected to a legitimate trusted network, mapped drives, and shared printers will not be accessible. Options A, B, and C are other examples of social-engineering attacks.

5.  The correct answer is **A**. Tailgating is when an unauthorized person pretends to be an employee, delivery person, or visitor and attempts to enter a secure area by closely following an authorized employee through a controlled access point, such as a door with an access card or a security checkpoint. Options B, C, and D are other types of social engineering.

6.  The correct answer is **A**. In a DDoS attack, the targeted network or system becomes overloaded and is unable to handle legitimate user requests, effectively denying service to legitimate users. DDoS attacks can involve thousands of connections. Botnets can be used to generate massive amounts of traffic. Option B does not involve thousands of connections, as a DoS could be created by a single malicious host. Option C refers to a vulnerability for which there is no remediation or patch. Option D involves an attacker spoofing an email address, IP address, or MAC address of another genuine host.

7.  The correct answer is **A**. An on-path attack refers to a type of network attack where an adversary gains control or inserts themselves into the communication path between two networked entities. This enables them to intercept, modify, or block network traffic flowing between these entities, allowing them to eavesdrop on sensitive information, manipulate data, or disrupt communication. This type of attack is also known as man in the middle (MiTM). Option B refers to a user who works for the organization that has malicious intent or is poorly trained and so poses a threat. Options C and D are used when an attacker targets a web application server to upload scripts or manipulate the database server (typically in an attempt to gain unauthorized access to the system).

8.  The correct answer is **C**. The main goal of an XSS attack is to manipulate the website's content and interact with the user's session. If the script can be uploaded to the web server, then other users will automatically run the script when they use a browser to visit the site. The malicious payload is identified by the use of arrowhead brackets, <>. Option A would involve the use of a spoofed network identity. Option B would use a different syntax, unique to the SQL language. A zero-day attack describes a vulnerability for which no patch is available.

9.  The correct answer is **D**. A zero-day attack is used to describe a vulnerability where there is no patch available. Options A, B, and C are described in other questions in this chapter.

10. The correct answer is **C**. In a SQL injection attack, attackers exploit vulnerabilities in a web application's input fields to manipulate the SQL queries executed by the application's database. In this case, the attacker has entered a malicious input into the login fields that alters the SQL query executed by the application. The condition '1' = '1' is always true, so the attacker is essentially bypassing the authentication process by manipulating the query to return results for any username and password combination. Option A, a brute-force attack, involves trying all possible combinations of usernames and passwords until the correct one is found. This log entry doesn't indicate repeated login attempts or trying various combinations. Option B, a dictionary attack, is similar to a brute-force attack but involves trying a list of common passwords or dictionary words. Option D, cross-site scripting (XSS), involves injecting malicious scripts into a web application, which then get executed by other users. It doesn't directly relate to unauthorized login attempts or manipulating database queries as seen in the provided log entry.

## 8.5 Given a scenario, manage and configure basic security settings in the Microsoft Windows OS

1.  The correct answer is **B**. This will both set the local NTFS permission and also share the folder on the network. Option A will not share the folder on the network. Option C, referring to read-only attributes, can be used to prevent a file or folder from being accidentally deleted. Option D would not share the folder on the network and would grant more permissions than required.

2.  The correct answer is **A**. All the required settings will be saved with a Microsoft account that is centrally managed and available. This also supports single sign-on (SSO). The account can be enabled through the Windows settings menu. Option B is not possible. Option C is a poor security choice and would still only create local accounts. Option D would only synchronize browser settings and would require that the user create a Microsoft account.

3.  The correct answer is **A, B**. Option A ensures that if the main user account is compromised, then an attacker will have limited privileges. Option B ensures the privileged account is exposed for short periods of time only. Option C is not a recommended best practice for the reasons mentioned previously. Option D is not going to work as the standard user will not have the required privileges.

4.  The correct answer is **B**. BitLocker to Go is intended to protect removable media. The USB drive will be encrypted and will require a BitLocker password or smart card to be used to view any content on the drive. Option A would require the installation of a third-party security suite, although it would support similar functionality. Option C offers no built-in security features. Option D is designed to prevent unauthorized configuration changes on a Windows device.

5.  The correct answer is **A**. EFS can enable a single file or an entire folder to be encrypted using AES symmetric encryption. The user who encrypts the folder will be the only user who will be able to decrypt the files contained within the folder. Additional users can be added at the owner's discretion. Option B is not appropriate as it does not allow a data owner to encrypt individual folders. Option C is used only for removable media. Option D sets permissions but does not encrypt the data.

6.  The correct answer is **B**. UAC is intended to prevent unauthorized configuration changes and will present the user with an option to use an administrator account or approve the action. Option A will pop up alert dialogs relating to suspicious files. Option C is not the answer, although an additional authentication factor could be required if a system detects a risky login event. Option D is not the answer as the user is making a configuration change on a network card, not the firewall.

7.  The correct answer is **A**. It is important to ensure all security updates and anti-virus definitions are kept up to date. In this case, the system was not able to be kept up to date, so the best action is to pull down all updates. Option B is not the best solution as the system may have more malware that has not been detected. Option C is not recommended when dealing with malware; the opposite is recommended (that you delete all restore points) to avoid re-infecting a system. Option D is only required as a last resort, perhaps when all other avenues of remediation have been attempted.

8.  The correct answer is **C**. When a firewall is blocking inbound connections to a port, then a scanner will show the port as being filtered. At the same time, we can see that the filtered port is associated with a database application (MySQL). Option A is not a good choice as it will leave the server unprotected from unwanted connections. Option B will not work as the problem seems to be with the application server. Option D is not an action that will solve the problem, as there is no evidence that the application is the problem.

## 8.6 Given a scenario, configure a workstation to meet best practices for security

1.  The correct answer is **A**. BitLocker will protect the data at rest. If the laptop is stolen, then the thief would have to know the BitLocker password. If they enter the wrong password, then the system will lock the attacker out. Option B would not protect sensitive data, only OS files. Option C would prevent the use of an authorized user account outside of core business hours. Option D would ensure a system is logged out if it is not being actively used.

2.  The correct answer is **B**. The least privilege policy is designed to minimize the potential damage or unauthorized access that can occur when a user's account is compromised or misused. By limiting user privileges, the policy reduces the attack surface and limits the ability of an attacker to move laterally within a system or network. Power Users is a group provided for backward compatibility. There are no privileges given to this group. Option C, disabling guest accounts, is a good security best practice but is not exactly what the question is asking for. Option D is a good security best practice as attackers will not know the name of the renamed administrator account.

3.  The correct answer is **B**. Including personal information such as your name or date of birth is not a best practice to create a strong password as personal information can be easily guessed. Option A is not the strongest option. A dictionary word could be used with a single capitalized character. However, combined with other password-hardening techniques, it can add to password complexity. Option C, incorporating special characters and numbers, will offer protection from simple password-guessing, dictionary, and rainbow table attacks. Option D, referring to longer passwords, is generally a more secure practice because it increases the number of possible combinations that attackers need to guess. However, longer passwords should also incorporate a mix of character types (letters, numbers, and special characters) for optimal security.

4.  The correct answer is **A**. UEFI includes a graphical user interface (GUI) that can be accessed through a mouse or touch input. This allows for easier configuration and management of system settings, such as boot options and hardware configurations. This replaces the older Binary Input/Output System (BIOS). To prevent a user from tampering with any settings, a password should be set. Options B, C, and D refer to the strengthening of passwords that will be used.

5.  The correct answer is **D**. A password manager is a software application or service that helps you securely store and manage your passwords. It provides a convenient way to generate, store, and retrieve complex passwords for different online accounts. The main purpose of a password manager is to improve security by eliminating the need to remember multiple passwords or to use weak and easily guessable passwords. Instead, you only need to remember a single master password or use other authentication methods, such as biometrics (fingerprint or face recognition), to unlock the password manager. A password manager will also protect passwords using encryption. None.

6.   The correct answer is **B**. Option B will restrict the ability of the contractors to log on to systems when there are other members of the payroll staff present. Option A would allow the contractors to log in at any time. Option C would have no effect as the contractors would have assigned accounts (you would never use the guest account for a privileged role). Option D is a good security best practice but does not address the question.

7.   The correct answer is **D**. A brute-force password attack is a technique used by hackers to gain unauthorized access to a system or account by systematically trying all possible combinations of passwords until the correct one is found. It is a straightforward and exhaustive method where the attacker uses automated tools to generate and try different passwords in rapid succession. Option A would use a wordlist or dictionary. Option B does not describe a password attack type. Option C is an example of a network packet sniffer, which can detect passwords sent unencrypted.

8.   The correct answer is **D**. Account lockout will prevent attacks against the interactive login process. Any automated attacks using wordlists or brute force will be highly unlikely to succeed. Option A does not prevent a password from being set that would match an entry in a wordlist. Option B, which refers to login hours restrictions, will not mitigate the threat if an attacker launches attacks during permitted hours. Option C will have no impact on other user accounts.

9.   The correct answer is **A**. By configuring autoplay settings for memory cards, the action can be set to do nothing. The card will be recognized but no automated actions will be taken. Option B would not help as it would make the presentation material unavailable. Option C refers to the wrong autoplay option as the media is a memory card. Option D may partially solve the problem but is not the best answer.

10.  The correct answer is **C**. By changing your password on a regular basis, you will reduce the risk of someone using stolen credentials to access your accounts, counteracting password-guessing or cracking attacks, and limit the impact of stolen passwords. Options A, B, and D are all unsecured ways of managing passwords.

11.  The correct answer is **A**. This would ensure the screens are locked after a period of inactivity (this can be as short as 1 minute). Option B is useful to remind users of their responsibilities but is not the most effective control. Option C is impractical. Option D does not solve the problem as the screen will still be visible.

12.  The correct answer is **B**. The password should be changed in the first instance, to protect the account. Option A is not good advice, although after changing the password, additional monitoring would be good advice. Option C is not practical as an account may be assigned encryption keys/certificates that cannot now be used. Option D is clearly not a recommended practice.

## 8.7 Explain common methods for securing mobile and embedded devices

1.  The correct answer is **C, E**. A screen lock will prevent unauthorized access to the mobile device and FDE ensures the data is protected. After a predetermined number of unsuccessful password attempts, the data is rendered unrecoverable. Options A and B protect a device when accessing network resources only. Option D is useful but will not have much effect if a device is lost or stolen.

2.  The correct answer is **C**. In a BYOD scenario, if an employee's personal device is lost or stolen, there is an increased risk of unauthorized individuals gaining access to sensitive corporate data stored on the device. Since BYOD devices are not under full control of the organization, it can be more challenging to implement robust security measures such as remote wiping or encryption. This risk highlights the importance of strong security policies and protocols for BYOD, such as password protection, device tracking, and data encryption. Option A is incorrect because compatibility issues with corporate applications can exist for both BYOD and company-owned business only (COBO), depending on the device and application requirements. Option B is incorrect because employee privacy and personal data compromise can happen in both BYOD and COBO scenarios if not properly managed. Option D is incorrect because phishing attacks and social engineering are not specific to COBO devices but can affect any device, regardless of ownership (including BYOD).

3.  The correct answer is **B**. The Public profile in Windows Firewall is the most restrictive. It is designed for use in public places where you have the least amount of trust in the network environment. It blocks many incoming connections and provides a higher level of security. Options A and C are trusted network profiles; they will not block incoming connections as strictly as the public profile. D is not a valid firewall profile.

4.  The correct answer is **A, C**. By deploying mobile device management (MDM), configuration settings can be enforced. Geofencing allows a virtual fence or boundary to be set when the device is geolocated within the fence, and then the settings can be enforced. Option B describes using a personal device in a work environment. Options D and E are good choices when the goal is to protect lost or stolen mobile devices, but not for this situation.

5.  The correct answer is **A, C**. Options A and C would satisfy the requirements for biometrics (something you are). Options B, D, and E would be something you know.

6.  The correct answer is **D**. IoT devices will connect to wireless networks and will be vulnerable if the default account password is not changed. Option A refers to a secure wireless protocol for personal area networks used in home automation. Option B is useful to provide a strong wireless signal. Option C is used to report on the location of a device using IP address or GPS coordinates.

## 8.8 Given a scenario, use common data destruction and disposal methods

1.  The correct answer is **C**. Degaussing will completely remove all data from magnetic media such as mechanical hard disk drives and backup tapes. It is not possible to reverse this process. Option A, erasing, does not remove all data remnants; recovery tools can be used to gain access to deleted or erased data. Option B, standard formatting, marks allocation units on a disk volume as free; data can be recovered from formatted volumes. Option D, wiping, erases the data but it can be recovered using certain software.

2.  The correct answer is **D**. Drilling would be a low-tech solution to achieve physical destruction. Drilling through disk platters will physically destroy the storage media. Options A and C require specialist equipment that can be expensive. Option B allows data to be recovered.

3.  The correct answer is **A**. A certification of destruction (CoD) is a document that verifies the complete and secure destruction of sensitive or confidential materials. It is typically issued by a professional shredding or destruction service provider to ensure compliance with legal and regulatory requirements, as well as to provide proof that the materials have been properly disposed of. Option B is used to deter unapproved removal or disclosure of sensitive data. Option C is not a certificate type; if an approved service provider incinerated printed materials, they would provide a CoD. Option D would be used to ensure a service provider meets targets using agreed-upon performance metrics.

4.  The correct answer is **A, C**. It is common that regulatory compliance will require highly classified documents to be sanitized using these two methods. Options B and D are applicable to electronic storage media.

## 8.9 Given a scenario, configure appropriate security settings on small office/home office (SOHO) wireless and wired networks

1.  The correct answer is **D**. Firmware updates on a small office/home office (SOHO) router serve multiple purposes. Firstly, they aim to improve the overall performance and stability of the router, ensuring it runs smoothly and efficiently. Secondly, firmware updates can introduce new features and functionalities, enhancing the router's capabilities. Lastly, and most importantly, firmware updates often address security vulnerabilities and bugs, providing necessary patches to safeguard against potential attacks or unauthorized access. It is crucial to keep the firmware up to date to protect the network and connected devices. Options A, B, and C on their own do not answer the question fully.

2.  The correct answer is **B**. A static wide-area network (WAN) IP, also known as a static public IP, is a fixed internet protocol (IP) address assigned to a device or network that is connected to the internet via a wide-area network. Option A may be something that could be used on the internal network so that a printer always gets assigned the same address. Option C allows for firewall exceptions to be added for internal devices such as gaming stations. Option D would only be required if there was a requirement for an internet-facing service such as an FTP server.

3. The correct answer is **C**. UPnP is a protocol that allows devices on a network to discover and communicate with each other without requiring a user to perform manual configuration. This simplifies tasks such as port opening for online gaming and accessing printers, media servers, and smart TVs. Option A is used to block web pages and email messages that contain inappropriate content. Option B will not affect the firewall rules in this case. Option D is not needed.

4. The correct answer is **B**. A screened subnet allows a semi-secure zone where a hardened host server can be placed. The server will be accessed from the internet through the firewall and will also be accessible from the internal network. Port forwarding will ensure the requests sent by external customers to the WAN IP address are routed currently to the FTP server on the screened subnet. Option A wouldn't be very useful in this case as we would not have more than one IP address in the screened subnet. Option C is definitely something that would ensure that the router was running the latest firmware but does not offer a solution to this question.

5. The correct answer is **A, D**. Without broadcasting the MAC address of the router and the assigned wireless network identifier, an attacker will have to use specialist equipment to detect the presence of the network. Manufacturers of network equipment use standard default administrator account names and passwords on products. These should always be changed. Option B is not needed as there is no requirement for an internet-facing FTP or WWW server. Option C is not something that is needed in this case and would reduce the security of the router.

6. The correct answer is **D**. In an area where there may be multiple wireless access points deployed, it is worthwhile investigating whether there are channels that are unused or have less congestion. Wireless controllers using the 2.4 GHz range only have the option for three non-overlapping channels. In this case, the other options all focus on security, not the speed or strength of the signal.

7. The correct answer is **A**. In a small business, such as a coffee shop, it is common to share the passkey with customers to provide access to free Wi-Fi. The most secure way to do this is to use simultaneous authentication of equals (SAE). This uses AES 256-bit encryption and prevents brute-force attacks against the key. Option B is not secure as WEP has been discontinued. WPA2 is an old standard and does not support SAE, so options C and D are incorrect.

## 8.10 Given a scenario, install and configure browsers and relevant security settings

1. The correct answer is **A, D**. When installing new software, it is recommended to always use a trusted site. If a user wants to download Google Chrome, for example, then it is best to visit the vendor site, not a third-party unknown site. Many software vendors publish the hash, or checksum, for the download file. This can be verified using a hashing utility on the user's workstation. Option B is not that important as a malicious download file could still be the same size as the genuine one. Option C describes a useful feature but does not ensure a trusted download and installation of a piece of software.

2. The correct answer is **A**. Adding a language translator as a browser extension is the most convenient and user-friendly solution for the company to help users translate websites into their native language. Browser extensions, such as Google Translate, allow users to translate web content directly within the browser without the need to copy and paste the content into a separate application. Option B, which refers to browser extensions, can provide the same functionality without requiring users to switch to a new browser. While support for HTML5 is important for modern web browsing, option C doesn't directly address the issue of translating websites into the user's native language. Option D, add support for additional languages to the Windows settings menu, is unrelated to the issue of translating websites.

3. The correct answer is **D**. By enabling an ad blocker, the browser will be able to render and display web pages much quicker. Option A is not really effective anymore as advertising content is embedded within pages, although it can block bogus popups that suggest a host system may have multiple malicious files. Options B and C are not designed to block advertising.

4. The correct answer is **A**. When browsing websites that are secure, the client browser will display a padlock symbol to show the user that the site has a valid certificate. Option B is incorrect as a certificate is not used with the HTTP protocol. Option C is not correct as a rating is not used. Option D allows browsing with no history being retained, which is not relevant to the question.

# Chapter 9: Software Troubleshooting

## 9.1 Given a scenario, troubleshoot common Windows OS problems

1. The correct answer is **A**. Outdated device drivers are a common cause of BSOD errors in Windows. When drivers are not up to date, they can conflict with the OS, leading to system instability and crashes. Options B, C, and D can also cause system issues, but outdated device drivers are specifically known to trigger BSOD errors more frequently.

2. The correct answer is **C**. Faulty RAM can cause BSOD errors, and the most effective solution is to replace the faulty RAM modules. Cleaning the computer's cooling fans (option A) may prevent overheating issues but will not directly address RAM-related errors. Updating the anti-virus software (option B) is unrelated to RAM errors. Re-installing the operating system (option D) is a more extensive troubleshooting step and is usually not required for resolving RAM-related BSOD errors.

3. The correct answer is **B**. The STOP error code displayed on a BSOD is designed to help identify the specific cause of the error. It provides a hexadecimal error code and often includes additional information that assists in troubleshooting and resolving the issue. Options A, C, and D do not accurately reflect the purpose of the STOP error code.

4. The correct answer is **B**. When a computer consistently shuts down after a brief period without displaying an error message, overheating is a common cause. Overheating can be due to a malfunctioning CPU fan, inadequate ventilation, or dust buildup. Power supply failure (option A) is less likely to cause consistent shutdowns without any error message. A virus or malware infection (option C) typically manifests as different symptoms, such as popups, system slowdowns, or unexpected behavior, rather than consistent shutdowns. A faulty motherboard (option D) can cause various issues, but it is not the most probable cause in this scenario.

5. The correct answer is **C**. One of the common reasons for a Windows service not starting is an incorrect service configuration. This can happen if the service is not set to start automatically, or if its dependencies are not properly configured. The service configuration should be checked to ensure that it is set correctly. While option A, insufficient disk space, can cause various issues on a computer, it is not directly related to a service not starting. If a service requires disk space to function properly, it may encounter problems once it is running, but it is not the primary reason for the service not starting. Option B, outdated device drivers, can lead to issues with hardware components, but they are not typically the cause of a service not starting. Services are software components that are separate from device drivers and their functionality. Option D, incompatible software installation, can cause conflicts and system instability, but it is unlikely to prevent a Windows service from starting. While conflicts between software components can occur, they are not a common cause for a service failing to start.

6. The correct answer is **A, C**. Option A, closing unnecessary applications, can help free up memory by releasing resources used by those applications. When the system is running low on memory, closing unused or unnecessary programs can alleviate the issue. Option C, adding more RAM to the system, is an effective solution for low-memory warnings. Increasing the physical RAM capacity provides more memory for the system to manage its workload. Option B, deleting temporary files, can help free up disk space but does not directly address low-memory warnings. Low-memory warnings are specifically related to insufficient RAM, not disk space. Option D, upgrading the processor, is incorrect because low-memory warnings are not directly related to the processor. Upgrading the processor may improve overall system performance but will not resolve low-memory warnings on its own.

7. The correct answer is **A**. This warning indicates that the system has encountered a severe issue that could lead to instability and is about to shut down. It is important to investigate and resolve the critical error to ensure the stability of the system. Option B, "Your anti-virus software has expired. Please renew your subscription," is not directly related to system instability. While it is important to keep anti-virus software up to date for security purposes, an expired subscription does not necessarily indicate system instability. Option C, "A new update is available for your web browser. Click here to install," is a notification for a web browser update. While it is recommended to keep software up to date for security reasons, a browser update is unlikely to directly indicate system instability. Option D, "Low disk space. Free up some space to optimize system performance," is a warning related to disk space, which can impact system performance. While low disk space may affect system stability in the long term, it is not an immediate indicator of system instability. It is more likely to impact system performance and storage capacity.

8. The correct answer is **B**. When the computer displays the "No OS found" message, it indicates that the system is unable to locate a valid OS. This can occur if the hard drive is not properly connected or if it has failed. In such cases, the computer cannot access the necessary files to start the OS. The other options (A, C, and D) may also cause boot-related issues, but they are less likely to directly result in the "No OS found" error. Option A is incorrect because if the Windows OS is missing or corrupted, it would typically display an error related to the OS, such as "Windows Boot Manager error." Option C is incorrect because incorrect BIOS settings could lead to booting issues, but they usually do not result in the specific error message "No OS found." Option D is incorrect because while viruses can cause various issues, they are less likely to directly result in the "No OS found" error. Viruses typically affect the functionality of the OS rather than completely preventing its detection.

9. The correct answer is **B**. A corrupted user profile can cause slow profile load times during login. When a user profile is corrupted, Windows may have difficulty loading the necessary settings and preferences, resulting in delays. The system resources (option A) are typically not the cause unless the computer is severely underpowered. Network connectivity issues (option C) would generally affect the user's ability to access network resources after login, but they are unlikely to directly impact the profile load times. Outdated device drivers (option D) can cause various issues, but they are not specifically related to slow profile load times.

10. The correct answer is **C**. Hardware clock malfunctions can lead to time drift problems as the system may not accurately track the passage of time. While incorrect time zone settings (option A) can cause time display discrepancies, a malware infection (option B) generally does not directly affect the system clock. Power outages (option D) may temporarily disrupt the system clock, but they are not a common cause of persistent time drift.

11. The correct answer is **B**. In the Windows Services management console, you can right-click on a service and choose the "Restart" option to restart the service. Option A, right clicking the service and selecting "Stop" and then "Start," is incorrect because it stops the service first and then starts it, which is different from a restart. Option C, double-clicking the service and selecting "Restart" from the toolbar, is incorrect because double-clicking a service typically opens the properties window for the service, not the option to restart it. Option D, right clicking the service and selecting "Pause" and then "Resume," is incorrect because it pauses and resumes the service, but it does not perform a restart.

12. The correct answer is **C**. When a system is rebooted, all running applications are terminated. This includes any unresponsive applications. Rebooting provides a fresh start and can help resolve issues with unresponsive applications. Rebooting does not reset configuration settings (option A). Rebooting does not automatically repair any issues (option D). Option B is not true as rebooting does have an effect on unresponsive applications.

13. The correct answer is **A**. When an application crashes immediately upon launch, it is essential to ensure that the computer meets the minimum system requirements specified by the application. Inadequate system resources can lead to crashes. Checking available disk space is important, but it is not the first step in this scenario unless the application explicitly requires a certain amount of free space (option B). Reviewing anti-virus software settings is a good practice, but it is not typically the primary cause of an application crashing immediately upon launch (option C). Compatibility mode settings are relevant if the application worked previously but stopped functioning after changes in the compatibility settings. However, it is not the initial step when the application crashes right at launch (option D).

14. The correct answer is **A**. The "boot device not found" error message typically indicates a problem with the boot loader, which is responsible for starting the OS. A corrupted boot loader can occur during an update process or due to other factors, preventing the system from booting properly. Option B, overheating CPU, can cause system instability and unexpected shutdowns, but it is not directly related to the "boot device not found" error. Option C, insufficient hard drive space, can impact system performance and prevent certain operations, but it is not the primary cause of the boot failure in this scenario. Option D, incorrect BIOS settings, can affect system functionality, but it is unlikely to result in the specific error message mentioned.

15. The correct answer is **A**. The installation of the new anti-virus software is causing BSOD errors, indicating a compatibility issue. To troubleshoot the problem, it is recommended to uninstall the anti-virus software and check whether the BSOD errors persist. If the errors cease after the uninstallation, alternative anti-virus software can be considered. Option B, upgrade the computer's RAM, does not typically resolve BSOD errors caused by anti-virus software compatibility. Option C, re-install the operating system, is an extreme measure and is not necessary for resolving compatibility issues with anti-virus software. Option D, replace the graphics card, is unlikely to resolve BSOD errors related to anti-virus software compatibility.

16. The correct answer is **A**. OS update failures can sometimes occur due to conflicts with temporary files or corrupted update data. Clearing temporary files helps eliminate potential issues and provides a clean environment for the update process. After clearing the temporary files, the user can retry the update to see whether the errors are resolved. Option B, install a different web browser, is not directly related to addressing OS update failures. Option C, upgrade the computer's power supply, is not generally connected to OS update failures. Option D, increase the screen resolution, does not address OS update failures and is unrelated to the update process.

17. The correct answer is **C**. When rolling back updates, it is important to create a system restore point. This allows you to revert your system to a previous state if any issues arise during the rollback process. System restore points capture the system's configuration and settings, enabling you to restore it to a known working state. Re-installing the latest updates is incorrect because the purpose of rolling back updates is to revert to a previous version, not to re-install the latest updates (option A). Disabling automatic updates is incorrect because disabling automatic updates does not address the process of rolling back updates. It simply prevents future updates from being installed automatically (option B). Increasing system resources is incorrect because it is unrelated to the process of rolling back updates. It pertains to improving system performance by allocating additional hardware resources, such as RAM or CPU, to address performance issues (option D).

18. The correct answer is **B**. When Windows fails to boot and displays a blue screen of death (BSOD), using System Restore to roll back to a previous working state is a recommended step. System Restore allows you to revert the system to a previously known good configuration, which can help resolve issues that caused the BSOD. Simply restarting the computer (option A) may not resolve the underlying issue. Re-installing all third-party applications (option C) is not necessary unless a specific application is causing the BSOD. Updating the computer's BIOS (option D) should be done cautiously and only if there is a specific indication that the BIOS update addresses the BSOD issue.

19. The correct answer is **C**. The correct answer is option C, when experiencing frequent application crashes. Running a Windows System File Checker can help identify and repair corrupted system files that may be causing frequent crashes. It is a troubleshooting step to address software-related issues. While hardware driver issues (option A) can also cause problems, they are better addressed by updating or re-installing the appropriate drivers. Running a file check is not directly related to installing new software updates (option B), although it can help ensure the stability of the system after updates. Performing a disk defragmentation (option D) is unrelated to running a Windows System File Checker, as defragmentation focuses on optimizing the storage layout on the disk.

20. The correct answer is **C**. Running the "sfc /scannow" command in Command Prompt initiates a Windows System File Checker. This command scans all protected system files and replaces incorrect versions with the correct Microsoft versions. The "sfc /scanfile" command (option A) is used to scan a specific file. "sfc /verifyonly" (option B) verifies the integrity of system files without making any repairs. "sfc /restorehealth" (option D) is used to repair system files using Windows Update as a source.

21. The correct answer is **C**. Windows reimaging can be used as a troubleshooting step when a computer is plagued by persistent crashes and blue screen errors. Reimaging can help eliminate software-related issues that might be causing system instability, providing a fresh and stable installation of Windows. Option A is incorrect because when a specific software application is not launching properly, it is usually an isolated issue related to that particular application. Troubleshooting steps specific to the application, such as re-installing or updating it, would be more appropriate. Option B is incorrect because an unstable internet connection is generally not resolved by using Windows reimaging. Troubleshooting network settings, checking hardware connections, or contacting the internet service provider would be more suitable for resolving internet connection issues. Option D is incorrect because adjusting the display resolution does not necessitate using Windows reimaging. Changing the display resolution is a configuration setting that can be adjusted within the OS without requiring a complete system re-installation.

## 9.2 Given a scenario, troubleshoot common personal computer (PC) security issues

1. The correct answer is **A**. The first step in troubleshooting network connectivity issues is to verify the physical network connections and cables. This includes checking whether the network cable is securely plugged into the PC and the router or switch. By ensuring the physical connections are intact, any issues related to loose or faulty connections can be identified and resolved. Updating anti-virus software (option B) is not directly related to network connectivity issues. Re-installing the OS (option C) is an extreme step and should be considered only if all other troubleshooting steps fail. Increasing the PC's RAM (option D) does not directly address network connectivity issues.

2.  The correct answer is **D**. False alerts regarding anti-virus protection can be caused by legitimate files being flagged as threats. By excluding the false positive files from anti-virus scans, the alerts will no longer appear, and the user can distinguish between genuine threats and false positives. Updating the anti-virus software (option A) may help improve its detection capabilities but may not directly address the false alert issue. Adjusting the settings of the firewall (option B) is unrelated to false alerts caused by the anti-virus software. Running a full system scan (option C) using an anti-virus program may detect threats but does not specifically address the false positive alerts.

3.  The correct answer is **B**. A ransomware infection is a type of malware that encrypts or alters the user's files and demands a ransom to restore access. This aligns with the user's report of altered or missing/renamed files. Phishing attacks (option A) typically involve tricking users into revealing sensitive information and are less likely to directly affect file integrity. Rootkit installations (option C) and unauthorized access by network intruders (option D) can potentially lead to file tampering, but a ransomware infection is the most common cause of files being altered or held hostage.

4.  The correct answer is **A**. Unwanted notifications within the OS can often be caused by unnecessary or malicious programs running at startup. By disabling startup programs, the technician can eliminate programs that may be responsible for generating unwanted notifications. Updating the BIOS (option B) is unrelated to OS notifications. Re-installing the OS (option C) is a drastic step and should be considered only if other troubleshooting methods fail. Cleaning the registry (option D) using a registry cleaner tool is unnecessary and may not directly address unwanted OS notifications.

5.  The correct answer is **B**. Often, issues with OS update failures can be resolved by restarting the PC and attempting to install the updates again. This can help reset any temporary glitches or conflicts that may be preventing successful updates. Disabling the anti-virus software (option A) may temporarily help in some cases, but it is not the first step to take. Re-installing the OS (option C) should be considered only if all other troubleshooting methods fail. Clearing the browser cache (option D) is unrelated to OS updates and would not resolve this particular issue.

6.  The correct answer is **A**. Adware or malware infections often result in the appearance of random or frequent pop-up advertisements on web browsers. These popups are usually unwanted and may lead to potentially harmful websites or downloads. Certificate warnings occur when a browser detects an issue with the security certificate of a website (option B). While certificate warnings may indicate potential security concerns, they are not directly associated with adware or malware infections. Option C, redirection, refers to instances where a web browser is automatically directed to a different website than the one intended by the user. While this can be caused by malware, it is not necessarily related to adware or malware infections alone. Slow internet speed can be caused by various factors, such as network congestion or issues with the internet service provider. While malware infections can impact internet performance, it is not a specific symptom associated with adware or malware infections (option D).

7. The correct answer is **C**. When a security certificate associated with a website expires, the browser generates certificate warnings to inform the user about the potential security risks. It is important to ensure that websites have up-to-date security certificates. An outdated browser can sometimes cause compatibility issues with new security certificates, but it is not the most likely cause for repeated certificate warnings (option A).While a firewall can block secure connections, it is unlikely to result in repeated certificate warnings (option B). Firewall-related issues typically prevent access to secure websites altogether rather than generating certificate warnings. DNS cache poisoning refers to an attack where incorrect or malicious information is inserted into the DNS cache. While this attack can lead to security issues, it is not the most likely cause for repeated certificate warnings (option D).

8. The correct answer is **C**. Browser hijacking is a form of malware attack where the settings of a web browser are modified without the user's consent, leading to frequent redirection to unwanted websites. This symptom is particularly associated with browser hijacking. Option A, random/frequent popups, can be associated with adware or malware infections but not specifically with browser hijacking. Certificate warnings can occur due to various reasons, including expired or invalid security certificates, but they are not directly linked to browser hijacking (option B). Option D, slow internet speed, can be caused by different factors, such as network congestion or performance issues, but it is not specifically associated with browser hijacking.

## 9.3 Given a scenario, use best practice procedures for malware removal

1. The correct answer is **A**. The best practice procedure for malware removal in this scenario is to disconnect the computer from the network to prevent further infection, perform a full system scan using updated anti-malware software to detect any malware, and then remove any detected malware. This approach ensures the thorough removal of the malicious software and helps restore the system's performance and stability. Option B is incorrect because manually deleting suspicious files and folders may not effectively remove all malware, and it does not address the potential for hidden or system-level malware. Option C is incorrect because re-installing the OS should be considered a last resort, as it involves significant time and effort. It should only be pursued if all other methods fail or if the system is severely compromised. Option D is incorrect because ignoring the issue can lead to further system instability, data loss, and potential security breaches. It is important to address malware infections promptly.

2.  The correct answer is **C**. The recommended practice for updating anti-malware software is to configure it to update automatically and regularly. This ensures that the software receives the latest virus definitions, security patches, and feature updates, providing the most effective protection against new and emerging threats. Option A is incorrect because disabling automatic updates can leave the system vulnerable to new threats if the software is not regularly updated. It is important to maintain up-to-date protection. Option B is incorrect because relying solely on manual updates prompted by the OS can lead to delays in receiving critical updates and leave the system exposed to malware attacks. Option D is incorrect because uninstalling and re-installing the software is not necessary for routine updates. Most anti-malware software offers in-app update functionality that does not require a complete re-install.

3.  The correct answer is **B**. It is important to investigate and verify malware symptoms before proceeding with the removal process because it allows for more accurate identification and selection of appropriate removal techniques. Different types of malware may exhibit different symptoms, and understanding these symptoms helps in determining the most effective course of action. The cost of malware removal can vary depending on factors such as the severity of the infection, the expertise required for removal, and the resources used, but it is not determined solely by investigating and verifying symptoms (option A). While investigating and verifying malware symptoms can provide some insights into the complexity of the infection, it does not directly help in estimating the time required to remove the malware (option C). The time required for removal depends on various factors, such as the nature of the malware, the extent of the infection, the efficiency of the removal tools, and the skill of the person performing the removal. Investigating and verifying malware symptoms may indirectly contribute to educating the end user about the potential risks of malware (option D). However, the primary purpose of investigating and verifying symptoms is to identify and select appropriate removal techniques. Educating the end user about malware risks is an important aspect but not directly related to the investigation and verification process.

4.  The correct answer is **A**. Regularly updating anti-virus software is crucial for staying protected against new malware threats. Updates often include the latest virus definitions, improved detection algorithms, and security enhancements, ensuring the anti-virus software can effectively identify and remove the latest malware variants. Option B, disable the system's user account control (UAC) feature, removes an important layer of defense against unauthorized system changes and can make the system more susceptible to malware infections. It is recommended to keep UAC enabled. Option C, share user credentials with trusted colleagues, can lead to unauthorized access, compromising the security of the system and increasing the risk of malware infections. User credentials should be kept confidential and not shared. Option D, enable all browser extensions and plugins by default, increases the attack surface and potential vulnerabilities, making the system more prone to malware infections. It is advisable to review and disable unnecessary or untrusted extensions and plugins to reduce the risk.

5.  The correct answer is **A**. Quarantining infected systems is necessary during the malware removal process to prevent the malware from spreading to other systems. By isolating the infected systems, the risk of further contamination is minimized, protecting other devices on the network. Option B, to disable System Restore in Windows, is not a primary reason for quarantining infected systems during the malware removal process. System Restore is a feature that allows users to revert their system's state to a previous point in time, which can be useful in case of system errors or issues. However, it is not directly related to quarantining infected systems. Option C, to create a restore point for future use, is also not a primary reason for quarantining infected systems. Restore points are typically created to provide a fallback option in case of system issues or changes. While it can be a good practice to create a restore point before performing malware removal, it is not the main purpose of quarantining infected systems. Option D, to schedule scans and run updates, is an important part of the malware removal process, but it is not directly related to quarantining infected systems. Quarantining infected systems is primarily done to isolate the malware and prevent its spread to other systems. Scans and updates can be performed after the quarantine to detect and remove the malware effectively.

6.  The correct answer is **B**. Disabling System Restore in Windows during malware removal is done primarily to remove any infected restore points. Malware can hide in these restore points, allowing it to survive even after the malware removal process. By disabling System Restore, all existing restore points are deleted, reducing the chances of the malware reappearing. Option A is incorrect because disabling System Restore does not directly prevent the malware from spreading to other systems. It mainly focuses on removing infected restore points. Option C is incorrect because disabling System Restore alone does not guarantee that the malware cannot re-infect the system. Other security measures, such as using reliable anti-virus software and updating system patches, are also necessary. Option D is not correct as System Restore does not directly speed up the malware removal process. It is primarily done to remove infected restore points rather than affect the speed of the removal process.

7.  The correct answer is **B**. When System Restore is disabled during malware removal, all existing restore points are deleted. This action helps remove any potential hiding places for the malware, making it harder for it to survive and re-infect the system. Disabling System Restore does not immediately delete the malware from the system. It primarily focuses on removing infected restore points rather than directly eliminating the malware (option A). Disabling System Restore does not directly isolate or prevent the malware from executing (option C). It primarily deals with removing infected restore points. Disabling System Restore does not make the system immune to further malware infections (option D). It is a precautionary step in the malware removal process, but additional security measures are required to ensure the system's ongoing protection.

8.  The correct answer is **C**. Educating the end user is crucial in reducing the likelihood of future malware incidents. By teaching the end user about safe browsing habits, recognizing phishing attempts, and avoiding suspicious downloads, they become more aware of potential threats and are less likely to fall victim to malware. This helps minimize the risk of re-infection. Option A is incorrect because educating the end user should not be done to shift the responsibility of malware removal to them entirely. It is a collaborative effort between the end user and IT professionals. Option B is incorrect because while enhancing the end user's technical skills can be beneficial, it is not the primary reason for educating them as part of the malware removal process. Option D is incorrect because creating a sense of panic and urgency is counterproductive. Educating the end user should focus on providing them with the necessary knowledge and tools to prevent malware incidents, rather than inducing panic.

9.  The correct answer is **C**. Educating the end user about malware removal can lead to faster incident response times. When end users are aware of potential malware threats and know how to report suspicious activities promptly, IT professionals can respond quickly and mitigate the impact of the incident. Option A is incorrect because educating the end user should not result in decreased user productivity. Instead, it should empower them to be proactive and take appropriate actions to prevent malware incidents. Option B is incorrect because the goal of educating the end user is to reduce reliance on IT support. By educating them about safe practices and self-help measures, end users can take more responsibility for their own security. Option D is incorrect because educating the end user about malware removal should lead to an increased likelihood of preventing data breaches, not the other way around.

10. The correct answer is **C**. Neglecting to educate the end user about malware removal can lead to a higher incidence of successful malware attacks. If end users are not aware of safe practices and do not know how to identify and report potential threats, they become more vulnerable to malware attacks. Option A is incorrect because neglecting to educate the end user does not necessarily result in increased IT budget allocation. While malware incidents can incur costs, allocating a higher budget may not address the root cause. Option B is incorrect because neglecting to educate the end user does not directly cause decreased system performance. Malware infections can impact system performance, but that is a consequence of the malware itself, not the lack of end user education. Option D is incorrect because neglecting to educate the end user does not directly cause decreased network bandwidth. Malware infections can consume network bandwidth if they engage in malicious activities, but that is a consequence of the malware itself, not the lack of end user education.

## 9.4 Given a scenario, troubleshoot common mobile OS and application issues

1.  The correct answer is **A**. Background app refresh is a feature that allows apps to refresh their content in the background, even when they are not actively being used. Enabling this feature for multiple apps can consume significant battery power, causing rapid battery drain. Option B is incorrect. Low screen brightness can conserve battery life, so it is unlikely to be the cause of the rapid battery drain. Option C is also incorrect. Mobile data usage affects data consumption but does not directly impact battery drain when the device is not actively using data. Option D is incorrect because overcharging the device can potentially damage the battery over time, but it does not cause immediate rapid battery drain.

2.  The correct answer is **C**. AirDrop requires both Bluetooth and Wi-Fi to be enabled on both devices for the file transfer to take place. Bluetooth is used for device discovery, and Wi-Fi is used for the actual file transfer. Option A is incorrect as AirDrop can work even when both devices are not connected to the same Wi-Fi network. It uses a combination of Bluetooth and Wi-Fi to establish a direct connection between devices. Option B is not correct as AirDrop can be used to transfer files between various Apple devices, including iPhones, iPads, and Mac computers. Option D is incorrect as AirDrop is exclusive to Apple devices and cannot be used to transfer files to non-Apple devices.

3.  The correct answer is **A**. Performing a soft reset on the device is the first troubleshooting step to attempt when a smartphone becomes unresponsive. This can be done by holding down the power button until the device restarts. It helps to clear temporary issues or software glitches that may be causing the unresponsiveness. Option B, clear the cache of all installed applications, may help with specific app-related issues, but it is not the most appropriate step for addressing a generally unresponsive device. Option C, re-install the mobile operating system, is a drastic measure that should be considered as a last resort when all other troubleshooting steps have failed. As many modern smartphones have non-removable batteries, option D may not be applicable. Even if the battery is removable, removing and reinserting it is not likely to resolve an unresponsiveness issue.

4.  The correct answer is **A**. Frequent battery drain is a common symptom of a malware-infected mobile device. Malware running in the background can consume system resources and drain the battery more quickly than usual. Option B, improved device performance, is not a common symptom of a malware-infected mobile device. Malware tends to slow down the device and negatively impact its performance. Option C, enhanced battery life, is also not a common symptom of a malware-infected mobile device. Malware typically increases battery drain rather than improving battery life. Option D, app icons rearranging automatically, can be caused by various factors, such as a user's unintentional actions or a bug in the OS, but it is not directly indicative of a malware infection.

5.  The correct answer is **A**. Near-field communication (NFC) enables contactless data exchange between two devices in close proximity. It allows devices to establish a connection by bringing them near each other, typically within a few centimeters. Option B, Bluetooth, is a wireless technology that enables data exchange between devices over short distances but not necessarily in close proximity or through contactless means. Option C, Wi-Fi, enables wireless communication between devices over longer distances and is not focused on contactless data exchange in close proximity. Option D, GPS (Global Positioning System), is a satellite-based navigation system used for determining the location and positioning of a device but does not facilitate contactless data exchange between devices.

6.  The correct answer is **B**. The first troubleshooting step to resolve the issue of the screen not autorotating on a mobile device is to check the screen rotation settings. Sometimes, the autorotate feature may be disabled in the device's settings, preventing the screen from automatically rotating. By verifying and adjusting the screen rotation settings, the issue can often be resolved without further action. While restarting the device can fix various issues, it may not specifically address the screen autorotation problem (option A). Checking the screen rotation settings is a more targeted approach. Option C, update the mobile operating system, can be beneficial for overall system stability and bug fixes, but it is less likely to directly resolve the specific issue of the screen not autorotating. It is not the most immediate troubleshooting step. Option D, perform a factory reset, should be considered as a last resort. It erases all data and settings on the device, which can be inconvenient and time-consuming. It should only be attempted if other troubleshooting steps have failed to resolve the issue.

7.  The correct answer is **B**. The most appropriate troubleshooting step to address a mobile device that randomly reboots while using an application is to update the OS to the latest version. This step is crucial as outdated OSs can cause compatibility issues, leading to system instability. Updating the OS ensures that any known bugs or vulnerabilities are addressed, providing a more stable environment for running applications. Option A, clear the cache and data of the application, might resolve issues related to the application's performance or data corruption, but it is unlikely to fix the problem of the device randomly rebooting. This step is more focused on resolving application-specific issues rather than system-wide problems. Option C, re-install the application, may help if the issue is isolated to that specific application, but if the device is randomly rebooting regardless of the application in use, re-installing the app is unlikely to solve the problem. Option D, factory reset the mobile device, should only be considered as a last resort. It erases all data and settings, returning the device to its original factory state. Performing a factory reset is a drastic step and should only be used when all other troubleshooting steps have failed to resolve the issue.

8.  The correct answer is **B**. Uninstalling unnecessary applications will free up storage space on the mobile device and allow the user to install new applications. Option A, clear the device cache, may improve performance but will not directly address the storage space issue. Option C, perform a factory reset, will erase all data and settings on the device, which is not necessary in this scenario. Option D, upgrade the device's operating system, is unrelated to the storage space problem.

9. The correct answer is **A, B**. Closing background applications can help conserve battery power by preventing unnecessary processes from running. Enabling battery optimization settings can also extend battery life. Option C, replace the device battery, is not necessary unless the battery is old or damaged. On many mobile devices, it is not possible to replace the battery. Option D, disable push email notifications, may reduce battery usage but is unlikely to be the primary cause of rapid battery drain.

10. The correct answer is **A**. Restarting the device is the initial troubleshooting step to address various software-related issues, including unresponsive touchscreens. Options B, C, and D – calibrate the touchscreen, update the device's firmware, and clean the touchscreen – are secondary steps that can be performed if the issue persists after restarting the device.

11. The correct answer is **B**. Uninstalling and re-installing the app can resolve app crashes caused by corrupted installation files. Option A, clear the app cache, can improve performance but may not directly address the crashes. Options C and D, update the device's operating system and restart the device, are general troubleshooting steps and may not specifically resolve the app-crashing issue.

12. The correct answer is **A**. Clearing app cache and data can help improve performance by removing temporary files and resetting app settings. Option B, perform a factory reset, would erase all data and settings, which should be avoided unless necessary. Option C, install a performance optimization app, may help but is not the first troubleshooting step. Option D, upgrade the device's memory (RAM), is unrelated to the slow performance issue.

13. The correct answer is **A, B**. Resetting the device's network settings can resolve Wi-Fi connectivity issues caused by misconfigured network settings. Forgetting and reconnecting to the Wi-Fi network is a less drastic step and can also help establish a stable connection. Option C, replace the device's Wi-Fi antenna, is unnecessary unless it is physically damaged. Option D, update the device's firmware, is a general troubleshooting step and may not specifically address the Wi-Fi connectivity problem.

14. The correct answer is **C**. Deleting unnecessary files and applications will free up storage space on the device and resolve the "Insufficient storage available" issue. Option A, clear the app cache, can also help, but it may not be sufficient in this case. Options C and D, move apps and data to an external storage device and upgrade the device's storage capacity, are possible solutions but not the first steps to consider.

15. The correct answer is **A, B**. Option A, update the device's firmware, can fix known issues and bugs that may cause frequent reboots and freezes. Option B, perform a factory reset, is a more drastic step and should be a step to consider if option A is unsuccessful. Option C, replace the device's battery, is unlikely to solve the problem. Option D, disable unnecessary background processes, can improve performance but may not directly address reboots and freezes.

## 9.5 Given a scenario, troubleshoot common mobile OS and application security issues

1. The correct answer is **B**. APK (Android Package Kit) is a file format used to distribute and install applications on Android devices. It contains all the necessary files and resources needed to run an Android application. Option A is incorrect because an APK file is not specifically used for storing music files. Option C is incorrect because APK files are not used on iOS devices; they are specific to the Android OS. Option D is incorrect because a system file responsible for managing network connections is not related to APK files.

2. The correct answer is **A**. Enabling developer mode on a mobile device grants access to advanced system settings and debugging features, allowing developers to test and troubleshoot applications more effectively. Option B is incorrect because the ability to install applications from unofficial sources is typically controlled by a separate setting called "Unknown sources" or "Allow installation from unknown sources." Option C is incorrect because enabling developer mode does not directly optimize battery life. Option D is incorrect because the screen resolution is generally fixed and cannot be increased by enabling developer mode.

3. The correct answer is **C**. Rooting an Android device grants the user administrative access and control over the OS. It allows for customization, installing custom ROM, and using advanced system-level features. Option A is incorrect because removing malicious applications does not require rooting the device. Option B is incorrect because rooting, if not done properly, can potentially compromise device security. Option D is incorrect because while rooting can provide certain performance benefits, it is not its primary purpose.

4. The correct answer is **A**. Jailbreaking refers to the process of bypassing software restrictions imposed by Apple on iOS devices. It allows users to access the root filesystem and install unauthorized applications. Option B is incorrect because bootlegging refers to the unauthorized reproduction or distribution of copyrighted material. Option C is incorrect because application spoofing involves creating a fake or imitation application to deceive users. Option D is incorrect because a malicious application is a type of harmful software that can compromise the security of a device, but it is not directly related to bypassing software restrictions.

5. The correct answer is **C**. A bootleg application is a term used to describe a pirated or unauthorized copy of a mobile application, typically obtained from unofficial sources. Option A is incorrect because APK is a file format used to distribute and install Android applications, but it does not specifically refer to pirated or unauthorized copies. Option B is incorrect because developer mode is an unrelated term. Option D is incorrect because root access refers to gaining administrative privileges on an Android device, which is not directly related to pirated or unauthorized copies of applications.

6.  The correct answer is **A**. High network traffic can cause a mobile device to have a sluggish response time, leading to delays in loading apps or web pages. Limited internet connectivity (option B) usually indicates a problem with the device's connection to the network but may not necessarily be related to high network traffic. A high number of ads (option C) is more likely to be caused by adware or malicious apps rather than high network traffic. Fake security warnings (option D) are typically associated with malware or phishing attempts, not specifically high network traffic.

7.  The correct answer is **A**. When a mobile device reaches its data usage limit, it may experience no internet connectivity until the limit is reset or additional data is purchased. Unexpected application behavior (option B) could be caused by various factors, but reaching a data usage limit is not directly related to this symptom. Leaked personal files/data (option C) suggests a security breach or privacy issue rather than a specific symptom of reaching a data usage limit. Sluggish response time (option D) could be a symptom of other issues but is not specifically related to reaching a data usage limit.

8.  The correct answer is **A**. A compromised mobile OS or application often exhibits slow device performance and frequent crashes because of malicious activities or vulnerabilities. This can indicate the presence of malware or unauthorized access. Option B suggests improved battery life and faster processing speed, which are not typical symptoms of a compromised mobile OS or application. Option C mentions enhanced security features and increased app compatibility, which are positive outcomes rather than symptoms of security issues. Option D suggests a smooth user interface and seamless multitasking, which are not directly related to security issues and compromises.

9.  The correct answer is **A**. Excessive battery usage can indicate a security issue with a mobile application, such as background processes or malicious activities consuming resources without the user's knowledge. It can be a symptom of malware or poorly optimized app code. Option B suggests regular software updates, which is generally considered a good practice for security but does not represent a security issue. Option C mentions limited app permissions, which actually contribute to better security by restricting access to sensitive device functions. Option D refers to encrypted data storage, which is a security feature rather than an issue.

10. The correct answer is **A**. Unexpected app crashes can be a symptom of a mobile OS vulnerability, where a flaw in the OS or its components causes apps to malfunction or terminate abruptly. These crashes can potentially be exploited by attackers. Option B mentions enhanced device performance, which is not a symptom of an OS vulnerability and is more likely a positive outcome. Option C suggests improved battery life, which is not typically associated with OS vulnerabilities. Option D refers to seamless network connectivity, which is not directly related to OS vulnerabilities and can occur even in secure systems.

11. The correct answer is **D**. Unauthorized app installations represent a common security issue with mobile devices. When users unknowingly install apps from untrusted sources or with malicious intent, it can lead to privacy breaches, data theft, or compromise of the device's security. Option A mentions weak network signal strength, which may affect connectivity but is not directly linked to security issues. Option B suggests strong device encryption, which is actually a security measure rather than an issue. Option C refers to regular backups of data, which are essential for data protection but not a security issue themself.

12. The correct answer is **A**. Unwanted pop-up advertisements can be a symptom of a mobile application security breach, indicating the presence of adware or malware. These advertisements can disrupt the user experience, compromise privacy, and potentially lead to further security issues. Option B mentions enhanced app functionality, which is not typically associated with security breaches. Option C suggests increased device storage capacity, which is unrelated to application security breaches. Option D refers to improved user experience, which may occur in well-designed applications but does not directly signify a security breach.

13. The correct answer is **A**. Excessive RAM utilization is a common indication of a security issue associated with mobile OSs. It can indicate memory leaks or poorly optimized processes, potentially leading to system instability and unauthorized access to sensitive information. Option B suggests prompt security updates, which is generally considered a good practice for addressing security issues rather than being a security issue. Option C mentions a secure boot process, which is a security feature rather than an issue. Option D refers to encrypted user data, which is a desirable security measure.

14. The correct answer is **A**. Application crashes upon launch can be a symptom of a mobile application vulnerability, indicating potential coding or implementation flaws that result in instability. Such vulnerabilities can be exploited by attackers to gain unauthorized access or perform malicious actions. Option B mentions faster battery charging, which is unrelated to application vulnerabilities. Option C suggests enhanced network connectivity, which is not typically associated with application vulnerabilities. Option D refers to increased app compatibility, which is a positive outcome rather than a symptom of vulnerabilities.

15. The correct answer is **C**. Outdated software versions represent a common security issue with mobile OSs. Failure to install software updates promptly can leave devices vulnerable to known exploits and security vulnerabilities that have been patched in newer versions. Option A mentions frequent app updates, which are generally considered beneficial for functionality and security. Option B suggests encrypted device backups, which actually contribute to better security rather than being a security issue. Option D highlights optimized power-saving features, which are unrelated to security issues with mobile OSs.

16. The correct answer is **A**. Unexpected data usage can be a symptom of a compromised mobile application, indicating unauthorized background activities, data exfiltration, or communication with malicious servers. It may result in additional charges, privacy breaches, or other security risks. Option B mentions improved device performance, which is not typically associated with compromised applications. Option C suggests enhanced battery longevity, which is not directly related to compromised applications. Option D refers to seamless app integration, which is unrelated to security compromises and can occur even in secure applications.

## Chapter 10: Operational Procedures

### 10.1 Given a scenario, implement best practices associated with documentation and support systems information management

1.  The correct answer is **C**. Splash screens are an effective way to communicate important information to users before they access a system. They can display regulatory compliance requirements, organization policies, and other essential information. By implementing splash screens, the company can ensure that users are informed and aware of the necessary guidelines and procedures. While password complexity rules are important for security (Option A), they are not directly related to regulatory compliance requirements or splash screens. Network segmentation is a technique used to divide a network into smaller segments for security and performance purposes (Option B). It is not directly related to splash screens or regulatory compliance requirements. Incident reports are typically used to document and track security incidents or system failures (Option D). While important for incident management, they are not directly related to regulatory compliance requirements or splash screens.

2.  The correct answer is **C**. Incident reports are the appropriate documents for recording detailed information about each incident that occurs during support activities. They provide a structured format to document the incident, including the nature of the issue, the steps taken to resolve it, and any relevant details. Incident reports are essential for tracking, analysis, and compliance purposes. Knowledge base articles contain information about common issues, solutions, and best practices (Option A). They are not specifically used for recording detailed information about individual incidents. Splash screens are typically used to display important information to users before accessing a system (Option B). They are not intended for recording incident details. Service-level agreements (SLAs) are contractual agreements between service providers and customers, defining the level of service expected (Option D). While SLAs may include incident management processes, they are not the primary documents for recording detailed incident information.

3.  The correct answer is **D**. Training employees on data handling and privacy policies is a best practice for complying with regulatory requirements related to incident reporting. By providing proper training, employees are equipped with the necessary knowledge and skills to handle incidents appropriately, ensuring compliance with regulatory guidelines. This includes understanding incident reporting procedures, incident classification, and the importance of documenting incidents accurately. While splash screens can be used for various purposes, such as displaying company logos or legal disclaimers, they are not directly related to incident reporting or regulatory compliance requirements (Option A). Vulnerability assessments are important for identifying security weaknesses in systems and networks (Option B). While they are crucial for overall security, they are not specific to incident reporting or regulatory compliance requirements. Encryption of sensitive customer data during transit is an essential security measure (Option C). However, it specifically focuses on protecting data during transmission and does not directly address incident reporting or regulatory compliance requirements.

4. The correct answer is **A**. Network diagrams provide visual representations of the network infrastructure and help support technicians understand the layout and connectivity, making them an essential part of the documentation for support system information management. The other choices are important but not directly related to support system information management.

5. The correct answer is **C**. A knowledge base is a centralized repository of information that contains troubleshooting guides, FAQs, and solutions to known issues. It serves as a valuable resource for support technicians when resolving customer problems. The other choices are unrelated to the purpose of a knowledge base.

6. The correct answer is **B**. When documenting a support request, it is crucial to include the date and time of the request. This information helps establish the order of requests and allows for proper tracking and prioritization. The other choices are irrelevant details that do not contribute to support system information management.

7. The correct answer is **C**. Regularly updating and reviewing documentation is a best practice to ensure that the information remains accurate and relevant. Storing documents in multiple physical locations may lead to version control issues (Option A). Sharing sensitive information via email can compromise security (Option B). Printing documentation unnecessarily wastes resources (Option D).

8. The correct answer is **B**. ServiceNow is an example of a ticketing system commonly used in support systems. It allows support technicians to create, track, and manage support tickets, ensuring efficient resolution of customer issues. The other choices are software applications unrelated to ticketing systems.

9. The correct answer is **C**. A service level agreement (SLA) in support system documentation defines the agreed-upon response and resolution times for support requests. It sets expectations for both the support provider and the customer. The other choices are not directly related to the purpose of an SLA.

10. The correct answer is **C**. A support system knowledge base article should include tested solutions to known issues. It should provide accurate and reliable information to assist support technicians in resolving customer problems. The other choices are irrelevant or inappropriate for inclusion in a knowledge base.

11. The correct answer is **C**. Organizing and categorizing support system documentation using color-coded labels helps improve accessibility and ease of navigation. It allows support technicians to quickly locate the relevant information they need. The other choices do not provide an efficient method of organization.

12. The correct answer is **A**. Salesforce is an example of a customer relationship management (CRM) system used in support systems. It helps manage customer information, interactions, and support requests, ensuring a streamlined customer support experience. The other choices are unrelated to CRM systems.

13. The correct answer is **C**. Creating an inventory list in support system documentation helps track spare parts and equipment available for repair and replacement. It ensures that support technicians have the necessary resources to address customer issues effectively. The other choices are unrelated to the purpose of an inventory list.

14. The correct answer is **B**. An acceptable use policy (AUP) is a set of rules and guidelines that define the acceptable and appropriate use of computer systems and networks within an organization. It outlines the expected behavior of users and helps protect against misuse or abuse of resources. AUPs typically cover topics such as authorized access, prohibited activities, confidentiality, and consequences for non-compliance. Option A is incorrect because backups of critical data are not directly related to an AUP. While data backup may be mentioned in other policies, an AUP specifically focuses on user behavior and system usage. Option C is incorrect because troubleshooting hardware issues is a separate topic from an AUP. Troubleshooting processes and procedures are covered under different policies or guidelines. Option D is incorrect because documenting software license agreements is not directly related to an AUP. Software license agreements are usually governed by legal and compliance policies rather than an AUP.

## 10.2 Explain basic change-management best practices

1. The correct answer is **C**. Documenting changes thoroughly is a basic change-management best practice because it helps maintain a record of all modifications made, making it easier to track and troubleshoot issues if they arise. Option A is incorrect because implementing changes without proper planning can lead to unexpected consequences and disruptions in the system. Option B is incorrect because communicating changes only after they have been implemented can cause confusion and resistance among users. Option D is incorrect because ignoring user feedback can result in overlooking important insights and requirements for successful change implementation.

2. The correct answer is **C**. Assessing and managing risks is a key element of change management. By identifying potential risks and implementing appropriate mitigation strategies, organizations can ensure a smoother transition during change implementation. Option A is incorrect because user involvement is crucial during change management to gather feedback, address concerns, and ensure user acceptance. Option B is incorrect because effective communication with stakeholders is essential for managing expectations and ensuring their understanding and support. Option D is incorrect because rushing the implementation process can lead to errors and overlook critical steps, increasing the likelihood of failure.

3.  The correct answer is **B**. Providing clear communication and training is a recommended practice for managing user resistance during change implementation. By keeping users informed about the changes and their benefits, and by providing adequate training, organizations can address concerns and increase user acceptance. Option A is incorrect because ignoring user concerns can lead to increased resistance and negatively impact the success of change implementation. Option C is incorrect because limiting user access to system documentation can hinder their understanding and ability to adapt to the changes effectively. Option D is incorrect because implementing changes abruptly without prior notice can cause confusion and resistance among users.

4.  The correct answer is **C**. The purpose of a change advisory board (CAB) is to evaluate and prioritize proposed changes. The CAB ensures that changes align with organizational goals, assesses their impact, and decides their priority for implementation. Option A is incorrect because approving all changes without review can lead to uncontrolled modifications and potential disruptions. Option B is incorrect because while the CAB may monitor the progress of change implementation, its primary purpose is to evaluate and prioritize proposed changes. Option D is incorrect because user involvement is important in the change process to gather feedback and ensure successful adoption.

5.  The correct answer is **C**. Temporary service disruptions are a common risk associated with change management. Implementing changes can sometimes result in system downtime or disruptions, affecting user productivity during the transition. Option A is incorrect because improved system performance is a potential benefit of change management rather than a risk. Option B is incorrect because increased user satisfaction is a desired outcome of successful change management. Option D is incorrect because enhanced security measures are typically a positive outcome of change management efforts.

6.  The correct answer is **B**. Performing regular backups is an example of a change management best practice for software deployments. Backups ensure that data can be restored if there are any issues or failures during the deployment process. Option A is incorrect because skipping the testing phase can lead to the deployment of faulty software and potential system disruptions. Option C is incorrect because implementing changes during peak hours can increase the impact on users and affect system availability. Option D is incorrect because effective user communication is crucial for managing expectations and ensuring a smooth transition.

7.  The correct answer is **B**. Conducting a thorough inventory assessment is an example of a change management best practice for hardware replacements. It ensures that organizations have accurate information about existing hardware, facilitating proper planning and decision-making during replacements. Option A is incorrect because ignoring user feedback can lead to overlooking important insights and requirements during hardware replacements. Option C is incorrect because implementing changes without testing can result in the deployment of faulty hardware and potential disruptions. Option D is incorrect because involving stakeholders in the process is essential for their understanding and support during hardware replacements.

8.  The correct answer is **C**. The purpose of a rollback plan in change management is to identify potential issues that may occur during the change implementation and outline the steps to revert back to the previous state if necessary. Option A is incorrect because the purpose of a rollback plan is not to prevent changes from being implemented but rather to provide a contingency plan if issues arise. Option B is incorrect because documenting the reasons for change implementation is important, but it is not the primary purpose of a rollback plan. Option D is incorrect because user feedback is valuable during the change process and should be considered, rather than excluded.

9.  The correct answer is **C**. Conducting regular risk assessments is a recommended practice for managing change-related risks. By periodically assessing potential risks associated with changes, organizations can proactively identify and mitigate them to minimize negative impacts. Option A is incorrect because avoiding risk assessment altogether can lead to overlooking potential risks and their consequences. Option B is incorrect because implementing changes without backup plans can result in unanticipated issues and difficulties during the change process. Option D is incorrect because ignoring risk mitigation strategies can leave organizations vulnerable to the negative impacts of potential risks.

10. The correct answer is **C**. Tailoring the message to the target audience is a key consideration when communicating changes to users during change management. Different users may have varying levels of technical knowledge and concerns, so customizing the communication helps ensure their understanding and acceptance. Option A is incorrect because providing vague and general information can lead to confusion and misunderstanding among users. Option B is incorrect because overemphasizing the negative aspects of the changes can create resistance and hinder user acceptance. Option D is incorrect because delaying communication until after the changes are implemented can cause uncertainty and negatively impact user readiness for the changes.

## 10.3 Given a scenario, implement workstation backup and recovery methods

1.  The correct answer is **A**. A full backup creates a complete copy of all data and settings, providing a comprehensive snapshot of the workstation at that particular moment. This method allows for a complete restoration in case of data loss. Option B only includes the data that has changed since the last full backup, not all data at a specific point in time. Option C only includes data that has changed since the last backup, which could be either a full or incremental backup, but it does not capture all data at a specific point in time. Option D is not a standard backup method. It refers to manually choosing specific files or folders for backup, not creating a complete snapshot of the workstation.

2. The correct answer is **A**. Bare-metal recovery involves restoring an entire workstation's operating system, applications, and data from a complete backup, often in situations where the system needs to be rebuilt from scratch or migrated to new hardware. Option B refers to restoring data or applications from backups stored in the cloud, but it does not address restoring the entire workstation's hard drive. Option C focuses on recovering individual files or folders rather than the entire workstation's hard drive. Option D is not a standard term. Incremental backups are used to restore only the data that has changed since the last backup, not the entire system.

3. The correct answer is **A**. Tape drives offer fast transfer rates compared to other backup storage media, but they tend to be costly compared to other options. Option B (external hard drives) is a popular backup medium due to its relatively fast transfer rate and cost-effectiveness compared to tape drives. Option C (network-attached storage (NAS)) provides a convenient and network-accessible backup solution, but its transfer rate will not be as fast as tape drives. Option D (cloud storage) is cost-effective and easy to scale, but transfer rates will be slower compared to tape drives, especially when dealing with large amounts of data.

4. The correct answer is **B**. An incremental backup is designed to only back up data that has changed since the last backup. This type of backup is designed to reduce backup time and requires less storage space. Option A (differential backup) backs up all data that has changed since the last full backup, not considering previous incremental backups. Option C (synthetic backup) is a method that creates a new full backup by combining a previous full backup and subsequent incremental backups. It does not directly address only backing up changed data since the last backup. Option D (continuous backup) involves backing up data in real-time as changes occur, ensuring minimal data loss in the event of a failure. It does not differentiate between full and incremental backups.

5. The correct answer is **A**. The grandfather-father-son rotation scheme involves using a set of backup media and cycling through them on a daily basis. The oldest backup is overwritten when the set becomes full. This scheme provides a combination of daily, weekly, and monthly backups. Option B (Tower of Hanoi) is a backup rotation scheme that uses a set of backup media, but it involves a more complex rotation pattern that includes multiple levels of backups based on specific rules. Option C (back up to disk) refers to storing backups on disk-based storage media but does not specify a rotation scheme. Option D (back up to tape) is a backup method that utilizes tape drives as the storage medium, but it does not imply a specific rotation scheme.

6. The correct answer is **C**. Snapshot backup provides the fastest recovery time when compared to other backup methods. Snapshots capture the state of the workstation's system and data at a specific point in time, allowing for quick restoration to that exact state. Option A (incremental backup) requires restoring data from multiple backups, including the last full backup and subsequent incremental backups, which can take longer. Option B (differential backup) also requires restoring data from multiple backups, including the last full backup and subsequent differential backups, which can be slower than snapshot backup. Option D (full backup) provides a complete copy of all data, but recovery time can be longer as it involves restoring all data rather than just the changes since the last backup.

7. The correct answer is **A**. Mirroring ensures data redundancy by creating identical copies of backups on different backup media simultaneously. This method enhances data availability and fault tolerance. Option B (replication) involves creating copies of data on different systems or locations, but it does not specifically refer to creating multiple copies of backups on different media. Option C (archiving) refers to the long-term storage of data that is no longer actively used but still needs to be retained for compliance or historical purposes. Option D (versioning) involves creating and storing multiple versions of a file or document to track changes over time but does not necessarily create multiple copies of backups.

8. The correct answer is **D**. Offsite backup involves storing backups in a location outside the primary site, providing protection against disasters or physical damage that could affect the original location. By storing backups in different geographical locations, data is safeguarded against localized events. Option A (cloud-based backup) offers remote storage of backups, but it does not inherently guarantee multiple copies across different geographical locations. Option B (tape backup) and Option C (disk-to-disk backup) can be used for offsite backup, but they do not inherently provide the highest level of data protection as they depend on the specific implementation and location of the backup media.

9. The correct answer is **A**. Image backup captures an exact copy of the workstation's operating system, applications, and data, allowing for quick restoration to a functional state. It creates a snapshot of the entire workstation's configuration. Option B (file-level backup) focuses on backing up individual files or folders rather than capturing the entire workstation's configuration. Option C (incremental backup) captures only the changes since the last backup, which might not include the full workstation's operating system and applications. Option D (differential backup) captures the changes since the last full backup, but it does not provide an exact copy of the entire workstation's configuration.

10. The correct answer is **A**. Continuous backup involves automatically backing up data in real time as changes occur. This method ensures minimal data loss in the event of a failure, as the backups are kept up to date at all times. Option B (synchronization backup) refers to maintaining identical copies of data in different locations, but it does not necessarily involve real-time backup. Option C (manual backup) refers to the process of manually initiating backups, which might not be as efficient or provide real-time data protection. Option D (snapshot backup) captures the state of the workstation at a specific point in time but does not continuously back up data as changes occur.

## 10.4 Given a scenario, use common safety procedures

1. The correct answer is **A**. Wearing an ESD (electrostatic discharge) wrist strap helps prevent static electricity from damaging computer components. It safely discharges any static electricity built up on your body. Option B (disconnecting the power supply without turning it off) can cause damage to the hardware and potentially harm the individual. Option C (handling circuit boards with bare hands) can introduce static electricity and damage sensitive components. Option D (standing on a wet surface) increases the risk of electric shock, which is hazardous when working with computer hardware.

2. The correct answer is **A**. Using compressed air to clean debris from fans and heatsinks helps maintain proper airflow and prevents overheating. It's important to clean the components safely and without causing damage. Option B (using a magnetized screwdriver) can potentially damage or interfere with sensitive electronic components. Option C (storing liquids near the computer) increases the risk of accidental spills, which can cause damage to the equipment. Option D (placing the computer on an unstable surface) increases the chances of it falling or toppling over, potentially causing damage.

3. The correct answer is **C**. Securing cables using cable ties or clips helps maintain an organized and tidy workspace, prevents tripping hazards, and protects the cables from damage due to pulling or tangling. Option A (pulling the cable from a distance) can cause stress on the connector and potentially damage it. Option B (bending the cable sharply) can lead to cable breakage or damage to the connector. Option D (leaving cables loose and tangled) increases the risk of tripping over them and can cause damage or disconnections.

4. The correct answer is **A**. Before opening a computer case, it is crucial to ensure the computer is turned off and unplugged. This eliminates the risk of electrical shock and protects both the technician and the hardware. Option B (wearing gloves) can increase the risk of static electricity discharge and potentially damage sensitive components. Option C (using a metal tool to open the case) can lead to accidental damage or short circuits if it comes into contact with live electrical components. Option D (keeping the case on a soft, cushioned surface) can interfere with proper ventilation and cooling, potentially causing overheating.

5. The correct answer is **A**. Following ergonomic practices, such as maintaining proper posture, using adjustable furniture, and taking regular breaks, helps prevent injuries such as musculoskeletal disorders and eye strain. Option B (wearing heavy jewelry and accessories) increases the risk of getting caught on components, causing damage or injury. Option C (using damaged tools) can lead to accidents, injuries, or damage to the hardware. It's important to use functional tools. Option D (skipping breaks and working for long periods without rest) can lead to fatigue, reduced focus, and increased chances of accidents or mistakes.

6.  The correct answer is **A**. Using an antistatic vacuum cleaner is a safe way to remove dust and debris from the inside of a computer. It helps prevent the buildup of static electricity and reduces the risk of damaging sensitive components. Option B (spraying cleaning solution directly onto components) can cause damage or short circuits. It's best to use a cleaning solution on a cloth or sponge first. Option C (cleaning the computer while it is still powered on) poses the risk of electrical shock and potential damage to the hardware. Option D (using a dry cloth to wipe the motherboard) can generate static electricity and potentially damage the components. It's better to use an antistatic cloth or cleaning solution.

7.  The correct answer is **A**. Disposing of old computer equipment should be done responsibly by recycling it according to local regulations. This helps prevent environmental contamination and ensures the proper handling of potentially hazardous materials. Option B (disassembling the equipment without protective gear) can expose individuals to potentially harmful substances or components, such as chemicals or sharp edges. Option C (throwing the equipment in regular household waste) can lead to improper disposal and can have negative environmental impacts. Option D (storing the equipment in a humid environment) can cause corrosion and damage to the components.

8.  The correct answer is **A**. When working with high-voltage equipment, it is essential to wear insulated gloves and safety glasses. These safety measures protect against electric shocks and potential eye injuries. Option B (working alone with high-voltage equipment) is not recommended. It's safer to have a colleague nearby or follow proper procedures for working with others in hazardous situations. Option C (using a metal ladder when working at heights) can create a risk of electric shock if it comes into contact with live electrical equipment. It's safer to use non-conductive ladders. Option D (using equipment with damaged cords) can be hazardous and may result in electrical shock or short circuits. Damaged cords should be repaired or replaced.

9.  The correct answer is **C**. In the event of a chemical spill near computer equipment, it is important to follow proper procedures for chemical cleanup. This may involve using appropriate safety equipment, containment measures, and contacting the appropriate authorities if necessary. Option A (shutting down the equipment immediately) may be necessary if there is an immediate risk of electrical damage, but the focus should be on addressing the chemical spill and ensuring safety. Option B (using a vacuum cleaner to remove the spill) can potentially spread the chemical or cause damage to the equipment. It's best to follow proper cleanup procedures. Option D (ignoring the spill and continuing to work) is not safe and can lead to potential damage to the equipment or harm to individuals in the area.

10. The correct answer is **A**. When installing or replacing computer hardware components, it is important to use proper lifting techniques for heavy components. This helps prevent strains, back injuries, and damage to the hardware. Option B (using excessive force when inserting connectors) can damage the connectors or the components themselves. It's important to use gentle pressure and ensure proper alignment. Option C (installing components in an unventilated area) can lead to overheating, which can damage the components and affect the overall performance of the system. Proper ventilation is essential. Option D (installing components without grounding yourself) increases the risk of static electricity discharge, which can damage sensitive components. It's important to ground yourself to prevent static electricity buildup.

## 10.5 Summarize environmental impacts and local environmental controls

1. The correct answer is **B**. Material Safety Data Sheets (MSDSs) are important documents that provide detailed information about potential hazards associated with specific materials. They outline the necessary precautions and safety measures to be followed when handling, using, or disposing of hazardous substances. The purpose of MSDSs is to ensure that individuals have access to accurate and relevant information to minimize the risks associated with hazardous materials. Option A is incorrect because transportation guidelines for hazardous materials are usually covered by separate regulations and documentation, such as the hazardous materials regulations (HMR). Option C is incorrect because the proper procedures for recycling electronic waste are typically outlined in different documents or guidelines, such as e-waste recycling regulations. Option D is incorrect because MSDSs do not certify the quality or durability of protective equipment. Such certifications are usually provided by relevant standards organizations or testing agencies.

2. The correct answer is **C**. The primary purpose of reviewing material safety data sheets (MSDSs) before handling or disposing of hazardous materials is to understand the potential health and safety risks associated with the materials. MSDSs provide crucial information about the hazards, precautions, and safe handling procedures for the substances involved. By reviewing the MSDSs, individuals can make informed decisions and take necessary precautions to minimize the risks to their health and safety. Option A focuses on the financial cost associated with the materials, which is not the primary purpose of reviewing MSDSs. Option B relates to the expiration date of the materials, which may be mentioned in the MSDSs but is not the primary purpose of reviewing it. Option D refers to identifying potential sources of the materials, which is unrelated to the primary purpose of reviewing MSDSs.

3. The correct answer is **C**. Recycling used batteries at designated centers or facilities ensures proper handling and environmentally friendly disposal. Option A is incorrect because throwing used batteries in the regular trash can lead to environmental pollution and the release of harmful chemicals. Option B is incorrect because while some electronics stores may offer battery disposal, it is not a standard practice, and not all stores have this service. Option D is incorrect because burying batteries in the backyard can contaminate the soil and pose risks to the environment and human health. Batteries should not decompose naturally in this manner.

4.  The correct answer is **C**. Returning used toner cartridges to the manufacturer or participating in a designated recycling program ensures they are properly recycled and disposed of in an environmentally responsible manner. Option A is incorrect because not all recycling bins are suitable for toner cartridge disposal, and improper recycling may harm the environment. Option B is incorrect because toner cartridges can contain harmful substances and should not be treated as regular trash. Option D is incorrect because burning toner cartridges releases toxic fumes and is highly hazardous.

5.  The correct answer is **A, B, and D**. Option A (selling devices to unknown parties) may lead to data breaches or unauthorized access to sensitive information. Option B (donating devices without properly wiping their data) may expose personal or confidential data to others. Option D (disassembling devices and disposing of their parts separately without proper knowledge) can lead to environmental damage, and some components may require specialized recycling facilities for safe disposal. Proper disposal of electronic devices and assets often involves data wiping, recycling, or returning them to the manufacturer or designated recycling programs. This ensures both data security and environmental protection. Option C (erasing all data before recycling or disposal) is essential to protect privacy; it is not a method to avoid.

6.  The correct answer is **A**. Temperature, humidity, and proper ventilation are important factors to consider for maintaining optimal equipment performance and longevity. Extreme temperatures can cause damage to sensitive components, while high humidity levels can lead to condensation and moisture-related issues. Proper ventilation ensures adequate airflow and helps prevent overheating. Option B – noise level, cable management, and power supply – are important considerations for a well-organized and efficient setup, but they are not directly related to temperature, humidity, and ventilation. Option C – lighting conditions, firewall settings, and antivirus software – are more focused on security and user experience rather than environmental factors. Option D – backup systems, network security, and data encryption – are essential for data protection but do not directly relate to temperature, humidity, and ventilation considerations.

7.  The correct answer is **A**. A UPS is specifically designed to provide backup power during power surges, under-voltage events, and power failures. It offers a continuous supply of power to connected devices, protecting them from potential damage or data loss. Option B, Power over Ethernet (PoE), refers to a technology that enables the delivery of power and data through an Ethernet cable to compatible devices, such as IP cameras or VoIP phones. This option is not directly related to protecting against power surges or failures. Option C, Network Attached Storage (NAS), is a storage device connected to a network that provides centralized file storage and sharing capabilities. While NAS devices may have some built-in surge protection, they are not primarily designed to protect against power surges or failures. Option D, Wireless Access Point (WAP), is a networking device that allows wireless devices to connect to a wired network. It is not designed to protect against power surges, under-voltage events, or power failures.

8. The correct answer is **A**. A surge protector, commonly referred to as a surge suppressor, is a specialized device created with the purpose of safeguarding electronic devices against sudden increases in voltage and power surges. Its primary function is to absorb and redirect excess electrical energy, shielding the connected devices from potential damage caused by these voltage spikes. By offering this protective barrier, surge protectors play a vital role in maintaining the longevity and reliability of electronic equipment. Option B, Uninterruptible Power Supply (UPS), is primarily used to provide backup power during power outages and protect against power failures. While some UPS models may have surge protection features, their primary function is not surge suppression. Option C, a power inverter, is used to convert DC power from a battery or other sources into AC power. It is not designed to suppress power surges or protect against voltage spikes. Option D, a power strip, is a device that provides multiple electrical outlets from a single power source. While some power strips may include surge protection features, not all power strips offer this functionality, and it is not their primary purpose.

9. The correct answer is **A**. A battery backup system, also known as an Uninterruptible Power Supply (UPS), is used to provide backup power to connected devices during power outages. It ensures that critical equipment remains operational and prevents data loss or damage caused by sudden power loss. Option B, increasing network bandwidth, is unrelated to the purpose of a battery backup system. Network bandwidth refers to the capacity of a network to transmit data. Option C, protecting against electromagnetic interference, is typically accomplished using devices such as shielding or filters. While a battery backup system may provide some level of protection against electrical noise, its primary purpose is to provide backup power. Option D, preventing power surges, is the function of a surge protector or surge suppressor, not a battery backup system.

10. The correct answer is **C**. Positioning the computer away from electrical interference helps reduce potential disruptions and ensures optimal performance. Placing the computer on an uneven surface (Option A) can cause stability issues and affect airflow. Locating the computer near direct sunlight (Option B) can lead to overheating and damage to the components. Stacking multiple computers on top of each other (Option D) can result in heat buildup and compromise ventilation.

11. The correct answer is **D**. Utilizing a vacuum designed for electronics is a suitable method for dust cleanup, as it minimizes the risk of static discharge and safely removes debris. Blowing compressed air directly into the components (Option A) can push the dust deeper into the system and potentially damage sensitive parts. Using a dry cloth to wipe the components (Option B) may cause static discharge and harm the computer. Applying water or liquid cleaning agents on the components (Option C) can lead to damage and short circuits.

## 10.6 Explain the importance of prohibited content/activity and privacy, licensing, and policy concepts

1.  The correct answer is **A**. The chain of custody is the process of documenting the handling and transfer of evidence during an incident response. It ensures the integrity and preservation of data by maintaining a clear record of who had control over the evidence at any given time. Option B, incident escalation, refers to the process of escalating an incident to a higher authority or management. Option C, password recovery, is unrelated to data integrity and preservation. Option D, data compression, is a technique used to reduce the size of data, but it does not directly address the importance of preserving data integrity during an incident response.

2.  The correct answer is **A**. When encountering prohibited content/activity during an incident response, it is important to inform management or law enforcement, if necessary. This ensures that appropriate actions are taken to address the issue and comply with legal requirements. Option B, continuing the investigation without involving anyone else, is not advisable as it may hinder the resolution of the incident. Option C, deleting the prohibited content/activity immediately, may compromise the chain of custody and hinder further investigation. Option D, performing a system reboot, is not a sufficient response to handling prohibited content/activity.

3.  The correct answer is **A**. Making a copy of a drive during an incident response is done to preserve data integrity and evidence. It ensures that the original data remains intact and can be analyzed without any modifications. Option B, speeding up the incident resolution process, may not be the primary purpose of making a drive copy. Option C, minimizing the impact on system performance, is unrelated to the need for preserving data integrity. Option D, reducing the risk of future incidents, is not directly addressed by making a drive copy.

4.  The correct answer is **A**. The concept that involves documenting the handling and transfer of evidence during an incident response is the chain of custody. It ensures a clear record of who had control over the evidence at any given time. Option B, incident containment, refers to the process of preventing an incident from spreading or causing further damage. Option C, data classification, is the process of categorizing data based on its sensitivity and importance. Option D, system hardening, involves implementing security measures to reduce vulnerabilities but does not directly relate to evidence handling.

5.  The correct answer is **D**. Documenting an incident during an incident response serves the purpose of creating a detailed record for analysis and accountability. It provides a comprehensive account of the incident, aiding in understanding the root cause and taking appropriate actions. Option A, providing a reference for future incidents, may be a secondary benefit but is not the primary purpose of documenting an incident. Option B, informing management of ongoing activities, may be necessary but is not the main purpose of documentation. Option C, facilitating collaboration with other teams, can be a benefit but is not the primary reason for documenting an incident.

6.  The correct answer is **C**. The end-user license agreement (EULA) outlines the permissions, restrictions, and liabilities associated with the use of software by an individual or organization. Option A, privacy policy, focuses on data protection. Option B, open source license, pertains to the distribution and modification of open source software. Option D, digital rights management (DRM), deals with copyright protection and access control to digital content.

7.  The correct answer is **A**. Personal use licenses typically require individual registration, allowing the software to be used by a single user for personal purposes. On the other hand, corporate use licenses are designed for organizations and allow the software to be used by multiple users within the organization. Option B, personal use licenses, are not defined by the length of the license. Option C, the restrictions within the terms of the license, may be different between personal and corporate licenses, often personal licenses are more restrictive. As for Option D, in some cases, a personal license may be free (with restricted use), but this is not always the case.

8.  The correct answer is **D**. Digital rights management (DRM) is a licensing concept that focuses on copyright protection and access control to digital content. It ensures that users comply with the terms of the software license and prevents unauthorized copying or distribution. Option A, open source license, refers to the distribution and modification of open-source software. Options B and C, valid license and non-expired license, pertain to the legal status of a license.

9.  The correct answer is **B**. Licensing, digital rights management (DRM), and the end-user license agreement (EULA) are designed to prevent the use of prohibited content/activity. They outline the permissible uses of software and help restrict or block access to content or activities that are deemed prohibited or illegal. Option A is incorrect. Licensing, DRM, and EULAs are implemented to prevent or control the sharing of prohibited content or activities, not to facilitate them. As for Option C, while those mechanisms can include monitoring features to track usage and ensure compliance with terms, their primary purpose is not to monitor and report prohibited content or activities. They aim to prevent such usage in the first place. For Option D, while EULAs and licensing agreements can specify consequences for violating terms, their main purpose is not to establish penalties. Their primary focus is on setting forth the rights, obligations, and restrictions related to the use of the software or content.

10. The correct answer is **B**. An open source license allows users to view, modify, and distribute the source code of software. It promotes collaboration, transparency, and community-driven development. As for Option A, a privacy policy outlines how an organization collects, uses, and manages user data. It is not related to software source code or licensing that allows code modification and distribution. For Option C, an EULA defines the terms and conditions under which software can be used; it typically does not grant users the right to view, modify, and distribute the source code. EULAs often restrict users from accessing the source code. For Option D, DRM is focused on protecting intellectual property rights, such as preventing unauthorized copying or distribution of digital content. It is not related to open access to source code for software development.

11. The correct answer is **A**. Regulated data refers to information that is subject to government regulations and restrictions. This type of data may include personal government-issued information, credit card transactions, healthcare data, and other sensitive information that requires special protection and compliance with specific policies. Option B is incorrect because regulated data is not freely accessible to the public. Option C is incorrect because regulated data is typically stored with encryption and security measures to ensure its protection. Option D is incorrect because regulated data is not necessarily shared among employees within an organization without proper authorization.

12. The correct answer is **B**. Personally identifiable information (PII) refers to data that can be used to identify an individual. Examples of PII include names, addresses, social security numbers, email addresses, and other similar personal details. Protecting PII is crucial for maintaining privacy and complying with privacy regulations. Option A is incorrect because social media posts and comments may contain personal opinions and information but do not necessarily qualify as PII. Option C is incorrect because publicly available company information does not necessarily involve personal details about individuals. Option D is incorrect because even non-sensitive email communication can potentially contain PII, such as email addresses and names.

13. The correct answer is **B**. When handling credit card transactions, one of the key concerns is securing cardholder data. It is crucial to protect credit card information to prevent unauthorized access, fraud, and identity theft. Compliance with industry standards such as the Payment Card Industry Data Security Standard (PCI DSS) is essential for safeguarding cardholder data. Option A is incorrect because while data availability is important, the primary concern with credit card transactions is data security. Option C is incorrect because maintaining accurate financial records is important but not the primary concern when handling credit card transactions. Option D is incorrect because while transaction speed is desirable, it is not the key concern when it comes to securing credit card transactions.

14. The correct answer is **B**. A driver's license number is an example of personal government-issued information. It is a unique identifier issued by the government to individuals for the purpose of driving legally. Protecting personal government-issued information is important to prevent identity theft and misuse. Option A is incorrect because social media account usernames are not government-issued personal information. Option C is incorrect because Wi-Fi network passwords are not personal government-issued information. Option D is incorrect because a home address is not directly government-issued personal information.

15. The correct answer is **B**. Data retention requirements refer to the policies and procedures for storing and managing data. It includes determining how long data should be retained, what types of data should be stored, and how data should be protected and disposed of when no longer needed. Compliance with data retention requirements is essential for regulatory compliance and effective data management. Option A is incorrect because data retention requirements are not related to the time it takes to process data. Option C is incorrect because data backup frequency is a separate concern from data retention requirements. Option D is incorrect because data transmission speed is not directly related to data retention requirements.

## 10.7 Given a scenario, use proper communication techniques and professionalism

1.  The correct answer is **C**. Active listening and paraphrasing the customer's concerns demonstrate professionalism by showing that you understand their needs and are actively engaged in finding a solution. Option A, interrupting the customer, may seem rude and dismissive. Option B, using technical jargon, can confuse the customer, and offering discounts or freebies (Option D) should only be considered if it aligns with company policies and the customer's issue.

2.  The correct answer is **A**. Maintaining eye contact and nodding in agreement are non-verbal cues that demonstrate active listening and engagement, which are professional communication behaviors. Option B, checking personal emails on a mobile device, is unprofessional and distracts from the conversation. Option C, speaking softly, shows consideration for others but does not address the question requirements (non-verbal). Option D, using slang terms and informal language, is inappropriate in a professional setting.

3.  The correct answer is **B**. Using "Dear [Recipient's First Name]," is the most appropriate and professional way to address the recipient in a business email. Options A and D are less formal and may not convey the necessary level of professionalism. Option C is an unusual way to address a business associate. It is more likely to be used in a legal undertaking (such as a court injunction).

4.  The correct answer is **C**. Utilizing visual aids, diagrams, and illustrations is the most effective way to convey complex technical information to a non-technical audience. Options A, B, and D are incorrect because using technical terms extensively can confuse the audience, relying solely on written documentation may not be easily understood, and speaking rapidly can overwhelm the audience and hinder comprehension.

5.  The correct answer is **B**. Option B demonstrates the use of professional language by describing the situation without being overly casual or judgmental. Options A, C, and D use unprofessional language and may not effectively address the customer's concerns.

6.  The correct answer is **C**. Offering alternative solutions and compromises demonstrates professionalism when handling a disagreement or conflict with a customer. Raising your voice, blaming the customer, or ignoring their concerns are unprofessional and can escalate the situation.

7.  The correct answer is **C**. Actively listening and respecting others' opinions is an example of appropriate professional behavior when interacting with colleagues. Options A, B, and D promote negative workplace dynamics and are considered unprofessional.

8.  The correct answer is **C**. Holding individual face-to-face meetings is the best communication method for delivering sensitive or confidential information. Options A, B, and D can compromise confidentiality and may not allow for personal attention or support.

9.  The correct answer is **B**. Keeping the microphone on mute when not speaking is an example of maintaining professionalism in a virtual meeting. Eating a meal on camera, using informal language in chat messages, and sharing irrelevant personal anecdotes are unprofessional and can disrupt the meeting.

10. The correct answer is **B**. Setting realistic expectations and providing updates is a professional approach to managing customer expectations. Overpromising can lead to disappointment, ignoring customer requests is unprofessional, and redirecting customers without addressing their concerns may be seen as dismissive.

11. The correct answer is **B**. Encrypting the customer's sensitive files and folders using strong encryption algorithms ensures their data remains confidential and protected. Option A is incorrect because regularly sharing the customer's data with colleagues compromises its confidentiality. Option C, uploading the customer's confidential data to a cloud storage service, increases the risk of unauthorized access. Option D, disposing of the customer's computer without securely wiping the hard drive, may expose their private materials to potential data breaches.

12. The correct answer is **C**. Implementing access controls on the printer ensures that only authorized individuals can use and access the customer's confidential materials, maintaining their security. Option A, sharing the printer's access credentials with other technicians, increases the risk of unauthorized access to the customer's confidential materials. Option B, disabling logging features, hampers the ability to track and investigate any potential privacy breaches. Option D, printing the customer's confidential documents in a public area, compromises their privacy and confidentiality.

13. The correct answer is **C**. Option C is the correct choice because implementing strong password policies and enabling full disk encryption on the customer's desktop computer provides an additional layer of security, ensuring the confidentiality of their materials. Option A, creating a shared user account with unrestricted access, compromises the confidentiality of the customer's materials. Option B, performing data backups without verifying the integrity and confidentiality of the backup media, may lead to potential data breaches. Option D, storing the customer's confidential files in publicly accessible folders, exposes them to unauthorized access.

## 10.8 Identify the basics of scripting

1. The correct answer is **C**. JavaScript is specifically designed for web development, allowing for dynamic and interactive elements on websites. Python, Bash, and PowerShell are commonly used scripting languages, allowing for automated tasks to be scheduled.

2. The correct answer is **D**. PowerShell is a scripting language developed by Microsoft for task automation and configuration management in Windows environments. Python, Bash, and JavaScript are not specifically designed for Windows automation.

3. The correct answer is **B**. Bash (Bourne Again SHell) is the default scripting language for Unix-like operating systems and is widely used for system administration tasks. Python, JavaScript, and PowerShell are not commonly used for this purpose.

4. The correct answer is **A**. Python is a versatile scripting language that can be used for various purposes, including web development, task automation, scientific computing, and data analysis. While Bash, JavaScript, and PowerShell have their own specific use cases, Python offers a broader range of applications.

5. The correct answer is **C**. JavaScript is primarily used for client-side scripting, allowing for dynamic and interactive elements on web pages. Python, Bash, and PowerShell are not typically used for this purpose.

6. The correct answer is **A**. Inadequate error handling can lead to unintended consequences such as introducing malware, changing system settings, or causing crashes. By implementing proper error handling mechanisms, script developers can minimize the risks and ensure safer execution of their scripts. Options B, C, and D are not directly related to the mentioned risks.

7. The correct answer is **B**. Implementing input validation and sanitization helps prevent malicious code injection through user input. It ensures that only expected and safe inputs are processed by the script, reducing the risk of unintentionally introducing malware. Regularly updating antivirus software (Option A) helps protect against known malware, but it does not directly address the risk associated with scripting. Options C and D are not recommended actions and can potentially introduce additional vulnerabilities.

8. The correct answer is **A**. Scripts that consume excessive memory resources can overload the browser or system, leading to crashes. This can occur when the script does not properly manage memory allocation or fails to release allocated resources. Options B, C, and D can cause performance issues but are not specifically related to mishandling of resources leading to crashes.

9. The correct answer is **C**. Downloading scripts from untrusted or unknown sources can lead to the inadvertent introduction of malware into the system. Option A is a good practice as reputable script repositories typically vet their content, reducing the risk of malware. Option B is also a good practice, but it doesn't directly address the concern of unintentionally introducing malware. Option D is a valid method to mitigate potential risks, but it doesn't specifically address the risk of malware.

10. The correct answer is **D**. When executing scripts, inadvertent changes to critical system settings may lead to system instability or malfunction. Options A, B, and C are positive outcomes that can result from intentional changes to system settings.

11. The correct answer is **C**. Optimizing resource usage in scripts helps avoid overloading system resources and reduces the likelihood of browser or system crashes. Options A and B are not directly related to preventing crashes due to resource mishandling. In fact, increasing script execution speed (Option A) could potentially exacerbate the issue. Option D is too extreme and may not be necessary if resource usage is properly optimized.

## 10.9 Given a scenario, use Remote access technologies

1. The correct answer is **A**. Microsoft Remote Assistance (MSRA) is the appropriate remote access technology to use in this scenario. MSRA allows a technician to remotely connect to a user's computer running a Windows operating system. Since the user and the technician are connected to the same network, MSRA can be used to troubleshoot and provide assistance without requiring additional configuration or access permissions. For Option B, VNC is a remote access technology commonly used for cross-platform remote access. However, in this scenario, since both the technician and the user are using a Windows operating system and are on the same network, using MSRA would be a more suitable choice. For Option C, RDP is a remote access technology that allows users to connect to a remote computer and control it as if they were sitting in front of it. While RDP is commonly used in various scenarios, in this particular situation where the technician and the user are on the same network, MSRA would be a more appropriate choice for troubleshooting and assistance. For Option D, SSH is a network protocol used for secure remote access to Unix-like systems. However, in this scenario where the technician needs to troubleshoot a Windows computer on the same network, MSRA would be the preferred remote access technology, as it is specifically designed for Windows systems and provides the necessary features for remote assistance.

2. The correct answer is **D**. Remote monitoring and management (RMM) is the most appropriate remote access technology for remotely monitoring and managing multiple devices in a network. RMM tools allow IT technicians to proactively monitor the health, performance, and security of devices from a centralized location. They provide features such as remote control, software deployment, patch management, and reporting, enabling efficient and effective management of remote devices. For Option A, VPNs are primarily used to establish secure connections between remote users and a private network. For Option B, RDP is a protocol that allows users to access and control a remote computer. For Option C, Telnet is a network protocol that allows remote access to devices using a command-line interface.

3. The correct answer is **B**. Remote Desktop Protocol (RDP) enables users to connect to and control their office computer remotely, providing access to files, applications, and resources. Option A, a virtual private network (VPN), is used to establish secure connections between networks, not necessarily for accessing individual computers remotely. Option C, Telnet, is a network protocol used for remote administration of devices, but it does not provide graphical remote desktop access. Option D, Secure Shell (SSH), is a cryptographic network protocol used for secure remote access, but it is primarily used for command-line access to devices rather than full desktop access.

4.  The correct answer is **A**. Remote Desktop Protocol (RDP) is the most suitable remote access technology for accessing a Windows server, as it provides graphical desktop access and control. Option B, File Transfer Protocol (FTP), is primarily used for transferring files between a client and a server, not for remote desktop access. Option C, Telnet, is a network protocol used for remote administration, but it does not provide graphical remote desktop access. Option D, Secure Shell (SSH), is commonly used for secure command-line access to Linux/Unix servers, but it may not provide graphical remote desktop access to Windows servers.

5.  The correct answer is **C**. Secure Shell (SSH) is the most appropriate remote access technology for connecting to a Linux server using a command-line interface, as it provides secure encrypted connections. Option A, Telnet, sends data in plain text, which can pose a security risk, and it does not provide encryption for remote access. Option B, Remote Desktop Protocol (RDP), is primarily used for graphical remote desktop access, not command-line access to Linux servers. Option D, the virtual private network (VPN), is used to establish secure connections between networks, but it does not directly provide command-line access to Linux servers.

6.  The correct answer is **A**. A virtual private network (VPN) is the most appropriate remote access technology for securely accessing a home network from a remote network, as it creates a secure tunnel between the user's device and the home network. Option B, Remote Desktop Protocol (RDP), is primarily used for remote desktop access within a network, and it may not be the most suitable option for remote access from a different network due to network configuration requirements. Option C, Telnet, is not a secure remote access technology and is generally not recommended for remote access purposes due to its lack of encryption and vulnerability to attacks. Option D, Secure Shell (SSH), is typically used for secure command-line access to servers, and while it can be used for remote access, a VPN is a more appropriate choice for accessing a home computer from a different network.

7.  The correct answer is **A**. Remote Desktop Protocol (RDP) commonly uses port 3389 by default for establishing remote desktop connections. Option B, File Transfer Protocol (FTP), commonly uses port 21 for control connections and port 20 for data connections, not port 3389. Option C, Telnet, typically uses port 23 for establishing remote terminal connections, not port 3389. Option D, Secure Shell (SSH), commonly uses port 22 for secure remote access, not port 3389.

8.  The correct answer is **A**. Apple Remote Desktop is the built-in remote access technology provided by Apple for remotely accessing Mac computers. Option B, Virtual Network Computing (VNC), is a cross-platform remote access technology and can be used to remotely access Mac computers, but Apple Remote Desktop is the built-in solution specifically designed for Mac-to-Mac remote access. Option C, Remote Desktop Protocol (RDP), is primarily used for Windows-based remote access, and while there are third-party clients available for Mac, it is not the built-in solution. Option D, Secure Shell (SSH), is used for secure command-line access to systems and does not provide graphical remote desktop access like Apple Remote Desktop.

9. The correct answer is **A**. A virtual private network (VPN) allows users to securely access their office network resources over the internet by establishing an encrypted connection. Remote Desktop Protocol (RDP) is primarily used for remote desktop access to individual computers rather than accessing network resources. Telnet is not a secure remote access technology and is generally not recommended for accessing network resources over the internet due to its lack of encryption and vulnerability to attacks. Secure Shell (SSH) is primarily used for secure command-line access to systems and may not provide the same level of network resource access as a VPN.

# Chapter 11: Mock Exam: Core 2 (220-1102)

1.  The correct answer is **B**. This is a reasonable first step for addressing a suspected malware infection. Antivirus apps can scan the device for malware and potentially remove it. However, it's important to use a reputable antivirus app and keep the device disconnected from the internet until the scan is complete to prevent further infection. Option A: This option is a drastic measure and should only be considered as a last resort. It will erase all data on the phone, including apps, settings, and personal data. It's not the most appropriate first step for malware removal. Option C: While disconnecting the smartphone from the internet can prevent further malware downloads or communication with command-and-control servers, it doesn't address the existing malware infection. This step should be combined with other actions, such as running a malware scan. Option D: Keeping the operating system and apps up to date is essential for security. However, this step alone may not remove existing malware. It's a good practice but should be combined with malware scanning and removal efforts.

2.  The correct answer is **D**. Once a change request has been approved by the change advisory board, the next logical step in the change process is sandbox testing. This is performed during the testing phase to isolate the change in a controlled environment and assess its impact on system functionality and performance. The purpose is to communicate the details of the approved change to the relevant stakeholders. Sandbox testing allows an organization to replicate a production environment. Option A: End user acceptance typically comes after the implementation of the change when end users are required to accept and adapt to the new or modified system. Option B: Risk analysis is generally conducted during the planning stage of the change process to identify potential risks and develop mitigation strategies. Option C: Stakeholder communication ensures that all parties involved are informed about the upcoming change, its potential impact, and any necessary actions or adjustments they may need to make. Effective stakeholder communication is crucial for maintaining transparency, minimizing disruptions, and ensuring a smooth implementation of the approved change.

3.  The correct answer is **A**. The most effective solution for the technician to implement in this scenario is to disable the browser's capability to send notifications to the Windows 10 Action Center. By doing so, the unwanted advertisement notifications originating from the browser will no longer appear within the Action Center, providing relief to the user. This solution directly targets the source of the notifications, ensuring a focused resolution. Option B: Performing a comprehensive antivirus scan on the computer is not the best solution in this case, as the reported notifications do not indicate malicious content. The issue seems to be related to browser notifications rather than a potential virus or malware infection. Option C: turning off all notifications within the Action Center, is a broad approach that might negatively impact the user's experience. It is preferable to address the specific issue of advertisement notifications from the web browser rather than disabling all notifications. Option D: transferring specific site notifications from the Allowed category to Block, might help manage notifications from specific websites, but it does not address the broader issue of advertisement notifications originating from the browser. Disabling the browser's ability to send notifications is a more comprehensive solution in this case.

4.   The correct answer is **D**. To address the issue of staff members frequently forgetting their passwords, implementing a single sign-on system with biometrics can be an effective solution. This approach allows users to authenticate themselves using unique physical characteristics, such as fingerprints or facial recognition, reducing the reliance on memorizing passwords and minimizing the chances of forgetting them. Option A is incorrect because enabling multifactor authentication adds an extra layer of security but does not directly address the problem of staff members forgetting their passwords. Option B is incorrect because increasing the failed login threshold may result in more unsuccessful login attempts before assistance is sought, but it does not address the underlying issue of forgotten passwords. Option C is incorrect because removing complex password requirements may make it easier for staff members to remember their passwords, but it also compromises the security of the system by weakening password strength and increasing vulnerability to unauthorized access.

5.   The correct answer is **B**. The most effective solution for dealing with a suspected rootkit is to utilize anti-malware software. Rootkits are sophisticated types of malware that can deeply embed themselves within the operating system, making them difficult to detect and remove. Anti-malware software is specifically designed to identify and eliminate such threats, providing the best chance of successfully removing the rootkit from the system. Option A, updating applications, may enhance security by patching vulnerabilities but may not directly address the rootkit issue. Option C, reinstalling the operating system, can be a drastic measure that should be considered only if other methods fail or the rootkit is exceptionally persistent. Option D, file restoration, may help recover compromised files but does not directly target the rootkit itself.

6.   The correct answer is **B**. Given the technology available in 2013 (at the time of writing), the most secure option for the wireless network would be WPA2 with AES encryption. WPA2 provides robust security measures, and Advanced Encryption Standard (AES) is a widely accepted and secure encryption algorithm for wireless communication. Although WPA3 and AES-256 or AES-128 are more recent advancements, they might not be supported by a 10-year-old wireless router. Therefore, selecting WPA2 with AES would offer the best available security configuration in this scenario. WPA2 was released in 2004. Option A, WPA3 with AES-128, offers a higher level of security than WPA2 with AES. However, choosing WPA3 with AES-256 provides even stronger encryption, making it the preferred choice for maximum security. It was released in 2018. Option C: WPA3 is the latest and most advanced Wi-Fi security protocol, providing strong protection against unauthorized access and attacks. AES-256 encryption ensures that the data transmitted over the network is securely encrypted with a robust encryption algorithm. It was released in 2018. Option D, WPA2 with TKIP, is not as secure as the other options. While WPA2 is still considered secure, TKIP is an old encryption method and has known vulnerabilities.

7. The correct answer is **C**. When assisting a user with updating Windows, the recommended approach for the call center technician is to guide the user through the process. In this case, the technician should instruct the user to click on the Search field, enter "Check for Updates," and then press the Enter key. This action initiates the Windows update process and allows the user to check for available updates and install them manually. Option A is incorrect because suggesting the use of a different system does not address the issue of updating Windows on the user's current device. Option B is incorrect and highly inappropriate as it involves sharing sensitive information (password) with the technician, which violates security protocols. Option D is incorrect because advising the user to wait for an upcoming automatic patch does not address the immediate need for updating Windows.

8. The correct answer is **A**. To ensure accurate association between the reported issue and the user, the technician should assign a unique ticket identifying number. This identifier makes it easier to track and manage the reported issue throughout the support process. Option B: This is not the best practice for associating a service ticket with a user. While protecting customer privacy is important, assigning a random ticket number without verifying the user's identity can lead to confusion and difficulty in resolving the issue. It's essential to link the ticket to the correct customer. Option C: Using the technician's personal identification is not a standard practice for associating service tickets with users. It could lead to confusion and is not a reliable way to track and resolve customer issues. Option D: Creating a generic ticket without associating it with any user is not an effective practice. It makes it challenging to provide personalized support and track issues for specific customers. Service tickets should always be associated with the appropriate user or customer to ensure a smooth resolution process.

9. The correct answer is **D**. The user's inability to log in to the network after an extended period of absence, with the network utilizing 802.1X and EAP-TLS for authentication on the wired network, can be attributed to various factors. However, the most probable cause in this scenario is an expired certificate. Since the user has been away for several months, it is possible that the certificate used for authentication has expired during that period, leading to the login issue. Option A is not directly related to the given situation involving network authentication and extended leave. Option B: Generally refers to services related to the operating system or applications, but it is not the primary cause of a login issue in this particular context. Option C is unrelated to network login issues caused by expired certificates.

10. The correct answer is **B**. To exclude specific folders from Windows search, the user should add those folders to the "Excluded Folders" list in the Windows search settings. This allows them to customize search preferences while keeping the search feature running. Option A: Disabling Windows Search Service will turn off the entire Windows search feature, which is not what the user wants. They want to exclude specific folders while keeping the search feature active. Option C: Deleting the folders will remove them from the hard drive entirely, which may not be what the user wants. They likely want to keep the folders but exclude them from search results. Option D: Reinstalling the entire operating system is a drastic and unnecessary step to exclude folders from Windows search. It would erase all data and settings, which is not the user's intention.

11. The correct answer is **B**. When the "cat" command is used in a Linux terminal with the filename "comptia.txt," it displays the content of that file on the terminal. It does not modify the file or create a new file. Therefore, option B is the correct answer. Option A is incorrect because executing the "cat" command does not replace the contents of the file with a new blank document. Option C is incorrect because the "cat" command does not perform any sorting operations on the contents of the file. Option D is incorrect because the "cat" command does not copy the contents of the file to another file.

12. The correct answer is **B**. This process, known as hard drive cloning, involves making an exact copy of the affected drives. By doing so, the original evidence remains intact and can be securely stored, ensuring its admissibility and maintaining the chain of custody. Option A: Encryption may be utilized for data protection but does not directly address evidence preservation. Option C: Contacting the cyber insurance company may be necessary for reporting incidents, but it does not specifically focus on evidence preservation. Option D: Informing law enforcement may be appropriate in certain cases, but creating hard drive duplicates is the primary action to preserve evidence in preparation for potential litigation.

13. The correct answer is **B**. To address the concerns of regularly modifying only a few files and limited storage space while mitigating regulatory requirements, the most effective backup method is incremental backup. Incremental backups only store the changes made since the last full or incremental backup, resulting in smaller backup sizes and quicker backup operations. This approach optimizes storage space utilization and reduces the time required for backup and restoration processes. Incremental backups allow the easy identification and restoration of specific modified files, minimizing potential data loss and downtime. Option A: A full backup would not be the best choice as it involves backing up all files and folders, regardless of whether they have been modified or not. This approach would consume significant storage space and require more time for backup operations. Option C: Off-site backup focuses on storing backup copies at a remote location for disaster recovery purposes. While it is a valuable strategy, it does not directly address the concerns of regularly modifying only a few files and limited storage space. Option D: Tape rotation has no bearing on the required storage space used for backups.

14. The correct answer is **A**. Setting a mobile device to silent or vibrate mode is a courteous practice when visiting a customer because it prevents incoming calls or notifications from causing disruptions or distractions during the visit. It shows respect for the customer's environment and ensures professional interaction. Option B: Setting the phone to silent or vibrate mode is not primarily done to conserve battery life. While it may have a minor impact on battery consumption, the main reason is to maintain a quiet and professional atmosphere during the customer visit. Option C: Setting the phone to silent mode does not prevent incoming calls from being recorded. Call recording settings are usually independent of the phone's audio settings and are controlled separately through specific apps or phone settings. Option D: Setting the phone to silent mode is unrelated to enabling location tracking for service records. Location tracking is typically a separate feature and is not affected by the phone's audio settings.

15. The correct answer is **D**. To handle the task of transferring a large number of files over an unreliable connection while allowing the ability to resume the process if the connection is interrupted, the recommended tool is Robocopy. Robocopy, short for "Robust File Copy," is a command-line utility designed for efficient file copying and mirroring. It includes features such as the ability to restart file transfers from where they left off in case of connection disruptions, making it an ideal choice for scenarios involving unreliable connections. Option A: System File Checker (sfc) is primarily used to scan and repair system files for errors, not for file transfers over an unreliable connection. Option B: Check Disk (chkdsk) is used for checking and repairing filesystem errors on a disk, not for file transfers. Option C: Git Clone (git clone) is a command used for cloning repositories from Git, a version control system. It is not intended for large file transfers over unreliable connections with the ability to resume the process if interrupted.

16. The correct answer is **D**. When implementing a new backup system, the initial backup that should be performed is a complete or full backup. A complete backup copies all data and files from the source system to the backup storage medium. This comprehensive backup captures the entire system and establishes a baseline for future backups. By starting with a complete backup, you ensure that all essential data and system configurations are securely stored, allowing efficient and effective restoration in the event of data loss or system failure. The full backup will clear the archive bit on all files, indicating that they have backed up. Option A: A copy backup can be made at any time; it is designed to backup all the files but does not set the archive bit. Option B: Mirror backups do not exist as a recognized backup type. This option is incorrect and not applicable in the context of backup and recovery. Option C: Differential backups capture the changes made since the last complete backup. Although differential backups are useful in subsequent backup cycles, they are not the initial backup type to be completed when installing a new backup and recovery system.

17. The correct answer is **A, B**. Option A is a valid recommendation. Installing a reputable ad blocker extension can effectively block unwanted pop-up ads and enhance the user's browsing experience by preventing intrusive ads from appearing. Option B is also a valid recommendation. Outdated browsers may have vulnerabilities that allow popups and other unwanted content to appear. Updating the browser to the latest version often includes security fixes that can help prevent such issues.  Option C: Disabling the firewall is not a recommended solution for dealing with popups. Firewalls play a critical role in protecting the computer from various online threats, including malware. Disabling the firewall would leave the computer vulnerable. Option D: Ignoring popups is not a recommended solution. While some popups may be harmless, others could be related to malicious activities or potentially unwanted programs (PUPs). It's essential to investigate and address the issue rather than ignore it. Option E: Downloading and running registry cleaner tools is not a recommended solution for dealing with popups. Registry cleaners can sometimes do more harm than good and are unlikely to address the root cause of pop-up issues. Option F: Resetting the computer to factory settings should be a last resort and is generally unnecessary for dealing with pop-ups. It would result in the loss of all user data and settings, which is a drastic measure that should only be considered if all other solutions fail.

18. The correct answer is **D**. When working with macOS, the ".dmg" file extension is commonly used for software installation. A DMG (disk image) file contains the necessary files and folders required for installing applications on macOS systems. Technicians often encounter DMG files when installing software or applications on Apple devices. The DMG file acts as a virtual disk that can be mounted, allowing access to the installer package contained within. Once mounted, the technician can initiate the installation process to install the software onto the macOS computer. There may be an option to have an application (possibly an installer) run automatically upon mounting a disk image, but that's not the norm. An .app file is similar to an .exe file in Windows and is mainly used for small programs and tools. Option A: ".pkg" is incorrect because it is typically used for package installers on macOS, not the actual software installation files. Option B: ".bat" is incorrect because it is a file extension used for batch files primarily in Windows environments, not macOS. Option C: ".msi" is incorrect because it is a file extension used for Windows Installer packages and is not commonly used for software installation on macOS.

19. The correct answer is **A, F**. The technician can take the following actions to address the issues. Option A: Clearing app cache and data can help resolve issues with crashing applications. Updating apps ensures you have the latest bug fixes and optimizations. Ensuring proper ventilation can prevent overheating. Option F: By closing down unneeded applications, memory will be freed up and background processing may be using extra system resources, contributing to the overheating. Option B: This is not the best solution. Performing a factory reset should be a last resort as it erases all data on the device. Installing third-party cooling apps may not always be effective and can sometimes cause more problems. Option C: Disabling automatic updates is not recommended as it can leave the device vulnerable to security issues. Limiting background processes may help with performance but might not resolve overheating or media playback issues. Option D: This is an extreme solution and not necessary in most cases. It should only be considered if the device is severely outdated or damaged. Option E: Ignoring the issues is not a recommended solution. Overheating and app crashes can be indicative of underlying problems that may worsen if left unaddressed.

20. The correct answer is **A**. This is the recommended action. Performing a System Restore allows the user to revert their computer's state to a previous point in time when it was working correctly. This can often resolve issues caused by system changes or updates. Option B: Reinstalling the entire Windows operating system is a drastic step and should be considered a last resort. It involves a lot of time and effort and may lead to data loss. System Restore is a less intrusive solution that should be tried first. Option C: While reinstalling the affected applications might resolve the issue if it's isolated to those specific applications, it won't address potential underlying system problems. System Restore is a more comprehensive solution that can address system-wide issues.

21. The correct answer is **C**. In order to ensure secure physical access to a data center, a proximity card reader can be employed. Proximity card readers utilize radio frequency identification (RFID) technology to grant authorized individuals access to restricted areas. These readers detect and validate proximity cards, also known as access cards or keycards, allowing entry to authorized personnel while restricting unauthorized individuals from entering the data center. Option A, perimeter barrier, refers to physical barriers such as fences or walls that enclose the data center premises but does not specifically address secure access control. Option B, an intrusion detection system, is designed to detect and alert against unauthorized entry or activities within a facility, but it does not directly address access control. Option D, a surveillance camera, plays a crucial role in monitoring and recording activities within the data center but does not directly control physical access to the facility.

22. The correct answer is **B**. When troubleshooting a slow computer, the Performance Monitor tool is a valuable asset for a technician. Performance Monitor allows the technician to monitor various system resources, such as CPU usage, memory utilization, disk activity, and network performance. By analyzing the data collected by Performance Monitor, the technician can identify resource bottlenecks or abnormal behavior that may be causing the slow performance. This enables them to pinpoint the specific area requiring attention and take appropriate measures to resolve the issue. Option A, System Optimizer, focuses on optimizing system performance but may not provide detailed insights into the specific causes of a slow computer. Option C, Registry Editor, is a tool that's used to modify the Windows registry and is not directly related to identifying performance issues. Option D, Task Scheduler, is primarily used for automating tasks and scheduling processes and does not provide real-time monitoring of system performance.

23. The correct answer is **A**. This string is most likely a checksum or hash value. It is used to verify the integrity of the downloaded software image. By comparing the calculated checksum of the downloaded file to this value, the technician can ensure that the file has not been tampered with during the download process. Option B: This string is not likely to be an encryption key. Encryption keys are generally longer and more complex, and they are used for encrypting and decrypting data, not for verifying the integrity of downloaded files. Option C: This string is not a product license key. Product license keys are typically alphanumeric and are used to activate or license software legally. They are not used for verifying the integrity of software downloads. Option D: This string is not a network port number. Network port numbers are used to specify a specific communication endpoint in networking protocols, such as TCP or UDP. They are not related to verifying the integrity of software downloads.

24. The correct answer is **A, B**. Option A: App whitelisting is a mobile device management (MDM) policy that allows administrators to specify which applications are allowed to be installed on mobile devices. By creating a whitelist of approved applications, you can prevent users from sideloading unapproved applications because only the apps on the whitelist can be installed. Option B: You can restrict users from sideloading apps by enforcing policies that only allow app installations from official app stores (such as Google Play or the Apple App Store). This prevents users from downloading and installing apps from unofficial or third-party sources. Option C: Enabling or disabling USB debugging control is more related to developer options and doesn't directly prevent the sideloading of unapproved applications. It's not a typical MDM policy for this purpose. Option D: Full device encryption is essential for data security but doesn't directly prevent users from sideloading applications. It's a security feature to protect data in case the device is lost or stolen. Option E: Enabling remote wipe is a security measure that protects data in case a device is lost or stolen. It doesn't directly prevent sideloading of applications. Option F: Geofencing is used to define geographical boundaries and trigger actions when a device enters or exits those boundaries. It's not directly related to preventing sideloading of applications.

25. The correct answer is **B**. The most likely reason why the technician is unable to join a Windows 10 laptop to a domain is because the laptop is running the Windows 10 Home edition. Windows 10 Home does not have the capability to join a domain; this functionality is only available in Windows 10 Professional or Enterprise editions. Option A: This option is incorrect because processor compatibility is typically not a determining factor for joining a domain. Option C: This option is incorrect because the absence of a touchscreen adapter would not be a reason that the laptop cannot be domain joined. Option D: The laptop being connected to a docking station is not directly related to the laptop's ability to join a domain.

26. The correct answer is **C**. The IT manager is likely to have concerns about the significant increase in network utilization caused by the larger size of CAD files being backed up to the software's cloud server. This increase in data transfer can put a strain on the network bandwidth and potentially affect the overall network performance. Option A is not the most likely concern for the IT manager in this scenario. While compatibility testing is important, it is not directly related to the storage of CAD file backups on the cloud server. Option B is not the primary concern here. While budget allocation for additional technician hours during installation is important, it is not the primary concern in this specific scenario. Option D is not the most likely concern for the IT manager. Although large update and installation files may pose challenges for local hard drives, it is not the primary concern mentioned in the question.

27. The correct answer is **C**. The incident described in the question is an example of impersonation. Impersonation occurs when someone fraudulently pretends to be another person or entity in order to deceive others. In this case, the caller is posing as a representative of a reputable bank, attempting to gain the trust of the company employee and potentially deceive them into revealing sensitive information or performing unauthorized actions. As the exploit involves the placing of a phone call, this could also be termed a Vishing exploit. Option A: Social engineering refers to the manipulation of individuals to gain unauthorized access or information. While impersonation can be a form of social engineering, it specifically involves pretending to be someone else. Option B: Phishing typically involves fraudulent emails or websites designed to deceive individuals into revealing sensitive information. Although the incident involves deception, it specifically describes a phone call, not an email or website. Option D: Identity theft involves stealing someone's personal information with the intention of using it for fraudulent purposes. While impersonation can be a component of identity theft, the incident described in the question does not specifically involve stealing the employee's identity.

28. The correct answer is **E**. An account lockout is a security measure typically implemented by computer systems to prevent unauthorized or malicious access to user accounts. If a user enters incorrect login credentials multiple times, their account may be locked out for a certain period of time or until it is manually unlocked by an administrator. This helps protect against dictionary or brute-force attacks, where an attacker repeatedly tries to guess login credentials in order to gain access to an account. Option A (two-factor authentication) is not the best choice for mitigating a dictionary attack specifically. While two-factor authentication enhances security overall, it does not directly address the dictionary attack issue. Option B: An IDS monitors network traffic and detects any suspicious activity or unauthorized access attempts. By analyzing patterns and signatures associated with dictionary attacks, the IDS can promptly alert network administrators, enabling them to take immediate action and prevent further unauthorized access. As this was during the night, it is likely there would be no staff to respond to the threat. Option C can improve password strength, but it alone cannot prevent a dictionary attack. Attackers can still guess complex passwords if they are present in the dictionary. Option D (network segmentation) is a security measure that isolates different parts of the network, but it may not directly mitigate a dictionary attack on a specific user's account. An IDS monitors network traffic and detects any suspicious activity or unauthorized access attempts. By analyzing patterns and signatures associated with dictionary attacks, the IDS can promptly alert network administrators, enabling them to take immediate action and prevent further unauthorized access.

29. The correct answer is **C**. To assist the manager in hiding the file and preventing accidental deletion by others, the technician should recommend using File Explorer. By modifying the file's properties, the user can mark it as hidden, making it less visible to other users accessing the shared drive. This provides an additional layer of protection and helps maintain the file's privacy and integrity. Option A: Disk Cleanup is used to free up disk space by removing unnecessary files, but it does not offer a feature to hide specific files. Option B: Task Scheduler is a tool used to automate tasks at specific times or events and does not provide functionality to hide files. Option D: Control Panel provides various system settings and configuration options, but it does not offer a direct solution for hiding files on shared drives.

30. The correct answer is **D**. Given the time constraint and the importance of resolving the issue promptly for the CEO, the technician should escalate the support ticket to higher-level technicians. By escalating the ticket, the technician ensures that the problem receives immediate attention from individuals with more expertise or resources to expedite the resolution process. Option A is incorrect because continuing research might consume additional time, which conflicts with the CEO's urgent need to have the device returned promptly. Option B is incorrect because restarting the diagnostic process would lead to redundant efforts, further delaying the resolution and not addressing the time-sensitive nature of the situation. Option C is incorrect because informing the CEO that the repair will take a few weeks is not a suitable course of action when there is an immediate need to return the device.

31. The correct answer is **A**. To maintain a consistent IP address for the server while adhering to the company's policy against static IP addresses, the technician should utilize IP address reservation through DHCP. By assigning a specific IP address to the server's MAC address within the DHCP server's configuration, the server will always receive the same IP address when it requests an IP address lease. This approach ensures that the server is easily identifiable and accessible on the network without relying on a static IP configuration. Option B: Network address translation (NAT) involves translating IP addresses between private and public networks and does not provide a solution for maintaining a consistent IP address for the server. Option C: Dynamic Name System (DNS) records associate domain names with IP addresses and are not directly related to ensuring a server maintains the same IP address. Option D: Virtual private network (VPN) configuration establishes secure connections over public networks and is not specifically relevant to maintaining a consistent IP address for a server.

32. The correct answer is **D**. The most efficient solution in this scenario would be setting up a virtual machine within the Windows OS to run Linux and the required application. This allows Windows and Linux applications to be run at the same time. Option A suggests utilizing a cloud environment. This will require network connections to the cloud provider. Option B: The Windows Linux Subsystem is a feature that can be installed on a Windows desktop computer. It allows basic command-line applications to be supported. However, it will not support all applications as it is an emulator, in contrast to a full installation of Linux with access to graphical applications. Option C: This approach will allow the user to swap between Linux and Windows as needed but will incur additional costs.

33. The correct answer is **A**. When working on internal computer components like processors and memory modules, it's crucial to prevent electrostatic discharge (ESD), which can damage sensitive electronic parts. Using an anti-static wrist strap helps to discharge any static electricity from your body, protecting the components. Option B: The order of upgrades is not necessarily critical as long as you follow proper procedures. However, this statement doesn't address the ESD concerns, which are essential for preventing damage during the upgrade process. Option C: Keeping the computers powered on during upgrades is not recommended. You should shut down and unplug the computers before making any hardware changes to avoid electrical hazards and ensure a safe upgrade process. Option D: This is incorrect. ESD precautions are essential during desktop upgrades, just as they are for laptops or any other electronic devices. Failing to take anti-static precautions can result in damaging the components, leading to costly repairs or replacements.

34. The correct answer is **B**. To enable speech recognition on a PC, the user should navigate to the Accessibility settings. Within the Accessibility settings, there is an option to enable speech recognition, allowing the user to interact with their computer using voice commands. Option A is incorrect as it primarily deals with language, date, time, and location settings. Option C is incorrect as it focuses on personalizing the display, themes, and visual aspects of the operating system. Option D is incorrect as it pertains to privacy settings and permissions for various applications and system features.

35. The correct answer is **D**. The acceptable use policy (AUP) should be updated to incorporate the new requirement of prohibiting cryptocurrency mining on work desktops. The AUP outlines the rules and guidelines for acceptable behavior and usage of company resources. By explicitly including this restriction in the AUP, the company can address the violation and prevent future instances. Option A: Enterprise mobility management (EMM) is not directly related to updating guidelines and policies regarding cryptocurrency mining on work desktops. EMM primarily focuses on managing mobile devices and their associated security and policies. Option B: A service level agreement (SLA) is a contractual agreement between a service provider and a customer, typically specifying the level of service and support to be provided. It does not specifically address updating guidelines and policies. Option C: Data loss prevention (DLP) is a set of technologies and practices aimed at preventing unauthorized disclosure or loss of sensitive data. While it is important for data protection, it does not directly relate to updating guidelines for cryptocurrency mining on work desktops.

36. The correct answer is **A**. This is the correct answer because one of the major benefits of moving to a 64-bit OS is the ability to access and utilize larger amounts of random access memory (RAM) than a 32-bit OS. This is particularly important for tasks such as video editing, 3D rendering, and other memory-intensive applications. Option B: This is not the primary benefit of moving to a 64-bit OS. While a 64-bit OS can offer performance improvements for certain tasks, the major advantage lies in its ability to address more RAM. Option C: The transition to a 64-bit OS primarily impacts memory access, and while it can indirectly benefit graphics performance by allowing for larger textures and smoother multitasking, it's not the primary benefit. Option D: The move to a 64-bit OS doesn't directly affect network connectivity or data transfer rates. These aspects are more dependent on network hardware and infrastructure.

37. The correct answer is **A**. The most likely cause of the issue is network connectivity problems. Since the laptop PC is functioning properly on the same network, it suggests that the network connection is not the root cause. However, the desktop PC's inability to log in to the domain and the technician's inability to access the secure intranet site indicate that there may be issues with network connectivity specific to the desktop PC. This can be due to factors such as network cable disconnection, faulty network adapter, or misconfiguration. Option B: Incorrect domain credentials would prevent both the laptop PC and the technician from accessing the domain, not just the desktop PC. Option C: Browser compatibility problems would typically affect the user's ability to access websites in general, rather than being specific to the secure intranet site. Option D: Firewall restrictions, while a possibility, would likely affect both the laptop PC and the technician's ability to access the secure intranet site, rather than being limited to the desktop PC.

38. The correct answer is **A**. Setting the network configuration to private allows access to shared files on the Windows firewall. Public profiles do not allow file and print sharing. Option B: Establishing a proxy server connection is not necessary for accessing shared drives on the network. Proxy servers are typically used for accessing the internet through an intermediary server, not for internal network file access. Option C: Granting the user with network administrator privileges is not required for accessing shared drives. Network administrator privileges are typically reserved for managing network resources and performing administrative tasks. Option D: Creating a shortcut to the shared drive's public documents is not the appropriate configuration for accessing files on a shared drive. The shortcut would only provide access to the public documents folder, limiting the user's ability to access other files on the shared drive.

39. The correct answer is **B**. To resize a partition on the internal storage drive of a computer running macOS, the technician should employ the Disk Utility tool. Disk Utility is a built-in utility in macOS that allows users to manage, format, and resize storage drives and partitions. With Disk Utility, the technician can easily modify the size of existing partitions to allocate space according to specific requirements. Option A: Activity Monitor is a utility used for monitoring system processes and resource usage, not for resizing partitions. Option C: Time Machine is a backup utility that enables users to create regular backups of their system, but it is not designed for partition resizing. Option D: Terminal is a command-line interface tool in macOS, primarily used for executing commands and scripts, but it is not specifically intended for resizing partitions.

40. The correct answer is **B**. The "Reset This PC" feature in Windows 10 allows you to reinstall Windows while keeping all previous user files and settings. It's a quick and efficient way to prepare a laptop for a new user while maintaining the base operating system. Option A: This is a valid method but not the most efficient for high staff turnover. Manually reinstalling Windows from installation media involves more time and effort compared to using built-in features such as "Reset This PC." Option C: Cloning the hard drive is not the best solution for re-purposing laptops for new staff members. It creates a copy of the existing system, including software and settings, which may not be suitable for a new user. It's also time-consuming. Option D: Windows 10 System Restore is designed to restore the system to its previous state, not to reinstall the operating system. It's not an efficient method for re-purposing laptops.

41. The correct answer is **A**. To resolve the issue of receiving unexpected pictures, the executive should set AirDrop to accept transfers solely from known contacts. This action restricts the reception of unsolicited files and ensures that only trusted sources can send content to the executive's iPhone during the flight. Option B is incorrect because disabling all wireless systems would hinder the executive's ability to use in-flight Wi-Fi for legitimate purposes. Option C is incorrect because discontinuing iMessage usage does not directly address the issue of receiving unexpected pictures through in-flight Wi-Fi. Option D is incorrect because limiting messages and calls to saved contacts only does not specifically address the problem of receiving unsolicited images during the flight.

42. The correct answer is **B**. The best solution for enhancing building security while allowing easy customer access is to install protective barriers such as bollards. Bollards are sturdy posts or barriers strategically placed around the building perimeter to physically prevent vehicles from breaching the area. They provide an effective physical deterrent and minimize the risk of unauthorized vehicle access, ensuring the safety of the premises. Option A, security personnel, may help with surveillance and monitoring but may not provide a sufficient physical barrier against vehicles. Option C, motion detection systems, are useful for detecting movement but do not directly address the issue of preventing vehicles from driving into the building. Option D, a controlled entryway or access control vestibule, primarily focuses on regulating access for individuals and may not offer the same level of protection against vehicle intrusions.

43. The correct answer is **A**. The best solution for addressing interference caused by nearby SSIDs is to adjust the channel settings of your wireless network. By changing the channel, you can avoid overlapping frequencies with neighboring networks and reduce interference. This allows your wireless network to operate on a clear and less congested channel, resulting in improved performance and reduced interference issues. Option B will definitely disrupt operations and is not a realistic option when considering the store may need to support wireless devices. Option C, switching the equipment off and then back on is not a solution to fix the problem. Option D, renaming the access point, does not directly resolve the interference issue caused by nearby SSIDs. Changing the access point name might be useful for identification purposes but does not mitigate the impact of interference on the wireless network.

44. The correct answer is **C**. Given the concerns regarding sensitive, legacy, unmaintained PII and the regulatory requirement for long-term data retention, the best approach would be to perform a complete backup of the data. Storing this backup on an offline, encrypted tape storage ensures that the data remains secure and protected from ransomware attacks. The transfer of data to offline storage provides an added layer of protection against potential data loss. Option A suggests a daily incremental backup to the corporate file server, which may not provide sufficient protection in case of a ransomware outbreak. Incremental backups only store changes since the last full backup, and in the event of an outbreak, the data could be compromised. Option B proposes using snapshots stored on a network-attached storage (NAS) device. While snapshots offer some level of data protection, they are still vulnerable to ransomware attacks if the NAS device itself becomes compromised. Option D suggests weekly, differential backups stored in a cloud-hosting provider. While offsite backups are good practice, differential backups only store changes since the last full backup, which may not provide adequate protection for sensitive data if a ransomware outbreak occurs.

45. The correct answer is **A**. Using a key combination to lock the computer when leaving the workstation is the best way for the police officer to quickly secure the workstation. This action immediately restricts access to the computer, ensuring that any sensitive or confidential information remains protected from unauthorized access during the officer's absence. Windows Key + L will lock the workstation. Option B: While ensuring the absence of unauthorized individuals is important for security, it does not provide an immediate and direct method of securing the workstation. Option C: Configuring a screensaver with an automatic lock after a set period of inactivity is a good security practice but may not be the most efficient solution when the officer needs to secure the workstation quickly. Option D: Turning off the monitor only addresses the issue of unauthorized visibility of information but does not provide a comprehensive solution to secure the entire workstation and its data.

46. The correct answer is **B, E**. To achieve automatic application boot-up upon logging in to a conference room computer, a technician would employ two specific options. First, utilizing the Task Scheduler feature allows them to schedule the application to launch automatically upon user login. Second, the Startup Folder option enables the technician to add a shortcut of the application to the system's designated startup folder, ensuring it initiates during the login process. Option A: Windows Explorer is a file management tool and does not pertain to the automatic launch of applications upon login. Option C: System Overview, or System Information, does not provide the functionality to enable automatic application boot-up on login. Option D: Programs and Features is unrelated to the task of initiating application launch during login. Option F: Device Manager deals with managing and configuring hardware devices and does not apply to the automatic launching of applications on login.

47. The correct answer is **A**. After resetting the user's password, enabling the requirement for the user to change the password at the next login adds an extra layer of security. This ensures that the user creates a new password unique to them and helps prevent unauthorized access to the account. Option B is incorrect because prohibiting the user from changing the password restricts their ability to enhance their account's security by regularly updating their password. Option C is incorrect because disabling the user's account would prevent them from accessing any resources or performing their tasks. It is an extreme measure that should be reserved for cases where there is a specific reason for disabling the account. Option D is incorrect because setting a password with no expiration date poses a security risk. Regularly changing passwords reduces the likelihood of compromised accounts and enhances overall security.

48. The correct answer is **C**. In this scenario, the most likely agreement being utilized is an end user license agreement (EULA). EULAs are commonly encountered when installing software and typically require users to scroll through the agreement text and click an "Accept" button to indicate their consent to the terms and conditions set forth by the software vendor. Option A, service level agreement, is incorrect because SLAs are usually related to service delivery and performance metrics between parties, rather than software installation agreements. Option B, non-disclosure agreement, is incorrect because NDAs are used to protect confidential information, not typically encountered during software installation. Option D, memorandum of understanding, is incorrect because MOUs are typically used to outline agreements or collaborations between organizations, not for software installation purposes.

49. The correct answer is **C**. Multi-factor authentication (MFA) involves the use of multiple authentication factors to verify the identity of a user. In this case, the combination of a one-time password (OTP) and a fingerprint scan serves as an example of MFA. The OTP provides a temporary code that is unique for each authentication attempt, adding an additional layer of security. Meanwhile, the fingerprint scan verifies the user's biometric data, such as their unique fingerprint pattern, adding another layer of authentication. Option A, voice recognition and facial recognition, are both components of biometric authentication but do not specifically represent MFA. Option B, username and password, are both something you know. Option D, password and PIN, represents a single-factor authentication method, not MFA.

50. The correct answer is **C**. In the given scenario, enabling hard drive encryption would be the best security practice. Hard drive encryption ensures that the data stored on the laptop's hard drive is protected by encrypting it with a strong encryption algorithm. This helps safeguard sensitive information even if the laptop is lost, stolen, or accessed by unauthorized individuals. By encrypting the hard drive, the data remains unreadable and inaccessible without the appropriate encryption key or password. Option A, PIN-based login, might provide an additional layer of security, but it does not offer the same level of protection as hard drive encryption when it comes to data confidentiality. Option B, quarterly password changes, is a good practice in general, but it may not be the most effective security measure for protecting data on a laptop that could be lost or stolen. Option D, physical laptop lock, is a physical security measure that helps prevent theft of the laptop, but it does not address the protection of data stored on the laptop's hard drive.

51. The correct answer is **D**. The fact that there is construction activity in the surrounding offices and the desktop not responding to the ping indicates that the most likely cause of the issue is a disconnected network cable. The construction activity might have caused physical disruption to the network infrastructure, resulting in the cable becoming disconnected. Option A is incorrect because the issue is specific to the user's desktop and not the DHCP server. Option B is incorrect because if the firewall was blocking network access, the ping request would not reach the desktop at all. Option C is incorrect because if the user's account was locked, they would still be able to connect to the network but might face authentication issues.

52. The correct answer is **A**. If the website has been verified to be online, the most likely cause of the issue lies with the user's browser. By deleting the browser history, any cached data or cookies that might be causing conflicts or preventing access to the website can be cleared, potentially resolving the issue. Option B is incorrect because clearing the DNS cache is more relevant for resolving issues related to domain name resolution. Option C is incorrect because flushing the ARP cache is more relevant for resolving network connectivity issues. Option D is incorrect because enabling JavaScript in the browser is not directly related to accessing a specific website.

53. The correct answer is **C**. To ensure files and user preferences are retained and perform the operation locally while migrating one station at a time, the most efficient method would be an in-place upgrade. An in-place upgrade allows the seamless transition from Windows 7 Pro to Windows 10 Pro while preserving user data and settings. Option A is incorrect because a master image is a pre-configured system image that is typically used for deploying multiple identical machines simultaneously. Option B is incorrect because a clean install would involve wiping out the existing operating system and user data, which goes against the requirement of retaining files and preferences. Option D, a server-based remote network installation (WDS), involves deploying the new operating system from a network location. This might not meet the requirement of performing the operation locally.

54. The correct answer is **A**. When there is a risk of data loss from lost or stolen laptops, the best recommendation is to enable full disk encryption. Full disk encryption ensures that even if the laptop falls into unauthorized hands, the data stored on the hard drive remains inaccessible without the encryption key. Option B is incorrect because while regular laptop backups are important for data protection, they do not directly address the risk of data loss from lost or stolen laptops. Option C is incorrect because while biometric authentication can enhance security, it may not be feasible for all laptop users and may impact user convenience. Option D is incorrect because while mandatory laptop tracking software can help in locating lost or stolen laptops, it does not directly protect the data stored on the laptops.

55. The correct answer is **C**. To achieve the highest level of wireless network security, the technician should implement WPA3. WPA3 is the latest security protocol, and it provides strong encryption algorithms and enhanced protection against unauthorized access. It offers improved security features compared to its predecessors, such as WPA2 and WEP. Option A, Wi-Fi Protected Setup (WPS), is incorrect because it introduces potential security vulnerabilities and should be disabled to ensure better security. Option B, Temporal Key Integrity Protocol (TKIP), is incorrect because it is an old security protocol that is less secure than WPA3. Option D, Wired Equivalent Privacy (WEP), is incorrect because it is an outdated and easily compromised security protocol. Option E, Media Access Control (MAC) filtering, is incorrect because it alone is not sufficient for providing comprehensive security and can be bypassed by attackers.

56. The correct answer is **B**. To address the reported slow performance and constant solid activity light on the hard drive, the FIRST step should be to use Performance Monitor to analyze resource utilization. This tool provides real-time monitoring and insights into the computer's performance, allowing you to identify any specific processes or applications that might be causing the slowdown. Option A is incorrect because checking Services in Control Panel primarily focuses on managing and configuring system services, not monitoring resource utilization. Option C is incorrect because running System File Checker is used to scan and restore Windows system files' integrity, which is not directly related to the reported performance issue. Option D is incorrect because Event Viewer is primarily used to review system events, logs, and errors, but it may not provide immediate insights into the resource utilization causing the slow performance.

57. The correct answer is **C**. Based on the symptoms described by the user, the most likely cause of the issue is a virus. Viruses are malicious software programs that can replicate and spread, causing various disruptions to the normal functioning of a computer system. In this case, the unauthorized opening of applications and browser redirects are common signs of a virus infection. Option A, keylogger, is incorrect because a keylogger is a type of software that records keystrokes on a computer, often used for malicious purposes like capturing sensitive information. While it can be a potential security concern, it does not directly explain the symptoms mentioned by the user. Option B, cryptominers, is incorrect because cryptominers are programs that are designed to use the computing power of a device to mine cryptocurrencies. While they can cause performance issues, they typically do not manifest in the form of unauthorized application openings or browser redirects. Option D, malware, is incorrect because malware is a general term that encompasses various types of malicious software, including viruses. While malware can indeed cause the reported symptoms, the specific term "virus" is a more accurate and suitable answer in this scenario.

58. The correct answer is **E**. To mitigate the issue of frequent micro power outages, the technician should utilize an uninterruptible power supply (UPS). Unlike surge suppressors that protect against voltage spikes, a UPS provides temporary power during short outages, ensuring the continuous operation of critical electronic devices. A UPS consists of a battery that automatically engages when a power outage occurs, supplying power until normal power is restored or allowing a controlled shutdown. This safeguards the connected equipment against potential data loss, hardware damage, and disruptions in productivity. Option A, surge suppressor, primarily protects against voltage spikes and power surges but does not provide backup power during outages. Option B, battery backup, is another term for Uninterruptible Power Supply (UPS), making it the correct answer in this scenario. Option C, CMOS battery, provides power to the computer's motherboard to retain BIOS settings but does not address power outages. Option D, generator backup, is a larger-scale solution typically used for extended power outages and is not necessary for short micro-outages.

59. The correct answer is **B**. In macOS, the default GUI and file manager for organizing, searching, and accessing files and folders is Finder. It provides a user-friendly interface and various features to navigate through the filesystem, perform file operations, and manage the overall file hierarchy. Option A, Disk Utility, is a utility in macOS used for disk management and performing tasks like formatting, partitioning, and repairing disks. It is not the default GUI and file manager. Option C, Dock, is a macOS feature that provides quick access to frequently used applications and files. While it is an essential component of the macOS interface, it is not the default GUI and file manager. Option D, FileVault, is a built-in encryption feature in macOS that protects data on the system's disk. However, it is not the default GUI and file manager in macOS.

60. The correct answer is **D**. The FAT32 filesystem format would be the best choice for ensuring the read and write compatibility of USB flash drives across several generations of Microsoft operating systems. FAT32 is a widely supported filesystem that can be accessed by various operating systems, including older versions of Windows, macOS, and Linux. It offers excellent compatibility and allows easy file sharing between different platforms. Option A, APFS (Apple File System), is the default filesystem used by Apple devices running macOS. While it provides advanced features and improved performance for macOS systems, it may not offer the same level of compatibility across different versions of Microsoft operating systems. Option B, ext4, is a popular filesystem used primarily in Linux operating systems. While it offers robust features and performance for Linux systems, it may not be as compatible with older versions of Microsoft operating systems. Option C, CDFS (Compact Disk File System), is a read-only filesystem format commonly used for optical disks. It is not suitable for USB flash drives and does not support write operations, making it incompatible with the requirements of the question.

61. The correct answer is **C**. The reason the malware is still present on the system even after performing a System Restore is that the malware has compromised the System Restore process itself. Malware can sometimes infiltrate and infect critical system files, making it difficult for the System Restore to fully eliminate the malicious software. In such cases, the malware can persist despite the restoration of previous system settings. Option A: Stating that a system patch disabled antivirus protection and the host firewall is incorrect because disabling these security measures would not explain why the malware is still present after a System Restore. Option B: Mentioning that the system updates did not include the latest anti-malware definitions is incorrect because it does not explain why the malware survived the System Restore process. Option D: This option suggests that the malware was installed before the creation of the System Restore point is incorrect because the System Restore is designed to revert the system to a previous point in time, regardless of when the malware was initially installed.

62. The correct answer is **A**. In this scenario, the most likely violation is the end user license agreement (EULA). The EULA typically specifies the terms and conditions for using the software, including limitations on the number of installations or the type of edition that can be used. If the technician discovered multiple copies of the home edition software installed on computers, it suggests a violation of the EULA by exceeding the permitted number of installations or using the software inappropriately. Option B, personally identifiable information (PII), refers to sensitive information that can identify an individual, such as their name, address, or social security number. PII is unrelated to the violation described in the question. Option C, digital rights management (DRM), pertains to technologies or measures used to protect copyrighted content from unauthorized distribution or use. It is not directly relevant to the violation of installing multiple copies of home edition software. Option D, open source agreement, refers to the terms and conditions of using open source software, which typically allows users to install and distribute the software freely. It is not applicable in this scenario as the violation is related to proprietary home edition software.

63. The correct answer is **B, D**. Preserving data from a hard drive for forensic analysis requires meticulous attention to detail and adherence to proper procedures. The two options that should be given the MOST consideration in this context are chain of custody and data integrity. Chain of custody is essential in maintaining the integrity and credibility of digital evidence. It involves documenting the custody, control, and transfer of evidence from the time it is acquired until it is presented in court. By ensuring a clear and unbroken chain of custody, the authenticity and admissibility of the preserved data can be upheld. Data integrity refers to the assurance that the preserved data remains unaltered and uncorrupted throughout the forensic analysis process. Measures such as using write-blockers, making bit-for-bit copies of the hard drive, and employing hash algorithms can help verify the integrity of the data. This is crucial for ensuring the accuracy and reliability of the forensic findings. Option A: Licensing agreements are legal agreements that govern the authorized use of software or intellectual property. While important in the broader context of software usage, they are not directly related to preserving data for forensic analysis. Option C: Incident management documentation pertains to recording and managing information about security incidents or breaches. While incident management is

important for handling security events, it is not directly related to preserving data from a hard drive for forensic analysis. Option E: Material safety data sheet (MSDS) contains information about the hazards and handling of specific chemicals or substances. While relevant in certain contexts, MSDS is not directly related to preserving data from a hard drive for forensic analysis. Option F: Retention requirements refer to the guidelines or regulations governing the retention and storage of data. While important for data management and compliance purposes, retention requirements are not directly related to preserving data specifically for forensic analysis.

64. The correct answer is **A.** The most likely tool a technician would use to remotely connect to a Linux desktop is Secure Shell (SSH). SSH is a widely used protocol that provides secure remote access and control to Linux systems. It allows technicians to establish a secure command-line connection to the remote Linux desktop, enabling them to perform troubleshooting tasks, execute commands, and administer the system remotely. Option B, VNC, is incorrect because while VNC can be used for remote desktop access, it is not natively designed for Linux and may require additional setup or compatibility measures. Option C, Remote Desktop Protocol (RDP), is incorrect because RDP is primarily used for remote access to Windows-based systems and is not natively designed for Linux. Option D, TeamViewer, is incorrect because although TeamViewer is a popular remote support tool, it is not specifically designed for Linux and may require additional installation steps or compatibility considerations.

65. The correct answer is **A.** The social engineering attack being attempted in this scenario is known as an "evil twin" attack. In an evil twin attack, an attacker sets up a rogue Wi-Fi access point that mimics a legitimate network, often using a similar or identical SSID. The intention is to deceive users into connecting to the malicious network, enabling the attacker to intercept sensitive information or perform other malicious activities. It is important for users to be cautious when connecting to public Wi-Fi networks and verify the legitimacy of the network before joining. Option B: Impersonation involves pretending to be someone else or a trusted entity to deceive individuals. While it can be a form of social engineering, it is not specifically related to the Wi-Fi network situation described. Option C: Insider threat refers to an attack or security breach caused by someone within the organization who has authorized access. It does not directly relate to the Wi-Fi network situation described. Option D: Whaling is a type of phishing attack that specifically targets high-profile individuals, such as executives or senior management, to trick them into revealing sensitive information. It is not directly related to the Wi-Fi network scenario described.

66. The correct answer is **B**. The most likely reason for the system not utilizing all the available RAM is that it is running on a 32-bit operating system. 32-bit operating systems have a maximum RAM capacity of approximately 4 GB, and any RAM installed beyond that limit will not be recognized or utilized. In this case, even though the technician installed 8 GB of RAM, the system's 32-bit operating system can only address and utilize up to 4 GB of RAM. To fully utilize the installed 8 GB of RAM, the system would need to be upgraded to a 64-bit operating system. Option A: Missing updates may affect system performance, but it is not directly related to the issue of RAM utilization. Option C: Malfunctioning RAM modules could cause issues, but in this case, the discrepancy is more likely due to the limitations of a 32-bit operating system. Option D: BIOS updates generally do not impact the recognition or utilization of RAM. The issue lies with the operating system's capacity.

67. The correct answer is **D**. The best method for returning the computer to service after a malware infection is to first reinstall the OS to ensure a clean and fresh installation, removing any traces of the malware. This step eliminates any infected files and configurations that may remain. Next, flashing the BIOS is recommended to restore the firmware to its original state, removing any malware that may have infected the BIOS. Finally, scanning the computer with on-premises antivirus software will help identify and eliminate any remaining malware threats, providing an additional layer of protection. Option A is incorrect because scanning the system with a Linux live disk may not be the most suitable method for removing malware from a corporate network computer as it may not have the necessary security and compatibility features. Option B is incorrect because flashing the BIOS and reformatting the drive alone does not address the malware infection. Without reinstalling the OS, the infected files and configurations may persist. Option C is incorrect because degaussing the hard drive is not an appropriate method for removing malware. Degaussing is the process of erasing magnetic media and is typically used for data destruction purposes, not for malware removal.

68. The correct answer is **A**. The most appropriate solution to address the issue of abnormally large desktop icons after a software patch deployment is to roll back the video card drivers. Video card drivers are responsible for rendering graphics on the screen, including the desktop icons. If the recently installed video card drivers are incompatible or causing display issues, rolling back to a previous version can restore the proper functionality and size of the icons. Option B, restoring the PC to factory settings, is an extreme measure that erases all user data and settings, reverting the system to its original state. This action should only be considered if other troubleshooting methods fail to resolve the issue. Option C, repairing the Windows profile, might address user-specific settings or configurations but is unlikely to resolve the issue with the desktop icons. The problem is more likely related to the video card drivers rather than the user's profile. Option D, reinstalling the Windows OS, is an extreme solution that should only be considered as a last resort. It involves reinstalling the entire OS, which can be time-consuming and may result in data loss. This action is unnecessary for resolving an issue with desktop icons and should be avoided unless all other options have been exhausted.

69. The correct answer is **D**. The term that defines the extent or boundaries of a change is the scope. The scope outlines the specific objectives, deliverables, and limits of a change project or initiative. It helps define what is included and excluded within the scope of the change, ensuring a clear understanding and effective management of the project's goals and boundaries. Option A, impact, is incorrect because it refers to the consequences or effects of a change, rather than specifying the range or boundaries of the change. Option B, purpose, is incorrect because it refers to the reason or objective behind the change, rather than its extent or boundaries. Option C, analysis, is incorrect because it pertains to the examination and evaluation of data or information, rather than defining the extent of a change.

70. The correct answer is **C**. To troubleshoot connection issues with a third-party USB adapter, a technician should utilize the devmgmt.msc tool. devmgmt.msc, also known as Device Manager, allows technicians to view and manage hardware devices connected to a computer. By opening Device Manager, the technician can verify if the USB adapter is recognized by the system and check for any associated driver issues. They can then proceed to update or reinstall the appropriate drivers, ensuring compatibility and resolving any connection problems. Option A, taskschd.msc, refers to the Task Scheduler, which is used for managing scheduled tasks and automated processes on a computer. It is not directly relevant to resolving connection issues with a USB adapter. Option B, eventvwr.msc, represents the Event Viewer, a tool used to view system logs and monitor system events. While it can be valuable for troubleshooting, it is not specifically designed for addressing USB adapter connection issues. Option D, diskmgmt.msc, pertains to Disk Management, a utility for managing disk drives and partitions on a computer. It does not directly address problems with USB adapter connectivity.

71. The correct answer is **D**. In this scenario, the most likely malware type being used is a keylogger. Keyloggers are designed to clandestinely record keystrokes made by users, capturing sensitive information such as passwords, credit card details, and other confidential data. By surreptitiously logging user input, keyloggers enable malicious actors to obtain unauthorized access to valuable information. Option A, cryptominers, is malicious software that exploits computer resources to mine cryptocurrencies. While they can affect system performance, they are not directly associated with capturing user input. Option B, rootkits, is stealthy malware that allows unauthorized access and control of a system while concealing its presence. While they can provide unauthorized access, they do not specifically focus on capturing user input. Option C, spear phishing, refers to a targeted form of phishing, where attackers deceive individuals into divulging sensitive information through deceptive emails or messages. Although it involves social engineering tactics, it does not directly involve capturing user input.

72. The correct answer is **C**. The best method for physically destroying SSDs that contain sensitive information is shredding. Shredding involves using specialized equipment to physically break the SSD into tiny pieces, rendering the data completely irretrievable. This method ensures the highest level of data destruction and mitigates the risk of unauthorized access or data recovery attempts. It is a recommended practice for organizations that handle sensitive information and need to comply with data privacy regulations. Option A, overwriting, is a method of securely erasing data from storage devices by overwriting it with random or predefined patterns. While overwriting can be effective for traditional hard drives, it is not as reliable for SSDs, as they employ wear leveling and other techniques that make it challenging to ensure complete data eradication. Option B, low-level formatting, is a process that prepares a storage device for initial use by configuring its filesystem structure. However, it does not guarantee data destruction and should not be relied upon as a secure method for disposing of SSDs containing sensitive information. Option D, deleting, refers to the act of removing data from a storage device. However, similar to wiping, standard deleting methods may not be sufficient to securely destroy data on SSDs. SSDs utilize wear leveling and other technologies that make it difficult to guarantee complete data removal solely through deleting.

73. The correct answer is **C**. To integrate Linux servers and desktops into Windows Active Directory environments, the correct option is C, Samba. Samba is an open source software suite that provides interoperability between Linux/Unix-based systems and Windows-based systems. It allows Linux servers and desktops to join Windows Active Directory domains, enabling seamless integration and sharing of resources such as file and print services. Option A, yum, is incorrect. yum is a package management command used in Linux distributions to install, upgrade, or remove software packages. It is not specifically related to integrating Linux systems with Windows Active Directory. Option B, CIFS, is incorrect. Common Internet File System (CIFS) is a network file-sharing protocol used by Windows operating systems. While it can be utilized for file sharing between Windows and Linux systems, it is not primarily used for integrating Linux systems into Windows Active Directory. Option D, chmod, is incorrect. chmod is a command-line utility used in Linux and Unix systems for setting access permissions on files. It does not have a direct role in integrating Linux systems with Windows Active Directory environments.

74. The correct answer is **D**. Before being granted login access to the network, a new employee must sign the acceptable use policy (AUP). The AUP outlines the rules and guidelines for utilizing the organization's network and technology resources. By signing the AUP, the employee acknowledges their understanding and agreement to abide by the policies set forth, ensuring responsible and secure use of the network. Option A: This is a document providing information about the properties, handling, and potential hazards of chemical substances. It is unrelated to network access. Option B: The EULA is a legal contract between the software provider and the end user, outlining the terms and conditions for software usage. While important, it is not directly related to network access. Option C: UAC is a security feature in operating systems that helps prevent unauthorized changes to the computer system. It is not a document that needs to be signed for network access.

75. The correct answer is **C**. To address the issue of an application failing to launch and displaying an error message indicating the need for repair, a technician should utilize the "Programs and Features" utility in Windows 10. This utility allows users to manage installed programs, including repairing or uninstalling problematic applications. By accessing "Programs and Features," the technician can initiate the repair process for the application in question, resolving the launch issue. Option A: The Device Manager utility in Windows 10 is used to manage hardware devices and their drivers, not for repairing applications. Option B: The Administrator Tools typically consist of various system management utilities, but they do not specifically address application repair. Option D: While the Recovery utility in Windows 10 allows for System Restore and troubleshooting, it is not directly involved in repairing specific applications.

76. The correct answer is **C**. When it comes to creating a secure tunnel that hides IP addresses and provides enhanced security for network traffic, the protocol of choice is the virtual private network (VPN). VPNs establish an encrypted connection between the user's device and a remote server, ensuring that all data transmitted between them remains confidential and secure. By routing network traffic through this encrypted tunnel, VPNs effectively protect the privacy and integrity of the data while concealing the user's IP address. Option A, DNS, is responsible for translating domain names into IP addresses. However, it does not provide the necessary encryption and security measures to establish a secure tunnel for network traffic or hide IP addresses. Option B, IPS, is a network security technology that detects and prevents malicious activities within a network. While IPS plays a crucial role in network security, it does not specifically create tunnels or hide IP addresses to secure network traffic. Option D, SSH, is a cryptographic network protocol that provides secure remote access to systems and secure file transfers. While SSH offers encryption and security for remote access, it does not specifically establish a tunnel for hiding IP addresses and securing all network traffic like a VPN does.

77. The correct answer is **B**. In this scenario, it is crucial for the technician to consult the corporate policies regarding the handling of sensitive information and off-site repairs. Corporate policies provide guidelines and procedures to ensure the protection of sensitive data during such situations. By checking the policies, the technician can make informed decisions on how to proceed with the repair process while maintaining the security and integrity of the sensitive information. Option A: remove the hard disk drive (HDD) and then send the computer for repair, may result in the loss of necessary data or make it difficult to diagnose and fix the issue effectively. It is important to follow established procedures to protect the data. Option C: delete sensitive information before the computer leaves the building, might be an option in certain cases, but it is essential to refer to corporate policies to determine the appropriate action to take. Option D: While obtaining authorization from the manager is important in certain situations, it is necessary to check the corporate policies first to ensure compliance with established procedures and guidelines for handling sensitive information.

78. The correct answer is **C**. To effectively manage documentation while creating a full inventory of the company's IT hardware, a technician should utilize asset tags and IDs. Asset tags and IDs provide a unique identification system that helps track and categorize each piece of hardware accurately. By affixing asset tags and assigning IDs to the equipment, the technician can easily associate specific hardware with corresponding documentation, such as purchase details, maintenance records, and warranty information. This ensures efficient inventory management and facilitates future hardware tracking and troubleshooting. Option A, checklist for new user setup, is not directly related to documentation management for IT hardware inventory. It pertains to the onboarding process of new users and their required setup procedures. Option B, user information, primarily refers to personal data and profiles of individual users. While user information may be useful for some aspects of IT management, it is not directly related to documentation management for hardware inventory. Option D, procurement life cycle, focuses on the overall process of acquiring new hardware, from the initial request to final deployment. While documentation is involved in the procurement life cycle, it does not specifically address the management of documentation for hardware inventory.

79. The correct answer is **D**. The user in this scenario is experiencing a social engineering attack known as vishing. Vishing is a type of attack where the attacker attempts to deceive individuals by phone calls, pretending to be a trusted entity such as a bank representative. They aim to extract sensitive information, such as account details or personal data, from unsuspecting victims. It is important for users to be cautious and never provide personal information over the phone unless they can verify the legitimacy of the caller. Option A, phishing, is a social engineering attack that typically occurs through email or fraudulent websites, aiming to trick users into revealing sensitive information. Option B, smishing, is a social engineering attack that occurs through text messages (SMS), where attackers deceive users into disclosing personal information or clicking on malicious links. Option C, whaling, is a specific type of phishing attack targeting high-profile individuals or executives within organizations, with the goal of obtaining sensitive information or access to valuable resources.

80. The correct answer is **B**. To manually set an IP address on a computer running macOS, the technician should use the "ifconfig" command. The "ifconfig" command allows the configuration and management of network interfaces, including the assignment of IP addresses. Option A, "ipconfig," is the command used in Windows operating systems to view and manage IP configurations. It is not applicable to macOS. Option C, "arpa," is the Address and Routing Parameter Area (ARPA) used in the context of the domain name system (DNS) and is not for setting IP addresses manually. Option D, "ping," is a command used to check network connectivity and latency by sending ICMP Echo Request packets. It does not configure IP addresses.

81. The correct answer is **C**. The correct term used to indicate that a vendor no longer supports a product, including the discontinuation of patches and updates, is end of life (EOL). When a product reaches its EOL, the vendor ceases to provide further support, leaving users without access to patches, updates, or technical assistance. This indicates that the product is no longer actively maintained or developed. Option A, AUP, stands for acceptable use policy, which refers to a set of rules or guidelines outlining acceptable behavior when using a particular service or resource. It does not indicate the end of vendor support for a product. Option B, EULA, stands for end user license agreement, which is a legal contract between the software vendor and the end user, specifying the terms and conditions of software usage. It does not indicate the end of vendor support for a product. Option D, UAC, stands for User Account Control, a security feature in Windows operating systems that prompts users for permission when performing certain system-level changes. It does not indicate the end of vendor support for a product.

82. The correct answer is **B**. WPA2 offers an advantage over WPA3 in terms of greater backward compatibility. WPA2 has been widely adopted and implemented in a vast array of devices, including older ones. When upgrading to WPA3, some older devices might not support the newer protocol, leading to connectivity issues. Therefore, opting for WPA2 can ensure that a wider range of devices can still connect securely to the network. Option A: This is not accurate. WPA3, compared to WPA2, offers a higher level of security due to its enhanced encryption methods and protection against some vulnerabilities. Option C: WPA3 has improved resistance to brute-force attacks through features such as Simultaneous Authentication of Equals (SAE), making it more secure against such attacks compared to WPA2. Option D: This is not the main advantage of WPA2 over WPA3. The support for larger device networks is not a defining feature when comparing the security advantages of these two protocols.

83. The correct answer is **A**. High disk usage with no specific application identified could indicate malware or a virus. Running a full antivirus scan is the first step in addressing this issue. Option B: Updating the graphics card driver may improve graphics-related performance issues but is unlikely to resolve high disk usage. Option C: Increasing the virtual memory size is not the first step in troubleshooting high disk usage. Option D: Clearing the browser cache may improve web browsing performance but is unlikely to resolve system-wide high disk usage.

84. The correct answer is **C**. WPA2 is the most secure option listed here. It provides strong encryption and is recommended for securing wireless networks. Option A: WEP is outdated and considered insecure. Option B: WPA is an improvement over WEP but not as secure as WPA2. Option D: WPS is a convenience feature, not an encryption method, and can have security vulnerabilities.

85. The correct answer is **A**. The "No bootable device found" error suggests that the computer is unable to find a bootable operating system. Checking the boot sequence in BIOS to ensure the correct boot device is selected is the first step in resolving this issue. Option B: RAM issues may cause startup problems but are less likely to result in this specific error message. Option C: Graphics card drivers do not typically affect the boot process. Option D: Internet connectivity is unrelated to boot errors.

86. The correct answer is **B**. When a device fails to connect to a Wi-Fi network, the first thing to check is the network password. It's possible that the user entered the wrong password. Option A: Bluetooth settings do not typically affect Wi-Fi connectivity. Option C: Cellular data usage is unrelated to Wi-Fi connectivity. Options D: App updates do not impact Wi-Fi network connections.

87. The correct answer is **C**. IMAP is designed for accessing emails from multiple devices while keeping them synchronized. It's the preferred choice for this scenario. Option A: POP3 downloads emails to a single device and doesn't synchronize them. Option B: SMTP is used for sending, not receiving, emails. Option D: HTTP is used for web browsing, not email access.

88. The correct answer is **B**. The symptoms of sluggish response time and an excessive number of ads are indicative of a bootleg/malicious application on an Android device. Such applications often contain adware or malware that can slow down the device and display unwanted ads. It's essential to identify and remove such applications to resolve these issues. Option A, developer mode enabled, typically does not cause sluggishness or excessive ads. It's more related to the development and debugging of apps. Option C, limited Internet connectivity, might cause some issues, but it wouldn't directly lead to sluggishness and excessive ads. Option D, unexpected application behavior, could be a result of a malicious application, but it doesn't directly explain the high number of ads and sluggish response time.

89. The correct answer is **A**. Fake security warnings appearing on an Android device could be a result of installing applications from untrusted sources or downloading APK files from unreliable websites. Such sources may contain malware or adware that triggers fake security alerts. It's crucial to install apps only from trusted sources such as the Google Play Store to prevent this issue. Option B, data-usage limit notification, is unrelated to fake security warnings. Option C, root access/jailbreak, could introduce security risks, but it's not directly related to fake security warnings. Option D, application spoofing, refers to deceptive practices related to app identity, not fake security warnings.

90. The correct answer is **B**. Limited internet connectivity can occur due to various reasons, such as network issues or incorrect Wi-Fi settings. While security concerns might be related, the primary issue here is connectivity rather than a specific security threat. Option A, developer mode enabled, is unlikely to directly cause limited internet connectivity. Option C, high network traffic, might slow down the connection but is not the primary cause of limited connectivity. Option D, leaked personal files/data, is unrelated to limited internet connectivity.

91. The correct answer is **C**. Unexpected application behavior can be caused by security concerns related to the source of Android packages (APKs). If users download and install APKs from untrusted sources, they risk installing malicious or poorly developed apps that can lead to crashes and other issues. Option A, high network traffic, can affect app performance but is not the primary cause of unexpected behavior. Option B, no internet connectivity, is unrelated to unexpected application behavior. Option D, root access/jailbreak, can introduce security risks but is not the primary cause of unexpected app behavior.

92. The correct answer is **D**. The persistent appearance of fake security warnings and a high number of ads, even when not using any applications, suggests the presence of a bootleg or malicious application on the device. Such applications often display ads and trigger fake security alerts as part of their malicious activities. Option A, limited internet connectivity, wouldn't directly cause fake security warnings and excessive ads. Option B, unexpected application behavior, could be a result of a malicious application, but it doesn't directly explain the high number of ads and fake security warnings. Option C, developer mode enabled, is unlikely to directly cause fake security warnings and ads when not using applications.

93. The correct answer is **D**. Exceeding data usage limits when not using data-intensive apps can be indicative of application spoofing. Malicious apps or malware may consume data in the background, simulating legitimate app usage. Identifying and removing such spoofed apps is crucial to resolving this issue. Option A, high network traffic, might increase data usage but is not the primary cause of exceeding data limits. Option B, data-usage limit notification, is a notification feature and not the cause of excessive data usage. Option C, root access/jailbreak, can introduce security risks but is not the primary cause of data overuse in this context.

# Index

# T

# U

www.packtpub.com

Subscribe to our online digital library for full access to over 7,000 books and videos, as well as industry leading tools to help you plan your personal development and advance your career. For more information, please visit our website.

## Why subscribe?

- Spend less time learning and more time coding with practical eBooks and Videos from over 4,000 industry professionals

- Improve your learning with Skill Plans built especially for you

- Get a free eBook or video every month

- Fully searchable for easy access to vital information

- Copy and paste, print, and bookmark content

At www.packtpub.com, you can also read a collection of free technical articles, sign up for a range of free newsletters, and receive exclusive discounts and offers on Packt books and eBooks.

# Other Books You May Enjoy

If you enjoyed this book, you may be interested in these other books by Packt:

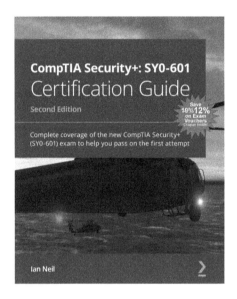

**CompTIA Security+: SY0-601 Certification Guide - Second Edition**

Ian Neil

ISBN: 978-1-80056-424-4

- Master cybersecurity fundamentals, from the CIA triad through to IAM
- Explore cloud security and techniques used in penetration testing
- Use different authentication methods and troubleshoot security issues
- Secure the devices and applications used by your company
- Identify and protect against various types of malware and viruses
- Protect yourself against social engineering and advanced attacks
- Understand and implement PKI concepts
- Delve into secure application development, deployment, and automation

**Official Google Cloud Certified Professional Cloud Security Engineer Exam Guide**

Ankush Chowdhary and Prashant Kulkarni

ISBN: 978-1-83546-886-9

- Understand how Google secures infrastructure with shared responsibility
- Use resource hierarchy for access segregation and implementing policies
- Utilize Google Cloud Identity for authentication and authorizations
- Build secure networks with advanced network features
- Encrypt/decrypt data using Cloud KMS and secure sensitive data
- Gain visibility and extend security with Google's logging and monitoring capabilities

## Share Your Thoughts

Now you've finished *CompTIA A+ Practice Tests Core 1 (220-1101) and Core 2 (220-1102)*, we'd love to hear your thoughts! Scan the QR code below to go straight to the Amazon review page for this book and share your feedback or leave a review on the site that you purchased it from.

```
https://packt.link/r/1837633185
```

Your review is important to us and the tech community and will help us make sure we're delivering excellent quality content.

# Coupon Code for CompTIA A+ Exam Vouchers and Labs

## Coupon Code for 13% Off on CompTIA A+ Exam Vouchers

Take advantage of the **13% discount** by following the below instructions:

1. Go to `https://www.testforless.store/comptia-a`.
2. Click the **Buy Now** button.
3. Add the **exam voucher** to your cart.
4. From your cart, verify your credentials and product details. Then, proceed to **check out**.
5. The **13% discount** is already applied. No promo code is required.

> **The discount for the exam voucher is only available in USD. If you are purchasing from other regions, the purchase will still be made in USD. Vouchers can only be used in the countries associated with the currency in which they are purchased. View the CompTIA's Currency restrictions (`https://wsr.pearsonvue.com/vouchers/pricelist/comptia.asp`) for further clarification.**

## Coupon Code for CompTIA A+ Labs

Get CompTIA A+ Labs for ~~$135~~ **$90** and improve your skill set through practice. Access labs for 12 months from the date of purchase and get hands-on experience in a variety of exam tasks and scenarios.

Take advantage of the labs discount by following the instructions below:

1. The following are the links for A+ Core 1 and Core 2 labs:
   - Core 1: `https://www.testforless.store/acore1`
   - Core 2: `https://www.testforless.store/acore2`
2. Click the **Get Now** button.
3. Add the **lab** to your cart.
4. From your cart, verify your credentials and product details. Then, proceed to **check out**.
5. The discount is already applied. No promo code is required.

www.ingramcontent.com/pod-product-compliance
Lightning Source LLC
Chambersburg PA
CBHW060646060326
40690CB00020B/4540